T0100521

Handbook of Computer Aided Verification

Handbook of Computer Aided Verification

Edited by
Jordan Dean

WILLFORD PRESS
www.willfordpress.com

Published by Willford Press,
118-35 Queens Blvd., Suite 400,
Forest Hills, NY 11375, USA

Copyright © 2023 Willford Press

This book contains information obtained from authentic and highly regarded sources. Copyright for all individual chapters remain with the respective authors as indicated. All chapters are published with permission under the Creative Commons Attribution License or equivalent. A wide variety of references are listed. Permission and sources are indicated; for detailed attributions, please refer to the permissions page and list of contributors. Reasonable efforts have been made to publish reliable data and information, but the authors, editors and publisher cannot assume any responsibility for the validity of all materials or the consequences of their use.

Trademark Notice: Registered trademark of products or corporate names are used only for explanation and identification without intent to infringe.

ISBN: 978-1-64728-440-4

Cataloging-in-publication Data

Handbook of computer aided verification / edited by Jordan Dean.
    p. cm.
Includes bibliographical references and index.
ISBN 978-1-64728-440-4
1. Computer software--Verification. 2. Electronic digital computers--Evaluation.
3. Computer programs--Verification. I. Dean, Jordan.
QA76.76.V47 H36 2023
005.14--dc23

For information on all Willford Press publications
visit our website at www.willfordpress.com

Contents

Preface

This book was inspired by the evolution of our times; to answer the curiosity of inquisitive minds. Many developments have occurred across the globe in the recent past which has transformed the progress in the field.

Computer aided verification (CAV) refers to the practice and theory of computer-assisted formal analysis of software and hardware systems. The purpose of formal verification is to increase the dependability and safety of software and hardware systems. CAV derives concepts and findings from logic, automata theory and graph theory, and combines theoretical and experimental aspects. Research in this field encompasses model checking, automated theorem proving, synthesis and testing. It includes numerous system models such as finite-state and infinite-state systems, probabilistic systems and hybrid systems. This book elucidates the concepts and innovative models around prospective developments with respect to computer aided verification. From theories to research to practical applications, studies related to all contemporary topics of relevance to this area of computer science have been included herein. The book will serve as a valuable source of reference for graduate and postgraduate students.

This book was developed from a mere concept to drafts to chapters and finally compiled together as a complete text to benefit the readers across all nations. To ensure the quality of the content we instilled two significant steps in our procedure. The first was to appoint an editorial team that would verify the data and statistics provided in the book and also select the most appropriate and valuable contributions from the plentiful contributions we received from authors worldwide. The next step was to appoint an expert of the topic as the Editor-in-Chief, who would head the project and finally make the necessary amendments and modifications to make the text reader-friendly. I was then commissioned to examine all the material to present the topics in the most comprehensible and productive format.

I would like to take this opportunity to thank all the contributing authors who were supportive enough to contribute their time and knowledge to this project. I also wish to convey my regards to my family who have been extremely supportive during the entire project.

Editor

Syntax-Guided Termination Analysis

Grigory Fedyukovich[(⊠)] [iD], Yueling Zhang, and Aarti Gupta

Princeton University, Princeton, USA
{grigoryf,yuelingz,aartig}@cs.princeton.edu

Abstract. We present new algorithms for proving program termination and non-termination using syntax-guided synthesis. They exploit the symbolic encoding of programs and automatically construct a formal grammar for symbolic constraints that are used to synthesize either a termination argument or a non-terminating program refinement. The constraints are then added back to the program encoding, and an off-the-shelf constraint solver decides on their fitness and on the progress of the algorithms. The evaluation of our implementation, called FREQ-TERM, shows that although the formal grammar is limited to the syntax of the program, in the majority of cases our algorithms are effective and fast. Importantly, FREQTERM is competitive with state-of-the-art on a wide range of terminating and non-terminating benchmarks, and it significantly outperforms state-of-the-art on proving non-termination of a class of programs arising from large-scale Event-Condition-Action systems.

1 Introduction

Originated from the field of program synthesis, an approach of syntax-guided synthesis (SyGuS) [2] has recently been applied [14,16] to verification of program safety. In general, a SyGuS-based method walks through a set of candidates, restricted by a formal grammar, and searches for a candidate that meets the predetermined specification. The distinguishing insight of [14,16], in which SyGuS discovers inductive invariants, is that a formal grammar need not necessarily be provided by the user (as in applications to program synthesis), but instead it could be automatically constructed on the fly from the symbolic encoding of the program being analyzed. Despite being incomplete, the approach shows remarkable practical success due to its ability to discover various facts about program behaviors whose syntactic representations are compact and look similar to the actual program statements.

Problems of proving and disproving program termination have a known connection to safety verification, e.g., [7,19,28,39,40]. In particular, to prove termination, a program could be augmented by a counter (or a set of counters) that is

---

This work was supported in part by NSF Grant 1525936.

Y. Zhang—Visiting Student Research Collaborator from East China Normal University, China.

initially assigned a reasonably large value and monotonically decreases at each iteration [38]. It remains to solve a safety verification task: to prove that the counter never goes negative. On the other hand, to prove that a program has only infinite traces, one could prove that the negation of a loop guard is never reachable, which boils down to another safety verification task. This knowledge motivates us not only to exploit safety verification as a subroutine in our techniques, but also to adapt successful methods across application domains.

We present a set of SyGuS-based algorithms for proving and disproving termination. For the former, our algorithm LINRANK adds a decrementing counter to a loop, iteratively guesses lower bounds on its initial value (using the syntactic patterns obtained from the code), which lead to the safety verification tasks to be solved by an off-the-shelf Horn solver. Existence of an inductive invariant guarantees termination, and the algorithm converges. Otherwise LINRANK proceeds to strengthening the lower bounds by adding another guess. Similarly, our algorithm LEXRANK deals with a system of extra counters ordered lexicographically and thus enables termination analysis for a wider class of programs.

For proving non-termination, we present a novel algorithm NONTERMREF that iteratively searches for a restriction on the loop guard, that *might lead* to infinite traces. Since safety verification cannot in general answer such queries, we build NONTERMREF on top of a solver for the validity of $\forall\exists$-formulas. In particular, we prove that if at the beginning of any iteration the desired restriction is fulfilled, then there exists a sequence of states from the beginning to the end of that iteration, and the desired restriction is fulfilled at the end of that iteration as well. Recent symbolic techniques [15] to handle quantifier alternation enabled us to prove non-termination of a large class of programs for which a reduction to safety verification is not effective.

These three algorithms are independent of each other, but they all rely on a generator of constraints that are further applied in different contexts. This distinguishes our work from most of the related approaches [7,18,20,23,30,32, 36,39,40]. The key insight, adapted from [14,16], is that the syntactical structures that appear in the program give rise to a formal grammar, from which many candidates could be sampled. Because the grammar is composed from a finite number of numeric constants, operators, and variable combinations, the number of sampled constraints is always finite. Furthermore, since our samples are syntactically close to the actual constructs which appear in the code, they often provide a practical guidance towards the proof of the task. Thus in the majority of cases, the algorithms converge with the successful result.

We have implemented our algorithms in a tool called FREQTERM, which utilizes solvers for Satisfiability Modulo Theory (SMT) [11,15] and satisfiability of constrained Horn clauses [16,24,26]. These automatic provers become more robust and powerful every day, which affects performance of FREQTERM only positively. We have evaluated FREQTERM on a range of terminating and non-terminating programs taken from SVCOMP[1] and on large-scale benchmarks

---

[1] Software Verification Competition.

arising from Event-Condition-Action systems[2] (ECA). Compared to state-of-the-art termination analyzers [18, 22, 30], FREQTERM exhibits a competitive runtime, and achieves several orders of magnitude performance improvement while proving non-termination of ECAs.

In the rest of the paper, we give background on automated verification (Sect. 2) and on SyGuS (Sect. 3); then we describe the application of SyGuS for proving termination (Sect. 4) and non-termination (Sect. 5). Finally, after reporting experimental results (Sect. 6), we overview related work (Sect. 7) and conclude the paper (Sect. 8).

2   Background and Notation

In this work, we formulate tasks arising in automated program analysis by encoding them to instances of the SMT problem [12]: for a given first-order formula φ and a background theory to decide whether there is an assignment m of values from the theory to variables in φ that makes φ true (denoted $m \models \varphi$). If every assignment to φ is also an assignment to some formula ψ, we write $\varphi \implies \psi$.

Definition 1. *A transition system P is a tuple $\langle V \cup V', Init, Tr \rangle$, where V is a vector of variables; V' is its primed copy; formulas Init and Tr encode the* initial states *and the* transition relation *respectively.*

We view *programs* as *transition systems* and throughout the paper use both terms interchangeably. An assignment s of values to all variables in V (or any copy of V such as V') is called a *state*. A trace is a (possibly infinite) sequence of states $s, s', \ldots$, such that (1) $s \models Init$, and (2) for each i, $s^{(i)}, s^{(i+1)} \models Tr$.

We assume, without loss of generality, that the transition-relation formula $Tr(V, V')$ is in Conjunctive Normal Form, and we split $Tr(V, V')$ to a conjunction $Guard(V) \wedge Body(V, V')$, where $Guard(V)$ is the maximal subset of conjuncts of Tr expressed over variables just from V, and every conjunct of $Body(V, V')$ can have appearances of variables from V and V'.

Intuitively, formula $Guard(V)$ encodes a loop guard of the program, whose loop body is encoded in $Body(V, V')$. For example, for a program shown in Fig. 1a, $V = \{x, y, K\}$, the $Guard = y < K \vee y > K$, and the entire encoding of the transition relation is shown in Fig. 1b.

Definition 2. *If each program trace contains a state s, such that $s \models \neg Guard$, then the program is called* terminating *(otherwise, it is called* non-terminating*).*

Tasks of proving termination and non-termination are often reduced to tasks of proving program safety. A *safety verification task* is a pair $\langle P, Err \rangle$, where $P = \langle V \cup V', Init, Tr \rangle$ is a program, and Err is an encoding of the *error states*. It has a solution if there exists a formula, called a *safe inductive invariant*, that implies $Init$, is closed under Tr, and is inconsistent with Err.

---

[2] Provided at http://rers-challenge.org/2012/index.php?page=problems.

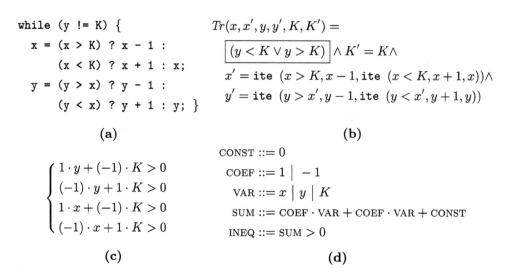

```
while (y != K) {
    x = (x > K) ? x - 1 :
        (x < K) ? x + 1 : x;
    y = (y > x) ? y - 1 :
        (y < x) ? y + 1 : y; }
```

$Tr(x, x', y, y', K, K') =$

$\boxed{(y < K \vee y > K)} \wedge K' = K \wedge$

$x' = \text{ite } (x > K, x - 1, \text{ite } (x < K, x + 1, x)) \wedge$

$y' = \text{ite } (y > x', y - 1, \text{ite } (y < x', y + 1, y))$

(a)   (b)

$$\begin{cases} 1 \cdot y + (-1) \cdot K > 0 \\ (-1) \cdot y + 1 \cdot K > 0 \\ 1 \cdot x + (-1) \cdot K > 0 \\ (-1) \cdot x + 1 \cdot K > 0 \end{cases}$$

CONST ::= 0

COEF ::= 1 | − 1

VAR ::= x | y | K

SUM ::= COEF · VAR + COEF · VAR + CONST

INEQ ::= SUM > 0

(c)   (d)

Fig. 1. (a): C-code; (b): transition relation Tr (in the framebox – *Guard*); (c): formulas S extracted from Tr and normalized; (d): grammar that generalizes S.

Definition 3. *Let* $P = \langle V \cup V', Init, Tr \rangle$; *a formula Inv is a* safe inductive invariant *if the following conditions hold:* (1) $Init(V) \implies Inv(V)$, (2) $Inv(V) \wedge Tr(V, V') \implies Inv(V')$, *and* (3) $Inv(V) \wedge Err(V) \implies \bot$.

If there exists a trace c (called a *counterexample*) that contains a state s, such that $s \models Err$, then the safety verification task does not have a solution.

3   Exploiting Program Syntax

The key driver of our termination and non-termination provers is a generator of constraints which help to analyze the given program in different ways. The source code often gives useful information, e.g., of occurrences of variables, constants, arithmetic and comparison operators, that could bootstrap the formula generator. We rely on the SyGuS-based algorithm [16] introduced for verifying program safety. It automatically constructs the grammar G based on the fixed set of formulas S obtained by traversing parse trees of $Init$, Tr, and Err. In our case, Err is not given, so G is based only on $Init$ and Tr.

For simplicity, we require formulas in S to have the form of inequalities composed from a linear combination over either V or V' and a constant (e.g., $x' < y' + 1$ is included, but $x' = x + 1$ is excluded). Then, if needed, variables are deprimed (e.g., $x' < y' + 1$ is replaced by $x < y + 1$), and formulas are normalized, such that all terms are moved to the left side (e.g., $x < y + 1$ is replaced by $x - y - 1 < 0$), the subtraction is rewritten as addition, $<$ is rewritten as $>$, and respectively $\le$ as $\ge$ (e.g., $x - y - 1 < 0$ is replaced by $(-1) \cdot x + y + 1 > 0$).

The entire process of creation of G is exemplified in Fig. 1. Production rules of G are constructed as follows: (1) the production rule for normalized inequalities

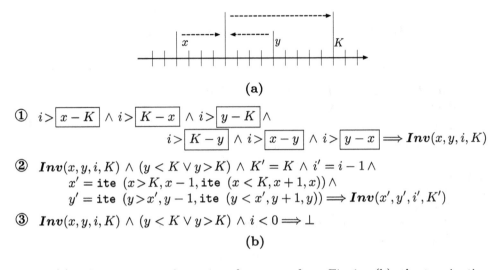

(a)

① $i > \boxed{x - K} \wedge i > \boxed{K - x} \wedge i > \boxed{y - K} \wedge$
$i > \boxed{K - y} \wedge i > \boxed{x - y} \wedge i > \boxed{y - x} \implies \boldsymbol{Inv}(x, y, i, K)$

② $\boldsymbol{Inv}(x, y, i, K) \wedge (y < K \vee y > K) \wedge K' = K \wedge i' = i - 1 \wedge$
$x' = \mathtt{ite}\ (x > K, x - 1, \mathtt{ite}\ (x < K, x + 1, x)) \wedge$
$y' = \mathtt{ite}\ (y > x', y - 1, \mathtt{ite}\ (y < x', y + 1, y)) \implies \boldsymbol{Inv}(x', y', i', K')$

③ $\boldsymbol{Inv}(x, y, i, K) \wedge (y < K \vee y > K) \wedge i < 0 \implies \bot$

(b)

Fig. 2. (a): The worst-case dynamics of program from Fig. 1a; (b): the termination-argument validity check (in the frameboxes – lower bounds $\{\ell_j\}$ for i).

(denoted INEQ) consists of choices corresponding to distinct types of inequalities in S, (2) the production rule for linear combinations (denoted SUM) consists of choices corresponding to distinct arities of inequalities in S, (3) production rules for variables, coefficients, and constants (denoted respectively VAR, COEF, and CONST) consist of choices corresponding respectively to distinct variables, coefficients, and constants that occur in inequalities in S. Note that the method of creation of G naturally extends to considering disjunctions and nonlinear arithmetic [16].

Choices in production rules of grammar G can be further assigned probabilities based on frequencies of certain syntactic features (e.g., frequencies of particular constants or combinations of variables) that belong to the program's symbolic encoding. In the interest of saving space, we do not discuss it here and refer the reader to [16]. The generation of formulas from G is performed recursively by sampling from probability distributions assigned to rules. Note that the choice of distributions affects only the order in which formulas are sampled and does not affect which formulas *can* or *cannot* be sampled in principle (because the grammar is fixed). Thus, without loss of generality, it is sound to assume that all distributions are uniform. In the context of termination analysis, we are interested in formulas produced by rules INEQ and SUM.

4 Proving Termination

We start this section with a motivating example and then proceed to presenting the general-purpose algorithms for proving program termination.

Example 1. The program shown in Fig. 1a terminates. It operates on three integer variables, x, y, and K: in each iteration y gets closer to x, and x gets closer

---

Algorithm 1. LINRANK(P): proving termination with linear termination argument

---

Input: $P = \langle V \cup V', \mathit{Init}, \mathit{Tr} \rangle$ where $\mathit{Tr} = \mathit{Guard} \wedge \mathit{Body}$
Output: $\mathit{res} \in \langle \text{TERMINATES}, \text{UNKNOWN} \rangle$

1 $V \leftarrow V \cup \{i\}; \quad V' \leftarrow V' \cup \{i'\};$
2 $\mathit{Tr} \leftarrow \mathit{Tr} \wedge i' = i - 1; \quad \mathit{Err} \leftarrow \mathit{Guard} \wedge i < 0;$
3 $G \leftarrow \text{GETGRAMMARANDDISTRIBUTIONS}(\mathit{Init}, \mathit{Tr});$
4 **while** CANSAMPLE(G) **do**
5      $\mathit{cand} \leftarrow \text{SAMPLE}(G, \text{SUM});$
6      $G \leftarrow \text{ADJUST}(G, \mathit{cand});$
7   **if** $\mathit{Init} \implies i > \mathit{cand}$ **then continue**;
8      $\mathit{Init} \leftarrow \mathit{Init} \wedge i > \mathit{cand};$
9   **if** ISSAFE($\mathit{Init}, \mathit{Tr}, \mathit{Err}$) **then return** TERMINATES;
10 **return** UNKNOWN;

---

to K. Thus, the total number of values taken by y before it equals K is no bigger than the maximal distance among x, y, and K (in the following, denoted Max). The worst-case dynamics happens when initially $x < y < K$ (shown in Fig. 2a), in other cases the program terminates even faster. To formally prove this, the program could be augmented by a so-called *termination argument*. For this example, it is simply a fresh variable i which is initially assigned Max (or any other value greater than Max) and which gets decremented by one in each iteration. The goal now is to prove that i never gets negative. Fig. 2b shows the encoding of this safety verification task (recall Definition 3). The existence of a solution to this task guarantees the safety of the augmented program, and thus, the termination of the original program. Most state-of-the-art Horn solvers are able to find a solution immediately.   □

The main challenge in preparing the termination-argument validity check is the generation of lower bounds $\{\ell_j\}$ for i in Init (e.g., conjunctions of the form $i > \ell_j$ in ① in Fig. 2b). We build on the insight that each ℓ_j could be constructed independently from the others, and then an inequality $i > \ell_j$ could be conjoined with Init, thus giving rise to a new safety verification task. For a generation of candidate inequalities, we utilize the algorithm from Sect. 3: all $\{\ell_j\}$ can be sampled from grammar G which is obtained in advance from Init and Tr.

For example, all six formulas in ① in Fig. 2b: $x - K, K - x, y - K, K - y, x - y$, and $y - x$ belong to the grammar shown in Fig. 1d. Note that for proving termination it is not necessary to have the most precise lower bounds. Intuitively, the larger the initial value of i, the more iterations it will stay positive. Thus, it is sound to try formulas which are not even related to actual lower bounds at all and keep them conjoined with Init.

4.1   Synthesizing Linear Termination Arguments

Algorithm 1 shows an *"enumerate-and-try"* procedure to search for a linear termination argument that proves termination of a program P. To initialize this search, the algorithm introduces an extra counter variable i and adds it to V (respectively, its primed copy i' gets added to V') (line 1).[3] Then the transition-relation formula Tr gets augmented by $i' = i - 1$, the decrement of the counter in the loop body. To specify a set of error states, Algorithm 1 introduces a formula Err (line 2): whenever the loop guard is satisfied and the value of counter i is negative. Algorithm 1 then starts searching for large enough lower bounds for i (i.e., a set of constraints over $V \cup \{i\}$ to be added to $Init$), such that no error state is ever reachable.

Before the main loop of our synthesis procedure starts, various formulas are extracted from the symbolic encoding of P and generalized to a formal grammar (line 3). The grammar is used for an iterative probabilistic sampling of candidate formulas (line 5) that are further added to the validity check of the current termination argument (line 8). In particular, each new constraint over i has the form $i > cand$, where $cand$ is produced by the SUM production rule described in Sect. 3. Once $Init$ is strengthened by this constraint, a new safety verification condition is compiled and checked (line 9) by an off-the-shelf Horn solver.

As a result of each safety check, either a formula satisfying Definition 3 or a counterexample cex witnessing reachability of an error state is generated. Existence of an inductive invariant guarantees that the conjunction of all synthesized lower bounds for i is large enough to prove termination, and thus Algorithm 1 converges. Otherwise, if grammar G still contains a formula that has not been considered yet, the synthesis loop iterates.

For the progress of the algorithm, it must keep track of the strength of each new candidate $cand$. That is, $cand$ should add more restrictions on i in $Init$. Otherwise, the outcome of the validity check (line 9) would be the same as in the previous iteration. For this reason, Algorithm 1 includes an important routine [16]: after each sampled candidate $cand$, it adjusts the probability distributions associated with the grammar, such that $cand$ could not be sampled again in the future iterations (line 6). Additionally, it checks (line 7) if a new constraint adds some value over the already accepted constraints. Consequently, our algorithm does not require explicit handing of counterexamples: if in each iteration $Init$ gets only stronger then current cex is invalidated. While in principle the algorithm could explicitly store cex and check its consistency with each new $cand$, however in our experiments it did not lead to significant performance gains.

Theorem 1. *If Algorithm 1 returns* TERMINATES *for program P, then P terminates.*

Indeed, the verification condition, which is proven safe in the last iteration of Algorithm 1, corresponds to some program P' that differs from P by the presence of variable i. The set of traces of P has a one-to-one correspondence with the

---

[3] Assume that initially set V does not contain i.

Algorithm 2. LexRank(P): proving termination with lexicographic termination argument

---

Input: $P = \langle V \cup V', Init, Tr \rangle$ where $Tr = Guard \wedge Body$
Output: $res \in \langle \text{TERMINATES}, \text{UNKNOWN} \rangle$

1   $V \leftarrow V \cup \{i,j\};$ $V' \leftarrow V' \cup \{i', j'\};$
2   $Err \leftarrow Guard \wedge i < 0;$ $jBounds \leftarrow \varnothing;$

3   $G, G', G'' \leftarrow$ GetGrammarAndDistributions($Init, Tr$);

4 **while** canSample(G) **or** canSample(G') **or** canSample(G'') **do**

5   **if** nondet() **then**
6         $cand \leftarrow$ sample(G, sum); $G \leftarrow$ adjust($G, cand$);
7         $Init \leftarrow Init \wedge i > cand;$
8   **if** nondet() **then**
9         $cand \leftarrow$ sample(G', sum); $G' \leftarrow$ adjust($G', cand$);
10        $Init \leftarrow Init \wedge j > cand;$
11   **if** nondet() **then**
12        $cand \leftarrow$ sample(G'', sum); $G'' \leftarrow$ adjust($G'', cand$);
13        $jBounds \leftarrow jBounds \cup \{j > cand\};$
14      $Tr' \leftarrow Tr \wedge ite(j > 0, i' = i \wedge j' = j - 1, i' = i - 1 \wedge \bigwedge_{b \in jBounds} b);$

15   **if** isSafe($Init, Tr', Err$) **then return** TERMINATES;
16 **return** UNKNOWN;

---

set of traces of P', such that each state reachable in P could be extended by a valuation of i to become a reachable state in P'. That is, P terminates iff P' terminates, and P' terminates by construction: i is initially assigned a reasonably large value, monotonically decreases at each iteration, and never goes negative.

We note that the loop in Algorithm 1 always executes only a finite number of iterations since G is constructed from the finite number of components, and in each iteration it gets adjusted to avoid re-sampling of the same candidates. However, an off-the-shelf Horn solver that checks validity of each candidate might not converge because the safety verification task is undecidable in general. To mitigate this obstacle, our implementation supports several state-of-the-art solvers and provides a flexibility to specify one to use.

4.2 Synthesizing Lexicographic Termination Arguments

There is a wide class of terminating programs for which no linear termination argument exists. A commonly used approach to handle them is via a search for a so-called lexicographic termination argument that requires introducing two or more extra counters. A SyGuS-based instantiation of such a procedure for two counters is shown in Algorithm 2 (more counters could be handled similarly). Algorithm 2 has a similar structure to Algorithm 1: the initial program gets augmented by counters, formula Err is introduced, lower bounds for counters are iteratively sampled and added to *Init* and *Tr*, and the verification condition is checked for safety.

The differences in Algorithm 2 are in how it handles two counters i and j, between which an implicit order is fixed. In particular, *Err* is still expressed over i only, but i gets decremented by one only when j equals zero (line 14). At the same time, j gets updated in each iteration: if it was equal to zero, it gets assigned a value satisfying the conjunction of constraints in an auxiliary set *jBounds*; otherwise it gets decremented by one. Algorithm 2 synthesizes *jBounds* as well as lower bounds for initial conditions over i and j. The sampling proceeds separately from three different grammars (lines 6, 9, and 12), and the samples are used in three different contexts (lines 7, 10, and 13 respectively). Optionally, Algorithm 2 could be parametrized by a synthesis strategy that gives interpretations for each of the NONDET() calls (lines 5, 8, and 11 respectively). In the simplest case, each NONDET() call is replaced by $\top$, which means that in each iteration Algorithm 2 needs to sample from all three grammars. Alternatively, NONDET() could be replaced by a method to identify only one grammar per iteration to be sampled from.

Theorem 2. *If Algorithm 2 returns* TERMINATES *for program P, then P terminates.*

The proof sketch for Theorem 2 is similar to the one for Theorem 1: an augmented program P' terminates by construction (due to a mapping of values of $\langle i, j \rangle$ into ordinals), and its set of traces has a one-to-one correspondence with the set of traces of P.

5 Proving Non-termination

In this section, we aim at solving the opposite task to the one in Sect. 4, i.e., we wish to witness infinite program traces and thus, to prove program non-termination. However, in contrast to a traditional search for a single infinite trace, it is often easier to search for groups of infinite traces.

Lemma 1. *Program $P = \langle V \cup V', Init, Tr \rangle$ where $Tr = Guard \wedge Body$ does not terminate if:*

1. *there exists a state s, such that $s \models Init$ and $s \models Guard$,*
2. *for every state s, such that $s \models Guard$, there exists a state s', such that $s, s' \models Tr$ and $s' \models Guard$.*

The lemma distinguishes a class of programs, for which the following holds. First, the loop guard is reachable from the set of initial states. Second, whenever the loop guard is satisfied, there exists a transition to a state in which the loop guard is satisfied again. Therefore, each initial state s, from which the loop guard is reachable, gives rise to at least one infinite trace that starts with s.

Note that for programs with deterministic transition relations (like, e.g., in Fig. 1a), the check of the second condition of Lemma 1 reduces to deciding the

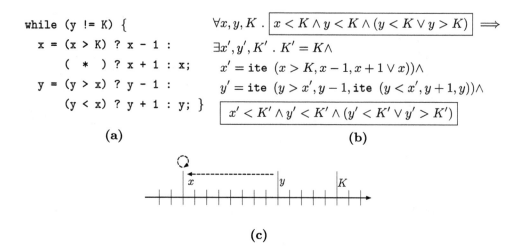

```
while (y != K) {
  x = (x > K) ? x - 1 :
    ( * ) ? x + 1 : x;
  y = (y > x) ? y - 1 :
    (y < x) ? y + 1 : y; }
```

$\forall x, y, K \,.\, \boxed{x < K \land y < K \land (y < K \lor y > K)} \implies$

$\exists x', y', K' \,.\, K' = K \land$

$x' = \text{ite}\ (x > K, x - 1, x + 1 \lor x)) \land$

$y' = \text{ite}\ (y > x', y - 1, \text{ite}\ (y < x', y + 1, y)) \land$

$\boxed{x' < K' \land y' < K' \land (y' < K' \lor y' > K')}$

(a)

(b)

(c)

Fig. 3. (a): A variant of program from Fig. 1a; (b): the valid $\forall\exists$-formula for its non-terminating refinement (in frameboxes – refined *Guard*-s); (c): an example of a non-terminating dynamics, when value of x (and eventually, y) never gets changed.

satisfiability of a quantifier-free formula since each state can be transitioned to exactly one state. But if the transition relation is non-deterministic, the check reduces to deciding validity of a $\forall\exists$-formula. Although handling quantifiers is in general hard, some recent approaches [15] are particularly tailored to solve this type of queries efficiently.

In practice, the conditions of Lemma 1 are too strict to be fulfilled for an arbitrary program. However, to prove non-termination, it is sufficient to constrain the transition relation as long as it preserves at least one original transition and only then to apply Lemma 1.

Definition 4. *Given programs* $P = \langle V \cup V', \textit{Init}, \textit{Tr} \rangle$, *and* $P' = \langle V \cup V', \textit{Init}, \textit{Tr}' \rangle$, *we say that* P' *is a* refinement *of* P *if* $\textit{Tr}' \implies \textit{Tr}$.

Intuitively, Definition 4 requires P and P' to operate over the same sets of variables and to start from the same initial states. Furthermore, each transition allowed by $\textit{Tr}'$ is also allowed by $\textit{Tr}$. One way to refine P is to restrict $\textit{Tr} = \textit{Guard} \land \textit{Body}$ by conjoining either *Guard*, or *Body*, or both with some extra constraints (called *refinement constraints*). In this work, we propose to sample them from our automatically constructed formal grammar (recall Sect. 3).

Example 2. Consider a program shown in Fig. 3a. It differs from the one shown in Fig. 1a by a non-deterministic choice in the second ite-statement. That is, y still moves towards x; but x moves towards K only when $x > K$, and otherwise x may always keep the initial value. The formal grammar generated for this program is the same as shown in Fig. 1d, and it contains constraints $x < K$ and $y < K$. Lemma 1 does not apply for the program as is, but it does after refining *Guard* with those constraints. In particular, the $\forall\exists$-formula in Fig. 3b is valid, and a witness to its validity is depicted in Fig. 3c: eventually both x and

---

Algorithm 3. NONTERMREF(P): proving non-termination

Input: $P = \langle V \cup V', Init, Tr \rangle$ where $Tr = Guard \wedge Body$
Output: $res \in \langle \text{TERMINATES}, \text{DOES NOT TERMINATE}, \text{UNKNOWN} \rangle$

1   **if** $Init(V) \wedge Guard(V) \implies \bot$ **then return** TERMINATES;

2    $Tr \leftarrow Tr \wedge \text{GETINVS}(Init, Tr)$;
3    $G \leftarrow \text{GETGRAMMARANDDISTRIBUTIONS}(Init, Tr)$;
4    $Refs \leftarrow \varnothing$; $Gramms \leftarrow \varnothing$; $Gramms.\text{PUSH}(G)$;

5   **while** $true$ **do**

6   **if** $\forall V \, . \, Guard(V) \wedge \bigwedge\limits_{r \in Refs} r(V) \implies$
           $\exists V' \, . \, Body(V, V') \wedge Guard(V') \wedge \bigwedge\limits_{r \in Refs} r(V')$ **then**

7   **return** DOES NOT TERMINATE;

8      $cand \leftarrow \top$;
9   **while** $Guard(V) \wedge \bigwedge\limits_{r \in Refs} r(V) \implies cand(V)$ **or**
           $Init(V) \wedge Guard(V) \wedge cand(V) \wedge \bigwedge\limits_{r \in Refs} r(V) \implies \bot$ **do**

10   **if** $Refs = \varnothing$ **and** $\neg\text{CANSAMPLE}(G)$ **then return** UNKNOWN;
11   **if** $Refs \neq \varnothing$ **and** $\neg\text{CANSAMPLE}(G)$ **then**
12          $Refs.\text{POP}()$;
13          $Gramms.\text{POP}()$;
14          $cand \leftarrow \top$; $G \leftarrow Gramms.\text{TOP}()$;
15   **continue**;
16        $cand \leftarrow \text{SAMPLE}(G, \text{INEQ})$;
17        $G \leftarrow \text{ADJUST}(G, cand)$;

18      $Refs.\text{PUSH}(cand)$;
19      $Gramms.\text{PUSH}(G)$;

---

y become equal and always remain smaller than K. Thus, the program does not terminate. □

5.1 Synthesizing Non-terminating Refinements

The algorithm for proving program's non-termination is shown in Algorithm 3. It starts with a simple satisfiability check (line 1) which filters out programs that never reach the loop body (thus they immediately terminate). Then, the transition relation Tr gets strengthened by auxiliary inductive invariants obtained with the help of the initial states $Init$ (line 2). The algorithm does not impose any specific requirements on the invariants (and it is sound even for a trivial invariant $\top$) and on a method that detects them. In many cases, auxiliary invariants make the algorithm converge faster. Similar to Algorithms 1–2, Algorithm 3 splits $Init$ and Tr to a set of formulas and generalizes them to a grammar. The difference lies in the type of formulas sampled from the grammar (INEQ vs SUM) and their use in the synthesis loop: Algorithm 3 treats sampled candidates as *refinement constraints* and attempts to apply Lemma 1 (line 6).

The algorithm maintains a stack of refinement constraints *Refs*. At the first iteration, *Refs* is empty, and thus the algorithm tries to apply Lemma 1 to the original program. For that application, a $\forall\exists$-formula is constructed and checked for validity. Intuitively the formula expresses the ability of *Body* to transition each state which satisfies *Guard* to a state which satisfies *Guard* as well. If the validity of $\forall\exists$-formula is proven, the algorithm converges (line 7). Otherwise, a refinement of P needs to be guessed. Thus, the algorithm samples a new formula (line 16) using the production rule INEQ, which is described in Sect. 3, pushes it to *Refs*, and iterates. Note that G permits formulas over V only (i.e., to restrict *Guard*), however, in principle it can be extended for sampling formulas over $V \cup V'$ (thus, to restrict *Body* as well).

For the progress of the algorithm, it must keep track of how each new candidate *cand* corresponds to constraints already belonging to *Refs*. That is, *cand* should not be implied by $Guard \wedge \bigwedge_{r \in Refs} r$ since otherwise the $\forall\exists$-formula in the next iteration would not change. Also, *cand* should not over-constrain the loop guard, and thus it is important to check that after adding *cand* to constraints from *Guard* and *Refs*, the loop guard is still reachable from the initial states. Both these checks are performed before the sampling (line 9). After the sampling, necessary adjustments on the probability distributions, assigned to the production rules of the grammar [16], are applied to ensure the same refinement candidates are not re-sampled again (line 17).

Because by construction G cannot generate conjunctions of constraints, the algorithm handles conjunctions externally. It is useful in case when a single constraint is not enough for application of Lemma 1, and it should be strengthened by another constraint. On the other hand, it also might be needed to withdraw some sampled candidates before converging. For this reason, Algorithm 3 maintains a stack *Gramms* of grammars and handles it synchronously with stack *Refs* (lines 12–14 and 18–19). When all candidates from a grammar were considered and were unsuccessful, the algorithm pops the latest candidate from *Refs* and rolls back to the grammar used in the previous iteration. Additionally, a maximum size of *Refs* can be specified to avoid considering too deep refinements.

Theorem 3. *If Algorithm 3 returns* DOES NOT TERMINATE *for program P, then P does not terminate.*

Indeed, constraints that belong to *Refs* in the last iteration of the algorithm give rise to a refinement P' of P, such that $P' = \langle V \cup V', Init, Tr \wedge \bigwedge_{r \in Refs} r \rangle$. The satisfiability check (line 9) and the validity check (line 6) passed, which correspond to the conditions of Lemma 1. Thus, P' does not terminate, and consequently it has an infinite trace. Finally, since P' refines P then all traces (including infinite ones) of P' belong to P, and P does not terminate as well.

5.2 Integrating Algorithms Together

With a few exceptions [30,39], existing algorithms address either the task of proving, or the task of disproving termination. The goal of this paper is to show that both tasks benefit from syntax-guided techniques. While an algorithmic integration of several orthogonal techniques is itself a challenging problem, it is not the focus of our paper. Still, we use a straightforward idea here. Since each presented algorithm has one big loop, an iteration of Algorithm 1 could be followed by an iteration of Algorithm 2 and in turn, by an iteration of Algorithm 3 (i.e., in a lockstep fashion). A positive result obtained by any algorithm forces all remaining algorithms to terminate. Based on our experiments, provided in detail in Sect. 6, the majority of benchmarks were proven either terminating or non-terminating by one of the algorithms within seconds. This justifies why the lockstep execution of all algorithms in practice would not bring a significant overhead.

6 Evaluation

We have implemented algorithms for proving termination and non-termination in a tool called FREQTERM[4]. It is developed on top of FREQHORN [16], uses it for Horn solving, and supports other Horn solvers, SPACER3 [26] and μZ [24], as well. To solve $\forall\exists$-formulas, FREQTERM uses the AE-VAL tool [15]. All the symbolic reasoning in the end is performed by the Z3 SMT solver [11].

FREQTERM takes as input a program encoded as a system of linear constrained Horn clauses (CHC). It supports any programming language, as long as a translator from it to CHCs exists. For encoding benchmarks to CHCs, we used SEAHORN v.0.1.0-rc3. To the best of our knowledge, FREQTERM is the only (non)-termination prover that supports a selection of Horn solvers in the backend. This allows the prover to leverage advancements in Horn solving easily.

We have compared FREQTERM against APROVE rev. c181f40 [18], ULTIMATE AUTOMIZER v.0.1.23 [22], and HIPTNT+ v.1.0 [30]. The rest of the section summarizes three sets of experiments. Sections 6.1 and 6.2 discuss the comparison on small but tricky programs, respectively terminating and non-terminating, which shows that our approach is applicable to a wide range of conceptually challenging problems. In Sect. 6.3, we target several large-scale benchmarks and show that FREQTERM is capable of significant pushing the boundaries of termination and non-termination proving. In total, we considered 856 benchmarks of various size and complexity. All experiments were conducted on a Linux SMP machine, Intel(R) Xeon(R) CPU E5-2680 v4 @ 2.40 GHz, 56 CPUs, 377 GB RAM.

6.1 Performance on Terminating Benchmarks

We considered **171** terminating programs[5] from the Termination category of SVCOMP and programs crafted by ourselves. Altogether, four tools in our experiment were able to prove termination of 168 of them within a timeout of 60 s and

---

[4] The source code of the tool is publicly.
[5] These benchmarks are available at https://goo.gl/MPimXE.

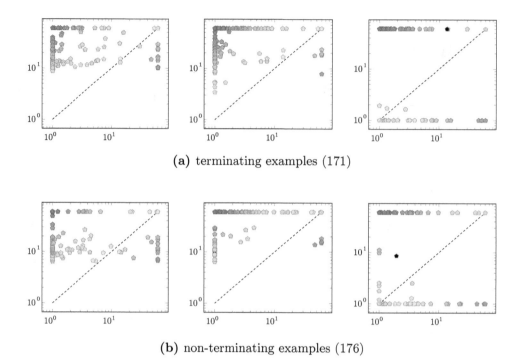

(a) terminating examples (171)

(b) non-terminating examples (176)

Fig. 4. FREQTERM vs respectively ULTIMATE AUTOMIZER, APROVE, and HIPTNT+.

left only three programs without a verdict. APROVE verified 76 benchmarks, HIPTNT+ 90 (including 3 that no other tool solved), ULTIMATE AUTOMIZER 105 (including 4 that no other tool solved). FREQTERM, implementing Algorithms 1–2 and relying on different solvers verified in total **155** (including **30** that no other tool solved). In particular, Algorithm 1 instantiated with SPACER3, proved termination of 88 programs, with μZ 79, and with FREQHORN 80. Algorithm 2 instantiated with SPACER3, proved termination of 92 programs, with μZ 109, and with FREQHORN 74.

A scatterplot with logarithmic scale on the axes in Fig. 4(a) shows comparisons of best running times of FREQTERM vs the running times of competing tools. Each point in a plot represents a pair of the FREQTERM run (x-axis) and the competing tool run (y-axis). Intuitively, green points represent cases when FREQTERM outperforms the competitor. On average, for programs solved by both FREQTERM and ULTIMATE AUTOMIZER, FREQTERM is 29 times faster (speedup calculated as a ratio of geometric means of the corresponding runs). In a similar setting, FREQTERM is 32 times faster than APROVE. However, FREQTERM is 2 times slower than HIPTNT+. The evaluation further revealed (in Sect. 6.3) that the latter tool is efficient only on small programs (around 10 lines of code each), and for large-scale benchmarks it exceeds the timeout.

6.2   Performance on Non-terminating Benchmarks

We considered **176** terminating programs[6] from the Termination category of
SVCOMP and programs crafted by ourselves. Altogether, four tools proved
non-termination of 172 of them: APROVE 35, HIPTNT+ 92, ULTIMATE
AUTOMIZER 123, and Algorithm 3 implemented in FREQTERM **152**. Additionally, we evaluated the effect of $\forall\exists$-solving in FREQTERM. For that reason, we
implemented a version of Algorithm 3 in which non-termination is reduced to
safety, but the conceptual SyGuS-based refinement generator remained the same.
This implementation used SPACER3 for proving that the candidate refinement
can never exit the loop. Among 176 benchmarks, such routine solved only 105,
which is 30% fewer than Algorithm 3. However, it managed to verify 8 benchmarks that Algorithm 3 could not verify (we believe, because SPACER3 was able
to add an auxiliary inductive invariant).

Logarithmic scatterplot in Fig. 4(b) shows comparisons of FREQTERM vs the
running times of competing tools. On average, FREQTERM is 41 times faster than
ULTIMATE AUTOMIZER, 73 times faster than APROVE, and exhibits roughly
similar runtimes to HIPTNT+ (again, here we considered only programs solved
by both tools). Based on these experiments, we conclude that currently FREQ-
TERM is more effective and more efficient at synthesizing non-terminating program refinements than at synthesizing terminating arguments.

6.3   Large-Scale Benchmarks

We considered some large-scale benchmarks for evaluation arising from Event-
Condition-Action (ECA) systems that describe reactive behavior [1]. We considered various modifications of five challenging ECAs[7]. Each ECA consists of one
large loop, where each iteration reads an input and modifies its internal state.
If an unexpected input is read, the ECA terminates.

In our first case study, we aimed to prove non-termination of the given ECAs,
i.e., that for any reachable internal state there exists an input value that would
keep the ECA alive. The main challenge appeared to be in the size of benchmarks
(up to 10000 lines of C code per loop) and reliance on an auxiliary inductive
invariant. With the extra support of SPACER3 to provide the invariant, FRE-
QTERM was able to prove non-termination of a wide range of programs. Among
all the competing tools, only ULTIMATE AUTOMIZER was able to handle these
benchmarks, but it verified only a small fraction of them within a 2 h timeout. In
contrast, FREQTERM solved 301 out of 302 tasks and outperformed ULTIMATE
AUTOMIZER by up to several orders of magnitude (i.e., from seconds to hours).
Table 1 contains a brief summary of our experimental evaluation.[8]

In our second case study, we instrumented the ECAs by adding extra conditions to the loop guards, thus imposing an implicit upper bound on the number

---

[6] These benchmarks are available at https://goo.gl/bZbuA2.

[7] These benchmarks are available at https://goo.gl/7mc2Ww.

[8] To calculate average timings, we excluded cases when the tool exceeded timeout.

Table 1. FREQTERM vs ULTIMATE AUTOMIZER on non-terminating ECAs (302).

Benchmarks			FREQTERM		ULTIMATE AUTOMIZER	
Class	# of tasks	Avg # of LoC	# solved	Avg time	# solved	Avg time
1 & 2	122	500	122	5 sec	3	27 min
3	60	1600	60	56 sec	0	∞
4	60	4700	60	9 min	6	82 min
5	60	10000	59	52 min	0	∞

Table 2. FREQTERM vs ULTIMATE AUTOMIZER on terminating ECAs (207).

Benchmarks			FREQTERM		ULTIMATE AUTOMIZER	
Class	# of tasks	Avg # of LoC	# solved	Avg time	# solved	Avg time
1 & 2	97	500	97	8 sec	96	73 sec
3	40	1600	40	3 min	12	56 min
4	35	4700	35	10 min	27	19 min
5	35	10000	34	65 min	19	99 min

of loop iterations, and applied tools to prove termination[9] (shown in Table 2). Again, only ULTIMATE AUTOMIZER was able to compete with FREQTERM, and interestingly it was more successful here than in the first case study. Encouragingly, FREQTERM solved all but one instance and was consistently faster.

7 Related Work

Proving Termination. A wide range of state-of-the-art methods are based on iterative reasoning driven by counterexamples [4,5,9,10,19,21,23,27,29,36] whose goal is to show that transitions cannot be executed forever. These approaches typically combine termination arguments, proven independently, but none of them leverages the syntax of programs during the analysis.

A minor range of tools of termination analyzers are based on various types of learning. In particular, [39] discovers a terminating argument from attempts to prove that no program state is terminating; [34] exploits information derived from tests, [37] guesses and checks transition invariants (over-approximations to the reachable transitive closure of the transition relation) from libraries of templates. The closest to our approach, [31] guesses and checks transition invariants using loop guards and branch conditions. In contrast, our algorithms guess lower bounds for auxiliary program counters and extensively use all available source code for guessing candidates.

---

[9] The task of adding interesting guards appeared to be non-trivial, so we were able to instrument only a part of all non-terminating benchmarks.

Proving Non-termination. Traditional algorithms, e.g. [3, 6, 8, 20, 22], are based on a search for lasso-shaped traces and a discovery of *recurrence sets*, i.e., states that are visited infinitely often. For instance, [32] searches for a geometric series in lasso-shaped traces. Our algorithm discovers *existential* recurrence sets and does not deal with traces at all: it handles their abstraction via a $\forall\exists$-formula.

A reduction to safety attracts significant attention here as well. In particular, [40] relies only on invariant generation to show that the loop guard is also satisfied, [19] infers weakest preconditions over inputs, under which program is non-terminating; and [7, 28] iteratively eliminate terminating traces through a loop by adding extra assumptions. In contrast, our approach does not reduce to safety, and thus does not necessarily require invariants. However, we observed that if provided, in practice they often accelerate our verification process.

Syntax-Guided Synthesis. SyGuS [2] is applied to various tasks related to program synthesis, e.g., [13, 17, 25, 33, 35, 41]. However, the formal grammar in those applications is typically given or constructed from user-provided examples. To the best of our knowledge, the only application of SyGuS to automatic program analysis was proposed by [14, 16], and it inspired our approach. Originally, the formal grammar, constructed from the verification condition, was iteratively used to guess and check only inductive invariants. In this paper, we showed that a similar reasoning is practical and easily transferable across applications.

8   Conclusion

We have presented new algorithms for synthesis of termination arguments and non-terminating program refinements. Driven by SyGuS, they iteratively generate candidate formulas which tend to follow syntactic patterns obtained from the source code. By construction, the number of possible candidates is always finite, thus the search space is always relatively small. The algorithms rely on recent advances in constraint solving, they do not depend on a particular backend engine, and thus performance of checking validity of a candidate can be improved by advancements in solvers. Our implementation FREQTERM is evaluated on a wide range of terminating and non-terminating benchmarks. It is competitive with state-of-the-art and it significantly outperforms other tools when proving non-termination of large-scale Event-Condition-Action systems.

In future work, it would be interesting to investigate synergetic ways of integrating the proposed algorithms together, as well as exploiting strengths of different backend Horn solvers for different verification tasks.

References

1. Almeida, E.E., Luntz, J.E., Tilbury, D.M.: Event-condition-action systems for reconfigurable logic control. IEEE Trans. Autom. Sci. Eng. 4(2), 167–181 (2007)
2. Alur, R., Bodík, R., Juniwal, G., Martin, M.M.K., Raghothaman, M., Seshia, S.A., Singh, R., Solar-Lezama, A., Torlak, E., Udupa, A.: Syntax-guided synthesis. In: FMCAD, pp. 1–17. IEEE (2013)

3. Bakhirkin, A., Piterman, N.: Finding recurrent sets with backward analysis and trace partitioning. In: Chechik, M., Raskin, J.-F. (eds.) TACAS 2016. LNCS, vol. 9636, pp. 17–35. Springer, Heidelberg (2016). https://doi.org/10.1007/978-3-662-49674-9_2

4. Balaban, I., Pnueli, A., Zuck, L.D.: Ranking abstraction as companion to predicate abstraction. In: Wang, F. (ed.) FORTE 2005. LNCS, vol. 3731, pp. 1–12. Springer, Heidelberg (2005). https://doi.org/10.1007/11562436_1

5. Brockschmidt, M., Cook, B., Fuhs, C.: Better termination proving through cooperation. In: Sharygina, N., Veith, H. (eds.) CAV 2013. LNCS, vol. 8044, pp. 413–429. Springer, Heidelberg (2013). https://doi.org/10.1007/978-3-642-39799-8_28

6. Brockschmidt, M., Ströder, T., Otto, C., Giesl, J.: Automated detection of non-termination and NullPointerExceptions for Java Bytecode. In: Beckert, B., Damiani, F., Gurov, D. (eds.) FoVeOOS 2011. LNCS, vol. 7421, pp. 123–141. Springer, Heidelberg (2012). https://doi.org/10.1007/978-3-642-31762-0_9

7. Chen, H.-Y., Cook, B., Fuhs, C., Nimkar, K., O'Hearn, P.: Proving nontermination via safety. In: Ábrahám, E., Havelund, K. (eds.) TACAS 2014. LNCS, vol. 8413, pp. 156–171. Springer, Heidelberg (2014). https://doi.org/10.1007/978-3-642-54862-8_11

8. Cook, B., Fuhs, C., Nimkar, K., O'Hearn, P.W.: Disproving termination with over-approximation. In: FMCAD, pp. 67–74. IEEE (2014)

9. Cook, B., Podelski, A., Rybalchenko, A.: Termination proofs for systems code. In: PLDI, pp. 415–426. ACM (2006)

10. Cook, B., See, A., Zuleger, F.: Ramsey vs. lexicographic termination proving. In: Piterman, N., Smolka, S.A. (eds.) TACAS 2013. LNCS, vol. 7795, pp. 47–61. Springer, Heidelberg (2013). https://doi.org/10.1007/978-3-642-36742-7_4

11. de Moura, L.M., Bjørner, N.: Z3: an efficient SMT solver. In: Ramakrishnan, C.R., Rehof, J. (eds.) TACAS 2008. LNCS, vol. 4963, pp. 337–340. Springer, Heidelberg (2008). https://doi.org/10.1007/978-3-540-78800-3_24

12. Detlefs, D., Nelson, G., Saxe, J.B.: Simplify: a theorem prover for program checking. J. ACM **52**(3), 365–473 (2005)

13. Fedyukovich, G., Ahmad, M.B.S., Bodík, R.: Gradual synthesis for static parallelization of single-pass array-processing programs. In: PLDI, pp. 572–585. ACM (2017)

14. Fedyukovich, G., Bodík, R.: Accelerating syntax-guided invariant synthesis. In: Beyer, D., Huisman, M. (eds.) TACAS 2018. LNCS, vol. 10805, pp. 251–269. Springer, Cham (2018). https://doi.org/10.1007/978-3-319-89960-2_14

15. Fedyukovich, G., Gurfinkel, A., Sharygina, N.: Automated discovery of simulation between programs. In: Davis, M., Fehnker, A., McIver, A., Voronkov, A. (eds.) LPAR 2015. LNCS, vol. 9450, pp. 606–621. Springer, Heidelberg (2015). https://doi.org/10.1007/978-3-662-48899-7_42

16. Fedyukovich, G., Kaufman, S., Bodík, R.: Sampling invariants from frequency distributions. In: FMCAD, pp. 100–107. IEEE (2017)

17. Galenson, J., Reames, P., Bodík, R., Hartmann, B., Sen, K.: CodeHint: dynamic and interactive synthesis of code snippets. In: ICSE, pp. 653–663. ACM (2014)

18. Giesl, J., et al.: Proving termination of programs automatically with AProVE. In: Demri, S., Kapur, D., Weidenbach, C. (eds.) IJCAR 2014. LNCS (LNAI), vol. 8562, pp. 184–191. Springer, Cham (2014). https://doi.org/10.1007/978-3-319-08587-6_13

19. Gulwani, S., Srivastava, S., Venkatesan, R.: Program analysis as constraint solving. In: PLDI, pp. 281–292. ACM (2008)

20. Gupta, A., Henzinger, T.A., Majumdar, R., Rybalchenko, A., Xu, R.: Proving non-termination. In: POPL, pp. 147–158. ACM (2008)
21. Harris, W.R., Lal, A., Nori, A.V., Rajamani, S.K.: Alternation for termination. In: Cousot, R., Martel, M. (eds.) SAS 2010. LNCS, vol. 6337, pp. 304–319. Springer, Heidelberg (2010). https://doi.org/10.1007/978-3-642-15769-1_19
22. Heizmann, M., et al.: Ultimate automizer with an on-demand construction of floyd-hoare automata. In: Legay, A., Margaria, T. (eds.) TACAS 2017. LNCS, vol. 10206, pp. 394–398. Springer, Heidelberg (2017). https://doi.org/10.1007/978-3-662-54580-5_30
23. Heizmann, M., Hoenicke, J., Podelski, A.: Termination analysis by learning terminating programs. In: Biere, A., Bloem, R. (eds.) CAV 2014. LNCS, vol. 8559, pp. 797–813. Springer, Cham (2014). https://doi.org/10.1007/978-3-319-08867-9_53
24. Hoder, K., Bjørner, N.: Generalized property directed reachability. In: Cimatti, A., Sebastiani, R. (eds.) SAT 2012. LNCS, vol. 7317, pp. 157–171. Springer, Heidelberg (2012). https://doi.org/10.1007/978-3-642-31612-8_13
25. Jha, S., Gulwani, S., Seshia, S.A., Tiwari, A.: Oracle-guided component-based program synthesis. In: ICSE, pp. 215–224. ACM (2010)
26. Komuravelli, A., Gurfinkel, A., Chaki, S.: SMT-based model checking for recursive programs. In: Biere, A., Bloem, R. (eds.) CAV 2014. LNCS, vol. 8559, pp. 17–34. Springer, Cham (2014). https://doi.org/10.1007/978-3-319-08867-9_2
27. Kroening, D., Sharygina, N., Tsitovich, A., Wintersteiger, C.M.: Termination analysis with compositional transition invariants. In: Touili, T., Cook, B., Jackson, P. (eds.) CAV 2010. LNCS, vol. 6174, pp. 89–103. Springer, Heidelberg (2010). https://doi.org/10.1007/978-3-642-14295-6_9
28. Larraz, D., Nimkar, K., Oliveras, A., Rodríguez-Carbonell, E., Rubio, A.: Proving non-termination using Max-SMT. In: Biere, A., Bloem, R. (eds.) CAV 2014. LNCS, vol. 8559, pp. 779–796. Springer, Cham (2014). https://doi.org/10.1007/978-3-319-08867-9_52
29. Larraz, D., Oliveras, A., Rodríguez-Carbonell, E., Rubio, A.: Proving termination of imperative programs using Max-SMT. In: FMCAD, pp. 218–225. IEEE (2013)
30. Le, T.C., Qin, S., Chin, W.: Termination and non-termination specification inference. In: PLDI, pp. 489–498. ACM (2015)
31. Lee, W., Wang, B.-Y., Yi, K.: Termination analysis with algorithmic learning. In: Madhusudan, P., Seshia, S.A. (eds.) CAV 2012. LNCS, vol. 7358, pp. 88–104. Springer, Heidelberg (2012). https://doi.org/10.1007/978-3-642-31424-7_12
32. Leike, J., Heizmann, M.: Geometric nontermination arguments. In: Beyer, D., Huisman, M. (eds.) TACAS 2018. LNCS, vol. 10806, pp. 266–283. Springer, Cham (2018). https://doi.org/10.1007/978-3-319-89963-3_16
33. Miltner, A., Fisher, K., Pierce, B.C., Walker, D., Zdancewic, S.: Synthesizing bijective lenses. PACMPL 2(POPL), 1:1–1:30 (2018)
34. Nori, A.V., Sharma, R.: Termination proofs from tests. In: ESEC/FSE, pp. 246–256. ACM (2013)
35. Panchekha, P., Torlak, E.: Automated reasoning for web page layout. In: OOPSLA, pp. 181–194. ACM (2016)
36. Podelski, A., Rybalchenko, A.: Transition invariants and transition predicate abstraction for program termination. In: Abdulla, P.A., Leino, K.R.M. (eds.) TACAS 2011. LNCS, vol. 6605, pp. 3–10. Springer, Heidelberg (2011). https://doi.org/10.1007/978-3-642-19835-9_2
37. Tsitovich, A., Sharygina, N., Wintersteiger, C.M., Kroening, D.: Loop summarization and termination analysis. In: Abdulla, P.A., Leino, K.R.M. (eds.) TACAS

2011. LNCS, vol. 6605, pp. 81–95. Springer, Heidelberg (2011). https://doi.org/10.1007/978-3-642-19835-9_9

38. Turing, A.M.: Checking a large routine. In: Report of a Conference on High Speed Automatic Calculating Machines (1949)

39. Urban, C., Gurfinkel, A., Kahsai, T.: Synthesizing ranking functions from bits and pieces. In: Chechik, M., Raskin, J.-F. (eds.) TACAS 2016. LNCS, vol. 9636, pp. 54–70. Springer, Heidelberg (2016). https://doi.org/10.1007/978-3-662-49674-9_4

40. Velroyen, H., Rümmer, P.: Non-termination checking for imperative programs. In: Beckert, B., Hähnle, R. (eds.) TAP 2008. LNCS, vol. 4966, pp. 154–170. Springer, Heidelberg (2008). https://doi.org/10.1007/978-3-540-79124-9_11

41. Wang, X., Dillig, I., Singh, R.: Program synthesis using abstraction refinement. PACMPL **2**, 63:1–63:30 (2018)

2

Model Checking Quantitative Hyperproperties

Bernd Finkbeiner, Christopher Hahn,
and Hazem Torfah[(✉)]

Reactive Systems Group, Saarland University,
Saarbrücken, Germany
{finkbeiner,hahn,torfah}@react.uni-saarland.de

Abstract. Hyperproperties are properties of sets of computation traces. In this paper, we study quantitative hyperproperties, which we define as hyperproperties that express a bound on the number of traces that may appear in a certain relation. For example, quantitative non-interference limits the amount of information about certain secret inputs that is leaked through the observable outputs of a system. Quantitative non-interference thus bounds the number of traces that have the same observable input but different observable output. We study quantitative hyperproperties in the setting of HyperLTL, a temporal logic for hyperproperties. We show that, while quantitative hyperproperties can be expressed in HyperLTL, the running time of the HyperLTL model checking algorithm is, depending on the type of property, exponential or even doubly exponential in the quantitative bound. We improve this complexity with a new model checking algorithm based on model-counting. The new algorithm needs only logarithmic space in the bound and therefore improves, depending on the property, exponentially or even doubly exponentially over the model checking algorithm of HyperLTL. In the worst case, the new algorithm needs polynomial space in the size of the system. Our Max#Sat-based prototype implementation demonstrates, however, that the counting approach is viable on systems with nontrivial quantitative information flow requirements such as a passcode checker.

1 Introduction

Model checking algorithms [17] are the cornerstone of computer-aided verification. As their input consists of both the system under verification and a logical formula that describes the property to be verified, they uniformly solve a wide range of verification problems, such as all verification problems expressible in linear-time temporal logic (LTL), computation-tree logic (CTL), or the modal μ-calculus. Recently, there has been a lot of interest in extending model checking from standard trace and tree properties to *information flow* policies like observational determinism or quantitative information flow. Such policies are called *hyperproperties* [21] and can be expressed in HyperLTL [18], an extension of LTL with trace quantifiers and trace variables. For example, *observational determinism* [47], the requirement that any pair of traces that have the same observable input also have the same observable output, can be expressed as the following HyperLTL formula: $\forall \pi. \forall \pi'. (\Box \pi =_I \pi') \rightarrow (\Box \pi =_O \pi')$ For many information flow policies of interest, including observational determinism, there is no longer a need for property-specific algorithms: it has been shown that the standard HyperLTL model checking algorithm [26] performs just as well as a specialized algorithm for the respective property.

The class of hyperproperties studied in this paper is one where, by contrast, the standard model checking algorithm performes badly. We are interested in *quantitative hyperproperties*, i.e., hyperproperties that express a bound on the number of traces that may appear in a certain relation. A prominent example of this class of properties is *quantitative non-interference* [43,45], where we allow some flow of information but, at the same time, limit the amount of information that may be leaked. Such properties are used, for example, to describe the correct behavior of a password check, where some information flow is unavoidable ("the password was incorrect"), and perhaps some extra information flow is acceptable ("the password must contain a special character"), but the information should not suffice to guess the actual password. In HyperLTL, quantitative non-interference can be expressed [18] as the formula $\forall \pi_0. \ \forall \pi_1 \dots \forall \pi_{2^c}. \left(\bigwedge_i \Box(\pi_i =_I \pi_0) \right) \rightarrow \left(\bigvee_{i \neq j} \Box(\pi_i =_O \pi_j) \right)$. The formula states that there do not exist $2^c + 1$ traces (corresponding to more than c bits of information) with the same observable input but different observable output. The bad performance of the standard model checking algorithm is a consequence of the fact that the $2^c + 1$ traces are tracked simultaneously. For this purpose, the model checking algorithm builds and analyzes a $(2^c + 1)$-fold self-composition of the system.

We present a new model checking algorithm for quantitative hyperproperties that avoids the construction of the huge self-composition. The key idea of our approach is to use *counting* rather than *checking* as the basic operation. Instead of building the self-composition and then *checking* the satisfaction of the formula, we add new atomic propositions and then *count* the number of sequences of evaluations of the new atomic propositions that satisfy the specification. Quantitative hyperproperties are expressions of the following form:

$$\forall \pi_1. \dots \forall \pi_k. \varphi \rightarrow (\# \sigma : X. \psi \vartriangleleft n),$$

where $\vartriangleleft \in \{\leq, <, \geq, >, =\}$. The universal quantifiers introduce a set of reference traces against which other traces can be compared. The formulas φ and ψ are HyperLTL formulas. The counting quantifier $\# \sigma : X. \psi$ counts the number of paths σ with different valuations of the atomic propositions X that satisfy ψ. The requirement that no more than c bits of information are leaked is the following quantitative hyperproperty:

$$\forall \pi. \# \sigma : O. \Box(\pi =_I \sigma) \leq 2^c$$

As we show in the paper, such expressions do not change the expressiveness of the logic; however, they allow us to express quantitative hyperproperties in exponentially more concise form. The counting-based model checking algorithm then maintains this advantage with a logarithmic counter, resulting in exponentially better performance in both time and space.

The viability of our counting-based model checking algorithm is demonstrated on a SAT-based prototype implementation. For quantitative hyperproperties of intrest, such as bounded leakage of a password checker, our algorithm shows promising results, as it significantly outperforms existing model checking approaches.

1.1 Related Work

Quantitative information-flow has been studied extensively in the literature. See, for example, the following selection of contributions on this topic: [1,14,19,32, 34,43]. Multiple verification methods for quantitative information-flow were proposed for sequential systems. For example, with static analysis techniques [15], approximation methods [35], equivalence relations [3,22], and randomized methods [35]. Quantitative information-flow for multi-threaded programs was considered in [11].

The study of quantitative information-flow in a reactive setting gained a lot of attention recently after the introduction of hyperproperties [21] and the idea of verifying the self-composition of a reactive system [6] in order to relate traces to each other. There are several possibilities to measure the amount of leakage, such as Shannon entropy [15,24,37], guessing entropy [3,34], and min-entropy [43]. A classification of quantitative information-flow policies as safety and liveness hyperproperties was given in [46]. While several verification techniques for hyperproperties exists [5,31,38,42], the literature was missing general approaches to quantitative information-flow control. SecLTL [25] was introduced as first general approach to model check (quantitative) hyperproperties, before HyperLTL [18], and its corresponding model checker [26], was introduced as a temporal logic for hyperproperties, which subsumes the previous approaches.

Using counting to compute the number of solutions of a given formula is studied in the literature as well and includes many probabilistic inference problems, such as Bayesian net reasoning [36], and planning problems, such as computing robustness of plans in incomplete domains [40]. State-of-the-art tools for propositional model counting are `Relsat` [33] and `c2d` [23]. Algorithms for counting models of temporal logics and automata over infinite words have been introduced in [27,28,44]. The counting of projected models, i.e., when some parts of the models are irrelevant, was studied in [2], for which tools such as `#CLASP` [2] and `DSharp_P` [2,41] exist. Our SAT-based prototype implementation is based on a reduction to a Max#SAT [29] instance, for which a corresponding tool exists.

Among the already existing tools for computing the amount of information leakage, for example, `QUAIL` [8], which analyzes programs written in a specific while-language and `LeakWatch` [12], which estimates the amount of leakage in

Java programs, `Moped-QLeak` [9] is closest to our approach. However, their approach of computing a symbolic summary as an Algebraic Decision Diagram is, in contrast to our approach, solely based on model counting, not maximum model counting.

2 Preliminaries

2.1 HyperLTL

HyperLTL [18] extends linear-time temporal logic (LTL) with trace variables and trace quantifiers. Let AP be a set of *atomic propositions*. A *trace* t is an infinite sequence over subsets of the atomic propositions. We define the set of traces $TR := (2^{AP})^{\omega}$. A subset $T \subseteq TR$ is called a *trace property* and a subset $H \subseteq 2^{TR}$ is called a *hyperproperty*. We use the following notation to manipulate traces: let $t \in TR$ be a trace and $i \in \mathbb{N}$ be a natural number. $t[i]$ denotes the i-th element of t. Therefore, $t[0]$ represents the starting element of the trace. Let $j \in \mathbb{N}$ and $j \geq i$. $t[i, j]$ denotes the sequence $t[i] \ t[i+1] \ldots t[j-1] \ t[j]$. $t[i, \infty]$ denotes the infinite suffix of t starting at position i.

HyperLTL Syntax. Let $\mathcal{V}$ be an infinite supply of trace variables. The syntax of HyperLTL is given by the following grammar:

$$\psi ::= \exists \pi.\psi \mid \forall \pi.\psi \mid \varphi$$
$$\varphi ::= a_{\pi} \mid \neg \varphi \mid \varphi \vee \varphi \mid \bigcirc \varphi \mid \varphi \, \mathcal{U} \, \varphi$$

where $a \in AP$ is an atomic proposition and $\pi \in \mathcal{V}$ is a trace variable. Note that atomic propositions are indexed by trace variables. The quantification over traces makes it possible to express properties like "on all traces ψ must hold", which is expressed by $\forall \pi. \ \psi$. Dually, one can express that "there exists a trace such that ψ holds", which is denoted by $\exists \pi. \ \psi$. The derived operators $\Diamond$, $\Box$, and $\mathcal{W}$ are defined as for LTL. We abbreviate the formula $\bigwedge_{x \in X}(x_{\pi} \leftrightarrow x_{\pi'})$, expressing that the traces π and π' are equal with respect to a set $X \subseteq AP$ of atomic propositions, by $\pi =_X \pi'$. Furthermore, we call a trace variable π free in a HyperLTL formula if there is no quantification over π and we call a HyperLTL formula φ closed if there exists no free trace variable in φ.

HyperLTL Semantics. A HyperLTL formula defines a *hyperproperty*, i.e., a set of sets of traces. A set T of traces satisfies the hyperproperty if it is an element of this set of sets. Formally, the semantics of HyperLTL formulas is given with respect to a *trace assignment* Π from $\mathcal{V}$ to TR, i.e., a partial function mapping trace variables to actual traces. $\Pi[\pi \mapsto t]$ denotes that π is mapped to t, with everything else mapped according to Π. $\Pi[i, \infty]$ denotes the trace assignment that is equal to $\Pi(\pi)[i, \infty]$ for all π.

$$\Pi \models_T \exists \pi. \psi \qquad \text{iff} \qquad \text{there exists } t \in T \ : \ \Pi[\pi \mapsto t] \models_T \psi$$

$$\Pi \models_T \forall \pi. \psi \qquad \text{iff} \qquad \text{for all } t \in T \ : \ \Pi[\pi \mapsto t] \models_T \psi$$

$$\Pi \models_T a_\pi \qquad \text{iff} \qquad a \in \Pi(\pi)[0]$$

$$\Pi \models_T \neg \psi \qquad \text{iff} \qquad \Pi \not\models_T \psi$$

$$\Pi \models_T \psi_1 \vee \psi_2 \qquad \text{iff} \qquad \Pi \models_T \psi_1 \text{ or } \Pi \models_T \psi_2$$

$$\Pi \models_T \bigcirc \psi \qquad \text{iff} \qquad \Pi[1, \infty] \models_T \psi$$

$$\Pi \models_T \psi_1 \,\mathcal{U}\, \psi_2 \qquad \text{iff} \qquad \text{there exists } i \geq 0 : \Pi[i, \infty] \models_T \psi_2$$
$$\text{and for all } 0 \leq j < i \text{ we have } \Pi[j, \infty] \models_T \psi_1$$

We say a set of traces T *satisfies* a HyperLTL formula φ if $\Pi \models_T \varphi$, where Π is the empty trace assignment.

2.2 System Model

A *Kripke structure* is a tuple $K = (S, s_0, \delta, AP, L)$ consisting of a set of states S, an initial state $s_0 \in S$, a transition function $\delta : S \to 2^S$, a set of *atomic propositions* AP, and a *labeling function* $L : S \to 2^{AP}$, which labels every state with a set of atomic propositions. We assume that each state has a successor, i.e., $\delta(s) \neq \emptyset$. This ensures that every run on a Kripke structure can always be extended to an infinite run. We define a *path* of a Kripke structure as an infinite sequence of states $s_0 s_1 \cdots \in S^\omega$ such that s_0 is the initial state of K and $s_{i+1} \in \delta(s_i)$ for every $i \in \mathbb{N}$. We denote the set of all paths of K that start in a state s with $Paths(K, s)$. Furthermore, $Paths^*(K, s)$ denotes the set of all path prefixes and $Paths^\omega(K, s)$ the set of all path suffixes. A *trace* of a Kripke structure is an infinite sequence of sets of atomic propositions $L(s_0), L(s_1), \cdots \in (2^{AP})^\omega$, such that s_0 is the initial state of K and $s_{i+1} \in \delta(s_i)$ for every $i \in \mathbb{N}$. We denote the set of all traces of K that start in a state s with $TR(K, s)$. We say that a Kripke structure K *satisfies* a HyperLTL formula φ if its set of traces satisfies φ, i.e., if $\Pi \models_{TR(K, s_0)} \varphi$, where Π is the empty trace assignment.

2.3 Automata over Infinite Words

In our construction we use automata over infinite words. A *Büchi automaton* is a tuple $\mathcal{B} = (Q, Q_0, \delta, \Sigma, F)$, where Q is a set of states, Q_0 is a set of initial states, $\delta : Q \times \Sigma \to 2^Q$ is a transition relation, and $F \subset Q$ are the accepting states. A run of $\mathcal{B}$ on an infinite word $w = \alpha_1 \alpha_2 \cdots \in \Sigma^\omega$ is an infinite sequence $r = q_0 q_1 \cdots \in Q^\omega$ of states, where $q_0 \in Q_0$ and for each $i \geq 0$, $q_{i+1} = \delta(q_i, \alpha_{i+1})$. We define $\mathbf{Inf}(r) = \{q \in Q \mid \forall i \exists j > i.\ r_j = q\}$. A run r is called accepting if $\mathbf{Inf}(r) \cap F \neq \emptyset$. A word w is accepted by $\mathcal{B}$ and called a *model* of $\mathcal{B}$ if there is an accepting run of $\mathcal{B}$ on w.

Furthermore, an *alternating automaton*, whose runs generalize from sequences to trees, is a tuple $\mathcal{A} = (Q, Q_0, \delta, \Sigma, F)$. Q, Q_0, Σ, and F are defined as above and $\delta : Q \times \Sigma \to \mathbb{B}^+ Q$ being a transition function, which maps a state and a symbol into a Boolean combination of states. Thus, a run(-tree) of an alternating Büchi automaton $\mathcal{A}$ on an infinite word w is a Q-labeled tree. A word w is accepted by $\mathcal{A}$ and called a *model* if there exists a run-tree T such that all paths p trough T are accepting, i.e., $\mathbf{Inf}(p) \cap F \neq \emptyset$.

A strongly connected component (SCC) in $\mathcal{A}$ is a maximal strongly connected component of the graph induced by the automaton. An SCC is called *accepting* if one of its states is an accepting state in $\mathcal{A}$.

3   Quantitative Hyperproperties

Quantitative Hyperproperties are properties of sets of computation traces that express a bound on the number of traces that may appear in a certain relation. In the following, we study quantitative hyperproperties that are specified in terms of HyperLTL formulas. We consider expressions of the following general form:

$$\forall \pi_1, \ldots, \pi_k.\ \varphi \rightarrow (\#\sigma : A.\ \psi \lhd n)$$

Both the universally quantified variables $\pi_1, \ldots, \pi_k$ and the variable σ after the *counting* operator $\#$ are trace variables; φ is a HyperLTL formula over atomic propositions AP and free trace variables $\pi_1 \ldots \pi_k$; $A \subseteq AP$ is a set of atomic propositions; ψ is a HyperLTL formula over atomic propositions AP and free trace variables $\pi_1 \ldots \pi_k$ and, additionally σ. The operator $\lhd \in \{<, \leq, =, >, \geq\}$ is a comparison operator; and $n \in \mathbb{N}$ is a natural number.

For a given set of traces T and a valuation of the trace variables $\pi_1, \ldots, \pi_k$, the term $\#\sigma : A.\ \psi$ computes the number of traces σ in T that differ in their valuation of the atomic propositions in A and satisfy ψ. The expression $\#\sigma : A.\ \psi \lhd n$ is *true* iff the resulting number satisfies the comparison with n. Finally, the complete expression $\forall \pi_1, \ldots, \pi_k.\ \varphi \rightarrow (\#\sigma : A.\ \psi \lhd n)$ is *true* iff for all combinations $\pi_1, \ldots, \pi_k$ of traces in T that satisfy φ, the comparison $\#\sigma : A.\ \psi \lhd n$ is satisfied.

Example 1 (Quantitative non-interference). Quantitative information-flow policies [13, 20, 30, 34] allow the flow of a bounded amount of information. One way to measure leakage is with *min-entropy* [43], which quantifies the amount of information an attacker can gain given the answer to a single guess about the secret. The *bounding problem* [45] for min-entropy is to determine whether that amount is bounded from above by a constant 2^c, corresponding to c bits. We assume that the program whose leakage is being quantified is deterministic, and assume that the secret input to that program is uniformly distributed. The bounding problem then reduces to determining that there is no tuple of $2^c + 1$ distinguishable traces [43, 45]. Let $O \subseteq AP$ be the set of observable outputs. A simple quantitative information flow policy is then the following quantitative hyperproperty, which bounds the number of distinguishable outputs to 2^c, corresponding to a bound of c bits of information:

$$\#\sigma : O.\ true \leq 2^c$$

A slightly more complicated information flow policy is quantitative non-interference. In quantitative non-interference, the bound must be satisfied for every individual input. Let $I \subseteq AP$ be the observable inputs to the system. Quantitative non-interference is the following quantitative hyperproperty[1]:

$$\forall \pi. \, \#\sigma \colon O. \; (\Box(\pi =_I \sigma)) \leq 2^c$$

For each trace π in the system, the property checks whether there are more than 2^c traces σ that have the same observable input as π but different observable output.

Example 2 (Deniability). A program satisfies *deniability* (see, for example, [7, 10]) when there is no proof that a certain input occurred from simply observing the output, i.e., given an output of a program one cannot derive the input that lead to this output. A deterministic program satisfies deniability when each output can be mapped to at least two inputs. A quantitative variant of deniability is when we require that the number of corresponding inputs is larger than a given threshold. Quantitative deniability can be specified as the following quantitative Hyperproperty:

$$\forall \pi. \, \#\sigma \colon I. \, (\Box(\pi =_O \sigma)) > n$$

For all traces π of the system we count the number of sequences σ in the system with different input sequences and the same output sequence of π, i.e., for the fixed output sequence given by π we count the number of input sequences that lead to this output.

4   Model Checking Quantitative Hyperproperties

We present a model checking algorithm for quantitative hyperproperties based on model counting. The advantage of the algorithm is that its runtime complexity is independent of the bound n and thus avoids the n-fold self-composition necessary for any encoding of the quantitative hyperproperty in HYPERLTL.

Before introducing our novel counting-based algorithm, we start by a translation of quantitative hyperproperties into formulas in HYPERLTL and establishing an exponential lower bound for its representation.

4.1   Standard Model Checking Algorithm: Encoding Quantitative Hyperproperties in HyperLTL

The idea of the reduction is to check a lower bound of n traces by existentially quantifying over n traces, and to check an upper bound of n traces by *universally* quantifying over $n + 1$ traces. The resulting HyperLTL formula can be verified using the standard model checking algorithm for HyperLTL [18].

---

[1] We write $\pi =_A \pi'$ short for $\pi_A = \pi'_A$ where π_A is the A-projection of π.

Theorem 1. *Every quantitative hyperproperty $\forall \pi_1, \ldots, \pi_k. \psi_\iota \to (\#\sigma : A. \psi \triangleleft n)$ can be expressed as a HyperLTL formula. For $\triangleleft \in \{\le\}(\{<\})$, the HyperLTL formula has $n + k + 1$(resp. $n + k$) universal trace quantifiers in addition to the quantifiers in ψ_ι and ψ. For $\triangleleft \in \{\ge\}(\{>\})$, the HyperLTL formula has k universal trace quantifiers and n (resp. $n + 1$) existential trace quantifiers in addition to the quantifiers in ψ_ι and ψ. For $\triangleleft \in \{=\}$, the HyperLTL formula has $k + n + 1$ universal trace quantifiers and n existential trace quantifiers in addition to the quantifiers in ψ_ι and ψ.*

Proof. For $\triangleleft \in \{\le\}$, we encode the quantitative hyperproperty $\forall \pi_1, \ldots, \pi_k. \psi_\iota \to (\#\sigma : A. \psi \triangleleft n)$ as the following HyperLTL formula:

$$\forall \pi_1, \ldots, \pi_k. \forall \pi'_1, \ldots, \pi'_{n+1}. \left(\psi_\iota \wedge \bigwedge_{i \ne j} \Diamond(\pi'_i \ne_A \pi'_j) \right) \to \left(\bigvee_i \neg\psi[\sigma \mapsto \pi'_i] \right)$$

where $\psi[\sigma \mapsto \pi'_i]$ is the HyperLTL formula ψ with all occurrences of σ replaced by π'_i. The formula states that there is no tuple of $n + 1$ traces $\pi'_1, \ldots, \pi'_{n+1}$ different in the evaluation of A, that satisfy ψ. In other words, for every $n + 1$ tuple of traces $\pi'_1, \ldots, \pi'_{n+1}$ that differ in the evaluation of A, one of the paths must violate ψ. For $\triangleleft \in \{<\}$, we use the same formula, with $\forall \pi'_1, \ldots, \pi'_n$ instead of $\forall \pi'_1, \ldots, \pi'_{n+1}$.

For $\triangleleft \in \{\ge\}$, we encode the quantitative hyperproperty analogously as the HyperLTL formula

$$\forall \pi_1, \ldots, \pi_k. \exists \pi'_1, \ldots, \pi'_n. \psi_\iota \to \left(\bigwedge_{i \ne j} \Diamond(\pi'_i \ne_A \pi'_j) \right) \wedge \left(\bigwedge_i \psi[\sigma \mapsto \pi'_i] \right)$$

The formula states that there exist paths $\pi'_1, \ldots, \pi'_n$ that differ in the evaluation of A and that all satisfy ψ. For $\triangleleft \in \{>\}$, we use the same formula, with $\exists \pi'_1, \ldots, \pi'_{n+1}$ instead of $\forall \pi'_1, \ldots, \pi'_n$. Lastly, for $\triangleleft \in \{=\}$, we encode the quantitative hyperproperty as a conjunction of the encodings for $\le$ and for $\ge$.

Example 3 (Quantitative non-interference in HyperLTL). As discussed in Example 1, quantitative non-interference is the quantitative hyperproperty

$$\forall \pi. \#\sigma : O. \square(\pi =_I \sigma) \le 2^c,$$

where we measure the amount of leakage with min-entropy [43]. The bounding problem for min-entropy asks whether the amount of information leaked by a system is bounded by a constant 2^c where c is the number of bits. This is encoded in HyperLTL as the requirement that there are no $2^c + 1$ traces distinguishable in their output:

$$\forall \pi_0. \forall \pi_1 \ldots \forall \pi_{2^c}. \left(\bigwedge_i \square(\pi_i =_I \pi_0) \right) \to \left(\bigvee_{i \ne j} \square(\pi_i =_O \pi_j) \right).$$

This formula is equivalent to the formalization of quantitative non-interference given in [26].

Model checking quantitative hyperproperties via the reduction to HyperLTL is very expensive. In the best case, when $\lhd \in \{\leq, <\}$, ψ_ι does not contain existential quantifiers, and ψ does not contain universal quantifiers, we obtain an HyperLTL formula without quantifier alternations, where the number of quantifiers grows linearly with the bound n. For m quantifiers, the HyperLTL model checking algorithm [26] constructs and analyzes the m-fold self-composition of the Kripke structure. The running time of the model checking algorithm is thus exponential in the bound. If $\lhd \in \{\geq, >, =\}$, the encoding additionally introduces a quantifier alternation. The model checking algorithm checks quantifier alternations via a complementation of Büchi automata, which adds another exponent, resulting in an overall doubly exponential running time.

The model checking algorithm we introduce in the next section avoids the n-fold self-composition needed in the model checking algorithm of HyperLTL and its complexity is independent of the bound n.

4.2 Counting-Based Model Checking Algorithm

A Kripke structure $K = (S, s_0, \tau, AP, L)$ violates a quantitative hyperproperty

$$\varphi = \forall \pi_1, \ldots, \pi_k. \ \psi_\iota \rightarrow (\#\sigma : A.\psi \lhd n)$$

if there is a k-tuple $t = (\pi_1, \ldots, \pi_k)$ of traces $\pi_i \in TR(K)$ that satisfies the formula

$$\exists \pi_1, \ldots, \pi_k. \ \psi_\iota \wedge (\#\sigma : A. \ \psi \,\overline{\lhd}\, n)$$

where $\overline{\lhd}$ is the negation of the comparison operator $\lhd$. The tuple t then satisfies the property ψ_ι and the number of $(k+1)$-tuples $t' = (\pi_1, \ldots, \pi_k, \sigma)$ for $\sigma \in TR(K)$ that satisfy ψ and differ pairwise in the A-projection of σ satisfies the comparison $\overline{\lhd} \ n$ (The A-projection of a sequence σ is defined as the sequence $\sigma_A \in (2^A)^\omega$, such that for every position i and every $a \in A$ it holds that $a \in \sigma_A[i]$ if and only if $a \in \sigma[i]$). The tuples t' can be captured by the automaton composed of the product of an automaton $A_{\psi_\iota \wedge \psi}$ that accepts all $k+1$ of traces that satisfy both ψ_ι and ψ and a $k + 1$-self composition of K. Each accepting run of the product automaton presents $k + 1$ traces of K that satisfy $\psi_\iota \wedge \psi$. On top of the product automaton, we apply a special counting algorithm which we explain in detail in Sect. 4.4 and check if the result satisfies the comparison $\overline{\lhd} \ n$.

Algorithm 1 gives a general picture of our model checking algorithm. The algorithm has two parts. The first part applies if the relation $\overline{\lhd}$ is one of $\{\geq, >\}$. In this case, the algorithm checks whether a sequence over AP_ψ (propositions in ψ) corresponds to infinitely many sequences over A. This is done by checking whether the product automaton B has a so-called *doubly pumped lasso*(DPL), a subgraph with two connected lassos, with a unique sequence over AP_ψ and different sequences over A. Such a doubly pumped lasso matches the same sequence over AP_ψ with infinitely many sequences over A (more in Sect. 4.4). If no doubly pumped lasso is found, a projected model counting algorithm is applied in the second part of the algorithm in order to compute either the maximum or the minimum value, corresponding to the comparison operator $\overline{\lhd}$. In the next subsections, we explain the individual parts of the algorithm in detail.

Algorithm 1. Counting-based Model Checking of Quantitative Hyperproperties

---

Input: Quantitative Hyperproperty $\varphi = \forall \pi_1 \ldots \pi_k.\ \psi_\iota \rightarrow (\#\sigma : A.\psi \lhd n)$, Kripke
    Structure $K = (S, s_0, \tau, AP, L)$
Output: $K \models \varphi$
 1: $B = QHLTL2BA(K, \pi_1, \ldots, \pi_k, \psi_\iota \wedge \psi)$
 2: /*Check Infinity*/
 3: **if** $\lhd \in \{\geq, >\}$ **then**
 4:    $ce = DPL(B)$
 5:   **if** $ce \neq \perp$ **then**
 6:     **return** ce
 7: /*Apply Projected Counting Algorithm*/
 8: **if** $\lhd \in \{\geq, >\}$ **then**
 9:    $ce = MaxCount(B, n, \lhd)$
10: **else**
11:    $ce = MinCount(B, n, \lhd)$
12: **return** ce

4.3 Büchi Automata for Quantitative Hyperproperties

For a quantitative hyperproperty $\varphi = \forall \pi_1 \ldots \pi_k.\ \psi_\iota \rightarrow (\#\sigma : A.\psi \lhd n)$ and a
Kripke structure $K = (S, s_0, \tau, AP, L)$, we first construct an alternating automa-
ton $A_{\psi_\iota \wedge \psi}$ for the HYPERLTL property $\psi_\iota \wedge \psi$. Let $A_{\psi_1} = (Q_1, q_{0,1}, \Sigma_2, \delta_1, F_1)$
and $A_{\psi_2} = (Q_2, q_{0,2}, \Sigma_2, \delta_2, F_2)$ be alternating automata for subformulas ψ_1 and
ψ_2. Let $\Sigma = 2^{AP_\varphi}$ where AP_φ are all indexed atomic propositions that appear
in φ. $A_{\psi_\iota \wedge \psi}$ is constructed using following rules[2]:

$\varphi = a_\pi$	$A_\varphi = (\{q_0\}, q_0, \Sigma, \delta, \emptyset)$ where $\delta(q_0, \alpha) = (a_\pi \in \alpha)$
$\varphi = \neg a_\pi$	$A_\varphi = (\{q_0\}, q_0, \Sigma, \delta, \emptyset)$ where $\delta(q_0, \alpha) = (a_\pi \notin \alpha)$
$\varphi = \psi_1 \wedge \psi_2$	$A_\varphi = (Q_1 \uplus Q_2 \uplus \{q_0\}, q_0, \Sigma, \delta, F_1 \uplus F_2)$ where $\delta(q, \alpha) = \delta_1(q_{0,1}, \alpha) \wedge \delta_2(q_{0,2}, \alpha)$ and $\delta(q, \alpha) = \delta_i(q, \alpha)$ when $q \in Q_i$ for $i \in \{1, 2\}$
$\varphi = \psi_1 \vee \psi_2$	$A_\varphi = (Q_1 \uplus Q_2 \uplus \{q_0\}, q_0, \Sigma, \delta, F_1 \uplus F_2)$ where $\delta(q, \alpha) = \delta_1(q_{0,1}, \alpha) \vee \delta_2(q_{0,2}, \alpha)$ and $\delta(q, \alpha) = \delta_i(q, \alpha)$ when $q \in Q_i$ for $i \in \{1, 2\}$
$\varphi = \bigcirc \psi_1$	$A_\varphi = (Q_1 \uplus \{q_0\}, q_0, \Sigma, \delta, F_1)$ where $\delta(q, \alpha) = q_{0,1}$ and $\delta(q, \alpha) = \delta_1(q, \alpha)$ for $q \in Q_1$
$\varphi = \psi_1 \mathcal{U} \psi_2$	$A_\varphi = (Q_1 \uplus Q_2 \uplus \{q_0\}, q_0, \Sigma, \delta, F_1 \uplus F_2)$ where $\delta(q_0, \alpha) = \delta_2(q_{0,2}, \alpha) \vee (\delta_1(q_{0,1}, \alpha) \wedge q_0)$ and $\delta(q, \alpha) = \delta_i(q, \alpha)$ when $q \in Q_i$ for $i \in \{1, 2\}$
$\varphi = \psi_1 \mathcal{R} \psi_2$	$A_\varphi = (Q_1 \uplus Q_2 \uplus \{q_0\}, q_0, \Sigma, \delta, F_1 \uplus F_2 \uplus \{q_0\})$ where $\delta(q_0, \alpha) = \delta_2(q_{0,2}, \alpha) \wedge (\delta_1(q_{0,1}, \alpha) \vee q_0)$ and $\delta(q, \alpha) = \delta_i(q, \alpha)$ when $q \in Q_i$ for $i \in \{1, 2\}$

For a quantified formula $\varphi = \exists \pi.\psi_1$, we construct the product automaton of
the Kripke structure K and the Büchi automaton of ψ_1. Here we reduce the
alphabet of the automaton by projecting all atomic proposition in AP_π away:

---

[2] The construction follows the one presented in [26] with a slight modification on
the labeling of transitions. Labeling over atomic proposition instead of the states
of the Kripke structure suffices, as any nondeterminism in the Kripke structure is
inherently resolved, because we quantify over trace not paths.

$\varphi = \exists \pi.\psi_1$	$A_\varphi = (Q_1 \times S \cup \{q_0\}, \Sigma \setminus AP_\pi, \delta, F_1 \times S)$
	where $\delta(q_0, \alpha) = \{(q', s') \mid q' \in \delta_1(q_{0,1}, \alpha \cup \alpha'), s' \in \tau(s_0), (L(s_0))_\pi =_{AP_\pi} \alpha'\}$
	and $\delta((q, s), \alpha) = \{(q', s') \mid q' \in \delta_1(q, \alpha \cup \alpha'), s' \in \tau(s), (L(s))_\pi =_{AP_\pi} \alpha'\}$

Given the Büchi automaton for the hyperproperty $\psi_\iota \wedge \psi$ it remains to construct the product with the $k+1$-self composition of K. The transitions of the automaton are defined over labels from $\Sigma = 2^{AP^*}$ where $AP^* = AP_\sigma \cup \bigcup_i AP_{\pi_i}$. $A_{\psi_\iota \wedge \psi}$. This is necessary to identify which transition was taken in each copy of K, thus, mirroring a tuple of traces in K. For each of the variables $\pi_1, \ldots \pi_k$ and σ we use following rule:

$\varphi = \exists \pi.\psi_1$	$A_\varphi = (Q_1 \times S \cup \{q_0\}, \Sigma, \delta, F_1 \times S)$
	where $\delta(q_0, \alpha) = \{(q', s') \mid q' \in \delta_1(q_{0,1}, \alpha), s' \in \tau(s_0), (L(s_0))_\pi =_{AP_\pi}\}$
	and $\delta((q, s), \alpha) = \{(q', s') \mid q' \in \delta_1(q, \alpha), s' \in \tau(s), (L(s))_\pi =_{AP_\pi}\}$

Finally, we transform the resulting alternating automaton to an equivalent Büchi automaton following the construction of Miyano and Hayashi [39].

4.4   Counting Models of ω-Automata

Computing the number of words accepted by a Büchi automaton can be done by examining its accepting lassos. Consider, for example, the Büchi automata over the alphabet $2^{\{a\}}$ in Fig. 1. The automaton on the left has one accepting lasso $(q_0)^\omega$ and thus has only one model, namely $\{a\}^\omega$. The automaton on the right has infinitely many accepting lassos $(q_0\{\})^i\{a\}(q_1(\{\} \vee \{a\}))^\omega$ that accept infinitely many different words all of the from $\{\}^*\{a\}(\{\} \vee \{a\})^\omega$. Computing the models of a Büchi automaton is insufficient for model checking quantitative hyperproperties as we are not interested in the total number of models. We rather *maximize*, respectively *minimize*, over sequences of subsets of atomic propositions *the number of projected models* of the Büchi automaton. For instance, consider the automaton given in Fig. 2. The automaton has infinitely many models. However, the maximum number of sequences $\sigma_b \in 2^{\{b\}}$ that correspond to accepting lassos in the automaton with a unique sequence $\sigma_a \in 2^{\{a\}}$ is two: For example, let n be a natural number. For any model of the automaton and for each sequence $\sigma_a := \{\}^n\{a\}(\{\})^\omega$ the automaton accepts the following two sequences: $\{b\}^n\{\}\{b\}^\omega$ and $\{b\}^\omega$. Formally, given a Büchi automaton $\mathcal{B}$ over AP and a set A, such that $A \subseteq AP$, an *A-projected model* (or projected model over A) is defined as a sequence $\sigma_A \in (2^A)^\omega$ that results in the A-projection of an accepting sequence $\upsilon \in (2^{AP})^\omega$.

Fig. 1. Büchi automata with one model (left) and infinitely many models (right).

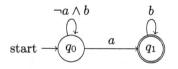

Fig. 2. A two-state Büchi automaton, such that there exist exactly two $\{b\}$-projected models for each $\{a\}$-projected sequence.

In the following, we define the maximum model counting problem over automata and give an algorithm for solving the problem. We show how to use the algorithm for model checking quantitative hyperproperties.

Definition 1 (Maximum Model Counting over Automata (MMCA)). *Given a Büchi automaton B over an alphabet 2^{AP} for some set of atomic propositions AP and sets $X, Y, Z \subseteq AP$ the maximum model counting problem is to compute*

$$\max_{\sigma_Y \in (2^Y)^\omega} |\{\sigma_X \in (2^X)^\omega \mid \exists \sigma_Z \in (2^Z)^\omega.\ \sigma_X \cup \sigma_Y \cup \sigma_Z \in L(B)\}|$$

where $\sigma \cup \sigma'$ is the point-wise union of σ and σ'.

As a first step in our algorithm, we show how to check whether the maximum model count is equal to infinity.

Definition 2 (Doubly Pumped Lasso). *For a graph G, a doubly pumped lasso in G is a subgraph that entails a cycles C_1 and another different cycle C_2 that is reachable from C_1.*

Fig. 3. Forms of doubly pumped lassos.

In general, we distinguish between two types of doubly pumped lassos as shown in Fig. 3. We call the lassos with periods C_1 and C_2 the lassos of the doubly pumped lasso. A doubly pumped lasso of a Büchi automaton B is one in the graph structure of B. The doubly pumped lasso is called accepting when C_2 has an accepting state. A more generalized formalization of this idea is given in the following theorem.

Theorem 2. *Let $B = (Q, q_0, \delta, 2^{AP}, F)$ be a Büchi automaton for some set of atomic propositions $AP = X \cup Y \cup Z$ and let $\sigma' \in (2^Y)^\omega$. The automaton B has infinitely many $X \cup Y$-projected models σ with $\sigma =_Y \sigma'$ if and only if B has an accepting doubly pumped lasso with lassos ρ and ρ' such that: (1) ρ is an accepting lasso (2) $tr(\rho) =_Y tr(\rho') =_Y \sigma'$ (3) The period of ρ' shares at least one state with ρ and (4) $tr(\rho) \neq_X tr(\rho')$.*

To check whether there is a sequence $\sigma' \in (2^Y)^\omega$ such that the number of $X \cup Y$-projected models σ of B with $\sigma =_Y \sigma'$ is infinite, we search for a doubly pumped lasso satisfying the constraints given in Theorem 2. This can be done by applying the following procedure:

Given a Büchi automaton $B = (Q, q_0, 2^{AP}, \delta, F)$ and sets $X, Y, Z \subseteq AP$, we construct the following product automaton $B_\times = (Q_\times, q_{\times,0}, 2^{AP} \times 2^{AP}, \delta_\times, F_\times)$ where: $Q_\times = Q \times Q$, $q_{\times,0} = (q_0, q_0)$, $\delta_\times = \{(s_1, s_2) \xrightarrow{(\alpha, \alpha')} (s_1', s_2') \mid s_1 \xrightarrow{\alpha} s_2, s_1' \xrightarrow{\alpha'} s_2', \alpha =_Y \alpha'\}$ and $F_\times = Q \times F$. The automaton B has infinitely many models σ' if there is an accepting lasso $\rho = (q_0, q_0)(\alpha_1, \alpha_1') \ldots ((q_j, q_j')(\alpha_{j+1}, \alpha_{j+1}') \ldots (q_k, q_k')(\alpha_{k+1}, \alpha_{k+1}'))$ in $B_\times$ such that: $\exists h \leq j. \, q_h' = q_j$, i.e., B has lassos ρ_1 and ρ_2 that share a state in the period of ρ_1 and $\exists h > j. \, \alpha_h \neq_X \alpha_h'$, i.e., the lassos differ in the evaluation of X in a position after the shared state and thus allows infinitely many different sequence over X for the a sequence over Y. The lasso ρ simulates a doubly pumped lasso in B satisfying the constraints of Theorem 2.

Theorem 3. *Given an alternating Büchi automaton $A = (Q, q_0, \delta, 2^{AP}, F)$ for a set of atomic propositions $AP = X \cup Y \cup Z$, the problem of checking whether there is a sequence $\sigma' \in (2^Y)^\omega$ such that A has infinitely many $X \cup Y$-projected models σ with $\sigma =_Y \sigma'$ is* PSPACE-*complete.*

The lower and upper bound for the problem can be given by a reduction from and to the satisfiability problem of LTL [4]. Due to the finite structure of Büchi automata, if the number of models of the automaton exceed the exponential bound $2^{|Q|}$, where Q is the set of states, then the automaton has infinitely many models.

Lemma 1. *For any Büchi automaton B, the number of models of B is less or equal to $2^{|Q|}$ otherwise it is ∞.*

Proof. Assume the number of models is larger than $2^{|Q|}$ then there are more than $2^{|Q|}$ accepting lassos in B. By the pigeonhole principle, two of them share the same $2^{|Q|}$-prefix. Thus, either they are equal or we found doubly pumped lasso in B.

Corollary 1. *Let a Büchi automaton B over a set of atomic propositions AP and sets $X, Y \subseteq AP$. For each sequence $\sigma_Y \in (2^Y)^\omega$ the number of $X \cup Y$-projected models σ with $\sigma =_Y \sigma_Y$ is less or equal than $2^{|Q|}$ otherwise it is ∞.*

From Corollary 1, we know that if no sequence $\sigma_Y \in (2^Y)^\omega$ matches to infinitely many $X \cup Y$-projected models then the number of such models is bound by $2^{|Q|}$. Each of these models has a run in B which ends in an accepting strongly connected component. Also from Corollary 1, we know that every model has a lasso run of length $|Q|$. For each finite sequence w_Y of length $|w_Y| = |Q|$ that reaches an accepting strongly connected component, we count the number $X \cup Y$-projected words w of length $|Q|$ with $w =_Y w_Y$ and that end in an accepting

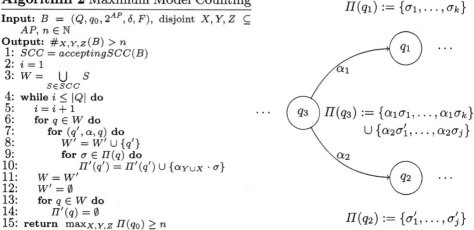

Algorithm 2 Maximum Model Counting

Input: $B = (Q, q_0, 2^{AP}, \delta, F)$, disjoint $X, Y, Z \subseteq$
  AP, $n \in \mathbb{N}$
Output: $\#_{X,Y,Z}(B) > n$
1: $SCC = acceptingSCC(B)$
2: $i = 1$
3: $W = \bigcup_{S \in SCC} S$
4: **while** $i \leq |Q|$ **do**
5:   $i = i + 1$
6:   **for** $q \in W$ **do**
7:     **for** (q', α, q) **do**
8:       $W' = W' \cup \{q'\}$
9:       **for** $\sigma \in \Pi(q)$ **do**
10:         $\Pi'(q') = \Pi'(q') \cup \{\alpha_{Y \cup X} \cdot \sigma\}$
11:   $W = W'$
12:   $W' = \emptyset$
13:   **for** $q \in W$ **do**
14:     $\Pi'(q) = \emptyset$
15: **return** $\max_{X,Y,Z} \Pi(q_0) \geq n$

$\Pi(q_1) := \{\sigma_1, \ldots, \sigma_k\}$

$\Pi(q_3) := \{\alpha_1\sigma_1, \ldots, \alpha_1\sigma_k\}$
$\cup \{\alpha_2\sigma_1', \ldots, \alpha_2\sigma_j'\}$

$\Pi(q_2) := \{\sigma_1', \ldots, \sigma_j'\}$

Fig. 4. Maximum Model Counting Algorithm (left) and a Sketch of a step in this algorithm (right): Current elements of our working set are $q_1, q_2 \in W$ and $q_3 \in W'$. If $i = 0$, i.e., we are in the first step of the algorithm, then q_1 and q_2 are states of accepting SCCs.

strongly connected component. This number is equal to the maximum model counting number.

Algorithm 2 describes the procedure. An algorithm for the minimum model counting problem is defined in similar way. The algorithm works in a backwards fashion starting with states of accepting strongly connected components. In each iteration i, the algorithm maps each state of the automaton with $X \cup Y$-projected words of length i that reach an accepting strongly connected component. After $|Q|$ iterations, the algorithm determines from the mapping of initial state q_0 a Y-projected word of length $|Q|$ with the maximum number of matching $X \cup Y$-projected words (Fig. 4).

Theorem 4. *The decisional version of the maximum model counting problem over automata (MMCA), i.e. the question whether the maximum is greater than a given natural number n, is in* $NP^{\#P}$.

Proof. Let a Büchi automaton over an alphabet 2^{AP} for a set of atomic propositions AP and sets $AP_X, AP_Y, AP_Z \subseteq AP$ and a natural number n be given. We construct a nondeterministic Turing Machine M with access to a $\#P$-oracle as follows: M guesses a sequence $\sigma_Y \in 2^{AP_Y}$. It then queries the oracle, to compute a number c, such that $c = |\{\sigma_X \in (2^{AP_X})^\omega \mid \exists \sigma_Z \in (2^{AP_Z})^\omega. \, \sigma_X \cup \sigma_Y \cup \sigma_Z \in L(B)\}|$, which is a $\#P$ problem [27]. It remains to check whether $n > c$. If so, M accepts.

The following theorem summarizes the main findings of this section, which establish, depending on the property, an exponentially or even doubly exponentially better algorithm (in the quantitative bound) over the existing model checking algorithm for HyperLTL.

Theorem 5. *Given a Kripke structure K and a quantitative hyperproperty φ with bound n, the problem whether $K \models \varphi$ can be decided in logarithmic space in the quantitative bound n and in polynomial space in the size of K.*

5   A Max#Sat-Based Approach

For existential HYPERLTL formulas ψ_ι and ψ, we give a more practical model checking approach by encoding the automaton-based construction presented in Sect. 4 into a propositional formula.

Given a Kripke structure $K = (S, s_0, \tau, AP_K, L)$ and a quantitative hyperproperty $\varphi = \forall \pi_1, \ldots, \pi_k.\ \psi_\iota \rightarrow (\#\sigma : A.\ \psi) \triangleleft n$ over a set of atomic propositions $AP_\varphi \subseteq AP_K$ and bound μ, our algorithm constructs a propositional formula ϕ such that, every satisfying assignment of ϕ uniquely encodes a tuple of lassos $(\pi_1, \ldots, \pi_k, \sigma)$ of length μ in K, where $(\pi_1, \ldots, \pi_k)$ satisfies ψ_ι and $(\pi_1, \ldots, \pi_k, \sigma)$ satisfies ψ. To compute the values $\max\limits_{(\pi_1, \ldots, \pi_k)} |\{\sigma_A \mid (\pi_1, \ldots, \pi_k, \sigma) \models \psi_\iota \wedge \psi\}|$ (in case $\triangleleft \in \{\leq, <\}$) or $\min\limits_{(\pi_1, \ldots, \pi_k)} |\{\sigma_A \mid (\pi_1, \ldots, \pi_k, \sigma) \models \psi_\iota \wedge \psi\}|$ (in case $\triangleleft \in \{\geq, >\}$), we pass ϕ to a maximum model counter, respectively, to a minimum model counter with the appropriate sets of counting and maximization, respectively, minimization propositions. From Lemma 1 we know that it is enough to consider lasso of length exponential in the size of φ. The size of ϕ is thus exponential in the size of φ and polynomial in the size of K.

The construction resembles the encoding of the bounded model checking approach for LTL [16]. Let $\psi_\iota = \exists \pi_1' \ldots \pi_{k'}'.\ \psi_\iota'$ and $\psi = \exists \pi_1'' \ldots \pi_{k''}''.\ \psi''$ and let AP_{ψ_ι} and AP_ψ be the sets of atomic propositions that appear in ψ_ι and ψ respectively. The propositional formula ϕ is given as a conjunction of the following propositional formulas: $\phi = \bigwedge_{i \leq k} [\![K]\!]_{\pi_i}^\mu \wedge [\![K]\!]_\sigma^\mu \wedge [\![\psi_\iota]\!]_\mu^0 \wedge [\![\psi]\!]_\mu^0$ where:

- μ is length of considered lassos and is equal to $\mu = 2^{|\psi_\iota' \wedge \psi''|} * |S|^{k+k'+k''+1} + 1$ which is one plus the size of the product automaton constructed from the $k + k' + k'' + 1$ self-composition and the automaton for $\psi_\iota \wedge \psi$. The "plus one" is to additionally check whether the number of models is infinite.
- $[\![K]\!]_\pi^k$ is the encoding of the transition relation of the copy of K where atomic propositions are indexed with π and up to an unrolling of length k. Each state of K can be encoded as an evaluation of a vector of $\log|S|$ unique propositional variables. The encoding is given by the propositional formula $I(\overrightarrow{v}_0^\pi) \wedge \bigwedge_{i=0}^{k-1} \tau(\overrightarrow{v}_i^\pi, \overrightarrow{v}_{i+1}^\pi)$ which encodes all paths of K of length k. The formula $I(\overrightarrow{v}_0^\pi)$ defines the assignment of the initial state. The formulas $\tau(\overrightarrow{v}_i^\pi, \overrightarrow{v}_{i+1}^\pi)$ define valid transitions in K from the ith to the $(i+1)$st state of a path.
- $[\![\psi_\iota]\!]_k^0$ and $[\![\psi]\!]_k^0$ are constructed using the following rules[3]:

---

[3] We omitted the rules for boolean operators for the lack of space.

	$i < k$	$i = k$
$[\![a_\pi]\!]_k^i$	a_π^i	$\bigvee_{j=0}^{k-1}(l_j \wedge a_\pi^j)$
$[\![\neg a_\pi]\!]_k^i$	$\neg a_\pi^i$	$\bigvee_{j=0}^{k-1}(l_j \wedge \neg a_\pi^j)$
$[\![\bigcirc \varphi_1]\!]_k^i$	$[\![\varphi_1]\!]_k^{i+1}$	$\bigvee_{j=0}^{k-1}(l_j \wedge [\![\varphi_1]\!]_k^j)$
$[\![\varphi_1 \mathcal{U} \varphi_2]\!]_k^i$	$[\![\varphi_2]\!]_k^i \vee ([\![\varphi_1]\!]_k^i \wedge [\![\varphi_1 \mathcal{U} \varphi]\!]_k^{i+1})$	$\bigvee_{j=0}^{k-1}(l_j \wedge \langle\varphi_1 \mathcal{U} \varphi_2\rangle_k^j)$
$\langle\varphi_1 \mathcal{U} \varphi_2\rangle_k^i$	$[\![\varphi_2]\!]_k^i \vee ([\![\varphi_1]\!]_k^i \wedge \langle\varphi_1 \mathcal{U} \varphi\rangle_k^{i+1})$	false
$[\![\varphi_1 \mathcal{R} \varphi_2]\!]_k^i$	$[\![\varphi_2]\!]_k^i \wedge ([\![\varphi_1]\!]_k^i \vee [\![\varphi_1 \mathcal{R} \varphi]\!]_k^{i+1})$	$\bigvee_{j=0}^{k-1}(l_j \wedge \langle\varphi_1 \mathcal{R} \varphi_2\rangle_k^j)$
$\langle\varphi_1 \mathcal{R} \varphi_2\rangle_k^i$	$[\![\varphi_2]\!]_k^i \wedge ([\![\varphi_1]\!]_k^i \vee \langle\varphi_1 \mathcal{R} \varphi\rangle_k^{i+1})$	true

in case of an existential quantifier over a trace variable π, we add a copy of the encoding of K with new variables distinguished by π:

$[\![\exists \pi.\varphi_1]\!]_k^i$	$[\![K]\!]_\pi^k \wedge [\![\varphi_1]\!]_k^i$

We define sets $X = \{a_\sigma^i \mid a \in A, i \leq k\}$, $Y = \{a^i \mid a \in AP_\psi \setminus A, i \leq k\}$ and $Z = P \setminus X \cup Y$, where P is the set of all propositions in ϕ. The maximum model counting problem is then $MMC(\phi, X, Y, Z)$.

5.1 Experiments

We have implemented the Max#Sat-based model checking approach from the last section. We compare the Max#Sat-based approach to the expansion-based approach using HYPERLTL [26]. Our implementation uses the MaxCount tool [29]. We use the option in MaxCount that enumerates, rather than approximates, the number of assignments for the counting variables. We furthermore instrumented the tool so that it terminates as soon as a sample is found that exceeds the given bound. If no sample is found after one hour, we report a timeout.

Table 1 shows the results on a parameterized benchmark obtained from the implementation of an 8bit passcode checker. The parameter of the benchmark is

Table 1. Comparison between the expansion-based approach (MCHyper) and the Max#Sat-based approach (MCQHyper). #max is the number of maximization variables (set Y). #count is the number of the counting variables (set X). TO indicates a time-out after 1 h.

Benchmark	Specification	MCHyper			MCQHyper			
		#Latches	#Gates	Time(sec)	#var	#max	#count	Time(sec)
Pwd_8bit	1bit_leak	9	55	0.3	97	16	2	1
	2bit_leak			0.4	176	32	4	1
	3bit_leak			1.3	336	64	8	2
	4bit_leak			97	656	128	16	4
	5bit_leak			TO	1296	256	32	8
	6bit_leak			TO	2576	512	64	335
	8bit_leak			TO	10256	2048	256	TO

the bound on the number of bits that is leaked to an adversary, who might, for example, enter passcodes in a brute-force manner. In all instances, a violation is found. The results show that the Max#Sat-based approach scales significantly better than the expansion-based approach.

6 Conclusion

We have studied quantitative hyperproperties of the form $\forall \pi_1, \ldots, \pi_k. \varphi \rightarrow (\#\sigma : A. \psi \triangleleft n)$, where φ and ψ are HyperLTL formulas, and $\#\sigma : A.\varphi \triangleleft n$ compares the number of traces that differ in the atomic propositions A and satisfy ψ to a threshold n. Many quantitative information flow policies of practical interest, such as quantitative non-interference and deniability, belong to this class of properties. Our new counting-based model checking algorithm for quantitative hyperproperties performs at least exponentially better in both time and space in the bound n than a reduction to standard HyperLTL model checking. The new counting operator makes the specifications exponentially more concise in the bound, and our model checking algorithm solves the concise specifications efficiently.

We also showed that the model checking problem for quantitative hyperproperties can be solved with a practical Max#SAT-based algorithm. The SAT-based approach outperforms the expansion-based approach significantly for this class of properties. An additional advantage of the new approach is that it can handle properties like deniability, which cannot be checked by MCHyper because of the quantifier alternation.

References

1. Alvim, M.S., Andrés, M.E., Palamidessi, C.: Quantitative information flow in interactive systems. J. Comput. Secur. **20**(1), 3–50 (2012)
2. Aziz, R.A., Chu, G., Muise, C.J., Stuckey, P.J.: #∃sat: projected model counting. In: Proceedings of the 18th International Conference on Theory and Applications of Satisfiability Testing - SAT 2015, Austin, TX, USA, 24–27 September 2015, pp. 121–137 (2015)
3. Backes, M., Köpf, B., Rybalchenko, A.: Automatic discovery and quantification of information leaks. In: 30th IEEE Symposium on Security and Privacy (S&P 2009), Oakland, California, USA, 17–20 May 2009, pp. 141–153 (2009)
4. Baier, C., Katoen, J.-P.: Principles of Model Checking (Representation and Mind Series). The MIT Press, Cambridge (2008)
5. Banerjee, A., Naumann, D.A.: Stack-based access control and secure information flow. J. Funct. Program. **15**(2), 131–177 (2005)
6. Barthe, G., D'Argenio, P.R., Rezk, T.: Secure information flow by self-composition. Math. Struct. Comput. Sci. **21**(6), 1207–1252 (2011)
7. Bindschaedler, V., Shokri, R., Gunter, C.A.: Plausible deniability for privacy-preserving data synthesis. PVLDB **10**(5), 481–492 (2017)
8. Biondi, F., Legay, A., Traonouez, L.-M., Wąsowski, A.: QUAIL: a quantitative security analyzer for imperative code. In: Sharygina, N., Veith, H. (eds.) CAV 2013. LNCS, vol. 8044, pp. 702–707. Springer, Heidelberg (2013). https://doi.org/10.1007/978-3-642-39799-8_49

9. Chadha, R., Mathur, U., Schwoon, S.: Computing information flow using symbolic model-checking. In: 34th International Conference on Foundation of Software Technology and Theoretical Computer Science, FSTTCS 2014, New Delhi, India, 15–17 December 2014, pp. 505–516 (2014)
10. Chakraborti, A., Chen, C., Sion, R.: Datalair: efficient block storage with plausible deniability against multi-snapshot adversaries. PoPETs **2017**(3), 179 (2017)
11. Chen, H., Malacaria, P.: Quantitative analysis of leakage for multi-threaded programs. In: Proceedings of the 2007 Workshop on Programming Languages and Analysis for Security, PLAS 2007, San Diego, California, USA, 14 June 2007, pp. 31–40 (2007)
12. Chothia, T., Kawamoto, Y., Novakovic, C.: LeakWatch: estimating information leakage from Java programs. In: Kutyłowski, M., Vaidya, J. (eds.) ESORICS 2014. LNCS, vol. 8713, pp. 219–236. Springer, Cham (2014). https://doi.org/10.1007/978-3-319-11212-1_13
13. Clark, D., Hunt, S., Malacaria, P.: Quantified interference for a while language. Electr. Notes Theor. Comput. Sci. **112**, 149–166 (2005)
14. Clark, D., Hunt, S., Malacaria, P.: Quantitative information flow, relations and polymorphic types. J. Log. Comput. **15**(2), 181–199 (2005)
15. Clark, D., Hunt, S., Malacaria, P.: A static analysis for quantifying information flow in a simple imperative language. J. Comput. Secur. **15**(3), 321–371 (2007)
16. Clarke, E., Biere, A., Raimi, R., Zhu, Y.: Bounded model checking using satisfiability solving. Form. Methods Syst. Des. **19**(1), 7–34 (2001)
17. Clarke, E.M., Emerson, E.A.: Design and synthesis of synchronization skeletons using branching time temporal logic. In: Kozen, D. (ed.) Logic of Programs 1981. LNCS, vol. 131, pp. 52–71. Springer, Heidelberg (1982). https://doi.org/10.1007/BFb0025774
18. Clarkson, M.R., Finkbeiner, B., Koleini, M., Micinski, K.K., Rabe, M.N., Sánchez, C.: Temporal logics for hyperproperties. In: Abadi, M., Kremer, S. (eds.) POST 2014. LNCS, vol. 8414, pp. 265–284. Springer, Heidelberg (2014). https://doi.org/10.1007/978-3-642-54792-8_15
19. Clarkson, M.R., Myers, A.C., Schneider, F.B.: Belief in information flow. In: 18th IEEE Computer Security Foundations Workshop, (CSFW-18 2005), Aix-en-Provence, France, 20–22 June 2005, pp. 31–45 (2005)
20. Clarkson, M.R., Myers, A.C., Schneider, F.B.: Quantifying information flow with beliefs. J. Comput. Secur. **17**(5), 655–701 (2009)
21. Clarkson, M.R., Schneider, F.B.: Hyperproperties. J. Comput. Secur. **18**(6), 1157–1210 (2010)
22. Cohen, E.S.: Information transmission in sequential programs. In: Foundations of Secure Computation, pp. 297–335 (1978)
23. Darwiche, A.: New advances in compiling CNF into decomposable negation normal form. In: Proceedings of the 16th European Conference on Artificial Intelligence, ECAI 2004, including Prestigious Applicants of Intelligent Systems, PAIS 2004, Valencia, Spain, 22–27 August 2004, pp. 328–332 (2004)
24. Denning, D.E.: Cryptography and Data Security. Addison-Wesley, Boston (1982)
25. Dimitrova, R., Finkbeiner, B., Kovács, M., Rabe, M.N., Seidl, H.: Model checking information flow in reactive systems. In: Kuncak, V., Rybalchenko, A. (eds.) VMCAI 2012. LNCS, vol. 7148, pp. 169–185. Springer, Heidelberg (2012). https://doi.org/10.1007/978-3-642-27940-9_12
26. Finkbeiner, B., Rabe, M.N., Sánchez, C.: Algorithms for model checking Hyper-LTL and HyperCTL*. In: Kroening, D., Pǎsǎreanu, C.S. (eds.) CAV 2015. LNCS,

vol. 9206, pp. 30–48. Springer, Cham (2015). https://doi.org/10.1007/978-3-319-21690-4_3

27. Finkbeiner, B., Torfah, H.: Counting models of linear-time temporal logic. In: Dediu, A.-H., Martín-Vide, C., Sierra-Rodríguez, J.-L., Truthe, B. (eds.) LATA 2014. LNCS, vol. 8370, pp. 360–371. Springer, Cham (2014). https://doi.org/10.1007/978-3-319-04921-2_29

28. Finkbeiner, B., Torfah, H.: The density of linear-time properties. In: D'Souza, D., Narayan Kumar, K. (eds.) ATVA 2017. LNCS, vol. 10482, pp. 139–155. Springer, Cham (2017). https://doi.org/10.1007/978-3-319-68167-2_10

29. Fremont, D.J., Rabe, M.N., Seshia, S.A.: Maximum model counting. In: Proceedings of the Thirty-First AAAI Conference on Artificial Intelligence, San Francisco, California, USA, 4–9 February 2017, pp. 3885–3892 (2017)

30. Gray III, J.W.: Toward a mathematical foundation for information flow security. In: Proceedings of the IEEE Symposium on Security and Privacy, pp. 210–234, May 1991

31. Hammer, C., Snelting, G.: Flow-sensitive, context-sensitive, and object-sensitive information flow control based on program dependence graphs. Int. J. Inf. Secur. 8(6), 399–422 (2009)

32. Gray III, J.W.: Toward a mathematical foundation for information flow security. In: IEEE Symposium on Security and Privacy, pp. 21–35 (1991)

33. Bayardo Jr., R.J., Schrag, R.: Using CSP look-back techniques to solve real-world SAT instances. In: Proceedings of the Fourteenth National Conference on Artificial Intelligence and Ninth Innovative Applications of Artificial Intelligence Conference, AAAI 1997, Providence, Rhode Island, 27–31 July 1997, pp. 203–208 (1997)

34. Köpf, B., Basin, D.A.: An information-theoretic model for adaptive side-channel attacks. In: Proceedings of the 2007 ACM Conference on Computer and Communications Security, CCS 2007, Alexandria, Virginia, USA, 28–31 October 2007, pp. 286–296 (2007)

35. Köpf, B., Rybalchenko, A.: Approximation and randomization for quantitative information-flow analysis. In: Proceedings of the 23rd IEEE Computer Security Foundations Symposium, CSF 2010, Edinburgh, United Kingdom, 17–19 July 2010, pp. 3–14 (2010)

36. Littman, M.L., Majercik, S.M., Pitassi, T.: Stochastic boolean satisfiability. J. Autom. Reason. 27(3), 251–296 (2001)

37. Malacaria, P.: Assessing security threats of looping constructs. In: Proceedings of the 34th ACM SIGPLAN-SIGACT Symposium on Principles of Programming Languages, POPL 2007, Nice, France, 17–19 January 2007, pp. 225–235 (2007)

38. Milushev, D., Clarke, D.: Incremental hyperproperty model checking via games. In: Riis Nielson, H., Gollmann, D. (eds.) NordSec 2013. LNCS, vol. 8208, pp. 247–262. Springer, Heidelberg (2013). https://doi.org/10.1007/978-3-642-41488-6_17

39. Miyano, S., Hayashi, T.: Alternating finite automata on ω-words. Theoret. Comput. Sci. 32(3), 321–330 (1984)

40. Morwood, D., Bryce, D.: Evaluating temporal plans in incomplete domains. In: Proceedings of the Twenty-Sixth AAAI Conference on Artificial Intelligence, 22–26 July 2012, Toronto, Ontario, Canada (2012)

41. Muise, C.J., McIlraith, S.A., Beck, J.C., Hsu, E.I.: DSHARP: fast d-DNNF compilation with sharpSAT. In: Kosseim, L., Inkpen, D. (eds.) AI 2012. LNCS (LNAI), vol. 7310, pp. 356–361. Springer, Heidelberg (2012). https://doi.org/10.1007/978-3-642-30353-1_36

42. Myers, A.C.: JFlow: practical mostly-static information flow control. In: Proceedings of the 26th ACM SIGPLAN-SIGACT Symposium on Principles of Program-

ming Languages, POPL 1999, San Antonio, TX, USA, 20–22 January 1999, pp. 228–241 (1999)

43. Smith, G.: On the foundations of quantitative information flow. In: de Alfaro, L. (ed.) FoSSaCS 2009. LNCS, vol. 5504, pp. 288–302. Springer, Heidelberg (2009). https://doi.org/10.1007/978-3-642-00596-1_21

44. Torfah, H., Zimmermann, M.: The complexity of counting models of linear-time temporal logic. Acta Informatica **55**(3), 191–212 (2016)

45. Yasuoka, H., Terauchi, T.: On bounding problems of quantitative information flow. In: Gritzalis, D., Preneel, B., Theoharidou, M. (eds.) ESORICS 2010. LNCS, vol. 6345, pp. 357–372. Springer, Heidelberg (2010). https://doi.org/10.1007/978-3-642-15497-3_22

46. Yasuoka, H., Terauchi, T.: Quantitative information flow as safety and liveness hyperproperties. Theor. Comput. Sci. **538**, 167–182 (2014)

47. Zdancewic, S., Myers, A.C.: Observational determinism for concurrent program security. In: Proceedings of CSF, p. 29. IEEE Computer Society (2003)

3

A Direct Encoding for NNC Polyhedra

(✉)

Anna Becchi and Enea Zaffanella

Department of Mathematical, Physical and Computer Sciences,
University of Parma, Parma, Italy
anna.becchi@studenti.unipr.it, enea.zaffanella@unipr.it

Abstract. We present an alternative Double Description representation for the domain of NNC (not necessarily closed) polyhedra, together with the corresponding Chernikova-like conversion procedure. The representation uses no slack variable at all and provides a solution to a few technical issues caused by the encoding of an NNC polyhedron as a closed polyhedron in a higher dimension space. A preliminary experimental evaluation shows that the new conversion algorithm is able to achieve significant efficiency improvements.

1 Introduction

The Double Description (DD) method [28] allows for the representation and manipulation of convex polyhedra by using two different geometric representations: one based on a finite collection of *constraints*, the other based on a finite collection of *generators*. Starting from any one of these representations, the other can be derived by application of a conversion procedure [10–12], thereby obtaining a DD pair. The procedure is incremental, capitalizing on the work already done when new constraints and/or generators need to be added to an input DD pair.

The DD method lies at the foundation of many software libraries and tools[1] which are used, either directly or indirectly, in research fields as diverse as bioinformatics [31,32], computational geometry [1,2], analysis of analog and hybrid systems [8,18,22,23], automatic parallelization [6,29], scheduling [16], static analysis of software [4,13,15,17,21,24].

In the classical setting, the DD method is meant to compute geometric representations for *topologically closed* polyhedra in an n-dimensional vector space. However, there are applications requiring the ability to also deal with linear *strict inequality constraints*, leading to the definition of *not necessarily closed* (NNC) polyhedra. For example, this is the case for some of the analysis tools developed for the verification of hybrid systems [8,18,22,23], static analysis tools such as Pagai [24], and tools for the automatic discovery of ranking functions [13].

The few DD method implementations providing support for NNC polyhedra (Apron and PPL) are all based on an *indirect* representation. The approach, proposed in [22,23] and studied in more detail in [3,5], encodes the strict inequality

---

[1] An incomplete list of available implementations includes cdd [19], PolyLib [27], Apron [25], PPL [4], 4ti2 [1], Skeleton [33], Addibit [20], ELINA [30].

constraints by means of an additional space dimension, playing the role of a *slack variable*; the new space dimension, usually denoted as ϵ, needs to be non-negative and bounded from above, i.e., the constraints $0 \leq \epsilon \leq 1$ are added to the topologically closed representation $\mathcal{R}$ (called ϵ-representation) of the NNC polyhedron $\mathcal{P}$. The main advantage of this approach is the possibility of reusing, almost unchanged, all of the well-studied algorithms and optimizations that have been developed for the classical case of closed polyhedra. However, the addition of a slack variable carries with itself a few technical issues.

- At the implementation level, more work is needed to make the ϵ dimension *transparent* to the end user.
- The ϵ-representation causes an *intrinsic overhead*: in any generator system for an ϵ-polyhedron, most of the "proper" points (those having a positive ϵ coordinate) need to be paired with the corresponding "closure" point (having a zero ϵ coordinate), almost doubling the number of generators.
- The DD pair in minimal form computed for an ϵ-representation $\mathcal{R}$, when reinterpreted as encoding the NNC polyhedron $\mathcal{P}$, typically includes many redundant constraints and/or generators, leading to inefficiencies. To avoid this problem, *strong minimization procedures* were defined in [3,5] that are able to detect and remove those redundancies. Even though effective, these procedures are not fully integrated into the DD conversion: they can only be applied *after* the conversion, since they interfere with incrementality. Hence, during the iterations of the conversion the ϵ-redundancies are not removed, causing the computation of bigger intermediate results.

In this paper, we pursue a different approach for the handling of NNC polyhedra in the DD method. Namely, we specify a *direct* representation, dispensing with the need of the slack variable. The main insight of this new approach is the separation of the (constraints or generators) geometric representation into two components, the skeleton and the non-skeleton of the representation, playing quite different roles: while keeping a geometric encoding for the skeleton component, we will adopt a combinatorial encoding for the non-skeleton one. For this new representation, we propose the corresponding variant of the Chernikova's conversion procedure, where both components are handled by respective processing phases, so as to take advantage of their peculiarities. In particular, we develop *ad hoc* functions and procedures for the combinatorial non-skeleton part.

The new representation and conversion procedure, in principle, can be integrated into any of the available implementations of the DD method. Our experimental evaluation is conducted in the context of the PPL and shows that the new algorithm, while computing the correct results for all of the considered tests, achieves impressive efficiency improvements with respect to the implementation based on the slack variable.

The paper is structured as follows. Section 2 briefly introduces the required notation, terminology and background concepts. Section 3 proposes the new representation for NNC polyhedra; the proofs of the stated results are in [7]. The extension of the Chernikova's conversion algorithm to this new representation is presented in Sect. 4. Section 5 reports the results obtained by the experimental evaluation. We conclude in Sect. 6.

2 Preliminaries

We assume some familiarity with the basic notions of lattice theory [9]. For a lattice $\langle L, \sqsubseteq, \bot, \top, \sqcap, \sqcup \rangle$, an element $a \in L$ is an *atom* if $\bot \sqsubset a$ and there exists no element $b \in L$ such that $\bot \sqsubset b \sqsubset a$. For $S \subseteq L$, the *upward closure* of S is defined as $\uparrow S \stackrel{\text{def}}{=} \{ x \in L \mid \exists s \in S \,.\, s \sqsubseteq x \}$. The set $S \subseteq L$ is *upward closed* if $S = \uparrow S$; we denote by $\wp_\uparrow(L)$ the set of all the upward closed subsets of L. For $x \in L$, $\uparrow x$ is a shorthand for $\uparrow \{x\}$. The notation for *downward closure* is similar. Given two posets $\langle L, \sqsubseteq \rangle$ and $\langle L^\sharp, \sqsubseteq^\sharp \rangle$ and two monotonic functions $\alpha \colon L \to L^\sharp$ and $\gamma \colon L^\sharp \to L$, the pair (α, γ) is a *Galois connection* [14] between L and $L^\sharp$ if $\forall x \in L, x^\sharp \in L^\sharp \colon \alpha(x) \sqsubseteq^\sharp x^\sharp \Leftrightarrow x \sqsubseteq \gamma(x^\sharp)$.

We write $\mathbb{R}^n$ to denote the Euclidean topological space of dimension $n > 0$ and $\mathbb{R}_+$ for the set of non-negative reals; for $S \subseteq \mathbb{R}^n$, $\mathrm{cl}(S)$ and $\mathrm{relint}(S)$ denote the topological closure and the relative interior of S, respectively. A topologically closed convex polyhedron (for short, closed polyhedron) is defined as the set of solutions of a finite system $\mathcal{C}$ of linear non-strict inequality and linear equality constraints; namely, $\mathcal{P} = \mathrm{con}(\mathcal{C})$ where

$$\mathrm{con}(\mathcal{C}) \stackrel{\text{def}}{=} \left\{ \boldsymbol{p} \in \mathbb{R}^n \mid \forall \beta = (\boldsymbol{a}^\mathsf{T} \boldsymbol{x} \bowtie b) \in \mathcal{C}, \bowtie \in \{\geq, =\} \,.\, \boldsymbol{a}^\mathsf{T} \boldsymbol{p} \bowtie b \right\}.$$

A vector $\boldsymbol{r} \in \mathbb{R}^n$ such that $\boldsymbol{r} \neq \boldsymbol{0}$ is a *ray* of a non-empty polyhedron $\mathcal{P} \subseteq \mathbb{R}^n$ if, $\forall \boldsymbol{p} \in \mathcal{P}$ and $\forall \rho \in \mathbb{R}_+$, it holds $\boldsymbol{p} + \rho \boldsymbol{r} \in \mathcal{P}$. The empty polyhedron has no rays. If both $\boldsymbol{r}$ and $-\boldsymbol{r}$ are rays of $\mathcal{P}$, then $\boldsymbol{r}$ is a *line* of $\mathcal{P}$. The set $\mathcal{P} \subseteq \mathbb{R}^n$ is a closed polyhedron if there exist finite sets $L, R, P \subseteq \mathbb{R}^n$ such that $\boldsymbol{0} \notin (L \cup R)$ and $\mathcal{P} = \mathrm{gen}(\langle L, R, P \rangle)$, where

$$\mathrm{gen}(\langle L, R, P \rangle) \stackrel{\text{def}}{=} \left\{ L\boldsymbol{\lambda} + R\boldsymbol{\rho} + P\boldsymbol{\pi} \in \mathbb{R}^n \mid \boldsymbol{\lambda} \in \mathbb{R}^\ell, \boldsymbol{\rho} \in \mathbb{R}_+^r, \boldsymbol{\pi} \in \mathbb{R}_+^p, \sum_{i=1}^p \pi_i = 1 \right\}.$$

When $\mathcal{P} \neq \emptyset$, we say that $\mathcal{P}$ is described by the *generator system* $\mathcal{G} = \langle L, R, P \rangle$. In the following, we will abuse notation by adopting the usual set operator and relation symbols to denote the corresponding component-wise extensions on systems. For instance, for $\mathcal{G} = \langle L, R, P \rangle$ and $\mathcal{G}' = \langle L', R', P' \rangle$, we will write $\mathcal{G} \subseteq \mathcal{G}'$ to mean $L \subseteq L'$, $R \subseteq R'$ and $P \subseteq P'$.

The DD method due to Motzkin et al. [28] allows combining the constraints and the generators of a polyhedron $\mathcal{P}$ into a DD pair $(\mathcal{C}, \mathcal{G})$: a *conversion* procedure [10–12] is used to obtain each description starting from the other one, also removing the redundant elements. For presentation purposes, we focus on the conversion from constraints to generators; the opposite conversion works in the same way, using duality to switch the roles of constraints and generators. We do not describe lower level details such as the *homogenization* process, mapping the polyhedron into a polyhedral cone, or the *simplification* step, needed for computing DD pairs in minimal form.

The conversion procedure starts from a DD pair $(\mathcal{C}_0, \mathcal{G}_0)$ representing the whole vector space and adds, one at a time, the elements of the input constraint system $\mathcal{C} = \{\beta_0, \ldots, \beta_m\}$, producing a sequence of DD pairs $\{(\mathcal{C}_k, \mathcal{G}_k)\}_{0 \le k \le m+1}$ representing the polyhedra

$$\mathbb{R}^n = \mathcal{P}_0 \xrightarrow{\beta_0} \ldots \xrightarrow{\beta_{k-1}} \mathcal{P}_k \xrightarrow{\beta_k} \mathcal{P}_{k+1} \xrightarrow{\beta_{k+1}} \ldots \xrightarrow{\beta_m} \mathcal{P}_{m+1} = \mathcal{P}.$$

At each iteration, when adding the constraint β_k to polyhedron $\mathcal{P}_k = \mathrm{gen}(\mathcal{G}_k)$, the generator system $\mathcal{G}_k$ is partitioned into the three components $\mathcal{G}_k^+$, $\mathcal{G}_k^0$, $\mathcal{G}_k^-$, according to the sign of the scalar products of the generators with β_k (those in $\mathcal{G}_k^0$ are the *saturators* of β_k); the new generator system for polyhedron $\mathcal{P}_{k+1}$ is computed as $\mathcal{G}_{k+1} \overset{\text{def}}{=} \mathcal{G}_k^+ \cup \mathcal{G}_k^0 \cup \mathcal{G}_k^\star$, where $\mathcal{G}_k^\star = \mathrm{comb\_adj}_{\beta_k}(\mathcal{G}_k^+, \mathcal{G}_k^-)$ and

$$\mathrm{comb\_adj}_{\beta_k}(\mathcal{G}_k^+, \mathcal{G}_k^-) \overset{\text{def}}{=} \{\, \mathrm{comb}_{\beta_k}(g^+, g^-) \mid g^+ \in \mathcal{G}_k^+, g^- \in \mathcal{G}_k^-, \mathrm{adj}_{\mathcal{P}_k}(g^+, g^-) \,\}.$$

Function 'comb_{β_k}' computes a linear combination of its arguments, yielding a generator that saturates the constraint β_k; predicate '$\mathrm{adj}_{\mathcal{P}_k}$' is used to select only those pairs of generators that are *adjacent* in $\mathcal{P}_k$.

The set $\mathbb{CP}_n$ of all closed polyhedra on the vector space $\mathbb{R}^n$, partially ordered by set inclusion, is a lattice $\langle \mathbb{CP}_n, \subseteq, \emptyset, \mathbb{R}^n, \cap, \uplus \rangle$, where the empty set and $\mathbb{R}^n$ are the bottom and top elements, the binary meet operator is set intersection and the binary join operator '$\uplus$' is the convex polyhedral hull. A constraint $\beta = (a^{\mathsf{T}} x \bowtie b)$ is said to be *valid* for $\mathcal{P} \in \mathbb{CP}_n$ if all the points in $\mathcal{P}$ satisfy β; for each such β, the subset $F = \{\, p \in \mathcal{P} \mid a^{\mathsf{T}} p = b \,\}$ is a *face* of $\mathcal{P}$. We write $cFaces_{\mathcal{P}}$ (possibly omitting the subscript) to denote the finite set of faces of $\mathcal{P} \in \mathbb{CP}_n$. This is a meet sublattice of $\mathbb{CP}_n$ and $\mathcal{P} = \bigcup\{\, \mathrm{relint}(F) \mid F \in cFaces_{\mathcal{P}} \,\}$.

When $\mathcal{C}$ is extended to allow for *strict* inequalities, $\mathcal{P} = \mathrm{con}(\mathcal{C})$ is an NNC (not necessarily closed) polyhedron. The set $\mathbb{P}_n$ of all NNC polyhedra on $\mathbb{R}^n$ is a lattice $\langle \mathbb{P}_n, \subseteq, \emptyset, \mathbb{R}^n, \cap, \uplus \rangle$ and $\mathbb{CP}_n$ is a sublattice of $\mathbb{P}_n$. As shown in [3, Theorem 4.4], a description of an NNC polyhedron $\mathcal{P} \in \mathbb{P}_n$ can be obtained by extending the generator system with a finite set C of *closure points*. Namely, for $\mathcal{G} = \langle L, R, C, P \rangle$, we define $\mathcal{P} = \mathrm{gen}(\mathcal{G})$, where

$$\mathrm{gen}(\langle L, R, C, P \rangle) \overset{\text{def}}{=} \left\{ L\lambda + R\rho + C\gamma + P\pi \in \mathbb{R}^n \;\middle|\; \begin{array}{l} \lambda \in \mathbb{R}^\ell, \rho \in \mathbb{R}_+^r, \\ \gamma \in \mathbb{R}_+^c, \pi \in \mathbb{R}_+^p, \pi \ne 0, \\ \sum_{i=1}^c \gamma_i + \sum_{i=1}^p \pi_i = 1 \end{array} \right\}.$$

For an NNC polyhedron $\mathcal{P} \in \mathbb{P}_n$, the finite set $nncFaces_{\mathcal{P}}$ of its faces is a meet sublattice of $\mathbb{P}_n$ and $\mathcal{P} = \bigcup\{\, \mathrm{relint}(F) \mid F \in nncFaces_{\mathcal{P}} \,\}$. Letting $\mathcal{Q} = \mathrm{cl}(\mathcal{P})$, the closure operator $\mathrm{cl} \colon nncFaces_{\mathcal{P}} \to cFaces_{\mathcal{Q}}$ maps each NNC face of $\mathcal{P}$ into a face of $\mathcal{Q}$. The image $\mathrm{cl}(nncFaces_{\mathcal{P}})$ is a join sublattice of $cFaces_{\mathcal{Q}}$ and its nonempty elements form an *upward closed subset*, which can be described by recording the minimal elements only (i.e., the atoms of the $nncFaces_{\mathcal{P}}$ lattice).

3   Direct Representations for NNC Polyhedra

An NNC polyhedron can be described by using an extended constraint system $\mathcal{C} = \langle C_=, C_\geq, C_> \rangle$ and/or an extended generator system $\mathcal{G} = \langle L, R, C, P \rangle$. These representations are said to be *geometric*, meaning that they provide a precise description of the position of their elements. For a closed polyhedron $\mathcal{P} \in \mathbb{CP}_n$, the use of completely geometric representations is an adequate choice. In the case of an NNC polyhedron $\mathcal{P} \in \mathbb{P}_n$ such a choice is questionable, since the precise geometric position of some of the elements is not really needed.

Example 1. Consider the NNC polyhedron $\mathcal{P} \in \mathbb{P}_2$ in the next figure, where the (strict) inequality constraints are denoted by (dashed) lines and the (closure) points are denoted by (unfilled) circles.

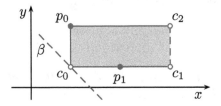

$\mathcal{P}$ is described by $\mathcal{G} = \langle L, R, C, P \rangle$, where $L = R = \emptyset$, $C = \{c_0, c_1, c_2\}$ and $P = \{p_0, p_1\}$. However, there is no need to know the position of point p_1, since it can be replaced by any other point on the open segment (c_0, c_1). Similarly, when considering the constraint representation, there is no need to know the exact slope of the strict inequality constraint β.

We now show that $\mathcal{P} \in \mathbb{P}_n$ can be more appropriately represented by integrating a geometric description of $\mathcal{Q} = \mathrm{cl}(\mathcal{P}) \in \mathbb{CP}_n$ (the *skeleton*) with a combinatorial description of $nncFaces_{\mathcal{P}}$ (the *non-skeleton*). We consider here the generator system representation; the extension to constraints will be briefly outlined in a later section.

Definition 1 (Skeleton of a generator system). *Let $\mathcal{G} = \langle L, R, C, P \rangle$ be a generator system in minimal form, $\mathcal{P} = \mathrm{gen}(\mathcal{G})$ and $\mathcal{Q} = \mathrm{cl}(\mathcal{P})$. The skeleton of $\mathcal{G}$ is $\mathcal{SK}_{\mathcal{Q}} = \mathrm{skel}(\mathcal{G}) \stackrel{\mathrm{def}}{=} \langle L, R, C \cup SP, \emptyset \rangle$, where $SP \subseteq P$ holds the points that can not be obtained by combining the other generators in $\mathcal{G}$.*

Note that the skeleton has no points at all, so that $\mathrm{gen}(\mathcal{SK}_{\mathcal{Q}}) = \emptyset$. However, we can define a variant function $\overline{\mathrm{gen}}(\langle L, R, C, P \rangle) \stackrel{\mathrm{def}}{=} \mathrm{gen}(\langle L, R, \emptyset, C \cup P \rangle)$, showing that the skeleton of an NNC polyhedron provides a non-redundant representation of its topological closure.

Proposition 1. *If $\mathcal{P} = \mathrm{gen}(\mathcal{G})$ and $\mathcal{Q} = \mathrm{cl}(\mathcal{P})$, then $\overline{\mathrm{gen}}(\mathcal{G}) = \overline{\mathrm{gen}}(\mathcal{SK}_{\mathcal{Q}}) = \mathcal{Q}$. Also, there does not exist $\mathcal{G}' \subset \mathcal{SK}_{\mathcal{Q}}$ such that $\overline{\mathrm{gen}}(\mathcal{G}') = \mathcal{Q}$.*

The elements of $SP \subseteq P$ are called *skeleton points*; the non-skeleton points in $P \setminus SP$ are redundant when representing the topological closure; these *non-skeleton points* are the elements in $\mathcal{G}$ that need not be represented geometrically.

Consider a point $\boldsymbol{p} \in \mathcal{Q} = \mathrm{cl}(\mathcal{P})$ (not necessarily in P). There exists a single face $F \in cFaces_{\mathcal{Q}}$ such that $\boldsymbol{p} \in \mathrm{relint}(F)$. By definition of function 'gen', point $\boldsymbol{p}$ behaves as a *filler* for $\mathrm{relint}(F)$ meaning that, when combined with the skeleton, it generates $\mathrm{relint}(F)$. Note that $\boldsymbol{p}$ also behaves as a filler for the relative interiors of all the faces in the set $\uparrow F$. The choice of $\boldsymbol{p} \in \mathrm{relint}(F)$ is actually arbitrary: any other point of $\mathrm{relint}(F)$ would be equivalent as a filler. A less arbitrary representation for $\mathrm{relint}(F)$ is thus provided by its own skeleton $\mathcal{SK}_F \subseteq \mathcal{SK}_{\mathcal{Q}}$; we say that $\mathcal{SK}_F$ is the *support* for the points in $\mathrm{relint}(F)$ and that any point $\boldsymbol{p}' \in \mathrm{relint}\big(\overline{\mathrm{gen}}(\mathcal{SK}_F)\big) = \mathrm{relint}(F)$ is a *materialization* of $\mathcal{SK}_F$.

In the following we will sometimes omit subscripts when clear from context.

Definition 2 (Support sets for a skeleton). *Let $\mathcal{SK}$ be the skeleton of an NNC polyhedron and let $\mathcal{Q} = \overline{\mathrm{gen}}(\mathcal{SK}) \in \mathbb{CP}_n$. The set of all supports for $\mathcal{SK}$ is defined as $\mathrm{NS}_{\mathcal{SK}} \stackrel{\mathrm{def}}{=} \{\, \mathcal{SK}_F \subseteq \mathcal{SK} \mid F \in cFaces_{\mathcal{Q}} \,\}$.*

We now define functions mapping a subset of the (geometric) points of an NNC polyhedron into the set of supports filled by these points, and vice versa.

Definition 3 (Filled supports). *Let $\mathcal{SK}$ be the skeleton of the polyhedron $\mathcal{P} \in \mathbb{P}_n$, $\mathcal{Q} = \mathrm{cl}(\mathcal{P})$ and NS be the corresponding set of supports. The abstraction function $\alpha_{\mathcal{SK}} \colon \wp(\mathcal{Q}) \to \wp_{\uparrow}(\mathrm{NS})$ is defined, for each $S \subseteq \mathcal{Q}$, as*

$$\alpha_{\mathcal{SK}}(S) \stackrel{\mathrm{def}}{=} \bigcup \{\, \uparrow \mathcal{SK}_F \mid \exists \boldsymbol{p} \in S, F \in cFaces \,.\, \boldsymbol{p} \in \mathrm{relint}(F) \,\}.$$

The concretization function $\gamma_{\mathcal{SK}} \colon \wp_{\uparrow}(\mathrm{NS}) \to \wp(\mathcal{Q})$, for each $\mathrm{NS} \in \wp_{\uparrow}(\mathrm{NS})$, is defined as

$$\gamma_{\mathcal{SK}}(NS) \stackrel{\mathrm{def}}{=} \bigcup \{\, \mathrm{relint}\big(\overline{\mathrm{gen}}(ns)\big) \;\big|\; ns \in NS \,\}.$$

Proposition 2. *The pair of functions $(\alpha_{\mathcal{SK}}, \gamma_{\mathcal{SK}})$ is a Galois connection. If $\mathcal{P} = \mathrm{gen}\big(\langle L, R, C, P \rangle\big) \in \mathbb{P}_n$ and $\mathcal{SK}$ is its skeleton, then $\mathcal{P} = (\gamma_{\mathcal{SK}} \circ \alpha_{\mathcal{SK}})(P)$.*

The non-skeleton component of a geometric generator system can be abstracted by '$\alpha_{\mathcal{SK}}$' and described as a combination of skeleton generators.

Definition 4 (Non-skeleton of a generator system). *Let $\mathcal{P} \in \mathbb{P}_n$ be defined by generator system $\mathcal{G} = \langle L, R, C, P \rangle$ and let $\mathcal{SK}$ be the corresponding skeleton component. The non-skeleton component of $\mathcal{G}$ is defined as $NS_{\mathcal{G}} \stackrel{\mathrm{def}}{=} \alpha_{\mathcal{SK}}(P)$.*

Example 2. Consider the generator system $\mathcal{G}$ of polyhedron $\mathcal{P}$ from Example 1. Its skeleton is $\mathcal{SK} = \langle \emptyset, \emptyset, \{c_0, c_1, c_2, p_0\}, \emptyset \rangle$, so that p_1 is not a skeleton point. By Definition 3, $NS_{\mathcal{G}} = \alpha_{\mathcal{SK}}(\{p_0, p_1\}) = \uparrow\{p_0\} \cup \uparrow\{c_0, c_1\}^2$ The minimal elements in $NS_{\mathcal{G}}$ can be seen to describe the atoms of $nncFaces_{\mathcal{P}}$, i.e., the 0-dimension face $\{p_0\}$ and the 1-dimension open segment (c_0, c_1).

The new representation is semantically equivalent to the fully geometric one.

---

[2] Since there are no rays and no lines, we adopt a simplified notation, identifying each support with the set of its closure points. Also note that $\mathrm{relint}(\{p_0\}) = \{p_0\}$.

Corollary 1. *For a polyhedron $\mathcal{P} = \text{gen}(\mathcal{G}) \in \mathbb{P}_n$, let $\langle \mathcal{SK}, NS \rangle$ be the skeleton and non-skeleton components for $\mathcal{G}$. Then $\mathcal{P} = \gamma_{\mathcal{SK}}(NS)$.*

4 The New Conversion Algorithm

The CONVERSION function in Pseudocode 1 incrementally processes each of the input constraints $\beta \in \mathcal{C}_{in}$ keeping the generator system $\langle \mathcal{SK}, NS \rangle$ up-to-date. The distinction between the skeleton and non-skeleton allows for a corresponding separation in the conversion procedure. Moreover, a few minor adaptations to their representation, discussed below, allow for efficiency improvements.

First, observe that every support $ns \in NS$ always includes all of the lines in the L skeleton component; hence, these lines can be left *implicit* in the representation of the supports in NS. Note that, even after removing the lines, each $ns \in NS$ is still a non-empty set, since it includes at least one closure point.

When lines are implicit, those supports $ns \in NS$ that happen to be single-tons[3] can be seen to play a special role: they correspond to the combinatorial encoding of the skeleton points in SP (see Definition 1). These points are not going to benefit from the combinatorial representation, hence we move them from the non-skeleton to the skeleton component; namely, $\mathcal{SK} = \langle L, R, C \cup SP, \emptyset \rangle$ is represented as $\mathcal{SK} = \langle L, R, C, SP \rangle$. The formalization presented in Sect. 3 is still valid, replacing '$\gamma_{\mathcal{SK}}$' with $\gamma'_{\mathcal{SK}}(NS) \overset{\text{def}}{=} \text{gen}(\mathcal{SK}) \cup \gamma_{\mathcal{SK}}(NS)$.

At the implementation level, each support $ns \in NS$ can be encoded by using a *set of indices* on the data structure representing the skeleton component $\mathcal{SK}$. Since NS is a finite upward closed set, the representation only needs to record its minimal elements. A support $ns \in NS$ is *redundant* in $\langle \mathcal{SK}, NS \rangle$ if there exists $ns' \in NS$ such that $ns' \subset ns$ or if $ns \cap SP \neq \emptyset$, where $\mathcal{SK} = \langle L, R, C, SP \rangle$. We write $NS_1 \oplus NS_2$ to denote the non-redundant union of $NS_1, NS_2 \subseteq \mathbb{NS}_{\mathcal{SK}}$.

4.1 Processing the Skeleton

Line 3 of CONVERSION partitions the skeleton $\mathcal{SK}$ into $\mathcal{SK}^+$, $\mathcal{SK}^0$ and $\mathcal{SK}^-$, according to the signs of the scalar products with constraint β. Note that the partition information is *logically* computed (no copies are performed) and it is stored in the $\mathcal{SK}$ component itself; therefore, any update to $\mathcal{SK}^+$, $\mathcal{SK}^0$ and $\mathcal{SK}^-$ directly propagates to $\mathcal{SK}$. In line 7 the generators in $\mathcal{SK}^+$ and $\mathcal{SK}^-$ are combined to produce $\mathcal{SK}^\star$, which is merged into $\mathcal{SK}^0$. These steps are similar to the ones for closed polyhedra, except that we now have to consider more kinds of combinations: the systematic case analysis is presented in Table 1. For instance, when processing a non-strict inequality $\beta_\geq$, if we combine a closure point in $\mathcal{SK}^+$ with a ray in $\mathcal{SK}^-$ we obtain a closure point in $\mathcal{SK}^\star$ (row 3, column 6). Since it is restricted to work on the skeleton component, this combination phase can safely apply the adjacency tests to quickly get rid of redundant elements.

---

[3] By 'singleton' here we mean a system $ns = \langle \emptyset, \emptyset, \{\boldsymbol{p}\}, \emptyset \rangle$.

Pseudocode 1. Incremental conversion from constraints to generators.

---

    function CONVERSION($\mathcal{C}_{in}$, $\langle \mathcal{SK}, \mathit{NS} \rangle$)

2:     **for all** $\beta \in \mathcal{C}_{in}$ **do**

        skel_partition(β, $\mathcal{SK}$);

4:         nonskel_partition($\langle \mathcal{SK}, \mathit{NS} \rangle$);

        if line $l \in \mathcal{SK}^+ \cup \mathcal{SK}^-$ **then** VIOLATING-LINE(β, l, $\langle \mathcal{SK}, \mathit{NS} \rangle$);

6:         **else**

            $\mathcal{SK}^\star \leftarrow$ comb_adj$_\beta$($\mathcal{SK}^+$, $\mathcal{SK}^-$); $\mathcal{SK}^0 \leftarrow \mathcal{SK}^0 \cup \mathcal{SK}^\star$;

8:             $\mathit{NS}^\star \leftarrow$ MOVE-NS(β, $\langle \mathcal{SK}, \mathit{NS} \rangle$);

            $\mathit{NS}^\star \leftarrow \mathit{NS}^\star \cup$ CREATE-NS(β, $\langle \mathcal{SK}, \mathit{NS} \rangle$);

10:            **if** is_equality(β) **then** $\langle \mathcal{SK}, \mathit{NS} \rangle \leftarrow \langle \mathcal{SK}^0, \mathit{NS}^0 \oplus \mathit{NS}^\star \rangle$;

           else if is_strict_ineq(β) **then**

12:               $\mathcal{SK}^0 \leftarrow$ points_become_closure_points($\mathcal{SK}^0$);

              $\langle \mathcal{SK}, \mathit{NS} \rangle \leftarrow \langle \mathcal{SK}^+ \cup \mathcal{SK}^0, \mathit{NS}^+ \oplus \mathit{NS}^\star \rangle$;

14:            **else** $\langle \mathcal{SK}, \mathit{NS} \rangle \leftarrow \langle \mathcal{SK}^+ \cup \mathcal{SK}^0, (\mathit{NS}^+ \cup \mathit{NS}^0) \oplus \mathit{NS}^\star \rangle$;

        PROMOTE-SINGLETONS($\langle \mathcal{SK}, \mathit{NS} \rangle$);

16:     **return** $\langle \mathcal{SK}, \mathit{NS} \rangle$;

Table 1. Case analysis for function 'comb$_\beta$' when adding an equality ($\beta_=$), a non-strict ($\beta_\geq$) or a strict ($\beta_>$) inequality constraint to a pair of generators from $\mathcal{SK}^+$ and $\mathcal{SK}^-$ (R = ray, C = closure point, SP = skeleton point).

	$\mathcal{SK}^+$	R	R	R	C	C	C	SP	SP	SP
	$\mathcal{SK}^-$	R	C	SP	R	C	SP	R	C	SP
$\beta_=$ or $\beta_\geq$	$\mathcal{SK}^\star$	R	C	SP	C	C	SP	SP	SP	SP
$\beta_>$	$\mathcal{SK}^\star$	R	C	C	C	C	C	C	C	C

4.2   Processing the Non-skeleton

Line 4 partitions the supports in NS by exploiting the partition information for the skeleton $\mathcal{SK}$, so that no additional scalar product is computed. Namely, each support $ns \in \mathit{NS}$ is classified as follows:

$$ns \in \mathit{NS}^+ \iff ns \subseteq (\mathcal{SK}^+ \cup \mathcal{SK}^0) \land ns \cap \mathcal{SK}^+ \neq \emptyset;$$

$$ns \in \mathit{NS}^0 \iff ns \subseteq \mathcal{SK}^0;$$

$$ns \in \mathit{NS}^- \iff ns \subseteq (\mathcal{SK}^- \cup \mathcal{SK}^0) \land ns \cap \mathcal{SK}^- \neq \emptyset;$$

$$ns \in \mathit{NS}^\pm \iff ns \cap \mathcal{SK}^+ \neq \emptyset \land ns \cap \mathcal{SK}^- \neq \emptyset.$$

This partitioning is consistent with the previous one. For instance, if $ns \in \mathit{NS}^+$, then for every possible materialization $\boldsymbol{p} \in \mathrm{relint}(\overline{\mathrm{gen}}(ns))$ the scalar product of $\boldsymbol{p}$ and β is strictly positive. The supports in $\mathit{NS}^\pm$ are those whose materializations can satisfy, saturate and violate the constraint β (i.e., the corresponding face *crosses* the constraint hyperplane).

In lines 8 and 9, we find the calls to the two main functions processing the non-skeleton component. A set $NS^\star$ of new supports is built as the union of the contributes provided by functions MOVE-NS and CREATE-NS.

Moving Supports. The MOVE-NS function, shown in Pseudocode 2, processes the supports in $NS^\pm$: this function "moves" the fillers of the faces that are crossed by the new constraint, making sure they lie on the correct side.

Let $ns \in NS^\pm$ and $F = \mathrm{relint}(\overline{\mathrm{gen}}(ns))$. Note that $ns = \mathcal{SK}_F$ *before* the addition of the new constraint β; at this point, the elements in $\mathcal{SK}^\star$ have been added to $\mathcal{SK}^0$, but this change still has to be propagated to the non-skeleton component NS. Therefore, we compute the *support closure* 'supp.cl$_{\mathcal{SK}}(ns)$' according to the updated skeleton $\mathcal{SK}$. Intuitively, supp.cl$_{\mathcal{SK}}(ns) \subseteq \mathcal{SK}$ is the subset of all the skeleton elements that are included in face F.

At the implementation level, support closures can be efficiently computed by exploiting the same *saturation information* used for the adjacency tests. Namely, for constraints $\mathcal{C}$ and generators $\mathcal{G}$, we can define

$$\mathrm{sat.inter}_{\mathcal{C}}(\mathcal{G}) \overset{\mathrm{def}}{=} \{\, \beta' \in \mathcal{C} \mid \forall g \in \mathcal{G} : g \text{ saturates } \beta' \,\},$$

$$\mathrm{sat.inter}_{\mathcal{G}}(\mathcal{C}) \overset{\mathrm{def}}{=} \{\, g \in \mathcal{G} \mid \forall \beta' \in \mathcal{C} : g \text{ saturates } \beta' \,\}.$$

Then, if $\mathcal{C}$ and $\mathcal{SK} = \langle L, R, C, SP \rangle$ are the constraint system and the skeleton generator system for the polyhedron, for each $ns \in NS$ we can compute [26]:

$$\mathrm{supp.cl}_{\mathcal{SK}}(ns) \overset{\mathrm{def}}{=} \mathrm{sat.inter}_{\mathcal{SK}}\big(\mathrm{sat.inter}_{\mathcal{C}}(ns)\big) \setminus L.$$

Face F is split by constraint β into F^+, F^0 and F^-. When β is a strict inequality, only F^+ shall be kept in the polyhedron; when the new constraint is a non-strict inequality, both F^+ and F^0 shall be kept. A minimal non-skeleton representation for these subsets can be obtained by *projecting* the support:

$$\mathrm{proj}^{\beta}_{\mathcal{SK}}(ns) \overset{\mathrm{def}}{=} \begin{cases} ns \setminus \mathcal{SK}^-, & \text{if } \beta \text{ is a strict inequality;} \\ ns \cap \mathcal{SK}^0, & \text{otherwise.} \end{cases}$$

To summarize, by composing support closure and projection in line 3 of MOVE-NS, each support in $NS^\pm$ is moved to the correct side of β.

Example 3. Consider $\mathcal{P} \in \mathbb{P}_2$ in the left hand side of the next figure.

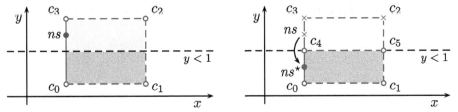

The skeleton $\mathcal{SK} = \langle \emptyset, \emptyset, C, \emptyset \rangle$ contains the closure points in $C = \{c_0, c_1, c_2, c_3\}$; the non-skeleton $NS = \{ns\}$ contains a single support $ns = \{c_0, c_3\}$, which makes sure that the open segment (c_0, c_3) is included in $\mathcal{P}$; the figure shows a single materialization for ns.

When processing $\beta = (y < 1)$, we obtain the polyhedron in the right hand side of the figure. In the skeleton phase of the CONVERSION function the adjacent skeleton generators are combined: c_4 (from $c_0 \in \mathcal{SK}^+$ and $c_3 \in \mathcal{SK}^-$) and c_5 (from $c_1 \in \mathcal{SK}^+$ and $c_2 \in \mathcal{SK}^-$) are added to $\mathcal{SK}^0$. Since the non-skeleton support ns belongs to $NS^\pm$, it is processed in the MOVE-NS function:

$$ns^* = \mathrm{proj}^\beta_{\mathcal{SK}}(\mathrm{supp.cl}_{\mathcal{SK}}(ns)) = \mathrm{proj}^\beta_{\mathcal{SK}}(\{c_0, c_3, c_4\}) = \{c_0, c_4\}.$$

In contrast, if we were processing the non-strict inequality $\beta' = (y \leq 1)$, we would have obtained $ns' = \mathrm{proj}^{\beta'}_{\mathcal{SK}}(\mathrm{supp.cl}_{\mathcal{SK}}(ns)) = \{c_4\}$. Since ns' is a singleton, it is upgraded to become a skeleton point by procedure PROMOTE-SINGLETONS. Hence, in this case the new skeleton is $\mathcal{SK} = \langle \emptyset, \emptyset, C, SP \rangle$, where $C = \{c_0, c_1, c_5\}$ and $SP = \{c_4\}$, while the non-skeleton component is empty.

Creating New Supports. Consider the case of a support $ns \in NS^-$ violating a non-strict inequality constraint β: this support has to be removed from NS. However, the upward closed set NS is represented by its minimal elements only so that, by removing ns, we are also implicitly removing other supports from the set $\uparrow ns$, including some that do not belong to NS^- and hence should be kept. Therefore, we have to explore the set of faces and detect those that are going to lose their filler: their minimal supports will be added to $NS^\star$. Similarly, when processing a non-strict inequality constraint, we need to consider the new faces introduced by the constraint: the corresponding supports can be found by projecting on the constraint hyperplane those faces that are possibly filled by an element in SP^+ or NS^+.

This is the task of the CREATE-NS function, shown in Pseudocode 2. It uses ENUMERATE-FACES as a helper:[4] the latter provides an enumeration of all the (higher dimensional) faces that contain the initial support ns. The new faces are obtained by adding to ns a new generator g and then composing the support closure and projection functions, as done in MOVE-NS. For efficiency purposes, a case analysis is performed so as to restrict the search area of the enumeration phase, by considering only the faces crossing the constraint.

Example 4. Consider $\mathcal{P} \in \mathbb{P}_2$ in the left hand side of the next figure, described by skeleton $\mathcal{SK} = \langle \emptyset, \emptyset, \{c_0, c_1, c_2\}, \{p\} \rangle$ and non-skeleton $NS = \emptyset$.

---

[4] This enumeration phase is inspired by the algorithm in [26].

Pseudocode 2. Helper functions for moving and creating supports.

---

    function MOVE-NS(β, $\langle \mathcal{SK}, NS \rangle$)
2:    $NS^\star \leftarrow \emptyset$;
    for all $ns \in NS^\pm$ **do** $NS^\star \leftarrow NS^\star \cup \{\mathrm{proj}^\beta_{\mathcal{SK}}(\mathrm{supp.cl}_{\mathcal{SK}}(ns))\}$;
4:    **return** $NS^\star$;
    function CREATE-NS(β, $\langle \mathcal{SK}, NS \rangle$)
6:    $NS^\star \leftarrow \emptyset$;
    let $\mathcal{SK} = \langle L, R, C, SP \rangle$;
8:    **for all** $ns \in NS^- \cup \{\{p\} \mid p \in SP^-\}$ **do**
        $NS^\star \leftarrow NS^\star \cup$ ENUMERATE-FACES(β, ns, $\mathcal{SK}^+$, $\mathcal{SK}$);
10:    **if** is_strict_ineq(β) **then**
        for all $ns \in NS^0 \cup \{\{p\} \mid p \in SP^0\}$ **do**
12:        $NS^\star \leftarrow NS^\star \cup$ ENUMERATE-FACES(β, ns, $\mathcal{SK}^+$, $\mathcal{SK}$);
    else
14:        **for all** $ns \in NS^+ \cup \{\{p\} \mid p \in SP^+\}$ **do**
        $NS^\star \leftarrow NS^\star \cup$ ENUMERATE-FACES(β, ns, $\mathcal{SK}^-$, $\mathcal{SK}$);
16:    **return** $NS^\star$;
    function ENUMERATE-FACES(β, ns, $\mathcal{SK}'$, $\mathcal{SK}$)
18:    $NS^\star \leftarrow \emptyset$; let $\mathcal{SK}' = \langle L', R', C', SP' \rangle$;
    for all $g \in (R' \cup C')$ **do** $NS^\star \leftarrow NS^\star \cup \{\mathrm{proj}^\beta_{\mathcal{SK}}(\mathrm{supp.cl}_{\mathcal{SK}}(ns \cup \{g\}))\}$;
20:    **return** $NS^\star$;
    procedure PROMOTE-SINGLETONS($\langle \mathcal{SK}, NS \rangle$)
22:    let $\mathcal{SK} = \langle L, R, C, SP \rangle$;
    for all $ns \in NS$ such that $ns = \langle \emptyset, \emptyset, \{c\}, \emptyset \rangle$ **do**
24:        $NS \leftarrow NS \setminus \{ns\}$; $C \leftarrow C \setminus \{c\}$; $SP \leftarrow SP \cup \{c\}$;

Pseudocode 3. Processing a line violating constraint β.

---

    procedure VIOLATING-LINE(β, l, $\langle \mathcal{SK}, NS \rangle$)
2:    split l into rays r^+ satisfying β and r^- violating β;
    $l \leftarrow r^+$;
4:    **for all** $g \in \mathcal{SK}$ **do** $g \leftarrow \mathrm{comb}_\beta(g, l)$;
    if is_equality(β) **then** $\mathcal{SK} \leftarrow \mathcal{SK}^0$;
6:    **if** is_strict_ineq(β) **then** STRICT-ON-EQ-POINTS(β, $\langle \mathcal{SK}, NS \rangle$);
    procedure STRICT-ON-EQ-POINTS(β, $\langle \mathcal{SK}, NS \rangle$)
8:    $NS^\star \leftarrow \emptyset$; let $\mathcal{SK}^0 = \langle L^0, R^0, C^0, SP^0 \rangle$;
    for all $ns \in NS^0 \cup \{\{p\} \mid p \in SP^0\}$ **do**
10:        $NS^\star \leftarrow NS^\star \cup$ ENUMERATE-FACES(β, ns, $\mathcal{SK}^+$, $\mathcal{SK}$);
    $\mathcal{SK}^0 \leftarrow$ points-become-closure-points($\mathcal{SK}^0$);
12:    $\langle \mathcal{SK}, NS \rangle \leftarrow \langle \mathcal{SK}^+ \cup \mathcal{SK}^0, NS^+ \oplus NS^\star \rangle$;

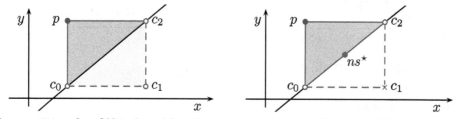

The partition for $\mathcal{SK}$ induced by the non-strict inequality is as follows:

$$\mathcal{SK}^+ = \langle \emptyset, \emptyset, \emptyset, \{p\}\rangle, \quad \mathcal{SK}^0 = \langle \emptyset, \emptyset, \{c_0, c_2\}, \emptyset\rangle, \quad \mathcal{SK}^- = \langle \emptyset, \emptyset, \{c_1\}, \emptyset\rangle.$$

There are no adjacent generators in $\mathcal{SK}^+$ and $\mathcal{SK}^-$, so that $\mathcal{SK}^\star$ is empty. When processing the non-skeleton component, the skeleton point in $\mathcal{SK}^+$ will be considered in line 15 of function CREATE-NS. The corresponding call to function ENUMERATE-FACES computes

$$ns^\star = \mathrm{proj}_{\mathcal{SK}}^\beta \left(\mathrm{supp.cl}_{\mathcal{SK}}(\{p\} \cup \{c_1\}) \right) = \mathrm{proj}_{\mathcal{SK}}^\beta (\{c_0, c_1, c_2, p\}) = \{c_0, c_2\},$$

thereby producing the filler for the open segment (c_0, c_2). The resulting polyhedron, shown in the right hand side of the figure, is thus described by the skeleton $\mathcal{SK} = \langle \emptyset, \emptyset, \{c_0, c_2\}, \{p\}\rangle$ and the non-skeleton $NS = \{ns^\star\}$.

It is worth noting that, when handling Example 4 adopting an entirely geometric representation, closure point c_1 needs to be combined with point p even if the two generators are *not* adjacent: this leads to a significant efficiency penalty. Similarly, an implementation based on the ϵ-representation will have to combine closure point c_1 with point p (and/or with some other ϵ-redundant points), because the addition of the slack variable makes them adjacent. Therefore, an implementation based on the new approach obtains a twofold benefit: first, the distinction between skeleton and non-skeleton allows for restricting the handling of non-adjacent combinations to the non-skeleton phase; second, thanks to the combinatorial representation, the non-skeleton component can be processed by using set index operations only, i.e., computing no linear combination at all.

Preparing for Next Iteration. In lines 10 to 15 of CONVERSION the generator system is updated for the next iteration. The new supports in $NS^\star$ are merged (using '$\oplus$' to remove redundancies) into the appropriate portions of the non-skeleton component. In particular, when processing a strict inequality, in line 12 the helper function

$$\text{points\_become\_closure\_points}(\langle L, R, C, SP\rangle) \stackrel{\mathrm{def}}{=} \langle L, R, C \cup SP, \emptyset\rangle$$

is applied to $\mathcal{SK}^0$, making sure that all of the skeleton points saturating β are transformed into closure points having the same position. The final processing step (line 15) calls helper procedure PROMOTE-SINGLETONS (see Pseudocode 2), making sure that all singleton supports get promoted to skeleton points.

Note that line 5 of CONVERSION, by calling procedure VIOLATING-LINE (see Pseudocode 3) handles the special case of a line violating β. This is just an optimization: the helper procedure STRICT-ON-EQ-POINTS can be seen as a tailored version of CREATE-NS, also including the final updating of $\mathcal{SK}$ and NS.

4.3 Duality

The definitions given in Sect. 3 for a geometric generator system have their dual versions working on a geometric *constraint* system. We provide a brief overview of these correspondences, which are summarized in Table 2.

Table 2. Correspondences between generator and constraint concepts.

	Generators	Constraints
Geometric skeleton		
singular	line	equality
non-singular	ray or closure point	non-strict inequality
semantics	$\mathrm{gen}(\mathcal{SK}) = \emptyset$	$\mathrm{con}(\mathcal{SK}) = \mathrm{cl}(\mathcal{P})$
Combinatorial non-skeleton		
abstracts	point	strict inequality
element role	face filler	face cutter
represents	upward closed set	downward closed set
encoding	minimal support	minimal support
singleton	skeleton point	skeleton strict inequality

For a non-empty $\mathcal{P} = \mathrm{con}(\mathcal{C}) \in \mathbb{P}_n$, the skeleton of $\mathcal{C} = \langle C_=, C_\geq, C_> \rangle$ includes the non-redundant constraints defining $\mathcal{Q} = \mathrm{cl}(\mathcal{P})$. Denoting by $SC_>$ the *skeleton strict inequalities* (i.e., those whose corresponding non-strict inequality is not redundant for $\mathcal{Q}$), we have $\mathcal{SK}_\mathcal{Q} \overset{\text{def}}{=} \langle C_=, C_\geq \cup SC_>, \emptyset \rangle$, so that $\mathcal{Q} = \mathrm{con}(\mathcal{SK}_\mathcal{Q})$. The *ghost* faces of $\mathcal{P}$ are the faces of the closure $\mathcal{Q}$ that do not intersect $\mathcal{P}$: $gFaces_\mathcal{P} \overset{\text{def}}{=} \{ F \in cFaces_\mathcal{Q} \mid F \cap \mathcal{P} = \emptyset \}$; thus, $\mathcal{P} = \mathrm{con}(\mathcal{SK}_\mathcal{Q}) \setminus \bigcup gFaces_\mathcal{P}$. The set $gFaces' \overset{\text{def}}{=} gFaces \cup \{\mathcal{Q}\}$ is a meet sublattice of $cFaces$; also, $gFaces$ is downward closed and can be represented by its *maximal* elements.

The skeleton support $\mathcal{SK}_F$ of a face $F \in cFaces_\mathcal{Q}$ is defined as the set of all the skeleton constraints that are saturated by all the points in F. Each face $F \in gFaces$ saturates a strict inequality $\beta_> \in C_>$: we can represent such a face using its skeleton support $\mathcal{SK}_F$ of which $\beta_>$ is a possible materialization. A constraint system non-skeleton component $NS \subseteq \mathbb{NS}$ is thus a combinatorial representation of the *strict inequalities* of the polyhedron.

Hence, the non-skeleton components for generators and constraints have a complementary role: in the case of generators they are face *fillers*, marking the minimal faces that are *included* in *nncFaces*; in the case of constraints they are face *cutters*, marking the maximal faces that are *excluded* from *nncFaces*. Note that the non-redundant cutters in *gFaces* are those having a *minimal* skeleton support, as is the case for the fillers.

As it happens with lines, all the equalities in $C_=$ are included in all the supports $ns \in NS$ so that, for efficiency, they are not represented explicitly.

After removing the equalities, a singleton $ns \in NS$ stands for a *skeleton strict inequality* constraint, which is better represented in the skeleton component, thereby obtaining $\mathcal{SK} = \langle C_=, C_\geq, SC_> \rangle$. Hence, a support $ns \in NS$ is redundant if there exists $ns' \in NS$ such that $ns' \subset ns$ or if $ns \cap SC_> \neq \emptyset$.

When the concepts underlying the skeleton and non-skeleton representation are reinterpreted as discussed above, it is possible to define a conversion procedure mapping a generator representation into a constraint representation which is very similar to the one from constraints to generators.

5   Experimental Evaluation

The new representation and conversion algorithms for NNC polyhedra have been implemented and tested in the context of the PPL (Parma Polyhedra Library). A full integration in the PPL domain of NNC polyhedra is not possible, since the latter assumes the presence of the slack variable ϵ. The approach, summarized by the diagram in Fig. 1, is to intercept each call to the PPL's conversion (working on ϵ-representations in $\mathbb{CP}_{n+1}$) and pair it with a corresponding call to the new algorithm (working on the new representations in $\mathbb{P}_n$).

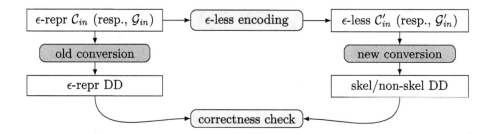

Fig. 1. High level diagram for the experimental evaluation (non-incremental case).

On the left hand side of the diagram we see the application of the standard PPL conversion procedure: the input ϵ-representation is processed by 'old conversion' so as to produce the output ϵ-representation DD pair. The 'ϵ-less encoding' phase produces a copy of the input without the slack variable; this is processed by 'new conversion' to produce the output DD pair, based on the new skeleton/non-skeleton representation. After the two conversions are completed, the outputs are checked for both semantic equivalence and non-redundancy. This final checking phase was successful on all the experiments performed, which include all of the tests in the PPL. In order to assess efficiency, additional code was added to measure the time spent inside the old and new conversion procedures, disregarding the input encoding and output checking phases. It is worth stressing that several experimental evaluations, including recent ones [2], confirm that the PPL is a state-of-the-art implementation of the DD method for a wide spectrum of application contexts.

The first experiment[5] on efficiency is meant to evaluate the *overhead* incurred by the new representation and algorithm for NNC polyhedra when processing topologically closed polyhedra, so as to compare it with the corresponding overhead incurred by the ϵ-representation. To this end, we considered the `ppl_lcdd` demo application of the PPL, which solves the *vertex/facet enumeration problem*. In Table 3 we report the results obtained on a selection of the test benchmarks[6] when using: the conversion algorithm for closed polyhedra (columns 2–3); the conversion algorithm for the ϵ-representation of NNC polyhedra (columns 4–5); and the new conversion algorithm for the new representation of NNC polyhedra (columns 6–7). Columns 'time' report the number of milliseconds spent; columns 'sat' report the number of saturation (i.e., bit vector) operations, in millions.

The results in Table 3 show that the use of the ϵ-representation for closed polyhedra incurs a significant overhead. In contrast, the new representation and algorithm go beyond all expectations: in almost all of the tests there is no overhead at all (that is, any overhead incurred is so small to be masked by the improvements obtained in other parts of the algorithm).

Table 3. Overhead of conversion for C polyhedra. Units: time (ms), sat (M).

test	closed poly		ϵ-repr		$\langle \mathcal{SK}, \mathcal{NS} \rangle$	
	time	sat	time	sat	time	sat
cp6.ext	21	1.1	47	5.3	13	1.1
cross12.ine	157	17.1	215	18.1	180	17.2
in7.ine	47	1.7	149	6.1	27	0.9
kkd38_6.ine	498	28.3	1870	113.2	218	14.2
kq20_11_m.ine	42	1.7	153	6.1	27	0.9
metric80_16.ine	39	2.3	76	5.4	25	2.0
mit31-20.ine	1109	88.7	35629	702.2	816	60.1
mp6.ine	86	6.4	215	17.9	72	8.0
reg600-5_m.ext	906	24.7	3062	119.1	723	14.0
sampleh8.ine	5916	307.4	42339	1420.7	3309	154.1
trunc10.ine	1274	91.7	5212	396.6	803	89.9

The second experiment is meant to evaluate the efficiency gains obtained in a more appropriate context, i.e., when processing polyhedra that are *not* topologically closed. To this end, we consider the same benchmark discussed in [3, Table 2],[7] which highlights the efficiency improvement resulting from the adoption of an *enhanced* evaluation strategy (where a knowledgeable user of the

---

[5] All experiments have been performed on a laptop with an Intel Core i7-3632QM CPU, 16 GB of RAM and running GNU/Linux 4.13.0-25.

[6] We only show the tests where PPL time on closed polyhedra is above 20 ms.

[7] The test `dualhypercubes.cc` is distributed with the source code of the PPL.

library explicitly invokes, when appropriate, the strong minimization procedures for ϵ-representations) with respect to the *standard* evaluation strategy (where the user simply performs the required computation, leaving the burden of optimization to the library developers). In Table 4 we report the results obtained for the most expensive test among those described in [3, Table 2], comparing the standard and enhanced evaluation strategies for the ϵ-representation (rows 1 and 2) with the new algorithm (row 3). For each algorithm we show in column 2 the total number of iterations of the conversion procedures and, in the next two columns, the median and maximum sizes of the representations computed at each iteration (i.e., the size of the intermediate results); in columns from 5 to 8 we show the numbers of incremental and non-incremental calls to the conversion procedures, together with the corresponding time spent (in milliseconds); in column 9 we show the time spent in strong minimization of ϵ-representations; in the final column, we show the overall time ratio, computed with respect to the time spent by the new algorithm.

Table 4. Comparing ϵ-representation based (standard and enhanced) computations for NNC polyhedra with the new conversion procedures.

algorithm	# iter	iter sizes		full conv		incr conv		ϵ-min	time
		median	max	num	time	num	time	time	ratio
ϵ-repr standard	1142	3706	7259	4	11	3	30336	27	1460.9
ϵ-repr enhanced	525	109	1661	7	204	0	—	29	11.2
$\langle \mathcal{SK}, \mathcal{NS} \rangle$ standard	314	62	180	4	6	3	15	—	1.0

Even though adopting the standard computation strategy (requiring no clever guess by the end user), the new algorithm obtains impressive time improvements, outperforming not only the standard, but also the enhanced computation strategy for the ϵ-representation. The reason for the latter efficiency improvement is that the enhanced computation strategy, when invoking the strong minimization procedures, interferes with incrementality: the figures in Table 4 confirm that the new algorithm performs three of the seven required conversions in an incremental way, while in the enhanced case they are all non-incremental. Moreover, a comparison of the iteration counts and the sizes of the intermediate results provides further evidence that the new algorithm is able to maintain a non-redundant description even *during* the iterations of a conversion.

6   Conclusion

We have presented a new approach for the representation of NNC polyhedra in the Double Description framework, avoiding the use of slack variables and distinguishing between the skeleton component, encoded geometrically, and the non-skeleton component, provided with a combinatorial encoding. We have proposed and implemented a variant of the Chernikova conversion procedure achieving significant efficiency improvements with respect to a state-of-the-art implementation of the domain of NNC polyhedra, thereby providing a solution to all the issues affecting the ϵ-representation approach. As future work, we plan to develop a full implementation of the domain of NNC polyhedra based on this new representation. To this end, we will have to reconsider each semantic operator already implemented by the existing libraries (which are based on the addition of a slack variable), so as to propose, implement and experimentally evaluate a corresponding correct specification based on the new approach.

References

1. 4ti2 team: 4ti2—a software package for algebraic, geometric and combinatorial problems on linear spaces. www.4ti2.de
2. Assarf, B., Gawrilow, E., Herr, K., Joswig, M., Lorenz, B., Paffenholz, A., Rehn, T.: Computing convex hulls and counting integer points with polymake. Math. Program. Comput. **9**(1), 1–38 (2017)
3. Bagnara, R., Hill, P.M., Zaffanella, E.: Not necessarily closed convex polyhedra and the double description method. Form. Asp. Comput. **17**(2), 222–257 (2005)
4. Bagnara, R., Hill, P.M., Zaffanella, E.: Applications of polyhedral computations to the analysis and verification of hardware and software systems. Theor. Comput. Sci. **410**(46), 4672–4691 (2009)
5. Bagnara, R., Ricci, E., Zaffanella, E., Hill, P.M.: Possibly not closed convex polyhedra and the Parma polyhedra library. In: Hermenegildo, M.V., Puebla, G. (eds.) SAS 2002. LNCS, vol. 2477, pp. 213–229. Springer, Heidelberg (2002). https://doi.org/10.1007/3-540-45789-5_17
6. Bastoul, C.: Code generation in the polyhedral model is easier than you think. In: Proceedings of the 13th International Conference on Parallel Architectures and Compilation Techniques (PACT 2004), Antibes Juan-les-Pins, France, pp. 7–16. IEEE Computer Society (2004)
7. Becchi, A., Zaffanella, E.: A conversion procedure for NNC polyhedra. CoRR, abs/1711.09593 (2017)
8. Benerecetti, M., Faella, M., Minopoli, S.: Automatic synthesis of switching controllers for linear hybrid systems: safety control. Theor. Comput. Sci. **493**, 116–138 (2013)
9. Birkhoff, G.: Lattice Theory. 3rd edn. Volume XXV of Colloquium Publications. American Mathematical Society, Providence (1967)
10. Chernikova, N.V.: Algorithm for finding a general formula for the non-negative solutions of system of linear equations. U.S.S.R. Comput. Math. Math. Phys. **4**(4), 151–158 (1964)
11. Chernikova, N.V.: Algorithm for finding a general formula for the non-negative solutions of system of linear inequalities. U.S.S.R. Comput. Math. Math. Phys. **5**(2), 228–233 (1965)
12. Chernikova, N.V.: Algorithm for discovering the set of all solutions of a linear programming problem. U.S.S.R. Comput. Math. Math. Phys. **8**(6), 282–293 (1968)
13. Colón, M.A., Sipma, H.B.: Synthesis of linear ranking functions. In: Margaria, T., Yi, W. (eds.) TACAS 2001. LNCS, vol. 2031, pp. 67–81. Springer, Heidelberg (2001). https://doi.org/10.1007/3-540-45319-9_6

14. Cousot, P., Cousot, R.: Systematic design of program analysis frameworks. In: Proceedings of the Sixth Annual ACM Symposium on Principles of Programming Languages, San Antonio, TX, USA, pp. 269–282 (1979)
15. Cousot, P., Halbwachs, N.: Automatic discovery of linear restraints among variables of a program. In: Conference Record of the Fifth Annual ACM Symposium on Principles of Programming Languages, Tucson, Arizona, pp. 84–96 (1978)
16. Doose, D., Mammeri, Z.: Polyhedra-based approach for incremental validation of real-time systems. In: Yang, L.T., Amamiya, M., Liu, Z., Guo, M., Rammig, F.J. (eds.) EUC 2005. LNCS, vol. 3824, pp. 184–193. Springer, Heidelberg (2005). https://doi.org/10.1007/11596356_21
17. Ellenbogen, R.: Fully automatic verification of absence of errors via interprocedural integer analysis. Master's thesis, School of Computer Science, Tel-Aviv University, Tel-Aviv, Israel, December 2004
18. Frehse, G.: PHAVer: algorithmic verification of hybrid systems past HyTech. Softw. Tools Technol. Transf. **10**(3), 263–279 (2008)
19. Fukuda, K., Prodon, A.: Double description method revisited. In: Deza, M., Euler, R., Manoussakis, I. (eds.) CCS 1995. LNCS, vol. 1120, pp. 91–111. Springer, Heidelberg (1996). https://doi.org/10.1007/3-540-61576-8_77
20. Genov, B.: The Convex Hull Problem in Practice: Improving the Running Time of the Double Description Method. Ph.D. thesis, University of Bremen, Germany (2014)
21. Gopan, D.: Numeric Program Analysis Techniques with Applications to Array Analysis and Library Summarization. Ph.D. thesis, University of Wisconsin, Madison, Wisconsin, USA, August 2007
22. Halbwachs, N., Proy, Y.-E., Raymond, P.: Verification of linear hybrid systems by means of convex approximations. In: Le Charlier, B. (ed.) SAS 1994. LNCS, vol. 864, pp. 223–237. Springer, Heidelberg (1994). https://doi.org/10.1007/3-540-58485-4_43
23. Halbwachs, N., Proy, Y.-E., Roumanoff, P.: Verification of real-time systems using linear relation analysis. Form. Methods Syst. Des. **11**(2), 157–185 (1997)
24. Henry, J., Monniaux, D., Moy, M.: PAGAI: a path sensitive static analyser. Electr. Notes Theor. Comput. Sci. **289**, 15–25 (2012)
25. Jeannet, B., Miné, A.: APRON: a library of numerical abstract domains for static analysis. In: Bouajjani, A., Maler, O. (eds.) CAV 2009. LNCS, vol. 5643, pp. 661–667. Springer, Heidelberg (2009). https://doi.org/10.1007/978-3-642-02658-4_52
26. Kaibel, V., Pfetsch, M.E.: Computing the face lattice of a polytope from its vertex-facet incidences. Comput. Geom. **23**(3), 281–290 (2002)
27. Loechner, V.: PolyLib: a library for manipulating parameterized polyhedra (1999). http://icps.u-strasbg.fr/PolyLib/
28. Motzkin, T.S., Raiffa, H., Thompson, G.L., Thrall, R.M.: The double description method. In: Contributions to the Theory of Games - Volume II, number 28 in Annals of Mathematics Studies, pp. 51–73. Princeton University Press, Princeton (1953)
29. Pop, S., Silber, G.-A., Cohen, A., Bastoul, C., Girbal, S., Vasilache, N.: GRAPHITE: Polyhedral analyses and optimizations for GCC. Technical Report A/378/CRI, Centre de Recherche en Informatique, École des Mines de Paris, Fontainebleau, France (2006)
30. Singh, G., Püschel, M., Vechev, M.T.: Fast polyhedra abstract domain. In: Proceedings of the 44th ACM SIGPLAN Symposium on Principles of Programming Languages, POPL 2017, Paris, France, pp. 46–59 (2017)

31. Terzer, M., Stelling, J.: Large-scale computation of elementary flux modes with bit pattern trees. Bioinformatics **24**(19), 2229–2235 (2008)
32. Terzer, M., Stelling, J.: Parallel extreme ray and pathway computation. In: Wyrzykowski, R., Dongarra, J., Karczewski, K., Wasniewski, J. (eds.) PPAM 2009. LNCS, vol. 6068, pp. 300–309. Springer, Heidelberg (2010). https://doi.org/10.1007/978-3-642-14403-5_32
33. Zolotykh, N.Y.: New modification of the double description method for constructing the skeleton of a polyhedral cone. Comput. Math. Math. Phys. **52**(1), 146–156 (2012)

4

Reactive Control Improvisation

Daniel J. Fremont$^{(\boxtimes)}$(iD) and Sanjit A. Seshia(iD)

University of California, Berkeley, USA
{dfremont,sseshia}@berkeley.edu

Abstract. Reactive synthesis is a paradigm for automatically building correct-by-construction systems that interact with an unknown or adversarial environment. We study how to do reactive synthesis when part of the specification of the system is that its behavior should be *random*. Randomness can be useful, for example, in a network protocol fuzz tester whose output should be varied, or a planner for a surveillance robot whose route should be unpredictable. However, existing reactive synthesis techniques do not provide a way to ensure random behavior while maintaining functional correctness. Towards this end, we generalize the recently-proposed framework of *control improvisation* (CI) to add reactivity. The resulting framework of *reactive control improvisation* provides a natural way to integrate a randomness requirement with the usual functional specifications of reactive synthesis over a finite window. We theoretically characterize when such problems are realizable, and give a general method for solving them. For specifications given by reachability or safety games or by deterministic finite automata, our method yields a polynomial-time synthesis algorithm. For various other types of specifications including temporal logic formulas, we obtain a polynomial-space algorithm and prove matching **PSPACE**-hardness results. We show that all of these randomized variants of reactive synthesis are no harder in a complexity-theoretic sense than their non-randomized counterparts.

1 Introduction

Many interesting programs, including protocol handlers, task planners, and concurrent software generally, are *open* systems that interact over time with an external environment. Synthesis of such *reactive systems* requires finding an implementation that satisfies the desired specification no matter what the environment does. This problem, *reactive synthesis*, has a long history (see [7] for a survey). Reactive synthesis from temporal logic specifications [19] has been particularly well-studied and is being increasingly used in applications such as hardware synthesis [3] and robotic task planning [15].

In this paper, we investigate how to synthesize reactive systems with *random behavior*: in fact, systems where *being random in a prescribed way is part of their specification*. This is in contrast to prior work on stochastic games where randomness is used to model uncertain environments or randomized strategies are merely allowed, not required. Solvers for stochastic games may incidentally produce randomized strategies to satisfy a functional specification (and some types of specification, e.g. multi-objective queries [4], may only be realizable by randomized strategies), but do not provide a general way to *enforce* randomness. Unlike most specifications used in reactive synthesis, our randomness requirement is a property of a system's *distribution* of behaviors, not of an individual behavior. While probabilistic specification languages like PCTL [12] can capture some such properties, the simple and natural randomness requirement we study here cannot be concisely expressed by existing languages (even those as powerful as SGL [2]). Thus, *randomized reactive synthesis* in our sense requires significantly different methods than those previously studied.

However, we argue that this type of synthesis is quite useful, because introducing randomness into the behavior of a system can often be beneficial, enhancing *variety*, *robustness*, and *unpredictability*. Example applications include:

- Synthesizing a black-box fuzz tester for a network service, we want a program that not only conforms to the protocol (perhaps only most of the time) but can generate many different sequences of packets: randomness ensures this.
- Synthesizing a controller for a robot exploring an unknown environment, randomness provides a low-memory way to increase coverage of the space. It can also help to reduce systematic bias in the exploration procedure.
- Synthesizing a controller for a patrolling surveillance robot, introducing randomness in planning makes the robot's future location harder to predict.

Adding randomness to a system in an *ad hoc* way could easily compromise its correctness. This paper shows how a randomness requirement can be integrated *into the synthesis process*, ensuring correctness as well as allowing trade-offs to be explored: how much randomness can be added while staying correct, or how strong can a specification be while admitting a desired amount of randomness?

To formalize randomized reactive synthesis we build on the idea of *control improvisation*, introduced in [6], formalized in [9], and further generalized in [8]. Control improvisation (CI) is the problem of constructing an *improviser*, a probabilistic algorithm which generates finite words subject to three constraints: a *hard constraint* that must always be satisfied, a *soft constraint* that need only be satisfied with some probability, and a *randomness constraint* that no word be generated with probability higher than a given bound. We define *reactive control improvisation* (RCI), where the improviser generates a word incrementally, alternating adding symbols with an adversarial environment. To perform synthesis in a finite window, we encode functional specifications and environment assumptions into the hard constraint, while the soft and randomness constraints allow us to tune how randomness is added to the system. The improviser obtained by solving the RCI problem is then a solution to the original synthesis problem.

The difficulty of solving reactive CI problems depends on the type of specification. We study several types commonly used in reactive synthesis, including reachability games (and variants, e.g. safety games) and formulas in the temporal logics LTL and LDL [5,18]. We also investigate the specification types studied in [8], showing how the complexity of the CI problem changes when adding reactivity. For every type of specification we obtain a randomized synthesis algorithm whose complexity matches that of ordinary reactive synthesis (in a finite window). This suggests that reactive control improvisation should be feasible in applications like robotic task planning where reactive synthesis tools have proved effective.

In summary, the main contributions of this paper are:

- The reactive control improvisation (RCI) problem definition (Sect. 3);
- The notion of *width*, a quantitative generalization of "winning" game positions that measures *how many ways* a player can win from that position (Sect. 4);
- A characterization of when RCI problems are realizable in terms of width, and an explicit construction of an improviser (Sect. 4);
- A general method for constructing efficient improvisation schemes (Sect. 5);
- A polynomial-time improvisation scheme for reachability/safety games and deterministic finite automaton specifications (Sect. 6);
- PSPACE-hardness results for many other specification types including temporal logics, and matching polynomial-space improvisation schemes (Sect. 7).

Finally, Sect. 8 summarizes our results and gives directions for future work.

2   Background

2.1   Notation

Given an alphabet Σ, we write $|w|$ for the length of a finite word $w \in \Sigma^*$, λ for the empty word, Σ^n for the words of length n, and $\Sigma^{\leq n}$ for $\cup_{0 \leq i \leq n} \Sigma^i$, the set of all words of length at most n. We abbreviate deterministic/nondeterministic finite automaton by DFA/NFA, and context-free grammar by CFG. For an instance $\mathcal{X}$ of any such formalism, which we call a *specification*, we write $L(\mathcal{X})$ for the language (subset of Σ^*) it defines (note the distinction between a language and a representation thereof). We view formulas of Linear Temporal Logic (LTL) [18] and Linear Dynamic Logic (LDL) [5] as specifications using their natural semantics on finite words (see [5]).

We use the standard complexity classes #P and PSPACE, and the PSPACE-complete problem QBF of determining the truth of a quantified Boolean formula. For background on these classes and problems see for example [1].

Some specifications we use as examples are *reachability games* [16], where players' actions cause transitions in a state space and the goal is to reach a target state. We group these games, *safety games* where the goal is to *avoid* a set of states, and *reach-avoid* games combining reachability and safety goals [20], together as *reachability/safety games* (RSGs). We draw reachability games as graphs in the usual way: squares are adversary-controlled states, and states with a double border are target states.

2.2   Synthesis Games

Reactive control improvisation will be formalized in terms of a 2-player game which is essentially the standard *synthesis game* used in reactive synthesis [7]. However, our formulation is slightly different for compatibility with the definition of control improvisation, so we give a self-contained presentation here.

Fix a finite alphabet Σ. The players of the game will alternate picking symbols from Σ, building up a word. We can then specify the set of winning plays with a language over Σ. To simplify our presentation we assume that players strictly alternate turns and that any symbol from Σ is a legal move. These assumptions can be relaxed in the usual way by modifying the winning set appropriately.

Finite Words: While reactive synthesis is usually considered over infinite words, in this paper we focus on synthesis in a finite window, as it is unclear how best to generalize our randomness requirement to the infinite case. This assumption is not too restrictive, as solutions of bounded length are adequate for many applications. In fuzz testing, for example, we do not want to generate arbitrarily long files or sequences of packets. In robotic planning, we often want a plan that accomplishes a task within a certain amount of time. Furthermore, planning problems with liveness specifications can often be segmented into finite pieces: we do not need an infinite route for a patrolling robot, but can plan within a finite horizon and replan periodically. Replanning may even be *necessary* when environment assumptions become invalid. At any rate, we will see that the bounded case of reactive control improvisation is already highly nontrivial.

As a final simplification, we require that all plays have length exactly $n \in \mathbb{N}$. To allow a range $[m, n]$ we can simply add a new padding symbol to Σ and extend all shorter words to length n, modifying the winning set appropriately.

Definition 2.1. *A* history *h is an element of $\Sigma^{\leq n}$, representing the moves of the game played so far. We say the game has* ended *after h if $|h| = n$; otherwise it is* our turn *after h if $|h|$ is even, and the* adversary's turn *if $|h|$ is odd.*

Definition 2.2. *A* strategy *is a function $\sigma : \Sigma^{\leq n} \times \Sigma \to [0, 1]$ such that for any history $h \in \Sigma^{\leq n}$ with $|h| < n$, $\sigma(h, \cdot)$ is a probability distribution over Σ. We write $x \leftarrow \sigma(h)$ to indicate that x is a symbol randomly drawn from $\sigma(h, \cdot)$.*

Since strategies are randomized, fixing strategies for both players does not uniquely determine a play of the game, but defines a *distribution* over plays:

Definition 2.3. *Given a pair of strategies (σ, τ), we can generate a random play $\pi \in \Sigma^n$ as follows. Pick $\pi_0 \leftarrow \sigma(\lambda)$, then for i from 1 to $n - 1$ pick $\pi_i \leftarrow \tau(\pi_0 \ldots \pi_{i-1})$ if i is odd and $\pi_i \leftarrow \sigma(\pi_0 \ldots \pi_{i-1})$ otherwise. Finally, put $\pi = \pi_0 \ldots \pi_{n-1}$. We write $P_{\sigma,\tau}(\pi)$ for the probability of obtaining the play π. This extends to a set of plays $X \subseteq \Sigma^n$ in the natural way: $P_{\sigma,\tau}(X) = \sum_{\pi \in X} P_{\sigma,\tau}(\pi)$. Finally, the set of* possible plays *is $\Pi_{\sigma,\tau} = \{\pi \in \Sigma^n \mid P_{\sigma,\tau}(\pi) > 0\}$.*

The next definition is just the conditional probability of a play given a history, but works for histories with probability zero, simplifying our presentation.

Definition 2.4. *For any history $h = h_0 \ldots h_{k-1} \in \Sigma^{\leq n}$ and word $\rho \in \Sigma^{n-k}$, we write $P_{\sigma,\tau}(\rho|h)$ for the probability that if we assign $\pi_i = h_i$ for $i < k$ and sample $\pi_k, \ldots, \pi_{n-1}$ by the process above, then $\pi_k \ldots \pi_{n-1} = \rho$.*

3   Problem Definition

3.1   Motivating Example

Consider synthesizing a planner for a surveillance drone operating near another, potentially adversarial drone. Discretizing the map into the 7×7 grid in Fig. 1 (ignoring the depicted trajectories for the moment), a route is a word over the four movement directions. Our specification is to visit the 4 circled locations in 30 moves without colliding with the adversary, assuming it cannot move into the 5 highlighted central locations.

Fig. 1. Improvised trajectories for a patrolling drone (solid) avoiding an adversary (dashed). The adversary may not move into the circles or the square.

Existing reactive synthesis tools can produce a strategy for the patroller ensuring that the specification is always satisfied. However, the strategy may be deterministic, so that in response to a fixed adversary the patroller will always follow the same route. Then it is easy for a third party to predict the route, which could be undesirable, and is in fact unnecessary if there are many other ways the drone can satisfy its specification.

Reactive control improvisation addresses this problem by adding a new type of specification to the *hard constraint* above: a *randomness requirement* stating that no behavior should be generated with probability greater than a threshold ρ. If we set (say) $\rho = 1/5$, then any controller solving the synthesis problem must be able to satisfy the hard constraint in at least 5 different ways, never producing any given behavior more than 20% of the time. Our synthesis algorithm can in fact compute the smallest ρ for which synthesis is possible, yielding a controller that is *maximally-randomized* in that the system's behavior is as close to a uniform distribution as possible.

To allow finer tuning of how randomness is introduced into the controller, our definition also includes a *soft constraint* which need only be satisfied with some probability $1-\epsilon$. This allows us to prefer certain safe behaviors over others. In our drone example, we require that with probability at least $3/4$, we do not visit a circled location twice.

These hard, soft, and randomness constraints form an instance of our reactive control improvisation problem. Encoding the hard and soft constraints as DFAs, our algorithm (Sect. 6) produced a controller achieving the smallest realizable $\rho = 2.2 \times 10^{-12}$. We tested the controller using the PX4 autopilot [17] to refine the generated routes into control actions for a drone simulated in Gazebo [14] (videos and code are available online [11]). A selection of resulting trajectories are shown in Fig. 1 (the remainder in Appendix A of the full paper [10]): starting from the triangles, the patroller's path is solid, the adversary's dashed. The left run uses an adversary that moves towards the patroller when possible. The right runs, with a simple adversary moving in a fixed loop, illustrate the randomness of the synthesized controller.

3.2 Reactive Control Improvisation

Our formal notion of randomized reactive synthesis in a finite window is a reactive extension of *control improvisation* [8,9], which captures the three types of constraint (hard, soft, randomness) seen above. We use the notation of [8] for the specifications and languages defining the hard and soft constraints:

Definition 3.1 ([8]). *Given* hard *and* soft *specifications* $\mathcal{H}$ *and* $\mathcal{S}$ *of languages over* Σ, *an* improvisation *is a word* $w \in L(\mathcal{H}) \cap \Sigma^n$. *It is* admissible *if* $w \in L(\mathcal{S})$. *The set of all* improvisations *is denoted* I, *and* admissible improvisations A.

Running Example. We will use the following simple example throughout the paper: each player may increment $(+)$, decrement $(-)$, or leave unchanged $(=)$ a counter which is initially zero. The alphabet is $\Sigma = \{+, -, =\}$, and we set $n = 4$. The hard specification $\mathcal{H}$ is the DFA in Fig. 2 requiring that the counter stay within $[-2, 2]$. The soft specification $\mathcal{S}$ is a similar DFA requiring that the counter end at a nonnegative value.

Then for example the word $++==$ is an admissible improvisation, satisfying both hard and soft constraints, and so is in A. The word $+-=-$ on the other hand satisfies $\mathcal{H}$ but not $\mathcal{S}$, so it is in I but not A. Finally, $+++-$ does not satisfy $\mathcal{H}$, so it is not an improvisation at all and is not in I.

A reactive control improvisation problem is defined by $\mathcal{H}$, $\mathcal{S}$, and parameters ϵ and ρ. A solution is then a strategy which ensures that the hard, soft, and randomness constraints hold against every adversary. Formally, following [8,9]:

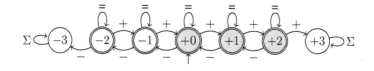

Fig. 2. The hard specification DFA $\mathcal{H}$ in our running example. The soft specification $\mathcal{S}$ is the same but with only the shaded states accepting.

Definition 3.2. *Given an* RCI *instance* $\mathcal{C} = (\mathcal{H}, \mathcal{S}, n, \epsilon, \rho)$ *with* $\mathcal{H}$, $\mathcal{S}$, *and* n *as above and* $\epsilon, \rho \in [0,1] \cap \mathbb{Q}$, *a strategy* σ *is an* improvising strategy *if it satisfies the following requirements for every adversary* τ:

Hard constraint: $P_{\sigma,\tau}(I) = 1$
Soft constraint: $P_{\sigma,\tau}(A) \geq 1 - \epsilon$
Randomness: $\forall \pi \in I, \ P_{\sigma,\tau}(\pi) \leq \rho$.

If there is an improvising strategy σ, *we say that* $\mathcal{C}$ *is* realizable. *An* improviser *for* $\mathcal{C}$ *is then an expected-finite time probabilistic algorithm implementing such a strategy* σ, *i.e. whose output distribution on input* $h \in \Sigma^{\leq n}$ *is* $\sigma(h, \cdot)$.

Definition 3.3. *Given an* RCI *instance* $\mathcal{C} = (\mathcal{H}, \mathcal{S}, n, \epsilon, \rho)$, *the* reactive control improvisation *(RCI) problem is to decide whether* $\mathcal{C}$ *is realizable, and if so to generate an improviser for* $\mathcal{C}$.

Running Example. Suppose we set $\epsilon = 1/2$ and $\rho = 1/2$. Let σ be the strategy which picks $+$ or $-$ with equal probability in the first move, and thenceforth picks the action which moves the counter closest to ± 1 respectively. This satisfies the hard constraint, since if the adversary ever moves the counter to ± 2 we immediately move it back. The strategy also satisfies the soft constraint, since with probability $1/2$ we set the counter to $+1$ on the first move, and if the adversary moves to 0 we move back to $+1$ and remain nonnegative. Finally, σ also satisfies the randomness constraint, since each choice of first move happens with probability $1/2$ and so no play can be generated with higher probability. So σ is an improvising strategy and this RCI instance is realizable.

We will study classes of RCI problems with different types of specifications:

Definition 3.4. *If* HSPEC *and* SSPEC *are classes of specifications, then the class of RCI instances* $\mathcal{C} = (\mathcal{H}, \mathcal{S}, n, \epsilon, \rho)$ *where* $\mathcal{H} \in$ HSPEC *and* $\mathcal{S} \in$ SSPEC *is denoted* RCI (HSPEC, SSPEC). *We use the same notation for the decision problem associated with the class, i.e., given* $\mathcal{C} \in$ RCI (HSPEC, SSPEC), *decide whether* $\mathcal{C}$ *is realizable. The size* $|\mathcal{C}|$ *of an RCI instance is the total size of the bit representations of its parameters, with* n *represented in unary and* ϵ, ρ *in binary.*

Finally, a *synthesis algorithm* in our context takes a specification in the form of an RCI instance and produces an implementation in the form of an improviser. This corresponds exactly to the notion of an improvisation scheme from [8]:

Definition 3.5 ([8]). *A polynomial-time improvisation scheme for a class $\mathcal{P}$ of RCI instances is an algorithm S with the following properties:*

Correctness: *For any $\mathcal{C} \in \mathcal{P}$, if $\mathcal{C}$ is realizable then $S(\mathcal{C})$ is an improviser for $\mathcal{C}$, and otherwise $S(\mathcal{C}) = \bot$.*

Scheme efficiency: *There is a polynomial $p : \mathbb{R} \to \mathbb{R}$ such that the runtime of S on any $\mathcal{C} \in \mathcal{P}$ is at most $p(|\mathcal{C}|)$.*

Improviser efficiency: *There is a polynomial $q : \mathbb{R} \to \mathbb{R}$ such that for every $\mathcal{C} \in \mathcal{P}$, if $G = S(\mathcal{C}) \neq \bot$ then G has expected runtime at most $q(|\mathcal{C}|)$.*

The first two requirements simply say that the scheme produces valid improvisers in polynomial time. The third is necessary to ensure that the improvisers themselves are efficient: otherwise, the scheme might for example produce improvisers running in time exponential in the size of the specification.

A main goal of our paper is to determine for which types of specifications there exist polynomial-time improvisation schemes. While we do find such algorithms for important classes of specifications, we will also see that determining the realizability of an RCI instance is often PSPACE-hard. Therefore we also consider *polynomial-space improvisation schemes*, defined as above but replacing time with space.

4   Existence of Improvisers

4.1   Width and Realizability

The most basic question in reactive synthesis is whether a specification is realizable. In *randomized* reactive synthesis, the question is more delicate because the randomness requirement means that it is no longer enough to ensure some property regardless of what the adversary does: there must be *many ways* to do so. Specifically, there must be at least $1/\rho$ improvisations if we are to generate each of them with probability at most ρ. Furthermore, at least this many improvisations must be *possible* given an unknown adversary: even if many exist, the adversary may be able to force us to use only a single one. We introduce a new notion of the size of a set of plays that takes this into account.

Definition 4.1. *The width of $X \subseteq \Sigma^n$ is $W(X) = \max_\sigma \min_\tau |X \cap \Pi_{\sigma,\tau}|$.*

The width counts how many distinct plays can be generated regardless of what the adversary does. Intuitively, a "narrow" game—one whose set of winning plays has small width—is one in which the adversary can force us to choose among only a few winning plays, while in a "wide" one we always have many safe choices available. Note that *which* particular plays can be generated depends on the adversary: the width only measures *how many* can be generated. For example, $W(X) = 1$ means that a play in X can always be generated, but possibly a different element of X for different adversaries.

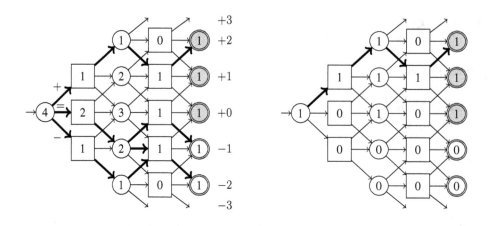

Fig. 3. Synthesis game for our running example. States are labeled with the widths of I (left) and A (right) given a history ending at that state.

Running Example. Figure 3 shows the synthesis game for our running example: paths ending in circled or shaded states are plays in I or A respectively (ignore the state labels for now). At left, the bold arrows show the 4 plays in I possible against the adversary that moves away from 0, and down at 0. This shows $W(I) \leq 4$, and in fact 4 plays are possible against any adversary, so $W(I) = 4$. Similarly, at right we see that $W(A) = 1$.

It will be useful later to have a *relative* version of width that counts how many plays are possible *from a given position*:

Definition 4.2. *Given a set of plays $X \subseteq \Sigma^n$ and a history $h \in \Sigma^{\leq n}$, the width of X given h is $W(X|h) = \max_\sigma \min_\tau |\{\pi \mid h\pi \in X \wedge P_{\sigma,\tau}(\pi|h) > 0\}|$.*

This is a direct generalization of "winning" positions: if X is the set of winning plays, then $W(X|h)$ counts the number of ways to win from h.

We will often use the following basic properties of $W(X|h)$ without comment (for lack of space this proof and the details of later proof sketches are deferred to Appendix B of the full paper [10]). Note that (3)–(5) provide a recursive way to compute widths that we will use later, and which is illustrated by the state labels in Fig. 3.

Lemma 4.1. *For any set of plays $X \subseteq \Sigma^n$ and history $h \in \Sigma^{\leq n}$:*

1. $0 \leq W(X|h) \leq |\Sigma|^{n-|h|}$;
2. $W(X|\lambda) = W(X)$;
3. *if $|h| = n$, then $W(X|h) = \mathbb{1}_{h \in X}$;*
4. *if it is our turn after h, then $W(X|h) = \sum_{u \in \Sigma} W(X|hu)$;*
5. *if it is the adversary's turn after h, then $W(X|h) = \min_{u \in \Sigma} W(X|hu)$.*

Now we can state the realizability conditions, which are simply that I and A have sufficiently large width. In fact, the conditions turn out to be exactly the same as those for non-reactive CI except that width takes the place of size [9].

Theorem 4.1. *The following are equivalent:*

(1) $\mathcal{C}$ is realizable.
(2) $W(I) \geq 1/\rho$ and $W(A) \geq (1-\epsilon)/\rho$.
(3) There is an improviser for $\mathcal{C}$.

Running Example. We saw above that our example was realizable with $\epsilon = \rho = 1/2$, and indeed $4 = W(I) \geq 1/\rho = 2$ and $1 = W(A) \geq (1-\epsilon)/\rho = 1$. However, if we put $\rho = 1/3$ we violate the second inequality and the instance is not realizable: essentially, we need to distribute probability $1 - \epsilon = 1/2$ among plays in A (to satisfy the soft constraint), but since $W(A) = 1$, against some adversaries we can only generate one play in A and would have to give it the whole $1/2$ (violating the randomness requirement).

The difficult part of the Theorem is constructing an improviser when the inequalities (2) hold. Despite the similarity in these conditions to the non-reactive case, the construction is much more involved. We begin with a general overview.

4.2   Improviser Construction: Discussion

Our improviser can be viewed as an extension of the classical random-walk reduction of uniform sampling to counting [21]. In that algorithm (which was used in a similar way for DFA specifications in [8,9]), a uniform distribution over paths in a DAG is obtained by moving to the next vertex with probability proportional to the number of paths originating at it. In our case, which plays are possible depends on the adversary, but the width still tells us *how many* plays are possible. So we could try a random walk using widths as weights: e.g. on the first turn in Fig. 3, picking $+$, $-$, and $=$ with probabilities $1/4$, $2/4$, and $1/4$ respectively. Against the adversary shown in Fig. 3, this would indeed yield a uniform distribution over the four possible plays in I.

However, the soft constraint may require a non-uniform distribution. In the running example with $\epsilon = \rho = 1/2$, we need to generate the single possible play in A with probability $1/2$, not just the uniform probability $1/4$. This is easily fixed by doing the random walk with a *weighted average* of the widths of I and A: specifically, move to position h with probability proportional to $\alpha W(A|h) + \beta(W(I|h) - W(A|h))$. In the example, this would result in plays in A getting probability α and those in $I \setminus A$ getting probability β. Taking α sufficiently large, we can ensure the soft constraint is satisfied.

Unfortunately, this strategy can fail if the adversary makes *more* plays available than the width guarantees. Consider the game on the left of Fig. 4, where $W(I) = 3$ and $W(A) = 2$. This is realizable with $\epsilon = \rho = 1/3$, but no values of α and β yield improvising strategies, essentially because an adversary moving from X to Z breaks the worst-case assumption that the adversary will minimize the number of possible plays by moving to Y. In fact, this instance is realizable but not by any memoryless strategy. To see this, note that all such strategies can be parametrized by the probabilities p and q in Fig. 4. To satisfy the randomness

Fig. 4. Reachability games where a naïve random walk, and all memoryless strategies, fail (left) and where no strategy can optimize either ϵ or ρ against every adversary simultaneously (right).

constraint against the adversary that moves from X to Y, both p and $(1-p)q$ must be at most $1/3$. To satisfy the soft constraint against the adversary that moves from X to Z we must have $pq + (1-p)q \geq 2/3$, so $q \geq 2/3$. But then $(1-p)q \geq (1-1/3)(2/3) = 4/9 > 1/3$, a contradiction.

To fix this problem, our improvising strategy $\hat{\sigma}$ (which we will fully specify in Algorithm 1 below) takes a simplistic approach: it tracks how many plays in A and I are expected to be possible based on their widths, and if more are available it ignores them. For example, entering state Z from X there are 2 ways to produce a play in I, but since $W(I|X) = 1$ we ignore the play in $I \setminus A$. Extra plays in A are similarly ignored by being treated as members of $I \setminus A$. Ignoring unneeded plays may seem wasteful, but the proof of Theorem 4.1 will show that $\hat{\sigma}$ nevertheless achieves the best possible ϵ:

Corollary 4.1. $\mathcal{C}$ *is realizable iff* $W(I) \geq 1/\rho$ *and* $\epsilon \geq \epsilon_{\text{opt}} \equiv \max(1 - \rho W(A), 0)$. *Against any adversary, the error probability of Algorithm 1 is at most* ϵ_{opt}.

Thus, if *any* improviser can achieve an error probability ϵ, ours does. We could ask for a stronger property, namely that against each adversary the improviser achieves the smallest possible error probability *for that adversary*. Unfortunately, this is impossible in general. Consider the game on the right in Fig. 4, with $\rho = 1$. Against the adversary which always moves up, we can achieve $\epsilon = 0$ with the strategy that at P moves to Q. We can also achieve $\epsilon = 0$ against the adversary that always moves down, but only with a *different* strategy, namely the one that at P moves to R. So there is no single strategy that achieves the optimal ϵ for every adversary. A similar argument shows that there is also no strategy achieving the smallest possible ρ for every adversary. In essence, optimizing ϵ or ρ in every case would require the strategy to depend on the adversary.

4.3   Improviser Construction: Details

Our improvising strategy, as outlined in the previous section, is shown in Algorithm 1. We first compute α and β, the (maximum) probabilities for generating elements of A and $I \setminus A$ respectively. As in [8], we take α as large as possible given $\alpha \leq \rho$, and determine β from the probability left over (modulo a couple corner cases).

Algorithm 1. the strategy $\hat{\sigma}$

1: $\alpha \leftarrow \min(\rho, 1/W(A))$ (or 0 instead if $W(A) = 0$)
2: $\beta \leftarrow (1 - \alpha W(A))/(W(I) - W(A))$ (or 0 instead if $W(I) - W(A) = 0$)
3: $m^A \leftarrow W(A)$, $m^I \leftarrow W(I)$
4: $h \leftarrow \lambda$
5: **while** the game is not over after h **do**
6:      **if** it is our turn after h **then**
7:         $m_u^A, m_u^I \leftarrow$ PARTITION(m^A, m^I, h) ▷ returns values for each $u \in \Sigma$
8:         for each $u \in \Sigma$, put $t_u \leftarrow \alpha m_u^A + \beta(m_u^I - m_u^A)$
9:         pick $u \in \Sigma$ with probability proportional to t_u and append it to h
10:        $m^A \leftarrow m_u^A$, $m^I \leftarrow m_u^I$
11:      **else**
12:         the adversary picks $u \in \Sigma$ given the history h; append it to h
    return h

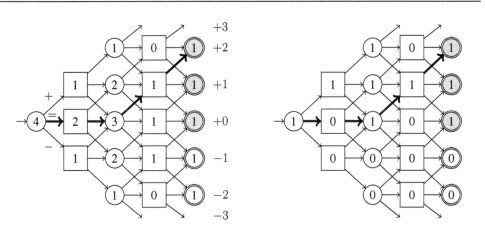

Fig. 5. A run of Algorithm 1, labeling states with corresponding widths of I (left) and A (right).

Next we initialize m^A and m^I, our expectations for how many plays in A and I respectively are still possible to generate. Initially these are given by $W(A)$ and $W(I)$, but as we saw above it is possible for more plays to become available. The function PARTITION handles this, deciding which m^A (resp., m^I) out of the available $W(A|h)$ ($W(I|h)$) plays we will use. The behavior of PARTITION is defined by the following lemma; its proof (in Appendix B [10]) greedily takes the first m^A possible plays in A under some canonical order and the first $m^I - m^A$ of the remaining plays in I.

Lemma 4.2. *If it is our turn after $h \in \Sigma^{\leq n}$, and $m^A, m^I \in \mathbb{Z}$ satisfy $0 \leq m^A \leq m^I \leq W(I|h)$ and $m^A \leq W(A|h)$, there are integer partitions $\sum_{u \in \Sigma} m_u^A$ and $\sum_{u \in \Sigma} m_u^I$ of m^A and m^I respectively such that $0 \leq m_u^A \leq m_u^I \leq W(I|hu)$ and $m_u^A \leq W(A|hu)$ for all $u \in \Sigma$. These are computable in poly-time given oracles for $W(I|\cdot)$ and $W(A|\cdot)$.*

Finally, we perform the random walk, moving from position h to hu with (unnormalized) probability t_u, the weighted average described above.

Running Example. With $\epsilon = \rho = 1/2$, as before $W(A) = 1$ and $W(I) = 4$ so $\alpha = 1/2$ and $\beta = 1/6$. On the first move, m^A and m^I match $W(A|h)$ and $W(I|h)$, so all plays are used and PARTITION returns $(W(A|hu), W(I|hu))$ for each $u \in \Sigma$. Looking up these values in Fig. 5, we see $(m_=^A, m_=^I) = (0, 2)$ and so $t(=) = 2\beta = 1/3$. Similarly $t(+) = \alpha = 1/2$ and $t(-) = \beta = 1/6$. We choose an action according to these weights; suppose $=$, so that we update $m^A \leftarrow 0$ and $m^I \leftarrow 2$, and suppose the adversary responds with $=$. From Fig. 5, $W(A| ==) = 1$ and $W(I| ==) = 3$, whereas $m^A = 0$ and $m^I = 2$. So PARTITION discards a play, say returning $(m_u^A, m_u^I) = (0, 1)$ for $u \in \{+, =\}$ and $(0, 0)$ for $u \in \{-\}$. Then $t(+) = t(=) = \beta = 1/6$ and $t(-) = 0$. So we pick $+$ or $=$ with equal probability, say $+$. If the adversary responds with $+$, we get the play $==++$, shown in bold on Fig. 5. As desired, it satisfies the hard constraint.

The next few lemmas establish that $\hat{\sigma}$ is well-defined and in fact an improvising strategy, allowing us to prove Theorem 4.1. Throughout, we write $m^A(h)$ (resp., $m^I(h)$) for the value of m^A (m^I) at the start of the iteration for history h. We also write $t(h) = \alpha m^A(h) + \beta(m^I(h) - m^A(h))$ (so $t(hu) = t_u$ when we pick u).

Lemma 4.3. *If $W(I) \geq 1/\rho$, then $\hat{\sigma}$ is a well-defined strategy and $P_{\hat{\sigma},\tau}(I) = 1$ for every adversary τ.*

Proof (sketch). An easy induction on h shows the conditions of Lemma 4.2 are always satisfied, and that $t(h)$ is always positive since we never pick a u with $t_u = 0$. So $\sum_u t_u = t(h) > 0$ and $\hat{\sigma}$ is well-defined. Furthermore, $t(h) > 0$ implies $m^I(h) > 0$, so for any $h \in \Pi_{\hat{\sigma},\tau}$ we have $\mathbb{1}_{h \in I} = W(I|h) \geq m^I(h) > 0$ and thus $h \in I$. □

Lemma 4.4. *If $W(I) \geq 1/\rho$, then $P_{\hat{\sigma},\tau}(A) \geq \min(\rho W(A), 1)$ for every τ.*

Proof (sketch). Because of the $\alpha m^A(h)$ term in the weights $t(h)$, the probability of obtaining a play in A starting from h is at least $\alpha m^A(h)/t(h)$ (as can be seen by induction on h in order of decreasing length). Then since $m^A(\lambda) = W(A)$ and $t(\lambda) = 1$ we have $P_{\hat{\sigma},\tau}(A) \geq \alpha W(A) = \min(\rho W(A), 1)$. □

Lemma 4.5. *If $W(I) \geq 1/\rho$, then $P_{\hat{\sigma},\tau}(\pi) \leq \rho$ for every $\pi \in \Sigma^n$ and τ.*

Proof (sketch). If the adversary is deterministic, the weights we use for our random walk yield a distribution where each play π has probability either α or β (depending on whether $m^A(\pi) = 1$ or 0). If the adversary assigns nonzero probability to multiple choices this only decreases the probability of individual plays. Finally, since $W(I) \geq 1/\rho$ we have $\alpha, \beta \leq \rho$. □

Proof (of Theorem 4.1). We use a similar argument to that of [8].

(1)⇒(2) Suppose σ is an improvising strategy, and fix any adversary τ. Then $\rho|\Pi_{\sigma,\tau} \cap I| = \sum_{\pi \in \Pi_{\sigma,\tau} \cap I} \rho \geq \sum_{\pi \in I} P_{\sigma,\tau}(\pi) = P_{\sigma,\tau}(I) = 1$, so $|\Pi_{\sigma,\tau} \cap I| \geq 1/\rho$. Since τ is arbitrary, this implies $W(I) \geq 1/\rho$. Since $A \subseteq I$, we also have $\rho|\Pi_{\sigma,\tau} \cap A| = \sum_{\pi \in \Pi_{\sigma,\tau} \cap A} \rho \geq \sum_{\pi \in A} P_{\sigma,\tau}(\pi) = P_{\sigma,\tau}(A) \geq 1 - \epsilon$, so $|\Pi_{\sigma,\tau} \cap A| \geq (1 - \epsilon)/\rho$ and thus $W(A) \geq (1 - \epsilon)/\rho$.

(2)⇒(3) By Lemmas 4.3 and 4.5, $\hat{\sigma}$ is well-defined and satisfies the hard and randomness constraints. By Lemma 4.4, $P_{\hat{\sigma},\tau}(A) \geq \min(\rho W(A), 1) \geq 1 - \epsilon$, so $\hat{\sigma}$ also satisfies the soft constraint and thus is an improvising strategy. Its transition probabilities are rational, so it can be implemented by an expected finite-time probabilistic algorithm, which is then an improviser for $\mathcal{C}$.

(3)⇒(1) Immediate. □

Proof (of Corollary 4.1). The inequalities in the statement are equivalent to those of Theorem 4.1 (2). By Lemma 4.4, we have $P_{\hat{\sigma},\tau}(A) \geq \min(\rho W(A), 1)$. So the error probability is at most $1 - \min(\rho W(A), 1) = \epsilon_{\text{opt}}$. □

5 A Generic Improviser

We now use the construction of Sect. 4 to develop a generic improvisation scheme usable with any class of specifications SPEC supporting the following operations:

Intersection: Given specs $\mathcal{X}$ and $\mathcal{Y}$, find $\mathcal{Z}$ such that $L(\mathcal{Z}) = L(\mathcal{X}) \cap L(\mathcal{Y})$.

Width Measurement: Given a specification $\mathcal{X}$, a length $n \in \mathbb{N}$ in unary, and a history $h \in \Sigma^{\leq n}$, compute $W(X|h)$ where $X = L(\mathcal{X}) \cap \Sigma^n$.

Efficient algorithms for these operations lead to efficient improvisation schemes:

Theorem 5.1. *If the operations on SPEC above take polynomial time (resp. space), then* RCI (SPEC, SPEC) *has a polynomial-time (space) improvisation scheme.*

Proof. Given an instance $\mathcal{C} = (\mathcal{H}, \mathcal{S}, n, \epsilon, \rho)$ in RCI (SPEC, SPEC), we first apply intersection to $\mathcal{H}$ and $\mathcal{S}$ to obtain $\mathcal{A} \in$ SPEC such that $L(\mathcal{A}) \cap \Sigma^n = A$. Since intersection takes polynomial time (space), $\mathcal{A}$ has size polynomial in $|\mathcal{C}|$. Next we use width measurement to compute $W(I) = W(L(\mathcal{H}) \cap \Sigma^n|\lambda)$ and $W(A) = W(L(\mathcal{A}) \cap \Sigma^n|\lambda)$. If these violate the inequalities in Theorem 4.1, then $\mathcal{C}$ is not realizable and we return $\perp$. Otherwise $\mathcal{C}$ is realizable, and $\hat{\sigma}$ above is an improvising strategy. Furthermore, we can construct an expected finite-time probabilistic algorithm implementing $\hat{\sigma}$, using width measurement to instantiate the oracles needed by Lemma 4.2. Determining $m^A(h)$ and $m^I(h)$ takes $O(n)$ invocations of PARTITION, each of which is poly-time relative to the width measurements. These take time (space) polynomial in $|\mathcal{C}|$, since $\mathcal{H}$ and $\mathcal{A}$ have size polynomial in $|\mathcal{C}|$. As $m^A, m^I \leq |\Sigma|^n$, they have polynomial bitwidth and so the arithmetic required to compute t_u for each $u \in \Sigma$ takes polynomial time. Therefore the total expected runtime (space) of the improviser is polynomial. □

Note that as a byproduct of testing the inequalities in Theorem 4.1, our algorithm can compute the best possible error probability ϵ_{opt} given $\mathcal{H}$, $\mathcal{S}$, and ρ (see Corollary 4.1). Alternatively, given ϵ, we can compute the best possible ρ.

We will see below how to efficiently compute widths for DFAs, so Theorem 5.1 yields a polynomial-time improvisation scheme. If we allow polynomial-*space* schemes, we can use a general technique for width measurement that only requires a very weak assumption on the specifications, namely testability in polynomial space:

Theorem 5.2. RCI (PSA, PSA) *has a polynomial-space improvisation scheme, where* PSA *is the class of polynomial-space decision algorithms.*

Proof (sketch). We apply Theorem 5.1, computing widths recursively using Lemmas 4.1, (3)–(5). As in the **PSPACE** QBF algorithm, the current path in the recursive tree and required auxiliary storage need only polynomial space.   □

6   Reachability Games and DFAs

Now we develop a polynomial-time improvisation scheme for RCI instances with DFA specifications. This also provides a scheme for reachability/safety games, whose winning conditions can be straightforwardly encoded as DFAs.

Suppose D is a DFA with states V, accepting states T, and transition function $\delta : V \times \Sigma \to V$. Our scheme is based on the fact that $W(L(D)|h)$ depends only on the state of D reached on input h, allowing these widths to be computed by dynamic programming. Specifically, for all $v \in V$ and $i \in \{0, \ldots, n\}$ we define:

$$
C(v, i) = \begin{cases}
\mathbb{1}_{v \in T} & i = n \\
\min_{u \in \Sigma} \; C(\delta(v, u), i+1) & i < n \land i \text{ odd} \\
\sum_{u \in \Sigma} C(\delta(v, u), i+1) & \text{otherwise.}
\end{cases}
$$

Running Example. Figure 6 shows the values $C(v, i)$ in rows from $i = n$ downward. For example, $i = 2$ is our turn, so $C(1, 2) = C(0, 3) + C(1, 3) + C(2, 3) = 1 + 1 + 0 = 2$, while $i = 3$ is the adversary's turn, so $C(-3, 3) = \min\{C(-3, 4)\} = \min\{0\} = 0$. Note that the values in Fig. 6 agree with the widths $W(I|h)$ shown in Fig. 5.

Lemma 6.1. *For any history* $h \in \Sigma^{\leq n}$, *writing* $X = L(D) \cap \Sigma^n$ *we have* $W(X|h) = C(D(h), |h|)$, *where* $D(h)$ *is the state reached by running* D *on* h.

Proof. We prove this by induction on $i = |h|$ in decreasing order. In the base case $i = n$, we have $W(X|h) = \mathbb{1}_{h \in X} = \mathbb{1}_{D(h) \in T} = C(D(h), n)$. Now take any history $h \in \Sigma^{\leq n}$ with $|h| = i < n$. By hypothesis, for any $u \in \Sigma$ we have $W(X|hu) = C(D(hu), i+1)$. If it is our turn after h, then $W(X|h) = \sum_{u \in \Sigma} W(X|hu) = \sum_{u \in \Sigma} C(D(hu), i+1) = C(D(h), i)$ as desired. If instead it is the adversary's turn after h, then $W(X|h) = \min_{u \in \Sigma} W(X|hu) = \min_{u \in \Sigma} C(D(hu), i+1) = C(D(h), i)$ again as desired. So by induction the hypothesis holds for any i.   □

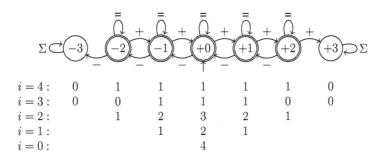

Fig. 6. The hard specification DFA $\mathcal{H}$ in our running example, showing how $W(I|h)$ is computed.

Theorem 6.1. $\mathrm{RCI}\,(\mathrm{DFA}, \mathrm{DFA})$ *has a polynomial-time improvisation scheme.*

Proof. We implement Theorem 5.1. Intersection can be done with the standard product construction. For width measurement we compute the quantities $C(v, i)$ by dynamic programming (from $i = n$ down to $i = 0$) and apply Lemma 6.1. □

7   Temporal Logics and Other Specifications

In this section we analyze the complexity of reactive control improvisation for specifications in the popular temporal logics LTL and LDL. We also look at NFA and CFG specifications, previously studied for non-reactive CI [8], to see how their complexities change in the reactive case.

For LTL specifications, reactive control improvisation is PSPACE-hard because this is already true of ordinary reactive synthesis in a finite window (we suspect this has been observed but could not find a proof in the literature).

Theorem 7.1. *Finite-window reactive synthesis for* LTL *is* PSPACE-*hard.*

Proof (sketch). Given a QBF $\phi = \exists x \forall y \ldots \chi$, we can view assignments to its variables as traces over a single proposition. In polynomial time we can construct an LTL formula ψ whose models are the satisfying assignments of χ. Then there is a winning strategy to generate a play satisfying ψ iff ϕ is true. □

Corollary 7.1. $\mathrm{RCI}\,(\mathrm{LTL}, \Sigma^*)$ *and* $\mathrm{RCI}\,(\Sigma^*, \mathrm{LTL})$ *are* PSPACE-*hard.*

This is perhaps disappointing, but is an inevitable consequence of LTL subsuming Boolean formulas. On the other hand, our general polynomial-space scheme applies to LTL and its much more expressive generalization LDL:

Theorem 7.2. $\mathrm{RCI}\,(\mathrm{LDL}, \mathrm{LDL})$ *has a polynomial-space improvisation scheme.*

Proof. This follows from Theorem 5.2, since satisfaction of an LDL formula by a finite word can be checked in polynomial time (e.g. by combining dynamic programming on subformulas with a regular expression parser). □

Thus for temporal logics polynomial-time algorithms are unlikely, but adding randomization to reactive synthesis does not increase its complexity.

The same is true for NFA and CFG specifications, where it is again PSPACE-hard to find even a single winning strategy:

Theorem 7.3. *Finite-window reactive synthesis for* NFA*s is* PSPACE-*hard.*

Proof (sketch). Reduce from QBF as in Theorem 7.1, constructing an NFA accepting the satisfying assignments of χ (as done in [13]).   □

Corollary 7.2. RCI (NFA, Σ^*) *and* RCI (Σ^*, NFA) *are* PSPACE-*hard.*

Theorem 7.4. RCI (CFG, CFG) *has a polynomial-space improvisation scheme.*

Proof. By Theorem 5.2, since CFG parsing can be done in polynomial time.   □

Since NFAs can be converted to CFGs in polynomial time, this completes the picture for the kinds of CI specifications previously studied. In non-reactive CI, DFA specifications admit a polynomial-time improvisation scheme while for NFAs/CFGs the CI problem is #P-equivalent [8]. Adding reactivity, DFA specifications remain polynomial-time while NFAs and CFGs move up to PSPACE.

Table 1. Complexity of the reactive control improvisation problem for various types of hard and soft specifications $\mathcal{H}$, $\mathcal{S}$. Here PSPACE indicates that checking realizability is PSPACE-hard, and that there is a polynomial-space improvisation scheme.

$\mathcal{H}\backslash\mathcal{S}$	RSG	DFA	NFA	CFG	LTL	LDL
RSG	poly-time					
DFA						
NFA						
CFG			PSPACE			
LTL						
LDL						

8 Conclusion

In this paper we introduced *reactive control improvisation* as a framework for modeling reactive synthesis problems where random but controlled behavior is desired. RCI provides a natural way to tune the amount of randomness while ensuring that safety or other constraints remain satisfied. We showed that RCI problems can be efficiently solved in many cases occurring in practice, giving a polynomial-time improvisation scheme for reachability/safety or DFA specifications. We also showed that RCI problems with specifications in LTL or LDL, popularly used in planning, have the PSPACE-hardness typical of bounded games, and gave a matching polynomial-space improvisation scheme. This scheme generalizes to any specification checkable in polynomial space, including NFAs, CFGs, and many more expressive formalisms. Table 1 summarizes these results.

These results show that, at a high level, finding a maximally-randomized strategy using RCI is no harder than finding any winning strategy at all: for specifications yielding games solvable in polynomial time (respectively, space), we gave polynomial-time (space) improvisation schemes. We therefore hope that in applications where ordinary reactive synthesis has proved tractable, our notion of randomized reactive synthesis will also. In particular, we expect our DFA scheme to be quite practical, and are experimenting with applications in robotic planning. On the other hand, our scheme for temporal logic specifications seems unlikely to be useful in practice without further refinement. An interesting direction for future work would be to see if modern solvers for quantified Boolean formulas (QBF) could be leveraged or extended to solve these RCI problems. This could be useful even for DFA specifications, as conjoining many simple properties can lead to exponentially-large automata. Symbolic methods based on constraint solvers would avoid such blow-up.

We are also interested in extending the RCI problem definition to unbounded or infinite words, as typically used in reactive synthesis. These extensions, as well as that to continuous signals, would be useful in robotic planning, cyberphysical system testing, and other applications. However, it is unclear how best to adapt our randomness constraint to settings where the improviser can generate infinitely many words. In such settings the improviser could assign arbitrarily small or even zero probability to every word, rendering the randomness constraint trivial. Even in the bounded case, RCI extensions with more complex randomness constraints than a simple upper bound on individual word probabilities would be worthy of study. One possibility would be to more directly control diversity and/or unpredictability by requiring the distribution of the improviser's output to be close to uniform after transformation by a given function.

Acknowledgements. The authors would like to thank Markus Rabe, Moshe Vardi, and several anonymous reviewers for helpful discussions and comments, and Ankush Desai and Tommaso Dreossi for assistance with the drone simulations. This work is supported in part by the National Science Foundation Graduate Research Fellowship Program under Grant No. DGE-1106400, by NSF grants CCF-1139138 and CNS-1646208, by DARPA under agreement number FA8750-16-C0043, and by TerraSwarm, one of six centers of STARnet, a Semiconductor Research Corporation program sponsored by MARCO and DARPA.

References

1. Arora, S., Barak, B.: Computational Complexity: A Modern Approach. Cambridge University Press, New York (2009)
2. Baier, C., Brázdil, T., Größer, M., Kučera, A.: Stochastic game logic. Acta Inf. **49**(4), 203–224 (2012)

3. Bloem, R., Galler, S., Jobstmann, B., Piterman, N., Pnueli, A., Weiglhofer, M.: Specify, compile, run: hardware from PSL. Electron. Notes Theor. Comput. Sci. **190**, 3–16 (2007). Proceedings of the 6th International Workshop on Compiler Optimization Meets Compiler Verification (COCV 2007). http://www.sciencedirect.com/science/article/pii/S157106610700583X
4. Chen, T., Forejt, V., Kwiatkowska, M., Simaitis, A., Wiltsche, C.: On stochastic games with multiple objectives. In: Chatterjee, K., Sgall, J. (eds.) MFCS 2013. LNCS, vol. 8087, pp. 266–277. Springer, Heidelberg (2013). https://doi.org/10.1007/978-3-642-40313-2_25
5. De Giacomo, G., Vardi, M.Y.: Linear temporal logic and linear dynamic logic on finite traces. In: Proceedings of the 23rd International Joint Conference on Artificial Intelligence. IJCAI 2013, pp. 854–860. AAAI Press (2013). http://dl.acm.org/citation.cfm?id=2540128.2540252
6. Donze, A., Libkind, S., Seshia, S.A., Wessel, D.: Control improvisation with application to music. Technical reports UCB/EECS-2013-183, EECS Department, University of California, Berkeley, Nov 2013. http://www2.eecs.berkeley.edu/Pubs/TechRpts/2013/EECS-2013-183.html
7. Finkbeiner, B.: Synthesis of reactive systems. In: Esparza, J., Grumberg, O., Sickert, S. (eds.) Dependable Software Systems Engineering. NATO Science for Peace and Security Series - D: Information and Communication Security, vol. 45, pp. 72–98. IOS Press, Amsterdam (2016)
8. Fremont, D.J., Donzé, A., Seshia, S.A.: Control improvisation. arXiv preprint (2017)
9. Fremont, D.J., Donzé, A., Seshia, S.A., Wessel, D.: Control improvisation. In: 35th IARCS Annual Conference on Foundations of Software Technology and Theoretical Computer Science (FSTTCS), pp. 463–474 (2015)
10. Fremont, D.J., Seshia, S.A.: Reactive control improvisation. arXiv preprint (2018)
11. Fremont, D.J., Seshia, S.A.: Reactive control improvisation website (2018). https://math.berkeley.edu/~dfremont/reactive.html
12. Hansson, H., Jonsson, B.: A logic for reasoning about time and reliability. Form. Asp. Comput. **6**(5), 512–535 (1994)
13. Kannan, S., Sweedyk, Z., Mahaney, S.: Counting and random generation of strings in regular languages. In: 6th Annual ACM-SIAM Symposium on Discrete Algorithms, pp. 551–557. SIAM (1995)
14. Koenig, N., Howard, A.: Design and use paradigms for Gazebo, an open-source multi-robot simulator. In: 2004 IEEE/RSJ International Conference on Intelligent Robots and Systems (IROS), vol. 3, pp. 2149–2154. IEEE (2004)
15. Kress-Gazit, H., Fainekos, G.E., Pappas, G.J.: Temporal-logic-based reactive mission and motion planning. IEEE Trans. Rob. **25**(6), 1370–1381 (2009)
16. Mazala, R.: Infinite games. In: Grädel, E., Thomas, W., Wilke, T. (eds.) Automata Logics, and Infinite Games. LNCS, vol. 2500, pp. 23–38. Springer, Heidelberg (2002). https://doi.org/10.1007/3-540-36387-4_2
17. Meier, L., Honegger, D., Pollefeys, M.: PX4: a node-based multithreaded open source robotics framework for deeply embedded platforms. In: 2015 IEEE International Conference on Robotics and Automation (ICRA), pp. 6235–6240. IEEE (2015)
18. Pnueli, A.: The temporal logic of programs. In: 18th Annual Symposium on Foundations of Computer Science (FOCS 1977), pp. 46–57. IEEE (1977)
19. Pnueli, A., Rosner, R.: On the synthesis of a reactive module. In: Proceedings of the 16th ACM SIGPLAN-SIGACT Symposium on Principles of Programming

Languages. POPL 1989, pp. 179–190. ACM, New York (1989). http://doi.acm.org/10.1145/75277.75293

20. Tomlin, C., Lygeros, J., Sastry, S.: Computing controllers for nonlinear hybrid systems. In: Vaandrager, F.W., van Schuppen, J.H. (eds.) HSCC 1999. LNCS, vol. 1569, pp. 238–255. Springer, Heidelberg (1999). https://doi.org/10.1007/3-540-48983-5_22

21. Wilf, H.S.: A unified setting for sequencing, ranking, and selection algorithms for combinatorial objects. Adv. Math. **24**(2), 281–291 (1977)

5

Controller Synthesis Made Real: Reach-Avoid Specifications and Linear Dynamics

Chuchu Fan$^{(\boxtimes)}$ⓘ, Umang Mathurⓘ, Sayan Mitraⓘ, and Mahesh Viswanathan

University of Illinois at Urbana Champaign,
Champaign, IL, USA
{cfan10,umathur3,mitras,
vmahesh}@illinois.edu

Abstract. We address the problem of synthesizing provably correct controllers for linear systems with reach-avoid specifications. Our solution uses a combination of an open-loop controller and a tracking controller, thereby reducing the problem to smaller tractable problems. We show that, once a tracking controller is fixed, the reachable states from an initial neighborhood, subject to any disturbance, can be over-approximated by a sequence of ellipsoids, with sizes that are independent of the open-loop controller. Hence, the open-loop controller can be synthesized independently to meet the reach-avoid specification for an initial neighborhood. Exploiting several techniques for tightening the over-approximations, we reduce the open-loop controller synthesis problem to satisfiability over quantifier-free linear real arithmetic. The overall synthesis algorithm, computes a tracking controller, and then iteratively covers the entire initial set to find open-loop controllers for initial neighborhoods. The algorithm is sound and, for a class of robust systems, is also complete. We present REALSYN, a tool implementing this synthesis algorithm, and we show that it scales to several high-dimensional systems with complex reach-avoid specifications.

1 Introduction

The controller synthesis question asks whether an input can be generated for a given system (or a plant) so that it achieves a given specification. Algorithms for answering this question hold the promise of automating controller design. They have the potential to yield high-assurance systems that are correct-by-construction, and even negative answers to the question can convey insights about unrealizability of specifications. This is not a new or a solved problem, but there has been resurgence of interest with the rise of powerful tools and compelling applications such as vehicle path planning [11], motion control [10, 23], circuits design [30] and various other engineering areas.

In this paper, we study synthesis for linear, discrete-time, plant models with bounded disturbance—a standard view of control systems [3,17]. We will consider *reach-avoid* specifications which require that starting from any initial state Θ, the controller has to drive the system to a target set G, while avoiding certain unsafe states or obstacles **O**. *Reach-avoid* specifications arise naturally in many domains such as autonomous and assisted driving, multi-robot coordination, and spacecraft autonomy, and have been studied for linear, nonlinear, as well as stochastic models [7,9,14,18].

Textbook control design methods address specifications like stability, disturbance rejection, asymptotic convergence, but they do not provide formal guarantees about reach-avoid specifications. Another approach is based on *discrete abstraction*, where a discrete, finite-state, symbolic abstraction of the original control system is computed, and a discrete controller is synthesized by solving a two-player game on the abstracted game graph. Theoretically, these methods can be applied to systems with nonlinear dynamics and they can synthesize controllers for a general class of LTL specifications. However, in practice, the discretization step leads to a severe state space explosion for higher dimensional models. Indeed, we did not find any reported evaluation of these tools (see related work) on benchmarks that go beyond 5-dimensional plant models.

In this paper, the controller we synthesize, follows a natural paradigm for designing controllers. The approach is to first design an *open-loop* controller for a single initial state $x_0 \in \Theta$ to meet the reach-avoid specification. This is called the reference trajectory. For the remaining states in the initial set, a *tracking controller* is combined, that drives these other trajectories towards the trajectory starting from x_0.

However, designing such a combined controller can be computationally expensive [32] because of the interdependency between the open-loop controller and the tracking controller. Our secret sauce in making this approach feasible, is to demonstrate that the two controllers can be synthesized in a decoupled way. Our strategy is as follows. We first design a tracking controller using a standard control-theoretical method called LQR (linear quadratic regulator) [5]. The crucial observation that helps decouple the synthesis of the tracking and open-loop controller, is that for such a combined controller, once the tracking controller is fixed, the set of states reached from the initial set is contained within a sequence of ellipsoidal sets [24] centered around the reference trajectory. The size of these ellipsoidal sets is solely dependent on the tracking controller, and is independent of the reference trajectory or the open-loop controller. On the flip side, the open-loop controller and the resulting reference trajectory can be chosen independent of the fixed tracking controller. Based on this, the problem of synthesizing the open-loop controller can be completely decoupled from synthesizing the tracking controller. Our open-loop controller is synthesized by encoding the problem in logic. The straightforward encoding of the synthesis problem results in a $\exists\forall$ formula in the theory of linear arithmetic. Unfortunately, solving large instances of such formulas using current SMT solvers is challenging. To overcome this, we exploit special properties of polytopes and hyper-rectangles, and reduce the original ∃∀-formula into the quantifier-free fragment of linear arithmetic (QF-LRA).

Our overall algorithm (Algorithm 1), after computing an initial tracking controller, iteratively synthesizes open-loop controllers by solving QF-LRA formulas for smaller subsets that cover the initial set. The algorithm will automatically identify the set of initial states for which the combined tracking+open-loop controller is guaranteed to work. Our algorithm is sound (Theorem 1), and for a class of robust linear systems, it is also complete (Theorem 2).

We have implemented the synthesis algorithm in a tool called REALSYN. Any SMT solver can be plugged-in for solving the open-loop problem; we present experimental results with Z3, CVC4 and Yices. We report the performance on 24 benchmark problems (using all three solvers). Results show that our approach scales well for complex models—including a system with 84-dimensional dynamics, another system with 3 vehicles (12-dimensional) trying to reach a common goal while avoiding collision with the obstacles and each other, and yet another system with 10 vehicles (20 dimensional) trying to maintain a platoon. REAL-SYN usually finds a controller within 10 min with the fastest SMT solver. The closest competing tool, Tulip [13,39], does not return any result even for some of the simpler instances.

Related Work. We briefly review related work on formal controller synthesis according to the plant model type, specifications, and approaches.

Plants and Specifications. In increasing order of generality, the types of plant models that have been considered for controller synthesis are double-integrator models [10], linear dynamical models [20,28,34,38], piecewise affine models [18,40], and nonlinear (possibly switched) models [7,25,31,33]. There is also a line of work on synthesis approaches for stochastic plants (see [1], and the references therein). With the exceptions noted below, most of these papers consider continuous time plant models, unlike our work.

There are three classes of specifications typically used for synthesis. In the order of generality, they are: (1) pure safety or invariance specifications [2,15,33], (2) reach-avoid [7,14,15,18,33], and (3) more general LTL and GR(1) [20,26,39] [16,38,40]. For each of these classes both bounded and unbounded-time variants have been considered.

Synthesis Tools. There is a growing set of controller synthesis algorithms that are available as implemented tools and libraries. This includes tools like CoSyMa [27], Pessoa [30], LTLMop [22,37], Tulip [13,39], SCOTS [31], that rely on the computation of some sort of a discrete (or symbolic) abstraction. Our trial with a 4-dimensional example on Tulip [13,39] did not finish the discretization step in one hour. LTLMop [22,37] handles GR(1) LTL specifications, which are more general than reach-avoid specifications considered in this paper, but it is designed for 2-dimensional robot models working in the Euclidean plane. An alternative synthesis approach generates mode switching sequences for switched system models [19,21,29,35,41] to meet the specifications. This line of work focuses on a finite input space, instead of the infinite input space we are considering in this paper. Abate et al. [2] use a controller template similar to the one considered in this paper for invariant specifications. A counter-example guided inductive synthesis (CEGIS) approach is used to first find a feedback controller for stabilizing the system. Since this feedback controller may not be safe for all initial states of the system, a separate verification step is employed to verify safety, or alternatively find a counter-example. In the latter case, the process is repeated until a valid controller is found. This is different from our approach, where any controller found needs no further verification. Several of the benchmarks are adopted from [2].

2   Preliminaries and Problem Statement

Notation. For a set A and a finite sequence σ in A^*, we denote the tth element of σ by $\sigma[t]$. $\mathbb{R}^n$ is the n-dimensional Euclidean space. Given a vector $x \in \mathbb{R}^n$, $x(i)$ is the ith component of x. We will use boldfaced letters (for example, $\mathbf{x}, \mathbf{d}, \mathbf{u}$, etc.,) to denote a sequence of vectors.

For a vector x, x^T is its transpose. Given an invertible matrix $M \in \mathbb{R}^{n \times n}$, $\|x\|_M \triangleq \sqrt{x^\mathsf{T} M^\mathsf{T} M x}$ is called the M-*norm* of x. For $M = I$, $\|x\|_M$ is the familiar 2-norm. Alternatively, $\|x\|_M = \|Mx\|_2$. For a matrix A, $A \succ 0$ means A is positive definite. Given two symmetric matrices A and B, $A \preceq B$ means $A - B$ is negative semi-definite. Given a matrix A and an invertible matrix M of the same dimension, there exists an $\alpha \geq 0$ such that $A^\mathsf{T} M^\mathsf{T} M A \preceq \alpha M^\mathsf{T} M$. Intuitively, α is the largest scaling factor that can be achieved by the linear transformation from x to Ax when using M for computing the norm, and can be found as the largest eigenvalue of the symmetric matrix $(MAM^{-1})^\mathsf{T}(MAM^{-1})$.

Given a vector $c \in \mathbb{R}^n$, an invertible matrix M, and a scalar value $r \geq 0$, we define $\mathcal{E}_r(c, M) \triangleq \{x \mid \|x - c\|_M \leq r\}$ to be the ellipsoid centered at c with radius r and shape M. $\mathcal{B}_r(c) \triangleq \mathcal{E}_r(c, I)$ is the ball of radius r centered at c. Given two vectors $c, v \in \mathbb{R}^n$, $\mathcal{R}_v(c) \triangleq \{x \mid \wedge_{i=1}^n c(i) - v(i) \leq x(i) \leq c(i) + v(i)\}$ is the rectangle centered at c with the length vector v. For a set $S \subseteq \mathbb{R}^n$, a vector $v \in \mathbb{R}^n$, and a matrix $M \in \mathbb{R}^{n \times n}$ we define $v \oplus S \triangleq \{x + v \mid x \in S\}$ and $M \otimes S \triangleq \{Mx \mid x \in S\}$. We say a set $S \subseteq \mathbb{R}^n$ is a polytope if there is a matrix $A^{m \times n}$ and a vector $b \in \mathbb{R}^m$ such that $S = \{x \mid Ax \leq b\}$, and denote by $vert(S)$ the set of vertices of S.

2.1   Discrete Time Linear Control Systems

An (n, m)-*dimensional discrete-time linear system* $\mathcal{A}$ is a 5-tuple $\langle A, B, \Theta, U, D \rangle$, where (i) $A \in \mathbb{R}^{n \times n}$ is called the *dynamic matrix*, (ii) $B \in \mathbb{R}^{n \times m}$ is called the *input matrix*, (iii) $\Theta \subseteq \mathbb{R}^n$ is a *set of initial states* (iv) $U \subseteq \mathbb{R}^m$ is the *space of inputs*, (v) $D \subseteq \mathbb{R}^n$ is the *space of disturbances*.

A *control sequence* for an (n, m)-dimensional system $\mathcal{A}$ is a (possibly infinite) sequence $\mathbf{u} = \mathbf{u}[0], \mathbf{u}[1], \ldots$, where each $\mathbf{u}[t] \in U$. Similarly, a *disturbance sequence* for $\mathcal{A}$ is a (possibly infinite) sequence $\mathbf{d} = \mathbf{d}[0], \mathbf{d}[1], \ldots$, where each $\mathbf{d}[t] \in D$. Given control $\mathbf{u}$ and disturbance $\mathbf{d}$, and an initial state $\mathbf{x}[0] \in \Theta$, the *execution of* $\mathcal{A}$ is uniquely defined as the (possibly infinite) sequence of states $\mathbf{x} = \mathbf{x}[0], \mathbf{x}[1], \ldots$, where for each $t > 0$,

$$\mathbf{x}[t+1] = A\mathbf{x}[t] + B\mathbf{u}[t] + \mathbf{d}[t]. \tag{1}$$

A *(state feedback) controller* for $\mathcal{A}$ is a function $g : \Theta \times \mathbb{R}^n \to \mathbb{R}^m$, that maps an initial state and a (current) state to an input. That is, given an initial state $x_0 \in \Theta$ and state $x \in \mathbb{R}^n$ at time t, the control input to the plant at time t is:

$$\mathbf{u}[t] = g(x_0, x). \tag{2}$$

This controller is allowed to use the memory of some initial state x_0 (not necessarily the current execution's initial state) for deciding the current state-dependent feedback. Thus, given an initial state $\mathbf{x}[0]$, a disturbance $\mathbf{d}$, and a state feedback controller g, Eqs. (1) and (2) define a unique execution $\mathbf{x}$ of $\mathcal{A}$. A state x is *reachable in t-steps* if there exists an execution $\mathbf{x}$ of $\mathcal{A}$ such that $\mathbf{x}[t] = x$. The set of all reachable states from $S \subseteq \Theta$ in exactly T steps using the controller g is denoted by $\mathsf{Reach}_{\mathcal{A},g}(S, T)$. When $\mathcal{A}$ and g are clear from the context, we write $\mathsf{Reach}(S, T)$.

2.2 Bounded Controller Synthesis Problem

Given a (n, m)-*dimensional discrete-time linear system* $\mathcal{A}$, a sequence $\mathbf{O}$ of *obstacles* or unsafe sets (with $\mathbf{O}[t] \subseteq \mathbb{R}^n$, for each t), a *goal* $G \subseteq \mathbb{R}^n$, and a time bound T, the *bounded time controller synthesis problem* is to find, a state feedback controller g such that for every initial state $\theta \in \Theta$ and disturbance $\mathbf{d} \in D^T$, the unique execution $\mathbf{x}$ of $\mathcal{A}$ with g, starting from $\mathbf{x}[0] = \theta$ satisfies (i) for all $t \leq T$, $\mathbf{u}[t] \in U$, (ii) for all $t \leq T$, $\mathbf{x}[t] \notin \mathbf{O}[t]$, and (iii) $\mathbf{x}[T] \in G$.

For the rest of the paper, we will assume that each of the sets in $\{\mathbf{O}[t]\}_{t \in \mathbb{N}}$, G and U are closed polytopes. Moreover, we assume that the pair (A, B) is controllable [3].

Example. *Consider a mobile robot that needs to reach the green area of an apartment starting from the entrance area, while avoiding the gray areas (Fig. 1). The robot's dynamics is described by a linear model (for example the navigation model from [12]). The obstacle sequence* $\mathbf{O}$ *here is static, that is,* $\mathbf{O}[t] = \mathbf{O}[0]$ *for all* $t \geq 0$. *Both* Θ *and* G *are rectangles. Although these sets are depicted in 2D, the dynamics of the robot may involve a higher dimensional state space.*

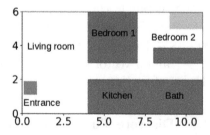

Fig. 1. The settings for controller synthesis of a mobile robot with reach-avoid specification.

In this example, there is no disturbance, but a similar problem can be formulated for an drone flying outdoors, in which case, the disturbance input would model the effect of wind. Time-varying obstacle sets are useful for modeling safety requirements of multi-robot systems.

3 Synthesis Algorithm

3.1 Overview

The controller synthesis problem requires one to find a state feedback controller that ensures that the trajectory starting from any initial state in Θ will meet the reach-avoid specification. Since the set of initial states Θ will typically be an infinite set, this requires the synthesized feedback controller g to have an effective representation. Thus, an "enumerative" representation, where a (separate) *open-loop controller* is constructed for each initial state, is not feasible — by an open-loop controller for initial state $x_0 \in \Theta$, we mean a control sequence $\mathbf{u}$ such that the corresponding execution $\mathbf{x}$ with $\mathbf{x}[0] = x_0$ and 0 disturbance satisfies the reach-avoid constraints. We, therefore, need a useful template that will serve as the representation for the feedback controller.

In control theory, one natural controller design paradigm is to first find a *reference execution* $\mathbf{x}_{\text{ref}}$ which uses an open-loop controller, then add a *tracking controller* which tries to force other executions $\mathbf{x}$ starting from different initial states $\mathbf{x}[0]$ to get close to $\mathbf{x}_{\text{ref}}$ by minimizing the distance between $\mathbf{x}_{\text{ref}}$ and $\mathbf{x}$. This form of controller combining open-loop control with tracking control is also proposed in [32] for reach-avoid specifications. The resulting trajectory under a combination of tracking controller plus reference trajectory can be described by the following system of equations.

$$
\begin{aligned}
\mathbf{u}[t] &= \mathbf{u}_{\text{ref}}[t] + K(\mathbf{x}[t] - \mathbf{x}_{\text{ref}}[t]), \text{with} \\
\mathbf{x}_{\text{ref}}[t+1] &= A\mathbf{x}_{\text{ref}}[t] + B\mathbf{u}_{\text{ref}}[t]
\end{aligned}
\tag{3}
$$

The tracking controller is given by the matrix K that determines the additive component of the input based on the difference between the current state and the reference trajectory. Once $\mathbf{x}_{\text{ref}}[0]$ and the open-loop control sequence $\mathbf{u}_{\text{ref}}$ is fixed, the value of $\mathbf{x}_{\text{ref}}[t]$ is determined at each time step $t \in \mathbb{N}$. Therefore, the controller g is uniquely defined by the tuple $\langle K, \mathbf{x}_{\text{ref}}[0], \mathbf{u}_{\text{ref}} \rangle$. We could rewrite the linear system in (3) as an augmented system

$$
\begin{bmatrix} \mathbf{x} \\ \mathbf{x}_{\text{ref}} \end{bmatrix}[t+1] = \begin{bmatrix} A + BK & -BK \\ 0 & A \end{bmatrix} \begin{bmatrix} \mathbf{x} \\ \mathbf{x}_{\text{ref}} \end{bmatrix}[t] + \begin{bmatrix} B & 0 \\ 0 & B \end{bmatrix} \begin{bmatrix} \mathbf{u}_{\text{ref}} \\ \mathbf{u}_{\text{ref}} \end{bmatrix}[t], + \begin{bmatrix} \mathbf{d} \\ 0 \end{bmatrix}[t].
$$

This can be rewritten as $\hat{\mathbf{x}}[t+1] = \hat{A}\hat{\mathbf{x}}[t] + \hat{B}\hat{\mathbf{u}}[t] + \hat{\mathbf{d}}[t]$. The closed-form solution is $\hat{\mathbf{x}}[t] = \hat{A}^t \hat{\mathbf{x}}[0] + \sum_{i=0}^{t-1} \hat{A}^{t-1-i}(\hat{B}\hat{\mathbf{u}}[i] + \hat{\mathbf{d}}[i])$. To synthesize a controller g of this form, therefore, requires finding $K, \mathbf{x}_{\text{ref}}[0], \mathbf{u}_{\text{ref}}$ such that the closed-form solution meets the reach-avoid specification. This is indeed the approach followed in [32], albeit in the continuous time setting. Observe that in the closed-form solution, $\hat{A}$, $\hat{\mathbf{u}}$, and $\hat{\mathbf{x}}[0]$ all depend on parameters that we need to synthesize. Therefore, solving such constraints involves polynomials whose degrees grow with the time bound. This is very expensive, and unlikely to scale to large dimensions and time bounds.

In this paper, to achieve scalability, we take a slightly different approach than the one where $K, \mathbf{x}_{\text{ref}}[0]$, and $\mathbf{u}_{\text{ref}}$ are simultaneously synthesized. We first synthesize a tracking controller K, *independent* of $\mathbf{x}_{\text{ref}}[0]$ and $\mathbf{u}_{\text{ref}}$, using the standard LQR method. Once K is synthesized, we show that, no matter what $\mathbf{x}_{\text{ref}}[0]$, and $\mathbf{u}_{\text{ref}}$ are, the state of the system at time t starting from x_0 is guaranteed to be contained within an ellipsoid centered at $\mathbf{x}_{\text{ref}}[t]$ and of radius that depends only on K, the initial distance between x_0 and $\mathbf{x}_{\text{ref}}[0]$, time t, and disturbance. Moreover, this radius is only a *linear* function of the initial distance (Lemma 1). Thus, if we can synthesize an open-loop controller $\mathbf{u}_{\text{ref}}$ starting from some state $\mathbf{x}_{\text{ref}}[0]$, such that ellipsoids centered around $\mathbf{x}_{\text{ref}}$ satisfy the reach-avoid specification, we can conclude that the combined controller will work correctly for all initial states in some ball around the initial state $\mathbf{x}_{\text{ref}}[0]$. The radius of the ball around $\mathbf{x}_{\text{ref}}[0]$ for which the controller is guaranteed to work, will depend on the radii of the ellipsoids around $\mathbf{x}_{\text{ref}}$ that satisfy the reach-avoid specification. This decoupled approach to synthesis is the first key idea in our algorithm.

Following the above discussion, crucial to the success of the decoupled approach is to obtain a tight characterization of the radius of the ellipsoid around $\mathbf{x}_{\text{ref}}[t]$ that contains the reach set, as a function of the initial distance — too conservative a bound will imply that the combined controller only works for a tiny set of initial states. The ellipsoid's shape and direction, which is characterized by a coordinate transformation matrix M, also affect the tightness of the over-approximations. We determine the shape and direction of the ellipsoids that give us the tightest over-approximation using an SDP solver (Sect. 3.4).

Synthesizing the tracking controller K, still leaves open the problem of synthesizing an open-loop controller for an initial state $\mathbf{x}_{\text{ref}}[0]$. A straightforward encoding of the problem of synthesizing a open-loop controller, that works for all initial states in some ball around $\mathbf{x}_{\text{ref}}[0]$, results in a $\exists\forall$-formula in the theory of real arithmetic. Unfortunately solving such formulas does not scale to large dimensional systems using current SMT solvers. The next key idea in our algorithm is to simplify these constraints. By exploiting special properties of polytopes and hyper-rectangles, we reduce the original $\exists\forall$-formula into the *quantifier-free* fragment of *linear* real arithmetic (QF-LRA) (Sect. 3.5).

Putting it all together, the overall algorithm (Algorithm 1) works as follows. After computing an initial tracking controller K, coordinate transformation M for optimal ellipsoidal approximation of reach-sets, it synthesizes open-loop controllers for different initial states by solving QF-LRA formulas. After each open-loop controller is synthesized, the algorithm identifies the set of initial states for which the combined tracking+open-loop controller is guaranteed to work, and removes this set from Θ. In each new iteration, it picks a new initial state not covered by previous combined controllers, and the process terminates when all of Θ is covered. Our algorithm is sound (Theorem 1)—whenever a controller is synthesized, it meets the specifications. Further, for robust systems (defined later in the paper), our algorithm is guaranteed to terminate when the system has a combined controller for all initial states (Theorem 2).

3.2 Synthesizing the Tracking Controller K

Given any open-loop controller $\mathbf{u}_{ref}$ and the corresponding reference execution $\mathbf{x}_{ref}$, by replacing in Eq. (1) the controller of Eq. (3) we get:

$$\mathbf{x}[t+1] = (A + BK)\mathbf{x}[t] - BK\mathbf{x}_{ref}[t] + B\mathbf{u}_{ref}[t] + \mathbf{d}[t]. \tag{4}$$

Subtracting $\mathbf{x}_{ref}[t+1]$ from both sides, we have that for any execution $\mathbf{x}$ starting from the initial states $\mathbf{x}[0]$ and with disturbance $\mathbf{d}$, the distance between $\mathbf{x}$ and $\mathbf{x}_{ref}$ changes with time as:

$$\mathbf{x}[t+1] - \mathbf{x}_{ref}[t+1] = (A + BK)(\mathbf{x}[t] - \mathbf{x}_{ref}[t]) + \mathbf{d}[t]. \tag{5}$$

With $A_c \triangleq A + BK$, $\mathbf{y}[t] \triangleq \mathbf{x}[t+1] - \mathbf{x}_{ref}[t+1]$, Eq. (5) becomes $\mathbf{y}[t+1] = A_c\mathbf{y}[t] + d[t]$. We want $\mathbf{x}[t]$ to be as close to $\mathbf{x}_{ref}[t]$ as possible, which means K should be designed to make $|\mathbf{y}[t]|$ converge to 0. Equivalently, K should be designed as a linear feedback controller such that A_c is stable[1]. Such a matrix K can be computed using classical control theoretic methods. In this work, we compute K as a linear (stable) feedback controller using LQR as stated in the following proposition.

Proposition 1 (LQR). *For linear system $\mathcal{A}$ with (A, B) to be controllable and 0 disturbance, fix any $Q, R \succ 0$ and let $J \triangleq \mathbf{x}^\mathsf{T}[T]Q\mathbf{x}[T] + \sum_{i=0}^{T-1}(\mathbf{x}^\mathsf{T}[i]Q\mathbf{x}[i] + \mathbf{u}^\mathsf{T}[i]R\mathbf{u}[i])$ be the corresponding quadratic cost. Let X be the unique positive definite solution to the discrete-time Algebraic Riccati Equation (ARE): $A^\mathsf{T}XA - X - A^\mathsf{T}XB(B^\mathsf{T}XB + R)^{-1}B^\mathsf{T}XA + Q = 0$, and $K \triangleq -(B^\mathsf{T}XB + R)^{-1}B^\mathsf{T}XA$. Then $A + BK$ is stable, and the corresponding feedback input minimizes J.*

Methods for choosing Q and R are outside the scope of this paper. We fix Q and R to be identity matrices for most examples. Roughly, for a given R, scaling up Q results in a K that makes an execution $\mathbf{x}$ converge faster to the reference execution $\mathbf{x}_{ref}$.

3.3 Reachset Over-Approximation with Tracking Controller

We present a method for over-approximating the reachable states of the system for a given tracking controller K (computed as in Proposition 1) and an open-loop controller $\mathbf{u}_{ref}$ (to be computed in Sect. 3.5).

Lemma 1. *Consider any $K \in \mathbb{R}^{m \times n}$, any initial set $S \subseteq \mathcal{E}_{r_0}(\mathbf{x}_{ref}[0], M)$ and disturbance $D \subseteq \mathcal{E}_\delta(0, M)$, where $r_0, \delta \geq 0$ and $M \in \mathbb{R}^{n \times n}$ is invertible.*

For any open-loop controller $\mathbf{u}_{ref}$ and the corresponding reference execution $\mathbf{x}_{ref}$,

$$Reach(S, t) \subseteq \mathcal{E}_{r_t}(\mathbf{x}_{ref}[t], M), \forall\, t \leq T, \tag{6}$$

where $r_t = \alpha^{\frac{t}{2}}r_0 + \sum_{i=0}^{t-1}\alpha^{\frac{i}{2}}\delta$, and $\alpha \geq 0$ is such that $(A+BK)^\mathsf{T}M^\mathsf{T}M(A+BK) \preceq \alpha M^\mathsf{T}M$.

---

[1] $A + BK$ has spectral radius $\rho(A + BK) < 1$.

Lemma 1 can be proved using the triangular inequality for the norm of Eq. (5). From Lemma 1, it follows that given a open-loop controller $\mathbf{u}_{ref}$ and the corresponding reference trajectory $\mathbf{x}_{ref}$, the reachable states from $S \subseteq \mathcal{E}_{r_0}(\mathbf{x}_{ref}[0], M)$ at time t can be over-approximated by an ellipsoid centered at $\mathbf{x}_{ref}[t]$ with size $r_t \triangleq \alpha^{\frac{t}{2}} r_0 + \sum_{i=0}^{t-1} \alpha^{\frac{i}{2}} \delta$. Here M is any invertible matrix that defines the shape of the ellipsoid and it influences the value of α. As the over-approximation (r_t) grows exponentially with t, it makes sense to choose M in a way that makes α small. In next section, we discuss how M and α are chosen to achieve this.

3.4 Shaping Ellipsoids for Tight Over-Approximating Hyper-rectangles

The choice of M and the resulting α may seem like a minor detail, but a bad choice here can doom the rest of the algorithm to be impractical. For example, if we fix M to be the identity matrix I, the resulting value of α may give over-approximations that are too conservative. Even if the actual executions are convergent to $\mathbf{x}_{ref}$ the resulting over-approximation can exponentially blow up.

We find the smallest exponential convergence/divergence rate (α) by solving for P in the following semi-definite program (SDP):

$$\min_{P \succ 0, \alpha \in \mathbb{R}} \alpha$$
$$\text{s.t} \quad (A + BK)^\intercal P(A + BK) \preceq \alpha P. \tag{7}$$

This gives M as the unique matrix such that $P = M^T M$.

In the rest of the paper, the reachset over-approximations will be represented by hyper-rectangles to allow us to efficiently use the existing SMT solvers. That is, the ellipsoids given by Lemma 1 have to be bounded by hyper-rectangles. For any coordinate transformation matrix M, the ellipsoid with unit size $\mathcal{E}_1(0, M) \subseteq \mathcal{R}_v(0)$, with $v(i) = \min_{x \in \mathcal{E}_1(0,M)} x(i)$. This $v(i)$ is also computed by solving an SDP. Similarly, $\mathcal{E}_r(0, M) \subseteq \mathcal{R}_{rv}(0)$. Therefore, from Lemma 1, it follows that Reach$(S, t) \subseteq \mathcal{R}_{r_t v}(\mathbf{x}_{ref}[t])$ with $r_t = \alpha^{\frac{t}{2}} r_0 + \sum_{i=0}^{t-1} \alpha^{\frac{i}{2}} \delta$ and v is the size vector of the rectangle bounding $\mathcal{E}_1(0, M)$. These optimization problems for computing M, α, and v have to be solved once per synthesis problem.

Example. *Continuing the previous example. Suppose robot is asked to reach the target set in 20 steps. Figure 2 shows the projection of the reachset on the robot's position with synthesized controller. The curves are the references executions $\mathbf{x}_{ref}$ from 2 initials cover and the rectangles are reachset over-approximations such that every execution of the system starting from each initial cover is guaranteed to be inside the rectangles at each time step.*

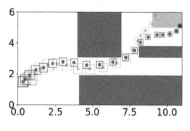

Fig. 2. Robot's position with the synthesized controllers using Algorithm 1.

3.5   Synthesis of Open-Loop Controller

In this section, we will discuss the synthesis of the open-loop controller $\mathbf{u}_{\mathsf{ref}}$ in $\langle K, \mathbf{x}_{\mathsf{ref}}[0], \mathbf{u}_{\mathsf{ref}}\rangle$. From the previous section, we know that given an initial set S, a tracking controller K, and an open-loop controller $\mathbf{u}_{\mathsf{ref}}$, the reachable set (under any disturbance) at time t is over-approximated by $\mathcal{R}_{r_t v}(\mathbf{x}_{\mathsf{ref}}[t])$. Thus, once we fix K and $\mathbf{x}_{\mathsf{ref}}[0]$, the problem of synthesizing a controller reduces to the problem of synthesizing an appropriate $\mathbf{u}_{\mathsf{ref}}$ such that the reachset over-approximations meet the reach-avoid specification. Indeed, for the rest of the presentation, we will assume a fixed K.

For synthesizing $\mathbf{u}_{\mathsf{ref}}$, we would like to formalize the problem in terms of constraints that will allow us to use SMT solvers. In the following, we describe the details of how this problem can be formalized as a quantifier-free first order formula over the theory of reals. We will then lay out specific assumptions and/or simplifications required to reduce the problem to QF-LRA theory, which is implemented efficiently in existing state-of-the-art SMT solvers. Most SMT solvers also provide the functionality of explicit model generation, and the concrete controller values can be read-off from the models generated when the constraints are satisfiable.

Constraints for Synthesizing $\mathbf{u}_{\mathsf{ref}}$. Let us fix an initial state x_0 and a radius r, defining a set of initial states $S = \mathcal{B}_r(x_0)$. The $\mathbf{u}_{\mathsf{ref}}$ synthesis problem can be stated as finding satisfying solutions for the formula $\phi_{\mathsf{synth}}(x_0, r)$.

$$
\begin{aligned}
\phi_{\mathsf{synth}}(x_0, r) \triangleq\ & \exists \mathbf{u}_{\mathsf{ref}}[0], \mathbf{u}_{\mathsf{ref}}[1], \dots \mathbf{u}_{\mathsf{ref}}[T{-}1], \\
& \exists \mathbf{x}_{\mathsf{ref}}[0], \mathbf{x}_{\mathsf{ref}}[1], \dots \mathbf{x}_{\mathsf{ref}}[T], \\
& \phi_{\mathsf{control}}(\mathbf{u}_{\mathsf{ref}}) \wedge \phi_{\mathsf{execution}}(\mathbf{u}_{\mathsf{ref}}, \mathbf{x}_{\mathsf{ref}}, x_0) \\
& \wedge \phi_{\mathsf{avoid}}(x_0, r, \mathbf{u}_{\mathsf{ref}}, \mathbf{x}_{\mathsf{ref}}) \wedge \phi_{\mathsf{reach}}(x_0, r, \mathbf{u}_{\mathsf{ref}}, \mathbf{x}_{\mathsf{ref}})
\end{aligned} \tag{8}
$$

where ϕ_{control} constrains the space of inputs, $\phi_{\mathsf{execution}}$ states that the sequence $\mathbf{x}_{\mathsf{ref}}$ is a reference execution following Eq. (3), ϕ_{avoid} specifies the safety constraint, ϕ_{reach} specifies that the system reaches G:

$$
\begin{aligned}
\phi_{\mathsf{control}}(\mathbf{u}_{\mathsf{ref}}) &\triangleq \bigwedge_{t=0}^{T-1} \mathbf{u}_{\mathsf{ref}}[t] \oplus \big(K \otimes \mathcal{R}_{r_t v}(0)\big) \subseteq U \\
\phi_{\mathsf{execution}}(\mathbf{u}_{\mathsf{ref}}, \mathbf{x}_{\mathsf{ref}}, x_0) &\triangleq (\mathbf{x}_{\mathsf{ref}}[0] = x_0) \wedge \bigwedge_{t=0}^{T-1} (\mathbf{x}_{\mathsf{ref}}[t+1] = A\mathbf{x}_{\mathsf{ref}}[t] + B\mathbf{u}_{\mathsf{ref}}[t]) \\
\phi_{\mathsf{avoid}}(x_0, r, \mathbf{u}_{\mathsf{ref}}, \mathbf{x}_{\mathsf{ref}}) &\triangleq \bigwedge_{t=0}^{T} \mathcal{R}_{r_t v}(\mathbf{x}_{\mathsf{ref}}[t]) \cap \mathbf{O}[t] = \varnothing \\
\phi_{\mathsf{reach}}(x_0, r, \mathbf{u}_{\mathsf{ref}}, \mathbf{x}_{\mathsf{ref}}) &\triangleq \mathcal{R}_{r_T v}(\mathbf{x}_{\mathsf{ref}}[T]) \subseteq G.
\end{aligned} \tag{9}
$$

As discussed in Sect. 3.2, the vector v and the constants $r_0, \dots, r_T$ are precomputed using the radius r of the initial ball.

We make a few remarks about this formulation. First, each of the formulas $\phi_{\mathsf{control}}, \phi_{\mathsf{avoid}}$ and ϕ_{reach} represent sufficient conditions to check for the existence of $\mathbf{u}_{\mathsf{ref}}$. Second, the constraints stated above belong to the (decidable) theory of reals. However, $\phi_{\mathsf{control}}, \phi_{\mathsf{avoid}}$ and ϕ_{reach}, and thus ϕ_{synth}, are not quantifier free as they use subset and disjointness checks. This is because for sets S, T

expressed as predicates $\varphi_S(\cdot)$ and $\varphi_T(\cdot)$, $S \cap T = \varnothing$ corresponds to the formula $\forall x \cdot \neg(\varphi_S(x) \wedge \varphi_T(x))$ and $S \subseteq T$ (or equivalently $S \cap T^c = \varnothing$) corresponds to the formula $\forall x \cdot \varphi_S(x) \implies \varphi_T(x)$.

Reduction to QF-LRA. Since the sets G and U are bounded polytopes, G^c and U^c can be expressed as finite unions of (possibly unbounded) polytopes. Thus, the subset predicates $\mathbf{u}_{\mathsf{ref}}[t] \oplus \left(K \otimes \mathcal{R}_{r_t v}(0)\right) \subseteq U$ in ϕ_{control} and $\mathcal{R}_{r_t v}(\mathbf{x}_{\mathsf{ref}}[t]) \subseteq G$ in ϕ_{reach} can be expressed as a disjunction over finitely many predicates, each expressing the disjointness of two polytopes.

The central idea behind eliminating the universal quantification in the disjointness predicates in ϕ_{avoid} or in the inferred disjointness predicates in ϕ_{reach} and ϕ_{control}, is to find a separating hyperplane that witnesses the disjointness of two polytopes. Let $P_1 = \{x \mid A_1 x \leq b_1\}$ and $P_2 = \{x \mid A_2 x \leq b_2\}$ be two polytopes such that P_1 is closed and bounded. Then, if there is an i for which each vertex v of P_1 satisfies $A_2^{(i)} v > b_2(i)$, we must have that $P_1 \cap P_2 = \varnothing$, where $A_2^{(i)}$ is the ith row vector of the matrix A_2. That is, such a check is sufficient to ensure disjointness. Thus, in the formula ϕ_{avoid}, in order to check if $\mathcal{R}_{r_t v}(\mathbf{x}_{\mathsf{ref}}[t])$ does not intersect with $\mathbf{O}[t]$, we check if there is a face of the polytope $\mathbf{O}[t]$ such that all the vertices of $\mathcal{R}_{r_t v}(\mathbf{x}_{\mathsf{ref}}[t])$ lie on the other side of the face. The same holds for each of the inferred predicates in ϕ_{reach} and ϕ_{control}. Eliminating quantifiers is essential to scale our analysis to large high dimensional systems.

Further, when the set G has a hyper-rectangle representation, the containment check $\mathcal{R}_{r_t v}(\mathbf{x}_{\mathsf{ref}}[T]) \subseteq G$ can directly be encoded as the conjunction of $O(n)$ linear inequalities, stating that for each dimension i, the lower and the upper bounds of $\mathcal{R}_{r_t v}(\mathbf{x}_{\mathsf{ref}}[t])$ in the ith dimension, satisfy $l'_i \leq l_i \leq u_i \leq u'_i$, where l'_i and r'_i represent the bounds for G in the ith dimension. Similarly, when $\mathbf{O}[t]$ has a rectangle representation, we can formulate the emptiness constraint $\mathcal{R}_{r_t v}(\mathbf{x}_{\mathsf{ref}}[t]) \cap \mathbf{O}[t] = \varnothing$ as $\bigvee_{i=1}^{n} (u_i < l'_i \vee l_i > u'_i)$, where l_i and u_i (resp. l'_i and u'_i) are the lower and upper bounds of $\mathcal{R}_{r_t v}(\mathbf{x}_{\mathsf{ref}}[t])$ (resp. $\mathbf{O}[t]$) in the ith dimension. Since such simplifications can exponentially reduce the number of constraints generated, they play a crucial for the scalability.

The constraints for checking emptiness and disjointness, as discussed above, only give rise to linear constraints, do not have the $\forall$ quantification over states, and is a sound transformation of ϕ_{synth} into QF-LRA. In Sect. 3.6 we will see that the reach set over-approximation can be made arbitrarily small when the disturbance is 0 by arbitrarily shrinking the size of the initial cover. Thus, these checks will also turn out to be sufficient to ensure that if there exists a controller, ϕ_{synth} is satisfiable.

Lemma 2. *Let $v \in \mathbb{R}^n$ and $r_0, \ldots, r_T \in \mathbb{R}$ be such that for any execution $\mathbf{x}_{\mathsf{ref}}$ starting at x_0, we have $\forall t \leq T \cdot \mathsf{Reach}(\mathcal{B}_r(x_0), t) \subseteq \mathcal{R}_{r_t v}(\mathbf{x}_{\mathsf{ref}}[t])$. If the formula $\phi_{\mathsf{synth}}(x_0, r)$ is satisfiable, then there is a control sequence $\mathbf{u}_{\mathsf{ref}}$ such that for every $x \in \mathcal{B}_r(x_0)$ and for every $\mathbf{d} \in \mathcal{D}^T$, the unique execution $\mathbf{x}$ defined by the controller $\langle K, x_0, \mathbf{u}_{\mathsf{ref}} \rangle$ and $\mathbf{d}$, starting at x satisfies $\mathbf{x}[T] \in G \wedge \forall t \leq T \cdot \mathbf{x}[t] \notin \mathbf{O}[t]$.*

We remark that a possible alternative for eliminating the $\forall$ quantifier is the use of Farkas' Lemma, but this gives rise to nonlinear constraints[2]. Indeed, in our experimental evaluation, we observed the downside of resorting to Farkas' Lemma in this problem.

3.6   Synthesis Algorithm Putting It All Together

The presentation in Sect. 3.5 describes how to formalize constraints to generate a control sequence that works for a subset of the initial set Θ. The overall synthesis procedure (Algorithm 1), first computes a tracking controller K, then generates open-loop control sequences and reference executions in order to cover the entire set Θ.

Algorithm 1. Algorithm for Synthesizing Combined Controller

1: **Input:** $\mathcal{A}, T, \mathbf{O}[0], \ldots, \mathbf{O}[T], G, Q, R$
2: $r^* \leftarrow$ diameter$(\Theta)/2$
3: $K, v, c_1, c_2 \leftarrow$ BLOATPARAMS$(\mathcal{A}, T, Q, R)$
4: cover $\leftarrow \varnothing$
5: controllers $\leftarrow \varnothing$
6: **while** $\Theta \not\subseteq$ cover **do**
7:     $\psi_{\mathsf{synth}} \leftarrow$ GETCONSTRAINTS$(\mathcal{A}, T, \mathbf{O}[0], \ldots, \mathbf{O}[T], G, v, c_1, c_2, r^*, \text{cover})$
8:     **if** CHECKSAT$(\psi_{\mathsf{synth}}) = $ SAT **then**
9:         $r, \mathbf{u}_{\mathsf{ref}}, \mathbf{x}_{\mathsf{ref}} \leftarrow$ MODEL(ψ_{synth})
10:         cover $\leftarrow$ cover $\cup\, \mathcal{B}_r(\mathbf{x}_{\mathsf{ref}}[0])$
11:         controllers $\leftarrow$ controllers $\cup\, \{\,(\,\langle K, \mathbf{x}_{\mathsf{ref}}[0], \mathbf{u}_{\mathsf{ref}}\rangle\,,\ \mathcal{B}_r(\mathbf{x}_{\mathsf{ref}}[0])\,)\,\}$
12:     **else**
13:         $r^* \leftarrow r^*/2$
14: **return** controllers;

The procedure BLOATPARAMS, computes a tracking controller K, a vector v and real valued parameters $\{c_1[t]\}_{t \leq T}$, $\{c_2[t]\}_{t \leq T}$, for the system $\mathcal{A}$ and time bound T with Q, R for the LQR method. Given any reference execution $\mathbf{x}_{\mathsf{ref}}$ and an initial set $\mathcal{B}_r(\mathbf{x}_{\mathsf{ref}}[0])$, the parameters computed by BLOATPARAMS can be used to over-approximate Reach$(\mathcal{B}_r(\mathbf{x}_{\mathsf{ref}}[0]), t)$ with the rectangle $\mathcal{R}_{v'}(\mathbf{x}_{\mathsf{ref}}[t])$, where $v' = (c_1[t]r + c_2[t])v$. The computation of these parameters proceeds as follows. Matrix K is determined using LQR (Proposition 1). Now we use Equation (7) to compute the matrix M and the rate of convergence α. Vector v is then computed such that $\mathcal{E}_1(0, M)$ is bounded by $\mathcal{R}_v(0)$. Let $r_{\mathsf{unit}} = \max_{x \in \mathcal{B}_1(0)} \|x\|_M$ and $\delta = \max_{d \in \mathcal{D}} \|d\|_M$. Then we have, $\mathcal{B}_r(x_0) \subseteq \mathcal{E}_{r \cdot r_{\mathsf{unit}}}(x_0, M)$ for any x_0. The constants $c_1[0], \ldots c_1[T], c_2[0], \ldots c_2[T]$ are computed as $c_1[t] = \alpha^{\frac{t}{2}} r_{\mathsf{unit}}$ and $c_2[t] = \sum_{i=0}^{t-1} \alpha^{\frac{i}{2}} \delta$; Sects. 3.2–3.4 establish the correctness guarantees of these

---

[2] Farkas' Lemma introduces auxiliary variables that get multiplied with existing variables $\mathbf{x}_{\mathsf{ref}}[0], \ldots, \mathbf{x}_{\mathsf{ref}}[T]$, leading to nonlinear constraints.

parameters. Clearly, these computations are independent of any reference executions $\mathbf{x}_{\text{ref}}$ and control sequences $\mathbf{u}_{\text{ref}}$.

The procedure GETCONSTRAINTS constructs the logical formula ψ_{synth} below such that whenever ψ_{synth} holds, we can find an initial radius r, and center x_0 in the set $\Theta \setminus \text{cover}$ and a control sequence $\mathbf{u}_{\text{ref}}$ such that any controlled execution starting from $\mathcal{B}_r(x_0)$ satisfies the reach-avoid requirements.

$$\psi_{\text{synth}} \triangleq \exists x_0 \, \exists r \cdot \left(x_0 \in \Theta \wedge x_0 \notin \text{cover} \wedge r > r^* \wedge \phi_{\text{synth}}(x_0, r) \right) \quad (10)$$

Recall that the constants $r_0, \ldots, r_T$ used in ϕ_{synth} are affine functions of r and thus ψ_{synth} falls in the QF-LRA fragment.

Line 8 checks for the satisfiability of ψ_{synth}. If satisfiable, we extract the model generated to get the radius of the initial ball, the control sequence $\mathbf{u}_{\text{ref}}$ and the reference execution $\mathbf{x}_{\text{ref}}$ in Line 9. The generated controller $\langle K, \mathbf{x}_{\text{ref}}[0], \mathbf{u}_{\text{ref}} \rangle$ is guaranteed to work for the ball $\mathcal{B}_r(\mathbf{x}_{\text{ref}}[0])$, which can be marked *covered* by adding it to the set cover. In order to keep all the constraints linear, one can further underapproximate $\mathcal{B}_r(\mathbf{x}_{\text{ref}}[0])$ with the rectangle $\mathcal{R}_w(\mathbf{x}_{\text{ref}}[0])$, where $w(i) = r/\sqrt{n}$ for each dimension $i \leq n$. If ψ_{synth} is unsatisfiable, then we reduce the minimum radius r^* (Line 13) and continue to look for controllers, until we find that $\Theta \subseteq \text{cover}$.

The set controllers is the set of pairs $(\langle K, x_0, \mathbf{u}_{\text{ref}} \rangle, S)$, such that the controller $\langle K, x_0, \mathbf{u}_{\text{ref}} \rangle$ drives the set S to meet the desired specification. Each time a new controller is found, it is added to the set controllers together with the initial set for which it works (Line 11). The following theorem asserts the soundness of Algorithm 1, and it follows from Lemmas 1 and 2.

Theorem 1. *If Algorithm 1 terminates, then the synthesized controller is correct. That is, (a) for each $x \in \Theta$, there is a $(\langle K, x_0, \mathbf{u}_{\text{ref}} \rangle, S) \in \text{controllers}$, such that $x \in S$, and (b) for each $(\langle K, x_0, \mathbf{u}_{\text{ref}} \rangle, S) \in \text{controllers}$, the unique controller $\langle K, x_0, \mathbf{u}_{\text{ref}} \rangle$ is such that for every $x \in S$ and for every $\mathbf{d} \in D^T$, the unique execution defined by $\langle K, x_0, \mathbf{u}_{\text{ref}} \rangle$ and $\mathbf{d}$, starting at x, satisfies the reach-avoid specification.*

Algorithm 1 ensures that, upon termination, every $x \in \Theta$ is covered, i.e., one can construct a combined controller that drives x to G while avoiding $\mathbf{O}$. However it may find multiple controllers for a point $x \in \Theta$. This non-determinism can be easily resolved by picking any controller assigned for x.

Below, we show that, under certain robustness assumptions on the system $\mathcal{A}$, G and the sets $\mathbf{O}$, and in the absence of disturbance Algorithm 1 terminates.

Robustly Controllable Systems. A system $\mathcal{A} = \langle A, B, \Theta, U, D \rangle$ is said to be ε-robustly controllable ($\varepsilon > 0$) with respect to the reach-avoid specification $(\mathbf{O}, G)$ and matrix K, if (a) $D = \{0\}$, and (b) for every initial state $\theta \in \Theta$ and for every open loop-controller $\mathbf{u}_{\text{ref}} \in U^T$ such that the unique execution starting from θ using the open-loop controller $\mathbf{u}_{\text{ref}}$ satisfies the reach-avoid specification, then with the controller $\langle K, \theta, \mathbf{u}_{\text{ref}} \rangle$ defined as in Equation (3), $\forall t \leq T, \text{Reach}(\mathcal{B}_\varepsilon(\theta), t) \cap \mathbf{O}[t] = \varnothing$ and $\text{Reach}(\mathcal{B}_\varepsilon(\theta), T) \subseteq G$, i.e., $\forall x \in \mathcal{B}_\varepsilon(\theta)$, the unique trajectory $\mathbf{x}$ defined by the controller $\langle K, \theta, \mathbf{u}_{ref} \rangle$ starting from x also satisfies the reach avoid specification.

Theorem 2. *Let $\mathcal{A}$ be ε-robust with respect to the reach-avoid specification $(\mathbf{O}, G)$ and K, for some $\varepsilon > 0$. If there is a controller for $\mathcal{A}$ that satisfies the reach-avoid specification, then Algorithm 1 terminates.*

When the system is robust, then (in the absence of any disturbance i.e., $D = \{0\}$), the sizes $r_0, r_1, \ldots, r_T$ of the hyper-rectangles that overapproximate reach-sets go arbitrarily close to 0 as the initial cover converges to a single point (as seen in Lemma 1). Therefore, the over-approximations can be made arbitrarily precise as r^* decreases. Moreover, as r^* approaches 0, Eq. (9) (with simplifications for QF-LRA), also becomes satisfiable whenever there is a controller. The correctness of Theorem 2 follows from both these observations.

4   RealSyn Implementation and Evaluation

4.1   Implementation

We have implemented our synthesis algorithm in a tool called REALSYN. REALSYN is written in Python. For solving Eq. (10) it can interface with any SMT solver through Python APIs. We present experimental results with Z3 (version 4.5.1) [6], Yices (version 2.5.4) [8], and CVC4 (version 1.5) [4]. REALSYN leverages the incremental solving capabilities of these solvers as follows: The constraints ψ_{synth} generated (line 8 in Algorithm 1) can be expressed as $\exists x_0, \exists r \cdot \psi_1 \wedge \psi_2$, where $\psi_1 \triangleq \phi_{synth}(x_0, r)$ and $\psi_2 \triangleq x_0 \in \Theta \wedge x_0 \notin \text{cover} \wedge r > r^*$. Since the bulk of the formula $\phi_{synth}(x_0, r)$ is in ψ_1 and it does not change across iterations, we can generate this formula only once, and push it on the context stack of the solvers. The formula ψ_2 is different across iterations, and can be pushed and popped out of the stack as required. This minimizes the time taken for generation of constraints.

4.2   Evaluation

We use 24 benchmark examples[3] to evaluate the performance of REALSYN with three different solvers on a standard laptop with Intel® Core™ i7 processor, 16 GB RAM, running Ubuntu 16.04. The results are reported in Table 1. The results are encouraging and demonstrate the effectiveness of using our approach and the feasibility of scalable controller synthesis for high dimensional systems and complex reach-avoid specifications.

Comparison With Other Tools. We considered other controller synthesis tools for possible comparison with REALSYN. In summary, CoSyMa [27], Pessoa [30], and SCOTS [31] do not explicitly support discrete-time sytems. LTLMop [22,37] is designed to analyze robotic systems in the (2-dimensional)

---

[3] The examples are available at https://github.com/umangm/realsyn.

Table 1. Controller synthesis using REALSYN and different SMT solvers. An explanation for the * marked entries can be found in Sect. 4.

	Model	n	m	Z3		CVC4		Yices	
				#iter	time(s)	#iter	time(s)	#iter	time(s)
1	1-robot	2	1	9	0.21	1	0.06	7	0.06
2	2-robot	4	2	164	12.62	11	0.31	183	2.26
3	running-example	4	2	N/A	T/O	N/A	T/O	1	319.97
4	1-car dynamic avoid	4	2	9	53.17	1	96.43	12	8.49
5	1-car navigation	4	2	18	7.49	1	3.05	17	6.73
6	2-car navigation	8	4	1	60.14	1	2668.2	1	4.07
7	3-car navigation	12	6	1	733.42	1	481.88	1	741.73
8	4-car platoon	8	4	1	0.37	1	0.21	1	0.15
9	8-car platoon	16	8	1	23.02	1	1.44	1	0.62
10	10-car platoon	20	10	1	459.36	1	20.93	1	7.74
11	Example	3	1	82	2.32	18	0.10	67	0.43
12	Cruise	1	1	1	0.06	1	0.03	1	0.02
13	Motor	2	1	1	0.10	1	0.06	1	0.03
14	Helicopter	3	1	81	2.31	13	0.08	70	0.38
15	Magnetic suspension	2	1	39	0.47	2	0.05	39	0.08
16	Pendulum	2	1	30	0.32	8	0.05	42	0.07
17	Satellite	2	1	40	0.46	5	0.05	32	0.06
18	Suspension	4	1	1	0.17	1	0.11	1	0.09
19	Tape	3	1	1	0.12	1	0.07	1	0.07
20	Inverted pendulum	2	1	39	0.49	2	0.05	39	0.09
21	Magnetic pointer	3	1	44	1.12	12	0.08	134	0.83
22	Helicopter	28	6	N/A (1*)	T/O (650*)	1	651.21	N/A	T/O
23	Building	48	1	1 (1*)	1936.03 (240*)	N/A	T/O	1	552.48
24	Pde	84	1	N/A (1*)	T/O (1800*)	1	8.48	1	8.87

Euclidean plane and thus not suitable for most of our examples. TuLiP [13,39] comes closest to addressing the same class of problems. TuLip relies on discretization of the state space and a receding horizon approach for synthesizing controllers for more general GR(1) specifications. However, we found TuLip succumbs to the state space explosion problem when discretizing the state space, and it did not work on most of our examples. For instance, TuLiP was unable to synthesize a controller for the 2-dimensional system '1-robot' (Table 1), and returned `unrealizable`. On the benchmark '2-robot' ($n = 4$), TuLip did not return any answer within 1 h. We checked these findings with the developers and they concurred that it is typical for TuLip to take hours even for 4-dimensional systems.

Benchmarks. Our benchmarks and their SMT encodings, could be of independent interest to the verification and SMT-community. Examples 1–10 are vehicle motion planning examples we have designed with reach-avoid specifications. Benchmarks 1–2 model robots moving on the Euclidean plane, where each robot is a 2-dimensional system and admits a 1-dimensional input. Starting from some initial region on the plane, the robots are required to reach the common goal area within the given time steps, while avoiding certain obstacles. For '2-robot', the robots are also required to maintain a minimum separation. Benchmarks 3–7 are discrete vehicular models adopted from [12]. Each vehicle is a 4-dimensional system with 2-dimensional input. Benchmark 3 is the system as our running example. Benchmark 4 describes one *ego* vehicle running on a two-lane road, trying to overtake a vehicle in front of it. The second vehicle serves as the obstacle. Benchmarks 5–7 are similar to Benchmark 2 where the vehicles are required to reach a common goal area while avoiding collision with the obstacles and with each other (inspired by a merge). The velocities and accelerations of the vehicles are also constrained in each of these benchmarks.

Benchmarks 8–10 model multiple vehicles trying to form a platoon by maintaining the safe relative distance between consecutive vehicles. The models are adopted (and discretized) from [32]. Each vehicle is a 2-dimensional system with 1-dimensional input. For the 4-car platoon model, the running times reported in Table 1 are much smaller than the time (5 min) reported in [32]. This observation aligns with our analysis in Sect. 3.1.

Benchmarks 11–21 are from [2]. The specification here is that the reach set has to be within a safe rectangle (that is, $G = true$). In [2] each model is discretized using 8 different time steps and here we randomly pick one for each model. In general, the running time of RealSyn is less than those reported in [2] (their reported machine had better configuration). On the other hand, the synthesized controller from [2] considers quantization errors, while our approach does not provide any guarantee for that.

Benchmarks 22–24 are a set of high dimensional examples adopted and discretized from [36]. Similar to previous ones, the only specification is that the reach sets starting from an initial state with the controller should be contained within a safe rectangle.

Synthesis Performance. In Table 1, columns 'n' and 'm' stand for the dimensions of the state space and input space. For each background solver, '#iter' is the number of iterations Algorithm 1 required to synthesize a controller, and 'time' is the respective running times. We specify a time limit of 1 h and report T/O (timeout) for benchmarks that do not finish within this limit. All benchmarks are synthesized for a specification with 10–20 steps.

In general, for low-dimensional systems (for example, in Benchmarks 11–21), each of the solvers finish quickly (in less than 1 s), with CVC4 and Yices outperforming Z3 on most benchmarks. The Yices solver is faster than the other two on most examples. Z3 was the slowest on most, except a few (e.g., Benchmark 3, 6) where CVC4 was much slower. The running time, in general, increases with the increase of the dimensionality but this relationship is far from simple. For example, the 84-dimensional Benchmark 24 was synthesized in less than 9 s by both CVC4 and Yices, possibly because the safety specification is rather simple for this problem.

The three solvers use different techniques for solving QF-LRA formulae with support for incremental solving. The default tactic in Z3 is such that it spends a large chunk of time when a constraint is pushed to the solver stack. In fact, for Benchmark 24, while the other two solvers finish within 9 s, Z3 did not finish pushing the constraints in the solver stack. When we disable incremental solving in Z3, the Benchmarks 22, 23 and 24 finish in about 650, 240 and 1800 s respectively (marked with *). The number of iterations widely vary across solvers, with CVC4 usually finishing in the fewest number of iterations. Despite the larger number of satisfiability queries, Yices manages to finish close to CVC4 on most examples.

5 Conclusion

We proposed a novel technique for synthesizing controllers for systems with discrete time linear dynamics, operating under bounded disturbances, and for reach-avoid specifications. Our approach relies on generating controllers that combine an open loop-controller with a tracking controller, thereby allowing a decoupled approach for synthesizing each component independently. Experimental evaluation using our tool REALSYN demonstrates the value of the approach when analyzing systems with complex dynamics and specifications.

There are several avenues for future work. This includes synthesis of combined controllers for nonlinear dynamical and hybrid systems, and for more general temporal logic specifications. Generating witnesses to show the absence of controllers is also an interesting direction.

References

1. Abate, A., Amin, S., Prandini, M., Lygeros, J., Sastry, S.: Computational approaches to reachability analysis of stochastic hybrid systems. In: Bemporad, A., Bicchi, A., Buttazzo, G. (eds.) HSCC 2007. LNCS, vol. 4416, pp. 4–17. Springer, Heidelberg (2007). https://doi.org/10.1007/978-3-540-71493-4_4
2. Abate, A., et al.: Automated formal synthesis of digital controllers for state-space physical plants. In: Majumdar, R., Kunvcak, V. (eds.) CAV 2017. LNCS, vol. 10426, pp. 462–482. Springer, Cham (2017). https://doi.org/10.1007/978-3-319-63387-9_23
3. Antsaklis, P.J., Michel, A.N.: A Linear Systems Primer, vol. 1. Birkhäuser Boston, Cambridge (2007)
4. Barrett, C., et al.: CVC4. In: Gopalakrishnan, G., Qadeer, S. (eds.) CAV 2011. LNCS, vol. 6806, pp. 171–177. Springer, Heidelberg (2011). https://doi.org/10.1007/978-3-642-22110-1_14
5. Boyd, S., Vandenberghe, L.: Convex Optimization (2004)
6. de Moura, L., Bjorner, N.: Z3: an efficient SMT solver. In: Ramakrishnan, C.R., Rehof, J. (eds.) TACAS 2008. LNCS, vol. 4963, pp. 337–340. Springer, Heidelberg (2008). https://doi.org/10.1007/978-3-540-78800-3_24

7. Ding, J., Tomlin, C.J.: Robust reach-avoid controller synthesis for switched nonlinear systems. In: Proceedings of the 49th IEEE Conference on Decision and Control, CDC 2010, 15–17 December 2010, Atlanta, Georgia, USA, pp. 6481–6486 (2010)

8. Dutertre, B.: Yices 2.2. In: Biere, A., Bloem, R. (eds.) CAV 2014. LNCS, vol. 8559, pp. 737–744. Springer, Cham (2014). https://doi.org/10.1007/978-3-319-08867-9_49

9. Esfahani, P.M., Chatterjee, D., Lygeros, J.: The stochastic reach-avoid problem and set characterization for diffusions. Automatica **70**, 43–56 (2016)

10. Fainekos, G.E., Girard, A., Kress-Gazit, H., Pappas, G.J.: Temporal logic motion planning for dynamic robots. Automatica **45**(2), 343–352 (2009)

11. Fainekos, G.E., Kress-Gazit, H., Pappas, G.J.: Hybrid controllers for path planning: a temporal logic approach. In: 2005 44th IEEE Conference on Decision and Control, and 2005 European Control Conference, CDC-ECC 2005, pp. 4885–4890. IEEE (2005)

12. Fehnker, A., Ivanvcić, F.: Benchmarks for hybrid systems verification. In: Alur, R., Pappas, G.J. (eds.) HSCC 2004. LNCS, vol. 2993, pp. 326–341. Springer, Heidelberg (2004). https://doi.org/10.1007/978-3-540-24743-2_22

13. Filippidis, I., Dathathri, S., Livingston, S.C., Ozay, N., Murray, R.M.: Control design for hybrid systems with tulip: the temporal logic planning toolbox. In: 2016 IEEE Conference on Control Applications, CCA 2016, Buenos Aires, Argentina, 19–22 September 2016, pp. 1030–1041 (2016)

14. Fisac, J.F., Chen, M., Tomlin, C.J., Sastry, S.S.: Reach-avoid problems with time-varying dynamics, targets and constraints. In: Proceedings of the 18th International Conference on Hybrid Systems: Computation and Control, HSCC 2015, Seattle, WA, USA, 14–16 April 2015, pp. 11–20 (2015)

15. Girard, A.: Controller synthesis for safety and reachability via approximate bisimulation. Automatica **48**(5), 947–953 (2012)

16. Gol, E.A., Lazar, M., Belta, C.: Language-guided controller synthesis for linear systems. IEEE Trans. Autom. Control **59**(5), 1163–1176 (2014)

17. Hespanha, J.P.: Linear Systems Theory. Princeton University Press, Princeton (2009)

18. Huang, Z., Wang, Y., Mitra, S., Dullerud, G.E., Chaudhuri, S.: Controller synthesis with inductive proofs for piecewise linear systems: an SMT-based algorithm. In: 54th IEEE Conference on Decision and Control, CDC 2015, Osaka, Japan, 15–18 December 2015, pp. 7434–7439 (2015)

19. Jha, S., Seshia, S.A., Tiwari, A.: Synthesis of optimal switching logic for hybrid systems. In: Proceedings of the 11th International Conference on Embedded Software, EMSOFT 2011, Part of the Seventh Embedded Systems Week, ESWeek 2011, Taipei, Taiwan, 9–14 October 2011, pp. 107–116 (2011)

20. Kloetzer, M., Belta, C.: A fully automated framework for control of linear systems from temporal logic specifications. IEEE Trans. Autom. Control **53**(1), 287–297 (2008)

21. Koo, T.J., Pappas, G.J., Sastry, S.: Mode switching synthesis for reachability specifications. In: Di Benedetto, M.D., Sangiovanni-Vincentelli, A. (eds.) HSCC 2001. LNCS, vol. 2034, pp. 333–346. Springer, Heidelberg (2001). https://doi.org/10.1007/3-540-45351-2_28

22. Kress-Gazit, H., Fainekos, G.E., Pappas, G.J.: Temporal logic based reactive mission and motion planning. IEEE Trans. Robot. **25**(6), 1370–1381 (2009)

23. Kress-Gazit, H., Lahijanian, M., Raman, V.: Synthesis for robots: guarantees and feedback for robot behavior. Ann. Rev. Control Robot. Auton. Syst. **1**(1) (2018)

24. Kurzhanskiy, A.A., Varaiya, P.: Ellipsoidal techniques for reachability analysis of discrete-time linear systems. IEEE Trans. Autom. Control **52**(1), 26–38 (2007)

25. Liu, J., Ozay, N., Topcu, U., Murray, R.M.: Synthesis of reactive switching proto-cols from temporal logic specifications. IEEE Trans. Autom. Control **58**(7), 1771–1785 (2013)

26. Majumdar, R., Mallik, K., Schmuck, A.-K.: Compositional synthesis of finite state abstractions. CoRR, abs/1612.08515 (2016)

27. Mouelhi, S., Girard, A., Gössler, G.: Cosyma: a tool for controller synthesis using multi-scale abstractions. In: Proceedings of The 16th International Conference on Hybrid Systems: Computation and Control, HSCC 2013, pp. 83–88, New York. ACM (2013)

28. Rami, M.A., Tadeo, F.: Controller synthesis for positive linear systems with bounded controls. IEEE Trans. Circuits Syst. **54**–**II**(2), 151–155 (2007)

29. Ravanbakhsh, H., Sankaranarayanan, S.: Robust controller synthesis of switched systems using counterexample guided framework. In: Proceedings of the 13th Inter-national Conference on Embedded Software, EMSOFT 2016, pp. 8:1–8:10, New York. ACM (2016)

30. Roy, P., Tabuada, P., Majumdar, R.: Pessoa 2.0: a controller synthesis tool for cyber-physical systems. In: Proceedings of the 14th International Conference on Hybrid Systems: Computation and Control, HSCC 2011, pp. 315–316, New York. ACM (2011)

31. Rungger, M, Zamani, M.: SCOTS: a tool for the synthesis of symbolic controllers. In: Proceedings of the 19th International Conference on Hybrid Systems: Compu-tation and Control, HSCC 2016, pp. 99–104, New York. ACM (2016)

32. Schürmann, B., Althoff, M.: Optimal control of sets of solutions to formally guaran-tee constraints of disturbed linear systems. In: 2017 American Control Conference, ACC 2017, Seattle, WA, USA, 24–26 May 2017, pp. 2522–2529 (2017)

33. Tabuada, P.: Verification and Control of Hybrid Systems - A Symbolic Approach. Springer, Heidelberg (2009). https://doi.org/10.1007/978-1-4419-0224-5

34. Tabuada, P., Pappas, G.J.: Linear time logic control of discrete-time linear systems. IEEE Trans. Autom. Control **51**(12), 1862–1877 (2006)

35. Taly, A., Gulwani, S., Tiwari, A.: Synthesizing switching logic using constraint solving. STTT **13**(6), 519–535 (2011)

36. Tran, H.D., Nguyen, L.V., Johnson, T.T.: Large-scale linear systems from order-reduction. In: ARCH@CPSWeek 2016, 3rd International Workshop on Applied Verification for Continuous and Hybrid Systems, Vienna, Austria, pp. 60–67 (2016)

37. Wong, K.W., Finucane, C., Kress-Gazit, H.: Provably-correct robot control with LTLMoP, OMPL and ROS. In: 2013 IEEE/RSJ International Conference on Intel-ligent Robots and Systems, Tokyo, Japan, 3–7 November 2013, p. 2073 (2013)

38. Wongpiromsarn, T., Topcu, U., Murray, R.M.: Receding horizon temporal logic planning. IEEE Trans. Autom. Control **57**(11), 2817–2830 (2012)

39. Wongpiromsarn, T., Topcu, U., Ozay, N., Xu, H., Murray, R.M.: TuLiP: a software toolbox for receding horizon temporal logic planning. In: Proceedings of the 14th International Conference on Hybrid Systems: Computation and Control, HSCC 2011, pp. 313–314, New York. ACM (2011)

40. Yordanov, B., Tumova, J., Cerna, I., Barnat, J., Belta, C.: Temporal logic control of discrete-time piecewise affine systems. IEEE Trans. Autom. Control **57**(6), 1491–1504 (2012)

41. Zhao, H., Zhan, N., Kapur, D.: Synthesizing switching controllers for hybrid sys-tems by generating invariants. In: Liu, Z., Woodcock, J., Zhu, H. (eds.) Theories of Programming and Formal Methods. LNCS, vol. 8051, pp. 354–373. Springer, Heidelberg (2013). https://doi.org/10.1007/978-3-642-39698-4_22

6

The Learnability of Symbolic Automata

George Argyros[1]([✉]) and Loris D'Antoni[2]

[1] Columbia University, New York, NY, USA
argyros@cs.columbia.edu
[2] University of Wisconsin-Madison, Madison, WI, USA
loris@cs.wisc.edu

Abstract. Symbolic automata (s-FAs) allow transitions to carry predicates over rich alphabet theories, such as linear arithmetic, and therefore extend classic automata to operate over infinite alphabets, such as the set of rational numbers. In this paper, we study the problem of the learnability of symbolic automata. First, we present MAT^*, a novel L^*-style algorithm for learning symbolic automata using membership and equivalence queries, which treats the predicates appearing on transitions as their own learnable entities. The main novelty of MAT^* is that it can take as input an algorithm Λ for learning predicates in the underlying alphabet theory and it uses Λ to infer the predicates appearing on the transitions in the target automaton. Using this idea, MAT^* is able to learn automata operating over alphabets theories in which predicates are efficiently learnable using membership and equivalence queries. Furthermore, we prove that a necessary condition for efficient learnability of an s-FA is that predicates in the underlying algebra are also efficiently learnable using queries and thus settling the learnability of a large class of s-FA instances. We implement MAT^* in an open-source library and show that it can efficiently learn automata that cannot be learned using existing algorithms and significantly outperforms existing automata learning algorithms over large alphabets.

1 Introduction

In 1987, Dana Angluin showed that finite automata *can be learned* in polynomial time using membership and equivalence queries [3]. In this learning model, often referred to as a *minimally adequate teacher* (MAT), the teacher can answer (*i*) whether a given string belongs to the target language being learned and (*ii*) whether a certain automaton is correct and accepts the target language, and provide a counterexample if the automaton is incorrect. Following this result, her L* algorithm has been studied extensively [16,17], it has been extended to several variants of finite automata [4,12,20] and has found many applications in program analysis [2,6,7] and program synthesis [25].

Recent work [6,11] developed algorithms which can efficiently learn s-FAs over certain alphabet theories. These algorithms operate using an underlying predicate learning algorithm which can learn partitions of the domain using predicates from counterexamples. While such results give sufficient conditions under which s-FAs can be efficiently learned, they do not provide any necessary conditions. More precisely, the following question remains open:

For what alphabet theories can s-FAs be efficiently learned?

In this paper, we make significant progress towards answering this question by providing new sufficient and necessary conditions for efficiently learning symbolic automata. More specifically, we present MAT^*, a new algorithm for learning s-FAs using membership and equivalence queries. The main novelty of MAT^* is that it can accept as input a MAT learning algorithm Λ for predicates in the underlying alphabet theory. Afterwards, MAT^* spawns instances of Λ to infer each transition in the target s-FA and efficiently answers membership and equivalence queries performed by Λ using the s-FA membership and equivalence oracles. The predicate learning algorithms do not need to learn entire partitions but individual predicates and therefore, MAT^* greatly simplifies the design of learning algorithms for s-FAs by allowing one to reuse existing learning algorithms for the underlying alphabet theory. Moreover, MAT^* allows the underlying predicate learning algorithms to perform *both* membership and equivalence queries, thus extending the class of efficiently learnable s-FAs to MAT-learnable alphabet theories—e.g., bit-vector predicates expressed as BDDs.

Furthermore, we show that a necessary condition for efficiently learning a symbolic automaton over a Boolean algebra is that the individual predicates in the algebra also have to be efficiently learnable. Moreover, we provide a characterization of the instances which are not efficiently learnable by our algorithm and conjecture that such instances are not learnable by any efficient algorithm.

We implement MAT^* in the open-source `symbolicautomata` library [1] and evaluate it on 15 regular-expression benchmarks, 1,500 s-FA benchmarks over bit-vector alphabets, and 18 synthetic benchmarks over infinite alphabets. Our results show that MAT^* can efficiently learn automata over different alphabet theories, some of which cannot be learned using existing algorithms. Moreover, for large finite alphabets, MAT^* significantly outperforms existing automata learning algorithms.

Contributions. In summary, our contributions are:

- MAT^*, the first algorithm for learning symbolic automata that operate over MAT-learnable alphabet theories—i.e., in which predicates can be learned using only membership and equivalence queries (Sect. 3).
- A soundness result for MAT^* and new necessary and sufficient conditions for the learnability of symbolic automata. Moreover, a characterization of the remaining class for which the learnability is not settled (Sect. 4).
- A modular implementation of MAT^* in an existing open-source library together with a comprehensive evaluation on existing and new automata-learning benchmarks (Sect. 6).

2 Background

2.1 Boolean Algebras and Symbolic Automata

In symbolic automata, transitions carry predicates over a decidable Boolean algebra. An *effective Boolean algebra* $\mathcal{A}$ is a tuple $(\mathfrak{D}, \Psi, \llbracket\_\rrbracket, \bot, \top, \vee, \wedge, \neg)$ where $\mathfrak{D}$ is a set of *domain elements*; Ψ is a set of *predicates* closed under the Boolean connectives, with $\bot, \top \in \Psi$; $\llbracket\_\rrbracket : \Psi \to 2^{\mathfrak{D}}$ is a *denotation function* such that (i) $\llbracket\bot\rrbracket = \emptyset$, (ii) $\llbracket\top\rrbracket = \mathfrak{D}$, and (iii) for all $\varphi, \psi \in \Psi$, $\llbracket\varphi \vee \psi\rrbracket = \llbracket\varphi\rrbracket \cup \llbracket\psi\rrbracket$, $\llbracket\varphi \wedge \psi\rrbracket = \llbracket\varphi\rrbracket \cap \llbracket\psi\rrbracket$, and $\llbracket\neg\varphi\rrbracket = \mathfrak{D} \setminus \llbracket\varphi\rrbracket$.

Example 1 (Equality Algebra). The *equality algebra* for an arbitrary set $\mathfrak{D}$ has predicates formed from Boolean combinations of formulas of the form $\lambda c. c = a$ where $a \in \mathfrak{D}$. Formally, Ψ is generated from the Boolean closure of $\Psi_0 = \{\varphi_a \mid a \in \mathfrak{D}\} \cup \{\bot, \top\}$ where for all $a \in \mathfrak{D}$, $\llbracket\varphi_a\rrbracket = \{a\}$. Examples of predicates in this algebra include $\lambda c. c = 5 \vee c = 10$ and $\lambda c. \neg(c = 0)$.

Definition 1 (Symbolic Finite Automata). *A symbolic finite automaton (s-FA) M is a tuple $(\mathcal{A}, Q, q_{init}, F, \Delta)$ where $\mathcal{A}$ is an effective Boolean algebra, called the* alphabet; *Q is a finite set of* states; *$q_{init} \in Q$ is the* initial state; *$F \subseteq Q$ is the set of* final states; *and $\Delta \subseteq Q \times \Psi_{\mathcal{A}} \times Q$ is the transition relation consisting of a finite set of* moves *or* transitions.

Characters are elements of $\mathfrak{D}_{\mathcal{A}}$, and *words* or *strings* are finite sequences of characters, or elements of $\mathfrak{D}_{\mathcal{A}}^*$. The empty word of length 0 is denoted by ϵ. A move $\rho = (q_1, \varphi, q_2) \in \Delta$, also denoted by $q_1 \xrightarrow{\varphi} q_2$, is a transition from the *source* state q_1 to the *target* state q_2, where φ is the *guard* or *predicate* of the move. For a state $q \in Q$, we denote by $\texttt{guard}(q)$ the set of guards for all moves from q. For a character $a \in \mathfrak{D}_{\mathcal{A}}$, an *a-move* of M, denoted $q_1 \xrightarrow{a} q_2$ is a move $q_1 \xrightarrow{\varphi} q_2$ such that $a \in \llbracket\varphi\rrbracket$.

An s-FA M is *deterministic* if, for all transitions $(q, \varphi_1, q_1), (q, \varphi_2, q_2) \in \Delta$, $q_1 \neq q_2 \to \llbracket\varphi_1 \wedge \varphi_2\rrbracket = \emptyset$—i.e., for each state q and character a there is at most one *a*-move out of q. An s-FA M is *complete* if, for all $q \in Q$, $\llbracket\bigvee_{(q,\varphi_i,q_i)\in\Delta} \varphi_i\rrbracket = \mathfrak{D}$—i.e., for each state q and character a there exists an *a*-move out of q. Throughout the paper we assume all s-FAs are deterministic and complete, since determinization and completion are always possible [10]. Given an s-FA $M = (\mathcal{A}, Q, q_{init}, F, \Delta)$ and a state $q \in Q$, we say a word $w = a_1 a_2 \cdots a_k$ is *accepted at state q* if, for $1 \leq i \leq k$, there exist moves $q_{i-1} \xrightarrow{a_i} q_i$ such that $q_{init} = q$ and $q_k \in F$.

For a deterministic s-FA M and a word w, we denote by $M_q[w]$ the state reached in M by w when starting at state q. When q is omitted we assume that execution starts at q_{init}. For a word $w = a_1 \cdots a_k$, we use $w[i..] = a_i \cdots a_k, w[..i] = a_1 \cdots a_i, w[i] = a_i$ to denote the suffix starting from the i-th position, the prefix up to the i-th position and the character at the i-th position respectively. We use $\mathbb{B} = \{\mathbf{T}, \mathbf{F}\}$ to denote the Boolean domain. A word w is called an *access string* for state $q \in Q$ if $M[w] = q$. For two states $q, p \in Q$, a word w is called a *distinguishing string*, if exactly one of $M_q[w]$ and $M_p[w]$ is final.

2.2   Learning Model

In this paper, we follow the notation from [17]. A concept is a Boolean function
$c : \mathfrak{D} \to \mathbb{B}$. A concept class $\mathcal{C}$ is a set of concepts which is represented using
representation class $\mathcal{R}$. By representation class we denote a fixed function from
strings to concepts in $\mathcal{C}$. For example, regular expressions, DFAs and NFAs are
different representation classes for the concept class of regular languages.

The learning model under which all learning algorithms in this paper operate
is called *exact learning from membership and equivalence queries* or learning
using a Minimal Adequate Teacher (MAT), and was originally introduced by
Angluin [3]. In this model, to learn an unknown concept $c \in \mathcal{C}$, a learning
algorithm has access to two types of queries:

Membership Query: In a membership query $\mathcal{O}(x)$, the input is $x \in \mathfrak{D}$ and
   the query returns the value $c(x)$ of the concept on given input x—i.e., **T** if x
   belongs to the concept and **F** otherwise.
Equivalence Query: In an equivalence query $\mathcal{E}(H)$, the input given is a
   hypothesis (or model) H. The query returns **T** if for every $x \in \mathfrak{D}$, $H(x) =$
   $c(x)$. Otherwise, an input $w \in \mathfrak{D}$ is returned such that $H(w) \neq c(w)$.

An algorithm is a learning algorithm for a concept class $\mathcal{C}$ if, for any $c \in \mathcal{C}$, the
algorithm terminates with a correct model for c after making a finite number of
membership and equivalence queries. In this paper, we will say that a learning
algorithm is *efficient* for a concept class $\mathcal{C}$ if it learns any concept $c \in \mathcal{C}$ using
a polynomial number of queries on the size of the representation of the target
concept in $\mathcal{R}$ and the length of the longest counterexample provided to the
algorithm.

An effective Boolean algebra $\mathcal{A} = (\mathfrak{D}, \Psi, [\![\_]\!], \bot, \top, \vee, \wedge, \neg)$ naturally defines
the concept class $2^{\mathfrak{D}}$ with representations in Ψ of predicates over the domain $\mathfrak{D}$.
We will say that an algorithm is a learning algorithm for the algebra $\mathcal{A}$ to denote
a learning algorithm that can efficiently learn predicates from the representation
class Ψ.

3   The MAT^* Algorithm

Our learning algorithm, MAT^*, can be viewed as a symbolic version of the
TTT algorithm for learning DFAs [16], but without discriminator finalization.
The learning algorithm accepts as input a membership oracle $\mathcal{O}$, an equivalence
oracle $\mathcal{E}$ as well as a learning algorithm Λ for the underlying Boolean algebra
used in the target s-FA $\mathcal{M}$. The algorithm uses a classification tree [17] to generate a partition of $\mathfrak{D}^*$ into equivalence classes which represent the states in the
target s-FA. Once a tree is obtained, we can use it to determine, for any word
$w \in \mathfrak{D}^*$, the state accessed by w in $\mathcal{M}$—i.e., what state the automaton reaches
when reading the word w. Then, we build an s-FA model $\mathcal{H}$, using the algebra
learning algorithm Λ to create models for each transition guard and utilizing
the classification tree in order to implement a membership oracle for Λ. Once a

---

Algorithm 1. S-FA-LEARN$(\mathcal{O}, \mathcal{E}, \Lambda)$ // s-FA Learning algorithm

---

Require: $\mathcal{O}$: membership oracle, $\mathcal{E}$: equivalence oracle, Λ: algebra learning algorithm.
   $T \leftarrow$ InitializeClassificationTree$(\mathcal{O})$
   $S_\Lambda \leftarrow$ InitializeGuardLearners(T, Λ)
   $\mathcal{H} \leftarrow$ GetSFAModel$(T, S_\Lambda, \mathcal{O})$
   while $\mathcal{E}(\mathcal{H}) \neq \mathbf{T}$ **do**
      $w \leftarrow$ GetCounterexample$(\mathcal{H})$
      $T, S_\Lambda \leftarrow$ ProcessCounterexample$(T, S_\Lambda, w, \mathcal{O})$
      $\mathcal{H} \leftarrow$ GetSFAModel$(T, S_\Lambda, \mathcal{O})$
   return H

---

model is generated, we check for equivalence and, given a counterexample, we
either update the classification tree with a new state and a corresponding distinguishing string, or propagate the counterexample into one of the instances of the
algebra learning algorithm Λ. The structure of MAT^* is shown in Algorithm 1.
In the rest of the section, we use the s-FA in Fig. 1 as a running example for our
algorithm.

3.1 The Classification Tree

The main data structure used by our learning
algorithm is the classification tree (CT) [17]. The
classification tree is a tree data structure used to
store the access and distinguishing strings for the
target s-FA so that all internal nodes of the tree
are labelled using a distinguishing string while
all leafs are labeled using access strings.

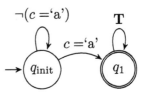

Fig. 1. An s-FA over equality algebra.

Definition 2. *A classification tree $T = (V, L, E)$ is a binary tree such that:*

- $V \subset \Sigma^*$ *is the set of nodes.*
- $L \subset V$ *is the set of leafs.*
- $E \subset V \times V \times \mathbb{B}$ *is the transition relation. For $(v, u, b) \in E$, we say that v is
  the parent of u and furthermore, if $b = \mathbf{T}$ (resp. $b = \mathbf{F}$) we say that u is the
  $\mathbf{T}$-child (resp. $\mathbf{F}$-child).*

Intuitively, given any internal node $v \in V$, any leaf l_T reached by following the
$\mathbf{T}$-child of v can be distinguished from any leaf l_F reached by the $\mathbf{F}$-child using
v. In other words, the membership queries for $l_T v$ and $l_F v$ produce different
results—i.e., $\mathcal{O}(l_T v) \neq \mathcal{O}(l_F v)$.

Tree Initialization. To initialize the CT data structure, we use a membership
query on the empty word ϵ. Then, we create a CT with two nodes, a root node
labeled with ϵ and one child also labeled with ϵ. The child of the root is either
a $\mathbf{T}$-child or $\mathbf{F}$-child, according to the result of the $\mathcal{O}(\epsilon)$ query.

The `sift` *Operation.* The main operation performed using the classification tree
is an operation called `sift` which allows one to determine, for any input word s,

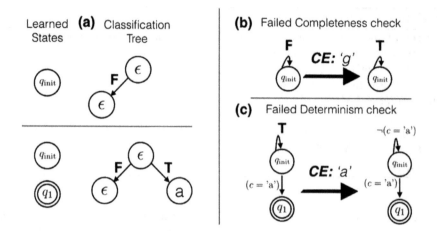

Fig. 2. (left) Classification tree and corresponding learned states for our running example. (right) Two different instances of failed partition verification checks that occured during learning and their respective updates on the given counterexamples (CE).

the state reached by s in the target s-FA. The $\mathtt{sift}(s)$ operation performs the following steps:

1. Set the current node to be the root node of the tree and let w be the label at the root. Perform a membership query on the word sw.
2. Let $b = \mathcal{O}(sw)$. Select the b-child of the current node and repeat step 2 until a leaf is reached.
3. Once a leaf is reached, return the access string with which the leaf is labelled.

Note that, until both children of the root node are added, we will have inputs that may not end up in any leaf node. In these cases our $\mathtt{sift}$ operation will return $\bot$ and MAT^* will add the queried input as a new leaf in the tree.

Once a classification tree is obtained, we use it to simulate a membership oracle for the underlying algebra learning algorithm Λ. This oracle is then used to infer models for the transitions and eventually construct an s-FA model. In Fig. 2 we show the classification tree and the corresponding states learned by the MAT^* algorithm during the execution on our running example from Fig. 1.

3.2 Building an s-FA Model

Assume we are given a classification tree $T = (V, L, E)$. Our next task is to use the tree along with the underlying algebra learning algorithm Λ to produce an s-FA model. The main idea is to spawn an instance of the Λ algorithm for each potential transition and then use the classification tree to answer membership queries posed by each Λ instance. Initially, we define an s-FA $\mathcal{H} = (\mathcal{A}, Q_{\mathcal{H}}, q_\epsilon, F_{\mathcal{H}}, \Delta_{\mathcal{H}})$, where $Q_{\mathcal{H}} = \{q_s \mid s \in L\}$—i.e. we create one state for each leaf of the classification tree T. Finally, for any $q \in Q_{\mathcal{H}}$, we have that $q \in F_{\mathcal{H}}$ if and only if $\mathcal{O}(q) = \mathbf{T}$. Next, we will show how to build the transition relation for $\mathcal{H}$. As mentioned above, our construction is based on the idea of spawning instances of Λ for each potential transition of the s-FA and then using the classification tree to decide, for each character, if the character satisfies the guard of the potential transition thus answering membership queries performed by the underlying algebra learner.

Guard Inference. To infer the set of guards in the transition relation $\Delta_{\mathcal{H}}$, we spawn, for each pair of states $(q_u, q_v) \in Q_{\mathcal{H}} \times Q_{\mathcal{H}}$, an instance $\Lambda^{(q_u, q_v)}$ of the algebra learning algorithm. We answer membership queries to $\Lambda^{(q_u, q_v)}$ as follows. Let $\alpha \in \mathfrak{D}$ be a symbol queried by $\Lambda^{(q_u, q_v)}$. Then, we return **T** as the answer to $\mathcal{O}(\alpha)$ if $\mathtt{sift}(u\alpha) = v$ and **F** otherwise. Once $\Lambda^{(q_u, q_v)}$ submits an equivalence query $\mathcal{E}(\phi)$ using a model ϕ, we suspend the execution of the algorithm and add the transition (q_u, ϕ, q_v) in $\Delta_{\mathcal{H}}$.

Partition Verification. Once all algebra learners have submitted a model through an equivalence query, we have a complete transition relation $\Delta_{\mathcal{H}}$. However, at this point there is no guarantee that for each state q the outgoing transitions from q form a partition of the domain $\mathfrak{D}$. Therefore, it may be the case that our s-FA model $\mathcal{H}$ is in fact non-deterministic and, moreover, that certain symbols do not satisfy any guard. Using such a model in an equivalence query would result in an *improper* learning algorithm and potential problems in the counterexample processing algorithm in Sect. 3.3. To mitigate this issue we perform the following checks:

Determinism check: For each state $q_s \in Q_{\mathcal{H}}$ and each pair of moves $(q_s, \phi_1, q_u), (q_s, \phi_2, q_v) \in \Delta_{\mathcal{H}}$, we verify that $[\![\phi_1 \wedge \phi_2]\!] = \emptyset$. Assume that a character α is found such that $\alpha \in [\![\phi_1 \wedge \phi_2]\!]$ and let $m = \mathtt{sift}(s\alpha)$. Then, it must be the case that the guard of the transition $q_s \rightarrow q_m$ must satisfy α. Therefore, we check if $m = u$ and $m = v$ and provide α as a counterexample to $\Lambda^{(q_s, q_u)}$ and $\Lambda^{(q_s, q_v)}$ respectively if the corresponding check fails.

Completeness check: For each state $q_u \in Q_{\mathcal{H}}$ let $S = \{\phi \mid (q, \phi, p) \in \Delta_{\mathcal{H}}\}$. We check that $[\![\bigvee_{\phi \in S} \phi]\!] = \mathfrak{D}$. If a symbol $h \notin [\![\bigvee_{\phi \in S} \phi]\!]$ is found then, let $v = \mathtt{sift}(uh)$. Following the same reasoning as above, we provide h as a counterexample to $\Lambda^{(q_u, q_v)}$.

These checks are iterated for each state until no more counterexamples are found. In Fig. 2 we demonstrate instances of failed determinism and completeness checks while learning our running example from Fig. 1 along with the corresponding updates on the predicates. For details regarding the equality algebra learner, see Sect. 5.

Optimizing the Number of Algebra Learning Instances. Note that in the description above, MAT^* spawns one instance of Λ for each possible transition between states in $\mathcal{H}$. To reduce the number of spawned algebra learning instances, we perform the following optimization: For each state q_s we initially spawn a single algebra learning instance $\Lambda^{(q_s, ?)}$. Let α be the first symbol queried by $\Lambda^{(q_s, ?)}$ and let $u = \mathtt{sift}(s\alpha)$. We return $\top$ as a query answer for α to $\Lambda^{(q_s, ?)}$ and set the target state for the instance to q_u, i.e. we convert the algebra learning instance to $\Lambda^{(q_s,q_u)}$. Afterwards, we keep a set $R = \{q_v \mid v = \mathtt{sift}(s\beta)\}$ for all $\beta \in \mathfrak{D}$ queried by the different algebra learning instances and generate new instances only for states $q_v \in R$ for which the guards are not yet inferred. Using this optimization, the total number of generated algebra learning instances never exceeds the number of transitions in the target s-FA.

3.3   Processing Counterexamples

For counterexample processing, we adapt the algorithm used in [6] in the setting of MAT^* . In a nutshell, our algorithm works similarly to the classic Rivest-Schapire algorithm [23] and the TTT algorithm [16] for learning DFAs, where a binary search is performed to locate the index in the counterexample where the executions of the model automaton and the target one diverge. However, once this breakpoint index is found, our algorithm performs further analysis to determine if the divergence is caused by an undiscovered state in our model automaton or because the guard predicate that consumes the breakpoint index character is incorrect.

Error Localization. Let w be a counterexample for a model $\mathcal{H}$ generated as described above. For each index $i \in [0..|w|]$, let $q_u = \mathcal{H}[w[..i]]$ be the state accessed by $w[..i]$ in $\mathcal{H}$ and let $\gamma_i = uw[i+1..]$. In other words, γ_i is obtained by first running w in $\mathcal{H}$ for i steps and then, concatenating the access string for the state reached in $\mathcal{H}$ with the word $w[i+1..]$. Note that, because initially the model $\mathcal{H}$ and the target s-FA start at the same state accessed by ϵ, the two machines are synchronized and therefore, $\mathcal{O}(\gamma_0) = \mathcal{O}(w)$. Moreover, since w is a counterexample, we have that $\mathcal{O}(\gamma_{|w|}) \neq \mathcal{O}(w)$. It follows that, there exists an index j, which we will refer to as *breakpoint*, for which $\mathcal{O}(\gamma_j) \neq \mathcal{O}(\gamma_{j+1})$. The counterexample processing algorithm uses a binary search on the index j to find such a breakpoint. For more information on the correctness of this method we refer the reader to [6, 23].

Breakpoint Analysis. Once we find an index j such that $\mathcal{O}(\gamma_j) \neq \mathcal{O}(\gamma_{j+1})$ we can conclude that the transition taken in $\mathcal{H}$ from $\mathcal{H}[w[..j]]$ with the symbol $w[j+1]$ is incorrect. In traditional algorithms for learning DFAs, the sole reason for having an incorrect transition would be that the transition is actually directed to a yet undiscovered state in the target automaton. However, in the symbolic setting we have to explore two different possibilities. Let $q_u = \mathcal{H}[w[..j]]$ be the state accessed in $\mathcal{H}$ by $w[..j]$, $q_v = \mathtt{sift}(uw[j+1])$ be the result of sifting $uw[j+1]$ in the classification tree and consider the transition $(q_u, \phi, q_v) \in \Delta_\mathcal{H}$. We use the guard ϕ to determine if the counterexample was caused by an invalid predicate guard or an undiscovered state in the target s-FA.

Case 1. Incorrect guard. Assume that $w[j+1] \notin \llbracket \phi \rrbracket$. Note that, ϕ was generated as a model by $\Lambda^{(q_u,q_v)}$ and therefore, a membership query from $\Lambda^{(q_u,q_v)}$ for a character α returns **T** if $\mathtt{sift}(u\alpha) = v$. Moreover, we have that $\mathtt{sift}(uw[j+1]) = v$. Therefore, if $w[j+1] \notin \llbracket \phi \rrbracket$, then $w[j+1]$ is a counterexample for the learning instance $\Lambda^{(q_u,q_v)}$ which produced ϕ. We proceed to supply $\Lambda^{(q_u,q_v)}$ with

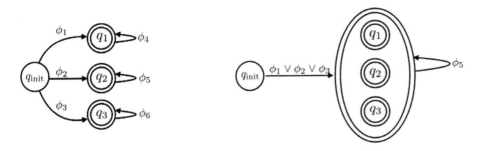

Fig. 3. (left) A minimal s-FA. (right) The s-FA corresponding to the classification tree of MAT^* with access strings for q_{init} and q_2 and a single distinguishing string ϵ.

the counterexample $w[j+1]$, update the corresponding guard and continue to generate a new s-FA model.

Case 2. Undiscovered state. Assume $w[j+1] \in [\![\phi]\!]$. It follows that ϕ is behaving as expected on the symbol $w[j+1]$ based on the current classification tree. We conclude that the state accessed by $w[..j+1]$ is in fact an undiscovered state in the target s-FA which we have to distinguish from the previously discovered states. Therefore, we proceed to add a new leaf in the tree to access this state. More specifically, we replace the leaf labelled with v with a sub-tree consisting of three nodes: the root is the word $w[j+1..]$, which is the distinguishing string for the states accessed by v and $uw[j+1]$. The **T**-child and **F**-child of this node are labelled with the words v and $uw[j]$ based on the results of $\mathcal{O}(v)$ and $\mathcal{O}(uw[j+1])$.

Finally, we have to take care of one last point: Once we add another state in the classification tree, certain queries that were previously directed to v may be directed to $uw[j]$ once we sift them down in the tree. This change implies that certain previous queries performed by algebra learning instances $\Lambda^{(q_s, q_v)}$ may be given invalid results and therefore, we can no longer guarantee correctness of the generated predicates. To solve this problem, we terminate all instances $\Lambda^{(q_s, q_v)}$ for all $q_s \in Q_{\mathcal{H}}$ and replace them with fresh instances of the algebra learning algorithm.

4   Correctness and Completeness of MAT^*

Given a learning algorithm Λ, we use $C_{\mathrm{m}}^{\Lambda}(n)$ to denote the number of membership queries and $C_{\mathrm{e}}^{\Lambda}(n)$ to denote the number of equivalence queries performed by Λ for a target concept with representation size n. In our analysis we will also use the following definitions:

Definition 3. *Let* $\mathcal{M} = (\mathcal{A}, Q, q_0, F, \Delta)$ *over a Boolean algebra* $\mathcal{A}$ *and let* $S \subseteq \Psi_{\mathcal{A}}$. *Then, we define:*

– *The maximum size of the union of predicates in* S *as* $\mathcal{U}(S) \stackrel{def}{=}$ $\max_{\Phi \subseteq S} |\bigvee_{\phi \in \Phi} \phi|$.

- *The maximum guard union size for $\mathcal{M}$ as $\mathcal{B}(\mathcal{M}) \overset{\text{def}}{=} \max_{q \in Q} \mathcal{U}(\textbf{guard}(q))$.*

The value $\mathcal{B}(\mathcal{M})$ denotes the maximum size that a predicate guard may take in any intermediate hypothesis produced by MAT^* during the learning process. Contrary to traditional L^*-style algorithms, the size of the intermediate hypothesis produced by MAT^* may fluctuate as we demonstrate in the following example.

Example 2. Consider the s-FA in the left side of Fig. 3. When we execute the MAT^* algorithm in this s-FA, and after an access string for q_2 is added to the classification tree, the tree will correspond to the s-FA shown on the right, in which the transition from q_{init} is taken over the union of the individual transitions in the target. Certain sequences of answers to equivalence queries can force MAT^* to first learn a correct model of $\phi_1 \vee \phi_2 \vee \phi_3$ before revealing a new state in the target s-FA.

We now state the correctness and query complexity of our algorithm.

Theorem 1. *Let $\mathcal{M} = (\mathcal{A}, Q, q_0, F, \Delta)$ be an s-FA, Λ be a learning algorithm $\mathcal{A}$ and let $k = \mathcal{B}(\mathcal{M})$. Then, MAT^* will learn $\mathcal{M}$ using Λ with $O(|Q|^2|\Delta|\mathcal{C}_m^\Lambda(k) + |Q|^2|\Delta|\mathcal{C}_e^\Lambda(k)\log m)$ membership and $O(|Q||\Delta|\mathcal{C}_e^\Lambda(k))$ equivalence queries, where m is the length of the longest counterexample given to MAT^*.*

Proof. First, we note that our counterexample processing algorithm only splits a leaf if there exists a valid distinguishing condition separating the two newly generated leafs. Therefore, the number of leafs in the discrimination tree is always at most $|Q|$. Next, note that each counterexample is processed using a binary search with complexity $O(\log m)$ to detect the breakpoint and, afterwards, either a new state is added or a counterexample is dispatched to the corresponding algebra learner.

Each classification tree $T = (V, L, E)$ defines a partition over $\mathfrak{D}^*$ and, therefore, an s-FA $\mathcal{H}_T$. In the worst case, MAT^* will learn $\mathcal{H}_T$ exactly before a new state in the target s-FA is revealed through an equivalence query. Since $\mathcal{H}_T$ is the result of merging states in the target s-FA, we conclude that the size of each predicate in $\mathcal{H}_T$ is at most k. It follows that, for each classification tree T, we can get at most $|\Delta_{\mathcal{H}_T}|\mathcal{C}_e^\Lambda(k)$ counterexamples until a new state is uncovered on the target s-FA. Note here, that our counterexample processing algorithm ensures that each counterexample will be either a valid counterexample for a predicate guard in $\mathcal{H}_T$ or it will uncover a new state. For each membership query performed by an underlying algebra learner, we have to sift a string in the classification tree which requires at most $|Q|$ membership queries. Therefore, the total number of membership queries performed for each candidate model $\mathcal{H}$ is bounded by $O(|\Delta|(|Q|\mathcal{C}_m^\Lambda(k) + \mathcal{C}_e^\Lambda(k))\log m)$ where m is the size of the longest counterexample so far. The number of equivalence queries is bounded by $O(|\Delta|\mathcal{C}_e^\Lambda(k))$. When a new state is uncovered, we assume that, in the worst case, all the algebra learners will be restarted (this is an overestimation) and therefore, the same process will be repeated at most $|Q|$ times giving us the stated bounds.

Note that the bounds on the number of queries stated in Theorem 1 are based on the worst-case assumption that we may have to restart *all* guard learning instances each time we discover a new state. In practice, we expect these bounds to be closer $O(|\Delta|\mathcal{C}_{\mathrm{m}}^{\Lambda}(k) + (|\Delta|\mathcal{C}_{\mathrm{e}}^{\Lambda}(k) + |Q|) \log m)$ membership and $O(|\Delta|\mathcal{C}_{\mathrm{e}}^{\Lambda}(k) + |Q|)$ equivalence queries.

Minimality of Learned s-FA. Since the MAT^* will only add a new state in the s-FA if a distinguishing sequence is found it follows that the total number of states in the s-FA is minimal. Moreover, MAT^* will not modify in any way the predicates returned by the underlying algebra learning instances. Therefore, if the size of the predicates returned by the Λ instances is minimal, MAT^* will maintain their minimality.

The following theorem shows that it is indeed not possible to learn s-FAs over a Boolean algebra that is not itself learnable.

Theorem 2. *Let $\Lambda^{s\text{-}FA}$ be an efficient learning algorithm for the algebra of s-FAs over a Boolean algebra $\mathcal{A}$. Then, the Boolean algebra $\mathcal{A}$ is efficiently learnable.*

Which s-FAs Are Efficiently Learnable? Theorem 2 shows that efficient learnability of an s-FA requires efficient learnability of the underlying algebra. Moreover, from Theorem 1 it follows that efficiently learnability using MAT^* depends on the following property of the underlying algebra:

Corollary 1. *Let $\mathcal{A}$ be an efficiently learnable Boolean algebra and consider the class $\mathcal{R}_{\mathcal{A}}^{s\text{-}FA}$ of s-FAs over $\mathcal{A}$. Then, $\mathcal{R}_{\mathcal{A}}^{s\text{-}FA}$ is efficiently learnable using MAT^* if and only if, for any set $S \subseteq \Psi_{\mathcal{A}}$ such that for any distinct $\phi, \psi \in S \implies [\![\phi \wedge \psi]\!] = \emptyset$, we have that $\mathcal{U}(S) = poly(|S|, \max_{\phi \in S} |\phi|)$.*

At this point we would like to point out that the above condition arises due to the fact that MAT^* is a congruence-based algorithm which successively computes hypothesis automata based on refining a set of access and distinguishing strings which is a common characteristic among all L^*-based algorithms. Therefore, this limitation of MAT^* is expected to be shared by any other algorithm in the same family. Given the fact that after three decades of research, L^*-based algorithms are the only known, provably efficient algorithms for learning DFAs (and subsequently s-FAs), we expect that expanding the class of learnable s-FAs is a very challenging task.

5   Learnable Boolean Algebras

We will now describe a number of interesting effective Boolean algebras which are efficiently learnable using membership and equivalence queries.

Boolean Algebras Over Finite Domains. Let $\mathcal{A}$ be any Boolean Algebra over a finite domain $\mathfrak{D}$. Then, any predicate $\phi \in \Psi$ can be learned using $|\mathfrak{D}|$ membership queries. More specifically, the learning algorithm constructs a predicate ϕ

accepting all elements in $\mathfrak{D}$ for which the membership queries return true as $\phi = \{c \mid c \in \mathfrak{D} \land \mathcal{O}(c) = \mathbf{T}\}$. Plugging this algebra learning algorithm into our algorithm, we get the TTT learning algorithm for DFAs without discriminator finalization [16]. This simple example demonstrates that algorithms for DFAs can be viewed as special cases of our s-FA learning algorithm for finite domains.

Equality Algebra. Consider the equality algebra defined in Example 1. Predicates in this algebra of size $|\phi| = k$ can be learned using $2k$ equivalence queries and no membership queries. Initially, the algorithm outputs the empty set $\bot$ as a hypothesis. In any subsequent step, the algorithm keeps a list of the counterexamples obtained so far in two sets $P, N \subseteq \mathfrak{D}$ such that P holds all the positive examples received so far and N holds all the negative examples. Afterwards, the algorithm finds the smallest hypothesis consistent with the counterexamples given. This hypothesis can be found efficiently as follows:

1. If $|P| > |N|$ then, $\phi = \lambda c. \neg(\bigvee_{d \in N} c = d)$.
2. If $|P| \leq |N|$ then, $\phi = \lambda c. (\bigvee_{d \in P} c = d)$.

It can be easily shown that the algorithm will find a correct hypothesis after at most $2k$ equivalence queries.

Other Algebras. The following Boolean algebras can be efficiently learned using membership and equivalence queries. All these algebras also have approximate fingerprints [3], which means that they are not learnable by equivalence queries alone. Thus, s-FAs over these algebras are not efficiently learnable by previous s-FA learning algorithms [6,11].

BDD algebra. The algebra of ordered binary decision diagrams (OBDDs) is efficiently learnable using a variant of the L* algorithm [22].
Tree automata algebra. Deterministic finite tree automata form an algebra which is also learnable using membership and equivalence queries [13].
s-FA algebra. s-FAs themselves form an effective Boolean algebra and therefore, s-FAs over s-FAs over learnable algebras are also learnable.

6   Evaluation

We have implemented MAT^* in the open-source `symbolicautomata` library [1], as well as the learning algorithms for boolean algebras over finite domains, equality algebras and BDD algebras as discussed in Sect. 5. Our implementation is fully modular: Once an algebra learning algorithm is defined in our library, it can be seamlessly plugged in as a guard learning algorithm for s-FAs. Since MAT^* is also an algebra learning algorithm, this allows us to easily learn automata over automata. All experiments were ran in a Macbook air with an 1.8 GHz Intel Core i5 and 8 GiB of memory. The goal of our evaluation is to answer the following research questions:

Q1: How does MAT^* perform on automata over large finite alphabets? (Subsect. 6.1)

Table 1. Evaluation of MAT^* on regular expressions.

ID	$|Q|$	$|\Delta|$	Memb	Equiv	R-CE	GU	D-CE	C-CE
RE.1	11	35	653	17	19	25	106	78
RE.2	24	113	7203	66	45	87	565	479
RE.3	11	15	483	11	16	16	59	45
RE.4	18	40	1745	17	33	32	188	164
RE.5	25	55	3180	22	48	45	244	211
RE.6	52	155	43737	588	104	640	3102	2953
RE.7	179	658	66477	1486	91	1398	7748	6540
RE.8	115	175	929261	299	206	390	28606	28354
RE.9	144	369	844213	699	261	817	30485	30135
RE.10	175	551	3228102	5346	286	5457	172180	170483
RE.11	6	9	3409	281	14	289	723	710
RE.12	10	14	1367	88	8	86	314	291
RE.13	29	46	20903	743	49	764	2637	2550
RE.14	8	13	5949	365	24	381	854	836
RE.15	8	15	661	82	2	76	228	198

Q2: How does MAT^* perform on automata over algebras that require both membership and equivalence queries? (Subsect. 6.2)
Q3: How does the size of predicates affect the performance of MAT^*? (Subsect. 6.3)

6.1 Equality Algebra Learning

In this experiment, we use MAT^* to learn s-FAs obtained from 15 regular expressions drawn from 3 domains: (1) Regular expressions used in web application sanitization frameworks such as in the CodeIgniter framework, (2) Regular expressions drawn from popular web application firewall ModSecurity and finally (3) Regular expressions from [18]. For this set of experiments we utilize as alphabet the entire UTF-16 (2^{16} characters) and used the equality algebra to represent predicates. Since the alphabet is finite, we also tried learning the same automata using TTT [16], the most efficient algorithm for learning finite automata over finite alphabets.

Results. Table 1 presents the results of MAT^*. The **Memb** and **Equiv** columns present the number of distinct membership and equivalence queries respectively. The **R-CE** column shows how many times a counterexample was reused, while the **GU** column shows the number of counterexamples that were used to update an underlying predicate (as opposed to adding a new state in the s-FA). Finally, **D-CE** shows the number of counterexamples provided to an underlying algebra learner due to failed determinism checks, while **C-CE** shows the number of counterexamples due to failed completeness checks. Note that these counterexamples did not require invoking the equivalence oracle.

Given the large alphabet sizes, TTT runs out of memory on all our benchmarks. This is not surprising since the number of queries required by TTT just to construct the *correct* model for a DFA with $128 = 2^7$ states is at least $|\Sigma||Q|\log|Q| = 2^{16} * 2^7 * 7 \approx 2^{26}$. We point out that a corresponding lower bound of $\Omega(|Q|\log|Q||\Sigma|)$ exists for the number of queries any DFA algorithm may perform and therefore, the size of the alphabet provides a fundamental limitation for any such algorithm.

Analysis. First, we observe that the performance of the algorithm is not always monotone in the number of states or transitions of the s-FA. For example, RE.10 requires more than 10x more membership and equivalence queries than RE.7 despite the fact that both the number of states and transitions of RE.10 are smaller. In this case, RE.10 has fewer transitions, but they contain predicates that are harder to learn—e.g., large character classes. Second, the completeness check and the corresponding counterexamples are not only useful to ensure that the generated guards form a partition but also to restore predicates after new states are discovered. Recall that, once we discover (split) a new state, a number of learning instances is discarded. Usually, the newly created learning instances will simply output $\perp$ as the initial hypothesis. At this point, completeness counterexamples are used to update the newly created hypothesis accordingly and thus save the MAT^* from having to rerun a large number of equivalence queries. Finally, we point out that the equality algebra learner made no special assumptions on the structure of the predicates such as recognizing character classes which are used in regular expressions and others. We expect that providing such heuristics can greatly improve the performance MAT^* in these benchmarks.

6.2   BDD Algebra Learning

In this experiment, we use MAT^* to learn s-FAs over a BDD algebra. We run MAT^* on 1,500 automata obtained by transforming Linear Temporal Logic over finite traces into s-FAs [9]. The formulas have 4 atomic propositions and the height in each BDD used by the s-FAs is four. To learn the underlying BDDs we use MAT^* with the learning algorithm for algebras over finite domains (see Sect. 5) since ordered BDDs can be seen as s-FAs over $\mathfrak{D} = \{0, 1\}$.

Figure 4 shows the number of membership (top left) and equivalence (top right) queries performed by MAT^* for s-FAs with different number of states. For this s-FAs, MAT^* is highly efficient with respect to both the number of membership and equivalence queries, scaling linearly with the number of states. Moreover, we note that the size of the set of transitions $|\Delta|$ does not drastically affect the overall performance of the algorithm. This is in agreement with the results presented in the previous section, where we argued that the difficulty of the underlying predicates and not their number is the primary factor affecting performance.

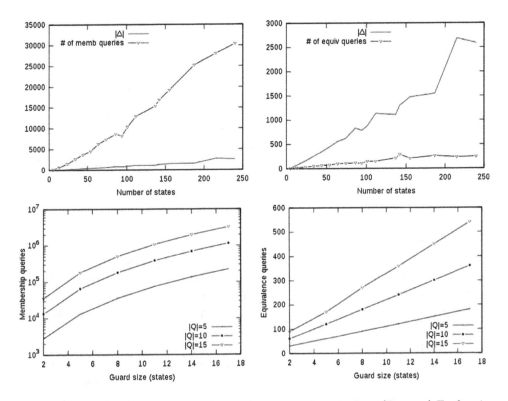

Fig. 4. (Top) Evaluation of MAT^* on s-FAs over a BDD algebra. (Bottom) Evaluation of MAT^* on s-FAs over an s-FA algebra. For an s-FA $\mathcal{M}_{m,n}$, the x-axis denotes the values of n. Different lines correspond to different values of m.

6.3 s-FA Algebra Learning

In this experiment, we use MAT^* to learn 18 s-FAs over s-FAs, which accept strings of strings. We evaluate the scalability of our algorithms when the difficulty of learning the underlying predicates increases. The possible internal s-FAs, which we will use as predicates, operate over the equality algebra and are denoted as I_k (where $2 \leq k \leq 17$). Each s-FA I_k accepts exactly one word $a \cdots a$ of length k and has $k+1$ states and $2k+1$ transitions. The external s-FAs are denoted as $\mathcal{M}_{m,n}$ (where $m \in \{5, 10, 15\}$ and $2 \leq n \leq 17$). Each s-FA $\mathcal{M}_{m,n}$ accepts exactly one word $s \cdots s$ of length m where each s is accepted by I_n.

Analysis. For simplicity, let's assume that we have the s-FA $\mathcal{M}_{n,n}$. Consider a membership query performed by one of the underlying algebra learning instances. Answering the membership query requires sifting a sequence in the classification tree of height at most n which requires $O(n)$ membership queries. Therefore, the number of membership queries required to learn each individual predicate is increased by a factor of $O(n)$. Moreover, for each equivalence query performed by an algebra learning instance, the s-FA learning algorithm has to pinpoint the counterexample to the specific algebra learning instance, a process which requires $\log m$ membership queries, where m is the length of the counterexample.

Therefore, we conclude that each underlying guard with n states will require a number of membership queries which is of the order of $O(n^3)$ at the worst and $O(n^2 \log n)$ queries at the best (since the CT has height $\Omega(\log n)$), ignoring the queries required for counterexample processing.

Figure 4 shows the number of membership (bottom left) and equivalence (bottom right) queries, which verify the theoretical analysis presented in the previous paragraph. Indeed, we see that in terms of membership queries, we have a very sharp increase in the number of membership queries which is in fact about quadratic in the number of states in the underlying guards. On the other hand, equivalence queries are not affected so drastically, and only increase linearly.

7   Related Work

Learning Finite Automata. The L* algorithm proposed by Dana Angluin [3] was the first to introduce the notion of minimally adequate teacher—i.e., learning using membership and equivalence queries—and was also the first for learning finite automata in polynomial time. Following Angluin's result, L* has been studied extensively [16,17], it has been extended to many other models—e.g., to nondeterministic automata [12] alternating automata [4]—and has found many applications in program analysis [2,5–7,24] and program synthesis [25]. Since finite automata only operate over finite alphabets, all the automata that can be learned using variants of L*, can also be learned using MAT^*.

Learning Symbolic Automata. The problem of scaling L^* to large alphabets was initially studied outside the setting of s-FAs using alphabet abstractions [14,15]. The first algorithm for symbolic automata over ordered alphabets was proposed in [20] but the algorithm assumes that the counterexamples provided to the learning algorithm are of minimal length. Argyros et al. [6] proposed the first algorithm for learning symbolic automata in the standard MAT model and also described the algorithm to distinguish counterexamples leading to new states from counterexamples due to invalid predicates which we adapt in MAT^*. Drews and D'Antoni [11] proposed a symbolic extension to the L^*algorithm, gave a general definition of learnability and demonstrated more learnable algebras such as union and product algebras. The algorithms in [6,11,19] are all extensions of L^* and assume the existence of an underlying learning algorithm capable of learning partitions of the domain from counterexamples. MAT^* does not require that the predicate learning algorithms are able to learn partitions, thus allowing to easily plug existing learning algorithms for Boolean algebras. Moreover, MAT^* allows the underlying algebra learning algorithms to perform both equivalence and membership queries, a capability not present in any previous work, thus expanding the class of s-FAs which can be efficiently learned.

Learning Other Models. Argyros et al. [6] and Botincan et al. [7] presented algorithms for learning restricted families of symbolic transducers—i.e., symbolic automata with outputs. Other algorithms can learn nominal [21] and register automata [8]. In these models, the alphabet is infinite but not structured (i.e., it does not form a Boolean algebra) and characters at different positions can be compared using binary relations.

Acknowledgements. The authors would like to thank the anonymous reviewers for their valuable comments. Loris D'Antoni was supported by National Science Foundation Grants CCF-1637516, CCF-1704117 and a Google Research Award. George Argyros was supported by the Office of Naval Research (ONR) through contract N00014-12-1-0166.

References

1. lorisdanto/symbolicautomata: Library for symbolic automata and symbolic visibly pushdown automata. https://github.com/lorisdanto/symbolicautomata/. Accessed 29 Jan 2018
2. Alur, R., Černý, P., Madhusudan, P., Nam, W.: Synthesis of interface specifications for java classes. SIGPLAN Not. **40**(1), 98–109 (2005)
3. Angluin, D.: Learning regular sets from queries and counterexamples. Inf. Comput. **75**(2), 87–106 (1987)
4. Angluin, D., Eisenstat, S., Fisman, D.: Learning regular languages via alternating automata. In: Proceedings of the 24th International Conference on Artificial Intelligence, IJCAI 2015, pp. 3308–3314. AAAI Press (2015)
5. Argyros, G., Stais, I., Jana, S., Keromytis, A.D., Kiayias, A.: SFADiff: automated evasion attacks and fingerprinting using black-box differential automata learning. In: Proceedings of the 2016 ACM SIGSAC Conference on Computer and Communications Security, pp. 1690–1701. ACM (2016)
6. Argyros, G., Stais, I., Kiayias, A., Keromytis, A.D.: Back in black: towards formal, black box analysis of sanitizers and filters. In: IEEE Symposium on Security and Privacy, SP 2016, 22–26 May 2016, San Jose, CA, USA, pp. 91–109 (2016)
7. Botincan, M., Babic, D.: Sigma*: symbolic learning of input-output specifications. In: The 40th Annual ACM SIGPLAN-SIGACT Symposium on Principles of Programming Languages, POPL 2013, 23–25 January 2013, Rome, Italy, pp. 443–456 (2013)
8. Cassel, S., Howar, F., Jonsson, B., Steffen, B.: Active learning for extended finite state machines. Formal Aspects Comput. **28**(2), 233–263 (2016)
9. D'Antoni, L., Kincaid, Z., Wang, F.: A symbolic decision procedure for symbolic alternating finite automata. arXiv preprint arXiv:1610.01722 (2016)
10. D'Antoni, L., Veanes, M.: The power of symbolic automata and transducers. In: Majumdar, R., Kunčak, V. (eds.) CAV 2017. LNCS, vol. 10426, pp. 47–67. Springer, Cham (2017). https://doi.org/10.1007/978-3-319-63387-9_3
11. Drews, S., D'Antoni, L.: Learning symbolic automata. In: Legay, A., Margaria, T. (eds.) TACAS 2017. LNCS, vol. 10205, pp. 173–189. Springer, Heidelberg (2017). https://doi.org/10.1007/978-3-662-54577-5_10
12. García, P., de Parga, M.V., Álvarez, G.I., Ruiz, J.: Learning regular languages using nondeterministic finite automata. In: Ibarra, O.H., Ravikumar, B. (eds.) CIAA 2008. LNCS, vol. 5148, pp. 92–101. Springer, Heidelberg (2008). https://doi.org/10.1007/978-3-540-70844-5_10
13. Habrard, A., Oncina, J.: Learning multiplicity tree automata. In: Sakakibara, Y., Kobayashi, S., Sato, K., Nishino, T., Tomita, E. (eds.) ICGI 2006. LNCS

(LNAI), vol. 4201, pp. 268–280. Springer, Heidelberg (2006). https://doi.org/10.1007/11872436_22

14. Howar, F., Steffen, B., Merten, M.: Automata learning with automated alphabet abstraction refinement. In: Jhala, R., Schmidt, D. (eds.) VMCAI 2011. LNCS, vol. 6538, pp. 263–277. Springer, Heidelberg (2011). https://doi.org/10.1007/978-3-642-18275-4_19

15. Isberner, M., Howar, F., Steffen, B.: Inferring automata with state-local alphabet abstractions. In: Brat, G., Rungta, N., Venet, A. (eds.) NFM 2013. LNCS, vol. 7871, pp. 124–138. Springer, Heidelberg (2013). https://doi.org/10.1007/978-3-642-38088-4_9

16. Isberner, M., Howar, F., Steffen, B.: The TTT algorithm: a redundancy-free approach to active automata learning. In: Bonakdarpour, B., Smolka, S.A. (eds.) RV 2014. LNCS, vol. 8734, pp. 307–322. Springer, Cham (2014). https://doi.org/10.1007/978-3-319-11164-3_26

17. Kearns, M.J., Vazirani, U.V.: An Introduction to Computational Learning Theory. MIT Press, Cambridge (1994)

18. Li, N., Xie, T., Tillmann, N., de Halleux, J., Schulte, W.: Reggae: automated test generation for programs using complex regular expressions. In: 2009 24th IEEE/ACM International Conference on Automated Software Engineering. ASE 2009, pp. 515–519. IEEE (2009)

19. Maler, O., Mens, I.-E.: A generic algorithm for learning symbolic automata from membership queries. In: Aceto, L., et al. (eds.) Models, Algorithms, Logics and Tools. LNCS, vol. 10460, pp. 146–169. Springer, Cham (2017). https://doi.org/10.1007/978-3-319-63121-9_8

20. Mens, I., Maler, O.: Learning regular languages over large ordered alphabets. Log. Methods Comput. Sci. 11(3) (2015)

21. Moerman, J., Sammartino, M., Silva, A., Klin, B., Szynwelski, M.: Learning nominal automata. In: Proceedings of the 44th ACM SIGPLAN-SIGACT Symposium on Principles of Programming Languages (POPL) (2017)

22. Nakamura, A.: An efficient query learning algorithm for ordered binary decision diagrams. Inf. Comput. 201(2), 178–198 (2005)

23. Rivest, R.L., Schapire, R.E.: Inference of finite automata using homing sequences. Inf. Comput. 103(2), 299–347 (1993)

24. Sivakorn, S., Argyros, G., Pei, K., Keromytis, A.D., Jana, S.: HVLearn: automated black-box analysis of hostname verification in SSL/TLS implementations. In: 2017 IEEE Symposium on Security and Privacy (SP), pp. 521–538. IEEE (2017)

25. Yuan, Y., Alur, R., Loo, B.T.: NetEgg: programming network policies by examples. In: Proceedings of the 13th ACM Workshop on Hot Topics in Networks, HotNets-XIII, pp. 20:1–20:7. ACM, New York (2014)

7

Space-Time Interpolants

Goran Frehse[1], Mirco Giacobbe[2(✉)], and Thomas A. Henzinger[2]

[1] Univ. Grenoble Alpes, CNRS, Grenoble INP, VERIMAG, Grenoble, France
[2] IST Austria, Klosterneuburg, Austria
mgiacobbe@ist.ac.at

Abstract. Reachability analysis is difficult for hybrid automata with affine differential equations, because the reach set needs to be approximated. Promising abstraction techniques usually employ interval methods or template polyhedra. Interval methods account for dense time and guarantee soundness, and there are interval-based tools that overapproximate affine flowpipes. But interval methods impose bounded and rigid shapes, which make refinement expensive and fixpoint detection difficult. Template polyhedra, on the other hand, can be adapted flexibly and can be unbounded, but sound template refinement for unbounded reachability analysis has been implemented only for systems with piecewise constant dynamics. We capitalize on the advantages of both techniques, combining interval arithmetic and template polyhedra, using the former to abstract time and the latter to abstract space. During a CEGAR loop, whenever a spurious error trajectory is found, we compute additional space constraints and split time intervals, and use these *space-time interpolants* to eliminate the counterexample. Space-time interpolation offers a lazy, flexible framework for increasing precision while guaranteeing soundness, both for error avoidance and fixpoint detection. To the best of out knowledge, this is the first abstraction refinement scheme for the reachability analysis over *unbounded* and *dense* time of affine hybrid systems, which is both *sound* and *automatic*. We demonstrate the effectiveness of our algorithm with several benchmark examples, which cannot be handled by other tools.

1 Introduction

Formal verification techniques can be used to either provide rigorous guarantees about the behaviors of a critical system, or detect instances of violating behavior if such behaviors are possible. Formal verification has become widely used in the design of software and digital hardware, but has yet to show a similar success for physical and cyber-physical systems. One of the reasons for this is a scarcity of suitable algorithmic verification tools, such as model checkers, which are formally sound, precise, and scale reasonably well. In this paper, we propose a novel verification algorithm that meets these criteria for systems with piecewise affine dynamics. The performance of the approach is illustrated experimentally on a number of benchmarks. Since systems with affine dynamics have been studied before, we first describe why the available methods and tools do not handle this class of systems sufficiently well, and then describe our approach and its core contributions.

Previous Approaches. The algorithmic verification of systems with continuous or discrete-continuous (hybrid) dynamics is a hard problem both in theory and practice. For piecewise constant dynamics (PCD), the continuous successor states (a.k.a. flow pipe) can be computed exactly, and the complexity is exponential in the number of variables [17, 19]. While in principle, any dynamics can be approximated arbitrarily well by PCD systems using an approach called hybridization [20], this requires partitioning of the state space, which often leads to prohibitive computational costs. For piecewise affine dynamics (PWA), one-step successors can be computed approximately using complex set representations. However, all published approaches suffer either from a possibly exponential increase in the complexity of the set representation, or from a possibly exponential increase in the approximation error as the considered time interval increases; this will be argued in detail in Sect. 4.

In addition to these theoretical obstacles, we note the following practical obstacles for the available tools and their performance in experiments. The only available model checkers that are (i) *sound* (i.e., they compute provable dense-time overapproximations), (ii) *unbounded* (i.e., they overapproximate the flow-pipe for an infinite time horizon), and (iii) *arbitrarily precise* (i.e., they support precision refinement) are, with one exception, limited to PCD systems, namely, HyTech [18], PHAVer [13], and Lyse [7]. The tool Ariadne [6] can deal with affine dynamics and is sound, unbounded, and precise. However, Ariadne discretizes the reachable state space with a rectangular grid. This invariably leads to an exponential complexity in terms of the number of variables. Other tools that are applicable to PWA systems do not meet our criteria in that they are either not formally sound (e.g., CORA [2], SpaceEx [15]), not arbitrarily precise because of templates or particular data structures (e.g., SpaceEx, Flow* [8], CORA), or limited to bounded model checking (e.g., dReach [24], Flow*). All the above tools exhibit fatal limitations in scalability or precision on standard PWA benchmarks; they typically work only on well-chosen examples. Note that while these tools do not meet the criteria we advance in this paper, they of course have strengths in other areas handling nonlinear and nondeterministic dynamics.

Our Approach. We view iterative abstraction refinement as critical for soundness and precision management, and fixpoint detection as critical for evaluating unbounded properties. We implement, for the first time, a CEGAR (counterexample-guided abstraction refinement) scheme in combination with a fixpoint detection criterion for PWA systems. Our abstraction refinement scheme manages complexity and precision trade-offs in a flexible way by decoupling time from space: the dense timeline is partitioned into a sequence of intervals that are refined individually and lazily, by splitting intervals, to achieve the necessary precision and detect fixpoints; state sets are overapproximated using template polyhedra that are also refined individually and lazily, by adding normal directions to templates; and both refinement processes are interleaved for optimal results, while maintaining soundness with each step. A similar approach was recently proposed for the limited class of PCA systems [7]; this paper can be seen as an extension of the approach to the class of piecewise affine dynamics.

With each iteration of the CEGAR loop, a spurious counterexample is removed by computing a proof of infeasibility in terms of a sequence of linear constraints in space and interval constraints in time, which we call a sequence of *space-time interpolants*. We use linear programming to construct a suitable sequence of space-time intervals and check for fixpoints. If a fixpoint check fails, we increase the time horizon by adding new intervals. The separation of time from space gives us the flexibility to explore different refinement strategies. Fine-tuning the iteration of space refinement (adding template directions), time refinement (splitting intervals), and fixpoint checking (adding intervals), we find that it is generally best to prefer fewer time intervals over fewer space constraints. Based on performance evaluation, we even expand individual intervals time when this is possible without sacrificing the necessary precision for removing a counterexample.

2 Motivating Example

The ordinary differential equation over the variables x and y

$$\begin{aligned}
\dot{x} &= 0.1x - y + 1.8 \\
\dot{y} &= x + 0.1y - 2.2
\end{aligned} \tag{1}$$

moves counterclockwise around the point $(2, 2)$ in an outward spiral. We center a box B (of side 0.92) on the same point and place a diagonal segment S close to the bottom right corner of B, without touching it (between $(2, 1)$ and $(3.5, 2)$; see Fig. 1). Then, we consider the problem of proving that every trajectory starting from any point in S never hits B. This is a time-unbounded reachability problem for a hybrid automaton with piecewise affine dynamics and two control modes. The first mode has the dynamics above (Eq. 1) and S as initial region. It has a transition to a second mode, which in its turn has B as invariant. The second mode is a bad mode, which all trajectories indeed avoid.

We tackle the reachability problem by abstraction refinement. In particular, we aim at automatically constructing an enclosure for the flowpipe—i.e., for the set of trajectories from S—which (i) avoids the bad state B and (ii) covers the continuous timeline up to infinity. Figure 1 shows three abstractions that result from different strategies for refining an initial space partition (i.e., template) and time partition (i.e., sequence of time intervals). All three refinement schemes start by enclosing S with an initial template polyhedron P, and then transforming P into a sequence of abstract flowpipe sections $\text{intflow}^{[\underline{t},\overline{t}]}(P)$, one for each interval $[\underline{t},\overline{t}]$ of an initial partitioning of the unbounded timeline. The computation of new flowpipe sections stops when a fixpoint is reached,—i.e., we reach a time threshold t^* whose flowpipe section closes a cycle with $\text{intflow}^{t^*}(P) \subseteq P$, sufficient condition for any further flowpipe section to be contained within the union of previously computed sections.

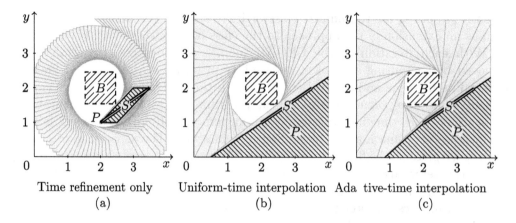

Fig. 1. Comparison of abstraction refinement methods for the ODE in Eq. 1, the segment S as initial region, and the box B as bad region. The polyhedron P is the template polyhedron of S, and the gray polyhedra are the flowpipe sections $\mathrm{intflow}^{[\underline{t},\overline{t}]}(P)$.

Refinement scheme (a) sticks to a fixed octagonal template P—i.e., to the normals of a regular octagon—and iteratively halves all time intervals until every flowpipe section avoids the bad set B. This is achieved at interval width $1/64$, but the computation does not terminate because no fixpoint is reached. Refinement scheme (b) splits time similarly but also computes a different, more accurate template for every iteration: first, an interval $[\underline{t},\overline{t}]$ is halved until it admits a halfspace interpolant —i.e., a halfspace H that $S \subseteq H$ and $\mathrm{intflow}^{[\underline{t},\overline{t}]}(H) \cap B = \emptyset$; then, a maximal set of linearly independent directions is chosen as template from the normals of the obtained halfspaces. Refinement scheme (b) succeeds at interval width $1/16$ to avoid B and reach a fixpoint; the latter at time 6.25, with $\mathrm{intflow}^{6.25}(P) \subseteq P$. Refinement scheme (c) modifies (b) by optimizing the refinement of the time partition: instead of halving time intervals, the maximal intervals which admit halfspace interpolants are chosen. This scheme produces a nonuniform time partitioning with an average interval width of about $1/8$, discovers five template directions, and finds a fixpoint in fewer steps.

Each iteration of the abstraction refinement loop consists of first abstracting the initial region into a template polyhedron, second solving the differential equation into a sequence of interval matrices, and finally transforming the template polyhedron using each of the interval matrices. We represent each transformation symbolically, by means of its support function. Then, we verify (i) the separation between every support function and the bad region, and (ii) the containment of any support function in the initial template polyhedron. The separation problem amounts to solving one LP, and the inclusion problem amounts to solving an LP in each template direction. If the separation fails, then we independently bisect each time that does not admit halfspace interpolants and expand each that does, until all are proven separated. Together, these halfspace interpolants form an infeasibility proof for the counterexample: a space-time interpolant. We forward the resulting new time intervals and halfspaces to the abstraction generator, and repeat, using the refined partitioning and the augmented template. If the inclusion fails, then we increase the time horizon by some amount Δ, and repeat. Once we succeed with both separation and inclusion, the system is proved safe.

This example shows the advantage of lazily refining *both* the space partitioning (i.e., the template) by adding directions, and the time partitioning, by splitting intervals.

3   Hybrid Automata with Piecewise Affine Dynamics

A hybrid automaton with piecewise affine dynamics consists of an n-dimensional vector x of real-valued variables and a finite directed multigraph (V, E), the control graph. We call it the control graph, the vertices $v \in V$ the control modes, and the edges $e \in E$ the control switches. We decorate each mode $v \in V$ with an initial condition $Z_v \subseteq \mathbb{R}^n$, a nonnegative invariant condition $I_v \subseteq \mathbb{R}^n_{\geq 0}$, and a flow condition given by the system of ordinary differential equations

$$\dot{x} = A_v x + b_v. \tag{2}$$

We decorate each switch $e \in E$ with a guard condition $G_e \subseteq \mathbb{R}^n$ and an update condition given the difference equations $x := R_e x + s_e$. All constraints I, G, and Z are conjuctions of rational linear inequalities, A and R are constant matrices, and b and s constant vectors of rational coefficients. In this paper, whenever an indexing of modes and switches is clear from the context, we index the respective constraints and transformations similarly, e.g., we abbreviate A_{v_i} with A_i.

A trajectory is a possibly infinite sequence of states $(v, x) \in V \times \mathbb{R}^n$ repeatedly interleaved first by a switching time $t \in \mathbb{R}_{\geq 0}$ and then by a switch $e \in E$

$$(v_0, x_0) t_0 (v_0, y_0) e_0 (v_1, x_1) t_1 (v_1, y_1) e_1 \ldots \tag{3}$$

for which there exists a sequence of solutions $\psi_0, \psi_1, \ldots : \mathbb{R} \to \mathbb{R}_n$ such that $\psi_i(0) = x_i$, $\psi_i(t_i) = y_i$ and they satisfy (i) the invariant conditions $\psi_i(t) \in I_i$ and (ii) the flow conditions $\dot{\psi}_i(t) = A_i \psi_i(t) + b_i$, for all $t \in [0, t_i]$. Moreover, $x_0 \in Z_0$, every switch e_i has source v_i, destination v_{i+1}, and the respective states satisfy (i) the guard condition $y_i \in G_i$ and (ii) the update $x_{i+1} = R_i y_i + s_i$. The maximal set of its trajectories is the semantics of the hybrid automaton, which is safe if none of them contains a special bad mode.

Every hybrid automaton with affine dynamics can be transformed into an equivalent hybrid automaton with linear dynamics, i.e., the special case where $b = 0$ on every mode. We obtain such transformation by adding one extra variable y, rewriting the flow of every mode into $\dot{x} = Ax + by$, and forcing y to be always equal to 1, i.e., invariant $y = 1$ and flow $\dot{y} = 0$ on every mode and update $y' = y$ on every switch. For this reason, in the following sections we discuss w.l.o.g. the reachability analysis of hybrid automata with linear dynamics.

4   Time Abstraction Using Interval Arithmetic

We abstract the reach set of the hybrid automaton with a union of convex polyhedra. In particular, we abstract the states that are reachable in a mode using a finite sequence of images of the initial region over a *time partitioning*, until a completeness threshold is reached. Thereafter, we compute the *template polyhedron* of each of the images that can take a switch. Then, we repeat in the destination mode and we continue until a fixpoint is found.

Precisely, a time partitioning T is a (possibly infinite) set of disjoint closed time intervals whose union is a single (possibly open) interval. For a finite set of directions $D \subseteq \mathbb{R}^n$, the D-polyhedron of a closed convex set X is the tightest polyhedral enclosure whose facets normals are in D. In the following, we associate every mode v to a template D_v and a time partitioning T_v of the time axis $\mathbb{R}_{\geq 0}$, we employ interval arithmetic for abstracting the continuous dynamics (Sect. 4.1), and on top of it we develop a procedure for hybrid dynamics (Sect. 4.2).

4.1   Continuous Dynamics

We consider w.l.o.g. a mode with ODE reduced to the linear form $\dot{x} = A_v x$, invariant I_v, and a given time interval $[\underline{t}, \overline{t}]$. Every linear ODE $\dot{x} = Ax$ has the unique solution

$$\psi(t) = \exp(At)\psi(0). \tag{4}$$

It follows (see also [16]) that the set of states reachable in v after exactly t time units from an initial region X is

$$\mathrm{flow}_v^t(X) \stackrel{\mathrm{def}}{=} \exp(A_v t)X \cap \bigcap_{0 \leq \tau \leq t} \exp(A_v(t-\tau))I_v, \tag{5}$$

Then, the flowpipe section over the time interval $[\underline{t}, \overline{t}]$ is

$$\mathrm{flow}_v^{[\underline{t}, \overline{t}]}(X) \stackrel{\mathrm{def}}{=} \cup\{\mathrm{flow}_v^t(X) \mid t \in [\underline{t}, \overline{t}]\}. \tag{6}$$

We note three straightforward but consequential properties of the reach set: (i) The accuracy of any convex abstraction depends on the size of the time interval: While $\mathrm{flow}_v^t(X)$ is convex for convex X, this is generally not the case for $\mathrm{flow}_v^{[\underline{t}, \overline{t}]}(X)$. (ii) We can prune the time interval whenever we detect that the reach set no longer overlaps with the invariant: If for any $t^* \geq 0$, $\mathrm{flow}_v^{t^*}(X) = \emptyset$, then for all $\overline{t} \geq t^*$, $\mathrm{flow}_v^{\overline{t}}(X) = \emptyset$ and $\mathrm{flow}_v^{[\underline{t}, \overline{t}]}(X) = \mathrm{flow}_v^{[\underline{t}, t^*]}(X)$. (iii) We can prune the time interval whenever we detect containment in the initial states: If $\mathrm{flow}_v^{t^*}(X) \subseteq X$, then $\mathrm{flow}_v^{[\underline{t}, \infty]}(X) = \mathrm{flow}_v^{[\underline{t}, t^*]}(X)$.

For given A and t, the matrix $\exp(At)$ can be computed with arbitrary, but only finite, accuracy. We resolve this problem by computing a rational interval matrix $[\underline{M}, \overline{M}]$, which we denote $\mathrm{intexp}(A, \underline{t}, \overline{t})$, such that for all $t \in [\underline{t}, \overline{t}]$ we have element-wise that

$$\exp(At) \in \mathrm{intexp}(A, \underline{t}, \overline{t}). \tag{7}$$

This interval matrix can be derived efficiently with a variety of methods [25], e.g., using a guaranteed ODE solver or using interval arithmetic. The width of the interval matrix can be made arbitrarily small at the price of increasing the number of computations and the size of the representation of the rational numbers. In our approach, we do not rely in a fixed accuracy of the interval matrix. Instead, we require that the accuracy increases as the width of the time interval goes to zero. That way, we don't need to introduce an extra parameter. To ensure progress in our refinement loop, we require that the interval matrix decreases monotonically when we split the time interval. Formally, if $[\underline{t}, \overline{t}] \subseteq [\underline{u}, \overline{u}]$ we require the element-wise inclusion $\mathrm{intexp}(A, \underline{t}, \overline{t}) \subseteq \mathrm{intexp}(A, \underline{u}, \overline{u})$. This can be ensured by intersecting the interval matrices with the original interval matrix after time splitting.

While the mapping with interval matrices is in general not convex [29], we can simplify the problem by assuming that all points of X are in the positive orthant. As long as X is bounded from below, this condition can be satisfied by inducing an appropriate coordinate change. Under the assumption that $X \subseteq \mathbb{R}^n_{\geq 0}$,

$$[\underline{M}, \overline{M}](X) = \{y \in \mathbb{R}^n \mid \underline{M}x \leq y \leq \overline{M}x \text{ and } x \in X\}. \tag{8}$$

Combining the above results, we obtain a convex abstraction of the flowpipe over a time interval as

$$\mathrm{intflow}_v^{[\underline{t}, \overline{t}]}(X) \stackrel{\mathrm{def}}{=} \mathrm{intexp}(A, \underline{t}, \overline{t})X \cap I_v. \tag{9}$$

The abstraction is conservative in the sense that $\mathrm{flow}_v^{[\underline{t}, \overline{t}]}(X) \subseteq \mathrm{intflow}_v^{[\underline{t}, \overline{t}]}(X)$. On the other hand, the longer is the time interval, the coarser is the abstraction. For this reason, we construct an abstraction of the flowpipe in terms of a union of convex approximations over a time partitioning. The abstract flowpipe over the time partitioning T is

$$\mathrm{intflow}_v^T(X) \stackrel{\mathrm{def}}{=} \cup\{\mathrm{intflow}_v^{[\underline{t}, \overline{t}]}(X) \mid [\underline{t}, \overline{t}] \in T\}. \tag{10}$$

Again, this is conservative w.r.t. the concrete flowpipe, i.e., for all time partitionings T it holds that $\mathrm{flow}_v^{\cup T}(X) \subseteq \mathrm{intflow}_v^T(X)$. Moreover, it is conservative w.r.t. any refinement of T, i.e., the time partitioning U refines T if $\cup U = \cup T$ and $\forall [\underline{u}, \overline{u}] \in U \colon \exists [\underline{t}, \overline{t}] \in T \colon [\underline{u}, \overline{u}] \subseteq [\underline{t}, \overline{t}]$, then $\mathrm{intflow}_v^U(X) \subseteq \mathrm{intflow}_v^T(X)$.

4.2 Hybrid Dynamics

We embed the flowpipe abstraction routine into a reachability algorithm that accounts for the switching induced by the hybrid automaton. The discrete post operator is the image of a set $Y \subseteq \mathbb{R}^n$ through a switch $e \in E$

$$\mathrm{jump}_e(Y) \stackrel{\mathrm{def}}{=} R_e(Y \cap G_e) \oplus \{s_e\}. \tag{11}$$

We explore the hybrid automaton constructing a set of abstract trajectories, namely sequences abstract states interleaved by time intervals and switches

$$(v_0, X_0)[\underline{t}_0, \overline{t}_0](v_0, Y_0)e_0(v_1, X_1)[\underline{t}_1, \overline{t}_1](v_1, Y_1)e_1 \ldots \tag{12}$$

input : Template $\{D_v\}$ and partitioning $\{T_v\}$ indexed by V
output: Optionally an abstract trajectory (counterexample)

1 **foreach** $v \in V$ *with nonempty* Z_v **do**
2 | push $(v, Z_v)[0, \Delta]$ into the stack W;
3 | add the D_v-polyhedron of Z_v to P_v;

4 **while** W *is not empty* **do**
5 | pop $\ldots (v, X)[\underline{t}, \overline{t}]$ from W;
6 | $P \leftarrow D_v$-polyhedron of X;
7 | **if** v *is bad and* $P \cap I_v$ *is nonempty* **then**   // check counterexample
8 | | **return** $\ldots (v, X)$;
9 | **foreach** $t^* \in \{\underline{t} + \delta, \underline{t} + 2\delta, \ldots, \overline{t}\}$ **do**   // find completeness threshold
10 | | **if** $intflow_v^{t^*}(P) \subseteq P_v$ **then break**;
11 | **if** $t^* = \overline{t}$ *and* $intflow_v^{\overline{t}}(P) \not\subseteq P_v$ **then**   // otherwise extend time horizon
12 | | push $\ldots (v, X)[\overline{t}, \overline{t} + \Delta]$ into W;
13 | **foreach** $[\underline{u}, \overline{u}] \in T_v$ *and* $[\underline{u}, \overline{u}] \cap [\underline{t}, t^*] \neq \emptyset$ **do**   // construct flowpipe
14 | | $Y \leftarrow intflow_v^{[\underline{u}, \overline{u}]}(P)$;
15 | | **foreach** $e \in E$ *with source* v *and destination* v' **do**
16 | | | $X' \leftarrow jump_e(Y)$;
17 | | | **if** $X' \subseteq P_{v'}$ **then continue**;
18 | | | push $\ldots (v, X)[\underline{u}, \overline{u}](v, Y)e(v', X')[0, \Delta]$ into W;
19 | | | add the $D_{v'}$-polyhedron of X' to $P_{v'}$;

Algorithm 1. Reachability procedure.

where $X_0, Y_0, \cdots \subseteq \mathbb{R}^n$ are nonempty sets of states that comply with template $\{D_v\}$ and partitioning $\{T_v\}$ in the following sense. First, $X_0 = Z_0$ and $X_{i+1} = jump_i(Y_i)$ for all $i \geq 0$. Second, $Y_i = intflow_i^{[\underline{t}_i, \overline{t}_i]}(P_i)$ for all $i \geq 0$, where P_i is the D_i-polyhedron of X_i and $[\underline{t}_i, \overline{t}_i] \in T_i$. The maximal set of abstract trajectories, the abstract semantics induced by $\{D_v\}$ and $\{T_v\}$, overapproximates the concrete semantics in the sense that every concrete trajectory (see Eq. 3) has an abstract trajectory that subsumes it, i.e., modes and switches match, $x_i \in X_i$, $t_i \in [\underline{t}_i, \overline{t}_i]$, and $y_i \in Y_i$, for all $i \geq 0$.

Computing the abstraction involves several difficulties. First, the trajectories might be not finitary. Indeed, this is unsolvable in theory, because the reachability problem is undecidable [21]. Second, the post operators are hard to compute. In particular, obtaining the sets X and Y in terms of conjunctions of linear inequalities in $\mathbb{R}^n$ requires eliminating quantifiers. In Algorithm 1, we present a procedure (which does not necessarily terminate) for tackling the first problem. In the next section, we show how to tackle the second using support functions.

We employ Algorithm 1 to explore the tree of abstract trajectories. We store in the stack W the leaves to process $\ldots (v, X)$, followed by a candidate interval $[\underline{t}, \overline{t}]$. For each leaf, we retrieve P, the template polyhedron of X. If it leads to a bad mode, we return, otherwise we search for a completeness threshold t^* between $\underline{t}$ excluded and $\overline{t}$, checking for inclusion in the union of visited polyhedra P_v. In case of failure, we extend the time horizon of Δ and push the next candidate to the stack. Then, we partition the time between $\underline{t}$ and t^*, construct the flowpipe, and process switching. Upon each successful switch, we augment $P_{v'}$ with the $D_{v'}$-polyhedron of the switching region X', avoiding to store redundant polyhedra. Notably, the latter operation is efficient because all polyhedra comply with the same template. For the same reason, we obtain efficient inclusion checks, which we implement by first computing the template polyhedron of the left hand side, and then comparing the constant terms of the respective linear inequalities.

In conclusion, this reachability procedure that takes a template $\{D_v\}$ and a partitioning $\{T_v\}$ and constructs a tree of reachable sets of states X and Y. It manipulates them through the post operators and overapproximate them into template polyhedra. In the next section, we discuss how to efficiently represent X and Y, so to efficiently compute their template polyhedra. In Sect. 6 we discuss how to discover appropriate $\{D_v\}$ and $\{T_v\}$, so to eliminate spurious counterexamples.

5   Space Abstraction Using Support Functions

Abstracting away time left us with the task of representing the state space of the hybrid automaton, namely the space of its variable valuations. Such sets consists of polyhedra emerging from operations such as intersections, Minkowski sums, and linear maps with simple or interval matrices. In this section, we discuss how to represent precisely all sets emerging from any of these operations by means of their support functions (Sect. 5.1) and then how to abstract them into template polyhedra (Sect. 5.2). In the next section, we discuss how to refine the abstraction.

5.1   Support Functions

The support function of a closed convex set $X \subseteq \mathbb{R}^n$ in direction $d \in \mathbb{R}^n$ consists of the maximizer scalar product of d over X

$$\rho_X(d) = \sup\{d^\mathsf{T} x \mid x \in X\}, \tag{13}$$

and, indeed, uniquely represents any closed convex set [28]. Classic work on the verification of hybrid automata with affine dynamic have posed a framework for the construction of support functions from basic set operations, but under the assumption of unboundedness and nonemptiness of the represented set, and with approximated intersection [16]. Indeed, if the set is empty then its support function is $-\infty$, while if it is unbounded an d points toward a direction of recession is $+\infty$, making the framework end up into undefined values. Such conditions turn out to be limiting in our context, first because we find desirable to represent unbounded sets so to accelerate the convergence to a fixpoint of the abstraction procedure, but most importantly because when encoding support functions for long abstract trajectories we might be not aware whether its concretization is infeasible. Checking this is a crucial element of a counterexample-guided abstraction refinement routine.

Recent work on the verification of hybrid automata with constant dynamics, i.e., with flows defined by constraints on the derivative only, provides us with a generalization of the classic support function framework which relaxes away the assumptions of boundedness and nonemptiness and yields precise intersection [7]. The framework encodes combinations of convex sets of states into LP (linear programs) which enjoy strong duality with their support function. Similarly, we encode the support function in direction d of any set X into the LP

$$\begin{aligned} &\text{minimize } c^\mathsf{T}\lambda \\ &\text{subject to } A\lambda = Bd, \end{aligned} \tag{14}$$

over the nonnegative vector of variables λ. The LP is dual to $\rho_X(d)$, which is to say that if the LP is infeasible then X is unbounded in direction d, and if the LP is unbounded then X is the empty set. Moreover, if the LP has bounded solution so does $\rho_X(d)$ and the solutions coincide.

The construction is inductive on operations between sets. For the base case, we recall that from duality of linear programming the support function of a polyhedron given by a system of inequalities $Px \le q$ is dual to the LP over $\lambda \ge 0$

$$\begin{aligned} &\text{minimize } q^\mathsf{T}\lambda \\ &\text{subject to } P^\mathsf{T}\lambda = d. \end{aligned} \tag{15}$$

Then, inductively, we assume that for the set $X \subseteq \mathbb{R}^n$ we are given an LP with the coefficients A_X, B_X, and c_X, and similarly for the set $Y \subseteq \mathbb{R}^n$. For the support functions of $X \oplus Y$, MX, and $X \cap Y$ we respectively construct the following LP over the nonnegative vectors of variables λ, μ, α, and β:

$$\begin{aligned} &\text{minimize } c_X^\mathsf{T}\lambda + c_Y^\mathsf{T}\mu \\ &\text{subject to } A_X\lambda = B_X d \text{ and } A_Y\mu = B_Y d, \end{aligned} \tag{16}$$

$$\begin{aligned} &\text{minimize } c_X^\mathsf{T}\lambda \\ &\text{subject to } A_X\lambda = B_X M^T d, \text{ and} \end{aligned} \tag{17}$$

$$\begin{aligned} &\text{minimize } c_X^\mathsf{T}\lambda + c_Y^\mathsf{T}\mu \\ &\text{subject to } A_X\lambda - B_X(\alpha - \beta) = 0 \text{ and} \\ &\qquad A_Y\mu + B_Y(\alpha - \beta) = B_Y d. \end{aligned} \tag{18}$$

Such construction follows as a special case of [7], which we extend with the support function of a map through an interval matrix.

The time abstraction of Sect. 4 additionally requires us to represent the map of sets of states through interval matrices. Precisely, we are given convex set of nonnegative values $X \subseteq \mathbb{R}^n_{\ge 0}$, the coefficients for the respective LP, an interval matrix $[\underline{M}, \overline{M}] \subseteq \mathbb{R}^{n \times n}$, and we aim at computing the support function of all values in X mapped by all matrices in $[\underline{M}, \overline{M}]$. To this end, we define the LP

$$\begin{aligned} &\text{minimize } c_X^\mathsf{T}\lambda \\ &\text{subject to } A_X\lambda + B_X(\underline{M}^\mathsf{T}\mu - \overline{M}^\mathsf{T}\nu) = 0 \text{ and} \\ &\qquad -\mu + \nu = d, \end{aligned} \tag{19}$$

over the vectors λ, μ, and ν of nonnegative variables. This linear program corresponds to the the dual of the interval matrix map in Eq. 8.

5.2   Computing Template Polyhedra

We represent all space abstractions X and Y in our procedure by their support functions. In particular, whenever set operations are applied, instead of solving the operation by removing quantifiers, we construct an LP. We delay solving it until we need to compute a template polyhedron. In that case, we compute the D-polyhedron of the set X by computing its support function in each of the directions in D, and constructing the intersection of halfspaces $\cap\{d^\mathsf{T}x \leq \rho_X(d) \mid d \in D\}$.

6   Abstraction Refinement Using Space-Time Interpolants

The reachability analysis of hybrid automata by means of the combination of interval arithmetic and support functions presented in Sects. 4 and 5 builds an overapproximation of the system dynamics. It is always sound for safety, but it may produce spurious counterexamples, due to an inherent lack of precision of the time abstraction and the polyhedral approximation. The level of precision is given by two factors, namely the choice of time partitioning and the choice of template directions, excluding the parameters for approximation of the exponential function, which we assume constant (see Sect. 4.1). In the following, we present a procedure to extract infeasibility proofs from spurious counterexamples. We produce them in the form of time partitions and bounding polyhedra, which we call space-time interpolants. Space-time interpolants can then be used to properly refine time partitioning and template directions.

Consider the bounded path $v_0, e_0, v_1, e_1, \ldots, v_k, e_k, v_{k+1}$ over the control graph and a sequence of dwell time intervals $[\underline{t}_0, \overline{t}_0], [\underline{t}_1, \overline{t}_1], \ldots, [\underline{t}_k, \overline{t}_k]$ emerging from an abstract trajectory. We aim at extracting a sequence $X_0, X_1, \ldots, X_{k+1}$ of (possibly nonconvex) polyhedra and a sequence $T_0, T_1, \ldots, T_k$ of refinements of the respective dwell times such that $Z_0 \subseteq X_0$, $\mathrm{jump}_0 \circ \mathrm{intflow}_0^{T_0}(X_0) \subseteq X_1$, $\ldots$, $\mathrm{jump}_k \circ \mathrm{intflow}_k^{T_k}(X_k) \subseteq X_{k+1}$, and $X_{k+1} \cap I_{k+1}$ is empty. In other words, we want every X_{i+1} to contain all states that can enter mode v_{i+1} after dwelling on v_i between $\underline{t}_i$ and $\overline{t}_i$ time, and the last to be separated from the invariant of mode v_{k+1}. Containment is to hold inductively, namely X_{i+1} has to contain what is reachable from X_i, and the time refinements T are to be chosen in such a way that containment holds in the abstraction. Then, we call the sequence $X_0, T_0, X_1, T_1, \ldots, X_k, T_k, X_{k+1}$ a sequence of space-time interpolants for the path and the dwell times above.

We compute a sequence of space-time interpolants by alternating multiple strategies. First, for the given sequence of dwell times, we attempt to extract a sequence of halfspace interpolants using linear programming (Sect. 6.1). In case of failure, we iteratively partition the dwell times in sets of smaller intervals, separating nonswitching from switching times and until every combination of intervals along the path admits halfspace interpolants (Sect. 6.2). We accumulate all halfspaces to form a sequence of unions of convex polyhedra that, together with the obtained time partitionings, will form a valid sequence of space-time interpolants. Finally, we refine the abstraction using the time partitionings and the outwards pointing directions of all computed halfspaces, in order to eliminate the spurious counterexample (Sect. 6.3).

6.1 Halfspace Interpolation

Halfspace interpolants are the special case of space-time interpolants where every polyhedron in the sequence is defined by a single linear inequality [1]. Indeed, they are the simplest kind of space-time interpolants, and, for the same reason, the ones that best generalize the reachable states along the path. Unfortunately, not all paths admit halfspace interpolants, but, if one such sequence exists, then it can be extrapolated from the solution of a linear program.

Consider a path $v_0, e_0, \ldots, v_{k+1}$ with the respective dwell times $[\underline{t}_0, \overline{t}_0], \ldots, [\underline{t}_k, \overline{t}_k]$. A sequence of halfspace interpolants consists of a sequence of sets $H_0, \ldots, H_{k+1}$ among either any halfspace, or the empty set, or the universe, such that $Z_0 \subseteq H_0$, $\mathrm{jump}_0 \circ \mathrm{intflow}_0^{[\underline{t}_0, \overline{t}_0]}(H_0) \subseteq H_1$, $\ldots$, $\mathrm{jump}_k \circ \mathrm{intflow}_k^{[\underline{t}_k, \overline{t}_k]}(H_k) \subseteq H_{k+1}$, and $H_{k+1} \cap I_{k+1}$ is empty. In contrast with general space-time interpolants, every time partition consists of a single time interval and therefore the support function of every post operator $\mathrm{jump} \circ \mathrm{intflow}^{[\underline{t}, \overline{t}]}$ can be encoded into a single LP (see Sect. 5). We exploit the encoding for extracting halfspace interpolants, similarly to a recent interpolation technique for PCD systems [7].

We encode the support function in direction d of the closure of the image of the post operators along the path, i.e., the set $\mathrm{jump}_k \circ \mathrm{intflow}_k^{[\underline{t}_k, \overline{t}_k]} \circ \cdots \circ \mathrm{jump}_0 \circ \mathrm{intflow}_0^{[\underline{t}_0, \overline{t}_0]}(Z_0)$, intersected with the invariant I_{k+1}. We obtain the following LP over the free vectors $\alpha_0, \ldots, \alpha_{k+1}$ and the nonnegative vectors $\beta, \delta_0, \ldots, \delta_k$, $\gamma_0, \ldots, \gamma_{k+1}$, $\mu_0, \ldots, \mu_k$, and $\nu_0, \ldots, \nu_k$:

$$
\begin{aligned}
\text{minimize} \quad & q_{Z_0}^{\mathsf{T}}\beta + \sum_{i=0}^{k}(q_{I_i}^{\mathsf{T}}\gamma_i + q_{G_i}^{\mathsf{T}}\delta_i + s_i^{\mathsf{T}}\alpha_{i+1}) + q_{I_{k+1}}^{\mathsf{T}}\gamma_{k+1} \\
\text{subject to} \quad & P_{Z_0}^{\mathsf{T}}\beta && = \alpha_0, \\
& \underline{M}_i^{\mathsf{T}}\mu_i - \overline{M}_i^{\mathsf{T}}\nu_i && = -\alpha_i && \text{for each } i \in [0..k], \quad (20) \\
& -\mu_i + \nu_i + P_{I_i}^{\mathsf{T}}\gamma_i + P_{G_i}^{\mathsf{T}}\delta_i = R_i^{\mathsf{T}}\alpha_{i+1} && \text{for each } i \in [0..k], \\
& P_{I_{k+1}}^{\mathsf{T}}\gamma_{k+1} && = -\alpha_{k+1} + d,
\end{aligned}
$$

where every system of inequalities $Px \leq q$ corresponds to the constraints of the respective init, guard, or invariant, every $R_i x + s_i$ is an update equation, and every interval matrix $[\overline{M}_i, \underline{M}_i] = \mathrm{intexp}(A_i, \underline{t}_i, \overline{t}_i)$. In general, one can check whether the closure is contained in a halfspace $a^{\mathsf{T}} x \leq b$ by setting the direction to its linear term $d = a$ and checking whether the objective function can equal its constant term b. In particular, we check for emptiness, which we pose as checking inclusion in $0x \leq -1$. Therefore, we set $d = 0$ and the objective function to equal -1. Upon affirmative answer, from the solution $\alpha_0^\star, \alpha_1^\star, \ldots, \nu_k^\star$ we obtain a valid sequence of halfspace interpolants whose i-th linear term is given by $\alpha_i^\star$ and i-th constant term is given by $q_{Z_0}^{\mathsf{T}}\beta^\star + \sum_{j=0}^{i-1}(q_{I_j}^{\mathsf{T}}\gamma_j^\star + q_{G_j}^{\mathsf{T}}\delta_j^\star + s_j^{\mathsf{T}}\alpha_{j+1}^\star)$.

input : sequence of intervals $[\underline{u}_0, \overline{u}_0], \ldots, [\underline{u}_j, \overline{u}_j]$
output: set of intervals

```
 1  b ← u_j;
 2  while b < ū_j do
 3  │   a ← b;
 4  │   b ← b + ε;
 5  │   c ← ū_j;
 6  │   if [u_0, ū_0], …, [u_{j-1}, ū_{j-1}], [a, b] does not admit halfspace interpolants then
 7  │   └   continue;
 8  │   if [u_0, ū_0], …, [u_{j-1}, ū_{j-1}], [a, c] admits halfspace interpolants then
 9  │   │   push [a, c] to the output;
10  │   └   return;
11  │   while c − b > ε do
12  │   │   if [u_0, ū_0], …, [u_{j-1}, ū_{j-1}], [a, ε⌊(b+c)/2ε⌋] admits halfspace interpolants then
13  │   │   │   b ← ε⌊(b+c)/2ε⌋;
14  │   │   else
15  │   │   └   c ← ε⌊(b+c)/2ε⌋;
16  └   push [a, b] to the output;
```

Algorithm 2. Nonswitching time partitioning.

6.2 Time Partitioning

Halfspace interpolation attempts to compute a sequence of enclosures that are convex for a sequence of sets that are not necessarily convex. Specifically, it requires each halfspace to enclose the set of solutions of a linear differential equation, which is nonconvex, by enclosing its convex overapproximation along a whole time interval. As a result, large time intervals produce large overapproximations, on which halfspace interpolation might be impossible. Likewise, shorter intervals produce tighter overapproximations, which are more likely to admit halfspace interpolants. In this section, we exploit such observation to enable interpolation over large time intervals. In particular, we properly partition the time into smaller subintervals and we treat each of them as a halfspace interpolation problem. Later, we combine the results to refine the abstraction.

Time partitioning is a delicate task in the whole abstraction refinement loop. In fact, while template refinement affects linearly the performance of the abstractor, partitioning time intervals that can switch induces branching in the search, possibly leading to an exponential blowup. For this reason, we partition time by narrowing down the switching time, for incremental precision, until no more is left. In particular, we use Algorithm 2 to compute a set N of maximal intervals that admit halfspace interpolants, by enlarging or narrowing them of ε amounts. We embed this procedure in Algorithm 3 which, along the sequence, excludes the time in N, constructing a set of intervals S that overapproximate the switching time. In particular, we construct the set with the widest possible intervals that are disjoint from N. Algorithm 3 succeeds when no more intervals are left, otherwise we half ε and reapply it to the sequences that are left to process.

input : sequence of intervals $[\underline{t}_0, \overline{t}_0], \ldots, [\underline{t}_k, \overline{t}_k]$
output: set of sequences of intervals

1 push $[\underline{t}_0, \overline{t}_0]$ to the queue Q;
2 **while** Q *is not empty* **do**
3   pop $[\underline{u}_0, \overline{u}_0], \ldots, [\underline{u}_j, \overline{u}_j]$ from Q;
4      $N \leftarrow$ nonswitching time partitioning of $[\underline{u}_0, \overline{u}_0], \ldots, [\underline{u}_j, \overline{u}_j]$;
5   **foreach** $[\underline{a}, \overline{a}] \in N$ **do**
6   push $[\underline{u}_0, \overline{u}_0], \ldots, [\underline{u}_{j-1}, \overline{u}_{j-1}], [\underline{a}, \overline{a}]$ to the output;
7   **if** $j = k$ **then**
8   **assert** $[\underline{u}_j, \overline{u}_j] \backslash \cup N = \emptyset$;
9   **continue**;
10     $S \leftarrow$ choose set of intervals that cover $[\underline{u}_j, \overline{u}_j] \backslash \cup N$;
11   **foreach** $[\underline{b}, \overline{b}] \in S$ **do**
12   push $[\underline{u}_0, \overline{u}_0], \ldots, [\underline{u}_{j-1}, \overline{u}_{j-1}], [\underline{b}, \overline{b}], [\underline{t}_{j+1}, \overline{t}_{j+1}]$ to Q;

Algorithm 3. Dwell time partitioning.

6.3 Abstraction Refinement

The procedures above construct sequences of time intervals $[\underline{u}_0, \overline{u}_0], \ldots, [\underline{u}_j, \overline{u}_j]$ that are included in $[\underline{t}_0, \overline{t}_0], \ldots, [\underline{t}_k, \overline{t}_k]$ and that, with the respective halfspace interpolants, this constitutes a proof of infeasibility for the counterexample. Yet, it does not form a sequence of space-time interpolants $X_0, T_0, \ldots, X_{k+1}$. We form each partitioning T_i by splitting $[\underline{t}_i, \overline{t}_i]$ in such a way each element of T_i is either contained in $[\underline{u}_i, \overline{u}_i]$ or disjoint from it, for all intervals $[\underline{u}_i, \overline{u}_i]$. Then, we refine the partitioning of mode v_i similarly. Each polyhedron X_i is a union of convex polyhedra, each of which is the intersection of all halfspaces H_i corresponding to some sequence $[\underline{u}_0, \overline{u}_0], \ldots, [\underline{u}_i, \overline{u}_i]$. Nevertheless, to refine the abstraction we do not need to construct X_i, but just to take the outward point directions of all H_i and add them to the template of v_i.

7 Experimental Evaluation

We implemented our method in C++ using GMP and Eigen for multiple precision linear algebra, Arb for interval arithmetic, and PPL for linear programming [5, 23]. In particular, all libraries we are using are meant to provide guaranteed solutions, as well as our implementation. We evaluate it on several instances of a *filtered oscillator* and a *rod reactor*, which are both parametric in the number of variables, and the latter in the number of modes too [15, 35]. We record several statistics from every execution of our tool: the number #cex of counterexamples found during the CEGAR loop, the number #dir of linearly independent directions and the average width of the time partitionings extracted from all space-time interpolants. Moreover, we independently measure three times. First, the time spent in finding counterexamples, namely the total time taken by inconclusive abstractions which returned a spurious counterexample. Second, the refinement time, that is the total time consumed by computing space-time interpolants. Finally, the verification time, that is the time spend in the last abstraction of the CEGAR loop, which terminates with a fixpoint proving the system safe. We compare the outcome and the performance of our tool against Ariadne which, to the best of our knowledge, is the only verification tool available that is numerically sound and time-unbounded [11].

Table 1. Statistics for the benchmark examples (oot when > 1000 s).

	# vars	# modes	# cex	# dirs	avg. width	cex. time	ref. time	ver. time	tot. time	Ariadne
filtosc_1st_ord	3	4	7	13	0.55	0.57	0.96	0.13	**1.66**	27.56
filtosc_2nd_ord	4	4	7	15	0.55	0.83	1.78	0.20	**2.81**	150.7
filtosc_3rd_ord	5	4	7	16	0.55	1.28	4.65	0.32	**6.25**	oot
filtosc_4th_ord	6	4	7	18	0.55	1.53	11.39	0.37	**13.29**	oot
filtosc_5th_ord	7	4	7	19	0.55	2.61	26.60	0.70	**29.37**	-
filtosc_6th_ord	8	4	7	18	0.55	4.56	101.8	1.29	**107.7**	-
filtosc_7th_ord	9	4	7	18	0.55	4.36	109.9	1.13	**114.6**	-
filtosc_8th_ord	10	4	7	17	0.55	5.92	150.9	1.54	**158.4**	-
filtosc_9th_ord	11	4	7	16	0.55	6.49	383.1	1.83	**391.3**	-
filtosc_10th_ord	12	4	7	17	0.55	12.84	428.87	3.73	**445.4**	-
filtosc_11th_ord	13	4	7	17	0.55	15.10	525.2	4.38	**544.6**	-
reactor_1_rod	2	4	11	3	0.11	5.24	10.64	1.59	**17.47**	oot
reactor_2_rods	3	5	9	7	0.79	5.68	5.36	2.33	**13.37**	oot
reactor_3_rods	4	6	12	13	1.07	14.46	13.94	13.13	**41.53**	-
reactor_4_rods	5	7	15	29	1.67	45.50	42.47	111.5	**199.9**	-
reactor_5_rods	6	8	16	31	1.81	73.77	27.36	696.46	**797.5**	-

The filtered oscillator is hybrid automaton with four modes that smoothens a signal x into a signal z. It has $k + 2$ variables and a system of $k + 2$ affine ODE, where k is the order of the filter. Table 1 shows the results, for a scaling of k up to the 11-th order. The first observation is that the CEGAR loop behaves quite similarly on all scalings: number of counterexamples, number of directions, and time partitionings are almost identical. On the other hand, the computation times show a growth, particularly in the refinement phase which dominates over abstraction and verification. This suggests us that our procedure exploits efficiently the symmetries of the benchmark. In particular, time partitioning seems unaffected. What affects the performance is linear programming, whose size depends on the number of variables of the system.

The rod reactor consists of a heating reactor tank and k rods each of which cools the tank for some amount of time, excluding each other. The hybrid automaton has one variable x for the temperature, k clock variables, one heating mode, one error mode, and k cooling modes. If the temperature reaches a critical threshold and no rod can intervene, it goes into an error. For this benchmark, we start with a simple template, the interval around x, and we discover further directions. Table 1 highlights two fundamental differences with the previous benchmark. First, the average width grows with the model size. This is because the heating mode requires finer time partitioning than the cooling modes. The cooling modes increase with the number of rods, and so does the average width over all time partitions. Second, while with the filtered oscillator the difficulty laid at interpolation, for the rod reactor interpolation is rather easy as well as finding counterexamples. Most of the time is spent in the verification phase, where all fixpoint checks must be concluded, without being interrupted by a counterexample. This shows the advantage of our lazy approach, which first processes the counterexamples and finally proves the fixpoint.

Our method outperforms Ariadne on all benchmarks. On the other hand, tools like Flow* and SpaceEx can be dramatically faster [9]. For instance, they analyze `filtosc_8th_ord` in resp. 9.1 s and 0.36 s (time horizon of 4 and jump depth of 10). This is hardly surprising, as our method has primarily been designed to comply with soundness and time-unboundedness, and pays the price for that.

8   Related Work

There is a rich literature on CEGAR approaches for hybrid automata, either abstracting to a purely discrete system [3,10,27,33,34] or to a hybrid automaton with simpler dynamics [22,30]. Both categories exploit the principle that the verification step is easier to carry out in the abstract domain. The abstraction entails a considerable loss of precision that can only be counteracted by increasing the number of abstract states. This leads to a state explosion that severely limits the applicability of such approaches. In contrast, our approach allows us to increase the precision by adding template directions, which does not increase the number of abstract states. The only case where we incur additional abstract states is when partitioning the time domain. This is a direct consequence of the nonconvexity of flowpipes of affine systems, and therefore seems to be unavoidable when using convex sets in abstractions. In [26], the abstraction consists of removing selected ODE entirely. This reduces the complexity, but does not achieve any fine-tuning between accuracy and complexity. Template reachability has been shown to be very effective in both scaling up reachability tasks to more efficient successor computations [15,31,32] and achieving termination even over unbounded time horizons [12]. The drawback of templates is the lack of accuracy, which may lead to an approximation error that accumulates excessively. Efforts to dynamically refine templates have so far not scaled well for affine dynamics [14]. A single-step refinement was proposed in [4], but as was illustrated in [7], the refinement needs to be inductive in order to exclude counterexamples in a CEGAR scheme.

9   Conclusion

We have developed an abstraction refinement scheme that combines the efficiency and scalability of template reachability with just enough precision to exclude all detected paths to the bad states. At each iteration of the refinement loop, only one template direction is added per mode and time-step. This does not increase the number of abstract states. Additional abstract states are only introduced when required by the nonconvexity of flowpipes of affine systems, a problem that we consider unavoidable. In contrast, existing CEGAR approaches for hybrid automata tend to suffer from state explosion, since refining the abstraction immediately requires additional abstract states. As our experiments confirm, our approach results in templates over very low complexity and terminates with an unbounded proof of safety after a relatively small number of iterations. Further research is required to extend this work to nondeterministic and nonlinear dynamics.

Acknowledgments. We thank Luca Geretti for helping us setting up Ariadne. This research was supported in part by the Austrian Science Fund (FWF) under grants S11402-N23 (RiSE/SHiNE) and Z211-N23 (Wittgenstein Award), by the European Commission under grant 643921 (UnCoVerCPS).

References

1. Albarghouthi, A., McMillan, K.L.: Beautiful interpolants. In: Sharygina, N., Veith, H. (eds.) CAV 2013. LNCS, vol. 8044, pp. 313–329. Springer, Heidelberg (2013). https://doi.org/10.1007/978-3-642-39799-8_22
2. Althoff, M.: An introduction to CORA 2015. In: Frehse, G., Althoff, M. (eds.) ARCH14-15. 1st and 2nd International Workshop on Applied veRification for Continuous and Hybrid Systems. EPiC Series in Computer Science, vol. 34, pp. 120–151. EasyChair (2015)
3. Alur, R., Dang, T., Ivančić, F.: Counterexample-guided predicate abstraction of hybrid systems. Theor. Comput. Sci. **354**(2), 250–271 (2006)
4. Asarin, E., Dang, T., Maler, O., Testylier, R.: Using redundant constraints for refinement. In: Bouajjani, A., Chin, W.-N. (eds.) ATVA 2010. LNCS, vol. 6252, pp. 37–51. Springer, Heidelberg (2010). https://doi.org/10.1007/978-3-642-15643-4_5
5. Bagnara, R., Hill, P.M., Zaffanella, E.: The Parma Polyhedra Library: toward a complete set of numerical abstractions for the analysis and verification of hardware and software systems. Sci. Comput. Program. **72**(1–2), 3–21 (2008)
6. Benvenuti, L., Bresolin, D., Collins, P., Ferrari, A., Geretti, L., Villa, T.: Assume-guarantee verification of nonlinear hybrid systems with Ariadne. Int. J. Robust Nonlinear Control **24**(4), 699–724 (2014)
7. Bogomolov, S., Frehse, G., Giacobbe, M., Henzinger, T.A.: Counterexample-guided refinement of template polyhedra. In: Legay, A., Margaria, T. (eds.) TACAS 2017. LNCS, vol. 10205, pp. 589–606. Springer, Heidelberg (2017). https://doi.org/10.1007/978-3-662-54577-5_34
8. Chen, X., Ábrahám, E., Sankaranarayanan, S.: Taylor model flowpipe construction for non-linear hybrid systems. In: RTSS 2012, pp. 183–192 (2012)
9. Chen, X., Schupp, S., Makhlouf, I.B., Ábrahám, E., Frehse, G., Kowalewski, S.: A benchmark suite for hybrid systems reachability analysis. In: Havelund, K., Holzmann, G., Joshi, R. (eds.) NFM 2015. LNCS, vol. 9058, pp. 408–414. Springer, Cham (2015). https://doi.org/10.1007/978-3-319-17524-9_29
10. Clarke, E., Fehnker, A., Han, Z., Krogh, B., Ouaknine, J., Stursberg, O., Theobald, M.: Abstraction and counterexample-guided refinement in model checking of hybrid systems. Int. J. Found. Comput. Sci. **14**(04), 583–604 (2003)
11. Collins, P., Bresolin, D., Geretti, L., Villa, T.: Computing the evolution of hybrid systems using rigorous function calculus. In: Proceedings of the 4th IFAC Conference on Analysis and Design of Hybrid Systems (ADHS12), Eindhoven, The Netherlands, pp. 284–290, June 2012

12. Dang, T., Gawlitza, T.M.: Template-based unbounded time verification of affine hybrid automata. In: Yang, H. (ed.) APLAS 2011. LNCS, vol. 7078, pp. 34–49. Springer, Heidelberg (2011). https://doi.org/10.1007/978-3-642-25318-8_6
13. Frehse, G.: PHAVer: algorithmic verification of hybrid systems past HyTech. STTT **10**(3), 263–279 (2008)
14. Frehse, G., Bogomolov, S., Greitschus, M., Strump, T., Podelski, A.: Eliminating spurious transitions in reachability with support functions. In: Proceedings of the 18th International Conference on Hybrid Systems: Computation and Control, pp. 149–158. ACM (2015)
15. Frehse, G., Le Guernic, C., Donzé, A., Cotton, S., Ray, R., Lebeltel, O., Ripado, R., Girard, A., Dang, T., Maler, O.: SpaceEx: scalable verification of hybrid systems. In: Gopalakrishnan, G., Qadeer, S. (eds.) CAV 2011. LNCS, vol. 6806, pp. 379–395. Springer, Heidelberg (2011). https://doi.org/10.1007/978-3-642-22110-1_30
16. Le Guernic, C., Girard, A.: Reachability analysis of hybrid systems using support functions. In: Bouajjani, A., Maler, O. (eds.) CAV 2009. LNCS, vol. 5643, pp. 540–554. Springer, Heidelberg (2009). https://doi.org/10.1007/978-3-642-02658-4_40
17. Halbwachs, N., Proy, Y.-E., Raymond, P.: Verification of linear hybrid systems by means of convex approximations. In: Le Charlier, B. (ed.) SAS 1994. LNCS, vol. 864, pp. 223–237. Springer, Heidelberg (1994). https://doi.org/10.1007/3-540-58485-4_43
18. Henzinger, T., Ho, P.H., Wong-Toi, H.: HyTech: a model checker for hybrid systems. Softw. Tools Technol. Transf. **1**, 110–122 (1997)
19. Henzinger, T.A.: The theory of hybrid automata. In: Inan, M.K., Kurshan, R.P. (eds.) Verification of Digital and Hybrid Systems, vol. 170, pp. 265–292. Springer, Heidelberg (2000). https://doi.org/10.1007/978-3-642-59615-5_13
20. Henzinger, T.A., Ho, P.H., Wong-Toi, H.: Algorithmic analysis of nonlinear hybrid systems. IEEE Trans. Autom. Control **43**, 540–554 (1998)
21. Henzinger, T.A., Kopke, P.W., Puri, A., Varaiya, P.: What's decidable about hybrid automata? In: Proceedings of the Twenty-Seventh Annual ACM Symposium on Theory of Computing, 29 May–1 June 1995, Las Vegas, Nevada, USA, pp. 373–382 (1995)
22. Jha, S.K., Krogh, B.H., Weimer, J.E., Clarke, E.M.: Reachability for linear hybrid automata using iterative relaxation abstraction. In: Bemporad, A., Bicchi, A., Buttazzo, G. (eds.) HSCC 2007. LNCS, vol. 4416, pp. 287–300. Springer, Heidelberg (2007). https://doi.org/10.1007/978-3-540-71493-4_24
23. Johansson, F.: Arb: efficient arbitrary-precision midpoint-radius interval arithmetic. IEEE Trans. Comput. **66**, 1281–1292 (2017)
24. Kong, S., Gao, S., Chen, W., Clarke, E.: dReach: δ-reachability analysis for hybrid systems. In: Baier, C., Tinelli, C. (eds.) TACAS 2015. LNCS, vol. 9035, pp. 200–205. Springer, Heidelberg (2015). https://doi.org/10.1007/978-3-662-46681-0_15
25. Moler, C., Van Loan, C.: Nineteen dubious ways to compute the exponential of a matrix, twenty-five years later. SIAM Rev. **45**(1), 3–49 (2003)
26. Nellen, J., Ábrahám, E., Wolters, B.: A CEGAR tool for the reachability analysis of PLC-controlled plants using hybrid automata. In: Bouabana-Tebibel, T., Rubin, S.H. (eds.) Formalisms for Reuse and Systems Integration. AISC, vol. 346, pp. 55–78. Springer, Cham (2015). https://doi.org/10.1007/978-3-319-16577-6_3
27. Ratschan, S., She, Z.: Safety verification of hybrid systems by constraint propagation-based abstraction refinement. ACM Trans. Embed. Comput. Syst. (TECS) **6**(1), 8 (2007)

28. Rockafellar, R.T.: Convex Analysis. Princeton University Press, Princeton (1970)
29. Rohn, J.: Systems of linear interval equations. Linear Algebra Appl. **126**, 39–78 (1989)
30. Roohi, N., Prabhakar, P., Viswanathan, M.: Hybridization based CEGAR for hybrid automata with affine dynamics. In: Chechik, M., Raskin, J.-F. (eds.) TACAS 2016. LNCS, vol. 9636, pp. 752–769. Springer, Heidelberg (2016). https://doi.org/10.1007/978-3-662-49674-9_48
31. Sankaranarayanan, S., Dang, T., Ivančić, F.: Symbolic model checking of hybrid systems using template polyhedra. In: Ramakrishnan, C.R., Rehof, J. (eds.) TACAS 2008. LNCS, vol. 4963, pp. 188–202. Springer, Heidelberg (2008). https://doi.org/10.1007/978-3-540-78800-3_14
32. Sankaranarayanan, S., Sipma, H.B., Manna, Z.: Scalable analysis of linear systems using mathematical programming. In: Cousot, R. (ed.) VMCAI 2005. LNCS, vol. 3385, pp. 25–41. Springer, Heidelberg (2005). https://doi.org/10.1007/978-3-540-30579-8_2
33. Segelken, M.: Abstraction and counterexample-guided construction of ω-automata for model checking of step-discrete linear hybrid models. In: Damm, W., Hermanns, H. (eds.) CAV 2007. LNCS, vol. 4590, pp. 433–448. Springer, Heidelberg (2007). https://doi.org/10.1007/978-3-540-73368-3_46
34. Sorea, M.: Lazy approximation for dense real-time systems. In: Lakhnech, Y., Yovine, S. (eds.) FORMATS/FTRTFT-2004. LNCS, vol. 3253, pp. 363–378. Springer, Heidelberg (2004). https://doi.org/10.1007/978-3-540-30206-3_25
35. Vaandrager, F.: Hybrid systems. Images of SMC Research, pp. 305–316 (1996)

8

Monitoring CTMCs by Multi-clock Timed Automata

Yijun Feng[1], Joost-Pieter Katoen[2]([✉]) [iD], Haokun Li[1]([✉]), Bican Xia[1]([✉]),
and Naijun Zhan[3,4]([✉]) [iD]

[1] LMAM and School of Mathematical Sciences, Peking University, Beijing, China
ker@protonmail.ch, xbc@math.pku.edu.cn
[2] RWTH Aachen University, Aachen, Germany
katoen@cs.rwth-aachen.de
[3] State Key Laboratory of Computer Science, Institute of Software,
Chinese Academy of Sciences, Beijing, China
znj@ios.ac.cn
[4] University of Chinese Academy of Sciences, Beijing, China

Abstract. This paper presents a numerical algorithm to verify continuous-time Markov chains (CTMCs) against multi-clock deterministic timed automata (DTA). These DTA allow for specifying properties that cannot be expressed in CSL, the logic for CTMCs used by state-of-the-art probabilistic model checkers. The core problem is to compute the probability of timed runs by the CTMC $\mathcal{C}$ that are accepted by the DTA $\mathcal{A}$. These likelihoods equal reachability probabilities in an embedded piecewise deterministic Markov process (EPDP) obtained as product of $\mathcal{C}$ and $\mathcal{A}$'s region automaton. This paper provides a numerical algorithm to efficiently solve the PDEs describing these reachability probabilities. The key insight is to solve an ordinary differential equation (ODE) that exploits the specific characteristics of the product EPDP. We provide the numerical precision of our algorithm and present experimental results with a prototypical implementation.

1 Introduction

Continuous-time Markov chains (CTMCs) [17] are ubiquitous. They are used to model safety-critical systems like communicating networks and power management systems, are key to performance and dependability analysis, and naturally describe chemical reaction networks. The algorithmic verification of CTMCs has received quite some attention. Aziz *et al.* [3] proved that verifying CTMCs against CSL (Continuous Stochastic Logic) is decidable. CSL is a probabilistic and timed branching-time logic that allows for expressing properties like "is the probability of a given chemical reaction within 50 time units at least 10^{-3}?". Baier *et al.* [5] gave efficient numerical algorithms for CSL model checking that nowadays provide the basis of CTMC model checking in PRISM [23], MRMC [22] and Storm [15], as well as GreatSPN [2]. Extensions of CSL to cascaded timed-until operators [27], conditional probabilities [19], and (simple) timed regular expressions [4] have been considered.

This paper considers the verification of CTMCs against *linear-time* real-time properties. These include relevant properties in the design of a gas burner [28], like "the probability that the duration of leaking is more than one twentieth over an interval with a length more than 20 s is less than 10^{-6}". Such real-time properties can be conveniently expressed by deterministic timed automata (DTA) [1]. The core problem in the verification of CTMC $\mathcal{C}$ against DTA $\mathcal{A}$ is to compute the probability of $\mathcal{C}$'s timed runs that are accepted by $\mathcal{A}$, i.e. $\Pr(\mathcal{C} \models \mathcal{A})$. Chen *et al.* [10,11] showed that this quantity equals the reachability probability in a piecewise deterministic Markov process (PDP) [14]. This PDP is obtained by taking the product of CTMC $\mathcal{C}$ and the region automaton of $\mathcal{A}$. Computing reachability probabilities in PDPs is a challenge.

Practical implementations of verifying CTMCs against DTA specifications are rare. Barbot *et al.* [7] showed that for *single-clock* DTA, the PDP is in fact a Markov regenerative process. (This observation is also at the heart of model-checking CSL^{TA} [16].) This implies that for single-clock DTA, off-the-shelf CSL model-checking algorithms can be employed resulting in an efficient procedure [7]. Mikeev *et al.* [24] generalised these ideas to infinite-state CTMCs obtained from stoichiometric equations, whereas Chen *et al.* [12] showed the theory to generalize verifying single-clock DTA to continuous-time Markov decision processes.

Multi-clock DTA are however much harder to handle. The characterisation of PDP reachability probabilities as the unique solution of a set of partial differential equations (PDEs) [10,11] does not give insight into an efficient computational procedure. With the notable exception of [25], verifying PDPs has not been considered. Fu [18] provided an algorithm to approximate the probabilities using finite difference methods and gave an error bound. This method hampers scalability and therefore was never implemented. The same holds for model-checking using other linear-time real-time formalisms such as MTL and timed automata [9], linear duration invariants [8], and probabilistic duration calculus [13]. All these multi-clock approaches suffer from scalability issues due to the low efficiency of solving PDEs and/or integral equations on which they heavily depend.

This paper presents a numerical technique to approximate the reachability probability in the product PDP. The DTA $\mathcal{A}$ is approximated by DTA $\mathcal{A}[t_f]$ which extends $\mathcal{A}$ with an additional clock that is never reset and that needs to be at most t_f when accepting. By increasing the time-bound t_f, DTA $\mathcal{A}[t_f]$ approximates $\mathcal{A}$ arbitrarily closely. We show that the set of PDPs characterizing the reachability probability in the embedded PDP of $\mathcal{C}$ and $\mathcal{A}[t_f]$ can be reduced to solving an ordinary differential equation (ODE). The specific characteristics of the product EPDP, in particular the fact that all clocks run at the same pace, are key to obtain these ODEs. Our numerical algorithm to solve the ODEs is based on computing the approximations in a backward manner using t_f and the sum of all clocks. The complexity of the resulting procedure is linear in the EPDP size, and exponential in $\lceil \frac{t_f}{\delta} \rceil$ where δ is the discretization step size. We show the approximations converges to the real solution of the ODEs at a linear speed of δ. Using a prototypical tool implementation we present some results on a number of case studies such as robot navigation with varying number of clocks in their specification. The experimental results show promising results for checking CTMCs against multi-clock DTA.

Organization of the Paper. Section 2 introduces basic notions including CTMCs, DTA, and PDPs. Section 3 presents the product of a CTMC and the region graph of a DTA and shows this is an embedded PDP. Section 4 derives the PDE (fixing some flaw in [10]), the reduction to the set of ODEs and presents the numerical algorithm to solve these ODEs. Section 5 presents the experimental results and Sect. 6 concludes.

2   Preliminaries

In this section, we introduce some basic notions which will be used later.

A probability space is denoted by a triple $(\Omega, \mathcal{F}, Pr)$, where Ω is a set of samples, $\mathcal{F}$ is a σ-algebra over Ω, and $Pr : \mathcal{F} \to [0,1]$ is a probability measure on $\mathcal{F}$ with $Pr(\Omega) = 1$. Let $\mathbb{P}_r(\Omega)$ denote the set of all probability measures over Ω. For a random variable X on the probability space, its expectation is denoted by $\mathbb{E}(X)$.

2.1   Continuous-Time Markov Chain (CTMC)

Definition 1 (CTMC). *A CTMC is a tuple* $\mathcal{C} = (S, \mathbf{P}, \alpha, AP, L, E)$, *where*

- S *is a finite set of states;*
- $\mathbf{P} : S \times S \to [0,1]$ *is the transition probability function, which is identified with the matrix* $\mathbf{P} \in [0,1]^{|S| \times |S|}$ *such that* $\sum_{t \in S} \mathbf{P}(s,t) = 1$, *for all* $s \in S$;
- $\alpha \in \mathbb{P}_r(S)$ *is the initial distribution;*
- AP *is a finite set of atomic propositions;*
- $L : S \to 2^{AP}$ *is a labeling function; and*
- $E : S \to \mathbb{R}_{>0}$ *is the exit rate function.*

We denote by $s \xrightarrow{t} s'$ a transition from state s to state s' after residing in state s for t time units. The probability of the occurrence of this transition within t time units is $\mathbf{P}(s, s') \int_0^t E(s) \exp^{-E(s)x} dx$, where $\int_0^t E(s) \exp^{-E(s)x} dx$ stands for the probability to leave state s in t time units, and $\mathbf{P}(s, s')$ for the probability to select the transition to s' from all transitions outgoing from s. A state s is called *absorbing* if $\mathbf{P}(s, s) = 1$. Given a CTMC $\mathcal{C}$, removing the exit rate function E results in a discrete-time Markov chain (DMTC), which is called *embedded* DTMC of $\mathcal{C}$. A CTMC $\mathcal{C}$ is called *irreducible* if there exists a unique stationary distribution α, such that $\alpha(s) > 0$ for all $s \in S$, and *weakly irreducible* if $\alpha(s)$ may be zero for some $s \in S$.

Definition 2 (CTMC Path). *Let* $\mathcal{C}$ *be a CTMC, a path* ρ *of* $\mathcal{C}$ *starting form* s_0 *with length* n *is a sequence* $\rho = s_0 \xrightarrow{t_0} s_1 \xrightarrow{t_1} \dots \xrightarrow{t_{n-1}} s_n \in S \times (\mathbb{R}_{>0} \times S)^n$. *The* set of paths in C with length n is denoted by $Path_n^C$; the set of all finite paths of C is $Path_{fin}^C = \cup_n Path_n^C$ and the set of infinite paths of C is $Path_{inf}^C = (S \times \mathbb{R}_{>0})^\omega$. We use $Path^C = Path_{fin}^C \cup Path_{inf}^C$ to denote all paths in C. As a convention, ε stands for the empty path.

Note that we assume the time to exit a state is strictly greater than 0. For an infinite path ρ, we use $Pref(\rho)$ to denote the set of its finite prefixes. For a (finite or infinite) path ρ with prefix $s_0 \xrightarrow{t_0} s_1 \xrightarrow{t_1} \dots$, the trace of the path is the sequence of states $trace(\rho) = s_0 s_1 \dots$. Let $\rho(n) = s_n$ be the n-th state in the path and $\rho[n] = t_n$ be the corresponding exit time for s_n. For a finite path $\rho = s_0 \xrightarrow{t_0} s_1 \xrightarrow{t_1} \dots \xrightarrow{t_{n-1}} s_n$, we use $T(\rho) = \sum_{i=0}^{n-1} t_i$ to denote the total time spent on this path if $n \geq 1$, otherwise $T(\rho) = 0$. For a time $t \leq T(\rho)$, $\rho(0 \dots t)$ denotes the prefix of ρ within t time units, i.e., $s_0 \xrightarrow{t_0} s_1 \xrightarrow{t_1} \dots \xrightarrow{t_{m-1}} s_m$ if there exists some $m \leq n$ with $\sum_{i=0}^{m-1} \rho[m] \leq t \wedge \sum_{i=0}^{m} \rho[m] > t$, otherwise ε.

A basic cylinder set $C(s_0, I_0, \dots, I_{n-1}, s_n)$ consists of all paths $\rho \in Path^C$ such that $\rho(i) = s_i$ for $0 \leq i \leq n$, and $\rho[i] \in I_i$ for $0 \leq i < n$. Then the σ−algebra $\mathcal{F}_{s_0}(C)$ associated with CTMC C and initial state s_0 is the smallest σ−algebra that contains all cylinder sets $C(s_0, I_0, \dots, I_{n-1}, s_n)$ with $\alpha(s_0) > 0$, and $\mathbf{P}(s_i, s_{i+1}) > 0$, for $1 \leq i \leq n$, and $I_0, \dots, I_{n-1}$ are non-empty intervals in $\mathbb{R}_{\geq 0}$. There is a unique probability measure Pr^C on the σ−algebra $\mathcal{F}_{s_0}(C)$, by which the probability for a cylinder set is given by

$$Pr^C(C(s_0, I_0, \dots, I_n, s_n)) = \alpha(s_0) \cdot \prod_{i=1}^{n} \int_{I_i} E(s_{i-1}) \exp^{-E(s_{i-1})x} dx \cdot \mathbf{P}(s_{i-1}, s_i)$$

Example 1. An example of CTMC is shown in Fig. 1, with $AP = \{a, b, c\}$ and initial state s_0. The exit rate r_i, $i = 0, 1, 2, 3$ and transition probability are shown in the figure.

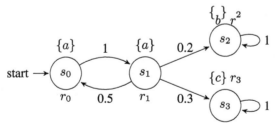

Fig. 1. An example of CTMC

2.2 Deterministic Timed Automaton (DTA)

A timed automaton is a finite state graph equipped with a finite set of non-negative real-valued clock variables, or clocks for short. Clocks can only be reset to zero, or proceed with rate 1 as time progresses independently. Let $\mathcal{X} = \{x_1, \ldots, x_n\}$ be a set of clocks. $\eta(x) : \mathcal{X} \to \mathbb{R}_{\geq 0}$ is a $\mathcal{X}$-valuation which records the amount of time since its last reset. Let $Val(\mathcal{A})$ be the set of all clock valuations of $\mathcal{A}$. For a subset $X \subseteq \mathcal{X}$, the reset of X, denoted as $\eta[X := 0]$, is the valuation η' such that $\eta'(x) = 0, \forall x \in X$, and $\eta'(x) = \eta(x)$, otherwise. For $d \in \mathbb{R}_{>0}$, $(\eta + d)(x) = \eta(x) + d$ for any clock $x \in \mathcal{X}$.

A clock constraint over $\mathcal{X}$ is a formula with the following form

$$g := x < c \mid x \leq c \mid x > c \mid x \geq c \mid x - y \geq c \mid g \wedge g,$$

where x, y are clocks, $c \in \mathbb{N}$. Let $Con(\mathcal{X})$ denote the set of clock constraints over $\mathcal{X}$. A valuation η satisfies a guard g, denoted as $\eta \models g$, iff $\eta(x) \bowtie c$ when g is $x \bowtie c$, where $\bowtie \in \{<, \leq, >, \geq\}$; and $\eta \models g_1$ and $\eta \models g_2$ iff $g = g_1 \wedge g_2$.

Definition 3 (DTA). *A DTA is a tuple* $\mathcal{A} = (\Sigma, \mathcal{X}, Q, q_0, Q_F, \hookrightarrow)$, *where*

- Σ *is a finite set of actions;*
- $\mathcal{X}$ *is a finite set of clocks;*
- Q *is a finite set of locations;*
- $q_0 \in Q$ *is the initial location;*
- $Q_F \subseteq Q$ *is the set of accepting locations;*
- $\hookrightarrow \in (Q \backslash Q_F) \times \Sigma \times Con(\mathcal{X}) \times 2^{\mathcal{X}} \times Q$ *is the transition relation, satisfying if* $q \xrightarrow{a,g,X} q'$ *and* $q \xrightarrow{a,g',X'} q''$ *with* $q' \neq q''$ *then* $g \cap g' = \emptyset$.

Each transition relation, or edge, $q \hookrightarrow q'$ in $\mathcal{A}$ is endowed with (a, g, X), where $a \in \Sigma$ is an action, $g \in Con(\mathcal{X})$ is the guard of the transition, and $X \subseteq \mathcal{X}$ is a set of clocks, which should be reset to 0 after the transition. An intuitive interpretation of the transition is that $\mathcal{A}$ can move from q to q' by taking action a and resetting all clocks in X to be 0 only if g is satisfied. There are no outgoing transitions from any accepting location in Q_F.

A finite timed path of $\mathcal{A}$ is of the form $\theta = q_0 \xrightarrow{a_0,t_0} q_1 \xrightarrow{a_1,t_1} \cdots \xrightarrow{a_{n-1},t_{n-1}} q_n$, where $t_i \geq 0$, for $i = 0, \ldots, n-1$. Moreover, there exists a sequence of transitions $q_j \xrightarrow{a_j,g_j,X_j} q_{j+1}$, for $0 \leq j \leq n-1$, such that $\eta_0 = \mathbf{0}$, $\eta_j + t_j \models g_j$ and $\eta_{j+1} = \eta_j[X_j := 0]$, where η_k denotes the clock valuation when entering q_k. θ is said to be *accepted by* $\mathcal{A}$ if there exists a state $q_i \in Q_F$ for some $0 \leq i \leq n$. As normal, it is assumed all DTA are non-Zeno [6], that is any circular transition sequence takes nonzero dwelling time.

A region is a set of valuations, usually represented by a set of clock constraints. Let $Reg(\mathcal{X})$ be the set of regions over $\mathcal{X}$. Given $\Theta, \Theta' \in Reg(\mathcal{X})$, Θ' is called a *successor* of Θ if for all $\eta \models \Theta$, there exists $t > 0$ such that $\eta + t \models \Theta'$ and $\forall t' < t, \eta + t' \models \Theta \vee \Theta'$. A region Θ satisfies a guard g, denoted as $\Theta \models g$, iff $\forall \eta \models \Theta$ implies $\eta \models g$. The reset operation on a region Θ is defined as $\Theta[X := 0] = \{\eta[X := 0] \mid \eta \models \Theta\}$. Then the region graph, viewed as a quotient transition system related to clock equivalence [6] can be defined as follows:

Definition 4 (Region Graph). *The region graph for DTA* $\mathcal{A} = (\Sigma, \mathcal{X}, Q, q_0, Q_F, \hookrightarrow)$ *is a tuple* $\mathcal{G}(\mathcal{A}) = (\Sigma, \mathcal{X}, \overline{Q}, \overline{q_0}, \overline{Q_F}, \mapsto)$, *where*

- $\overline{Q} = Q \times Reg(\mathcal{X})$ *is the set of states;*
- $\overline{q_0} = (q_0, \mathbf{0}) \in \overline{Q}$ *is the initial state;*
- $\overline{Q_F} \subseteq Q_F \times Reg(\mathcal{X})$ *is the set of final states;*
- $\mapsto \subseteq \overline{Q} \times ((\Sigma \times 2^{\mathcal{X}}) \cup \{\lambda\}) \times \overline{Q}$ *is the transition relation satisfying*
  - $(q, \Theta) \xmapsto{\lambda} (q, \Theta')$ *if* Θ' *is a successor of* Θ*;*
  - $(q, \Theta) \xmapsto{a,X} (q', \Theta'')$ *if there exists* $g \in Con(\mathcal{X})$ *and transition* $q \xrightarrow{a,g,X} q'$ *such that* $\Theta \models g$ *and* $\Theta'' = \Theta[X := 0]$*.*

Example 2 (Adapted from [10]*).* Figure 2 presents an example of DTA and Fig. 3 gives its region graph, in which double circle and double rectangle stand for final states, respectively.

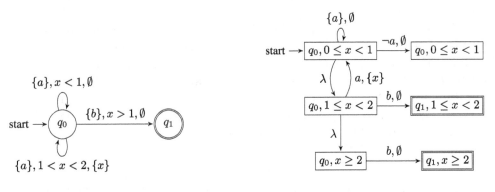

Fig. 2. A DTA $\mathcal{A}$　　　　　　　**Fig. 3.** The region graph of $\mathcal{A}$

2.3 Piecewise-Deterministic Markov Process (PDP)

Piecewise-deterministic Markov Processes (PDPs for short) [14] cover a wide range of stochastic models in which the randomness appears as discrete events at fixed or random times, whose evolution is deterministically governed by an ODE system between these times. A PDP consists of a mixture of deterministic motion and random jumps between a finite set of locations. During staying in a location, a PDP evolves deterministically following a flow function, which is a solution to an ODE system between these times. A PDP can jump between locations either randomly, in which case the residence time of a location is governed by an exponential distribution, or when the location invariant is violated. The successor state of the jump follows a probability measure depending on the current state. A PDP is right-continuous and has the strong Markov property [14].

Definition 5 (PDP [14]**).** *A PDP is a tuple* $\mathcal{Q} = (Z, \mathcal{X}, Inv, \phi, \Lambda, \mu)$ *with*

- *Z is a finite set of locations;*
- *$\mathcal{X}$ is a finite set of variables;*
- *$Inv : Z \to 2^{\mathbb{R}^{|\mathcal{X}|}}$ is an invariant function;*

- $\phi : Z \times \mathbb{R}^{|\mathcal{X}|} \times \mathbb{R}_{\geq 0} \to \mathbb{R}^{|\mathcal{X}|}$, is a flow function, which is a solution of a system of ODEs with Lipschitz continuous vector fields;
- $\Lambda : \mathbb{S} \to \mathbb{R}_{>0}$ is an exit rate function;
- $\overline{\mathbb{S}} \to \mathbb{P}_r(\mathbb{S})$, is the transition probability function, where $\mathbb{S} = \{\xi := (z, \eta) \mid z \in Z, \eta \models Inv(z)\}$ is the state space for $\mathcal{Q}$, $\overline{\mathbb{S}}$ is the closure of $\mathbb{S}$, $\mathbb{S}^o = \{(z, \eta) \mid z \in Z, \eta \models Inv(z)^o\}$ is the interior of $\mathbb{S}$, in which $Inv(z)^o$ stands for the interior of $Inv(z)$, and $\partial \mathbb{S} = \cup_{z \in Z} \{z\} \times \partial Inv(z)$ is the boundary of $\mathbb{S}$, in which $\partial Inv(z) = \overline{Inv(z)} \backslash Inv^o$ and $\overline{Inv(z)}$ is the closure of $Inv(z)$.

For any $\xi = (z, \eta) \in \mathbb{S}$, there is an $\delta(\xi) > 0$ such that $\Lambda(z, \phi(z, \eta, t))$ is integrable on $[0, \delta(\xi))$. $\mu(\xi)(A)$ is measurable for any $A \in \mathcal{F}(\mathbb{S})$, where $\mathcal{F}(\mathbb{S})$ is the smallest $\sigma-$algebra generated by $\{\cup_{z \in Z} z \times A_z \mid A_z \in \mathcal{F}(Inv(z))\}$ and $\mu(\xi)(\{\xi\}) = 0$.

There are two ways to take transitions between locations in PDP $\mathcal{Q}$. A PDP $\mathcal{Q}$ is allowed to stay in a current location z only if $Inv(z)$ is satisfied. During its residence, the valuation η evolves time-dependently according to the flow function. Let $\xi \oplus t = (z, \phi(z, \eta, t))$ be the successor state of $\xi = (z, \eta)$ after residing t time units in z. Thus, $\mathcal{Q}$ is piecewise-deterministic since its behavior is determined by the flow function ϕ in each location. In a state $\xi = (z, \eta)$ with $\eta \models Inv(z)^o$, the PDP $\mathcal{Q}$ can either evolve to a state $\xi' = \xi \oplus t$ by delaying t time units, or take a Markovian jump to $\xi'' = (z'', \eta'') \in \mathbb{S}$ with probability $\mu(\xi)(\{\xi''\})$. When $\eta \models \partial Inv(z)$, $\mathcal{Q}$ is forced to take a boundary jump to $\xi'' = (z'', \eta'') \in \mathbb{S}$ with probability $\mu(\xi)(\{\xi''\})$.

3   Reduction to the Reachability Probability of EPDP

As proved in [10], model-checking of a given CTMC $\mathcal{C}$ against a linear real-time property expressed by a DTA $\mathcal{A}$, i.e., determining $Pr(\mathcal{C} \models \mathcal{A})$, can be reduced to computing the reachability probability of the product of $\mathcal{C}$ and $\mathcal{G}(\mathcal{A})$. This can be further reduced to computing the reachability probability of the embedded PDP (EPDP) of the product. But how to efficiently compute the reachability probability of the EPDP still remains challenging, as existing approaches [7,10,16] can only handle DTA with one clock. We will attack this challenge in this paper. For self-containedness, we reformulate the reduction reported in [10] in this section.

A path $\rho = s_0 \xrightarrow{t_0} s_1 \xrightarrow{t_1} \dots$ of CTMC $\mathcal{C}$ is accepted by DTA $\mathcal{A}$ if $\hat{\rho} = q_0 \xrightarrow{L(s_0), t_0} q_1 \xrightarrow{L(s_1), t_1} \dots \xrightarrow{L(s_{n-1}), t_{n-1}} q_n$ induced by some ρ's prefix is an accepting path of $\mathcal{A}$. Then $Pr(\mathcal{C} \models \mathcal{A}) = Pr\{\rho \in Path^{\mathcal{C}} \mid \rho \text{ is accepted by } \mathcal{A}\}$.

Definition 6 (Product Region Graph [7]). *The product of CTMC $\mathcal{C} = (S, \mathbf{P}, \alpha, AP, L, E)$ and the region graph of DTA $\mathcal{G}(\mathcal{A}) = (\Sigma, \mathcal{X}, \overline{Q}, \overline{q_0}, \overline{Q_F}, \mapsto)$, denoted by $\mathcal{C} \otimes \mathcal{G}(\mathcal{A})$, is a tuple $(\mathcal{X}, V, \alpha', V_F, \rightharpoonup, \Lambda)$, where*

- $V = S \times \overline{Q}$ is the state space;
- $\alpha'(s, \overline{q_0}) = \alpha(s)$ is the initial distribution;
- $V_F = S \times \overline{Q_F}$ is the set of accepting states;
- $\rightharpoonup \subseteq V \times (([0, 1] \times 2^{\mathcal{X}}) \cup \{\lambda\}) \times V$ is the smallest relation satisfying

- $(s, \overline{q}) \xrightarrow{\lambda} (s, \overline{q'})$ *(called* delay transition*), if* $\overline{q} \xmapsto{\lambda} \overline{q'}$;
- $(s, \overline{q}) \xrightarrow{p, X} (s'', \overline{q''})$ *(called* Markovian transition*), if* $\mathbf{P}(s, s'') = p, p > 0$ *and* $\overline{q} \xmapsto{L(s), X} \overline{q''}$;

- $\Lambda : V \to \mathbb{R}_{>0}$ *is the exit rate function, where*

$$\Lambda(s, \overline{q}) = \begin{cases} E(s) & \textit{if there exists a Markovian transition from } (s, \overline{q}) \\ 0 & \textit{otherwise} \end{cases}$$

Remark 1. Note that the definition of region graph here is slightly different from the usual one in the sense that Markovian transitions starting from a boundary do not contribute to the reachability probability. Therefore we can merge the boundary into its unique delay successor.

Example 3 (Adapted from [10]*).* Figure 4 shows the product region graph of CTMC $\mathcal{C}$ in Example 1 and DTA $\mathcal{A}$ in Example 2. The graph can be split into three subgraphs in a column-wise manner, where all transitions within a subgraph are probabilistic, all transitions evolve to the next subgraph are delay transitions, and transitions with reset lead to a state in the first subgraph. For conciseness, the location v_9 stands for all nodes that may be reached by a Markovian transition yet cannot reach an accepting node.

Proposition 1 ([10])**.** *For CTMC $\mathcal{C}$ and DTA $\mathcal{A}$, $Pr(\mathcal{C} \models \mathcal{A})$ is measurable and*

$$Pr(\mathcal{C} \models \mathcal{A}) = Pr^{\mathcal{C} \otimes \mathcal{G}(\mathcal{A})}\{Path^{\mathcal{C} \otimes \mathcal{G}(\mathcal{A})}(\Diamond \overline{Q_F})\}.$$

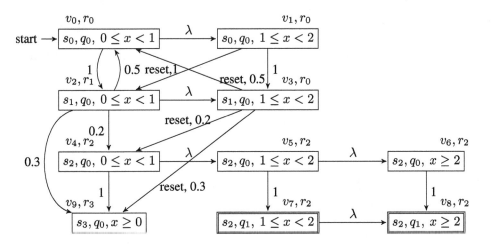

Fig. 4. Product region graph $\mathcal{C} \otimes \mathcal{G}(\mathcal{A})$ of CTMC $\mathcal{C}$ in Example 1 and DTA $\mathcal{A}$ in Example 2

When treated as a stochastic process, $\mathcal{C} \otimes \mathcal{G}(\mathcal{A})$ can be interpreted as a PDP. In this way, computing the reachability probability of Q_F in $\mathcal{C} \otimes \mathcal{G}(\mathcal{A})$ can be reduced to computing the time-unbounded reachability probability in the EPDP of $\mathcal{C} \otimes \mathcal{G}(\mathcal{A})$.

Definition 7 (EPDP, [7]). *Given $\mathcal{C} \otimes \mathcal{G}(\mathcal{A}) = (\mathcal{X}, V, \alpha', V_F, \rightharpoonup, \Lambda)$, the EPDP $\mathcal{Q}^{\mathcal{C} \otimes \mathcal{A}}$ is a tuple $(\mathcal{X}, V, Inv, \phi, \Lambda, \mu)$ where for any $v = (s, (q, \Theta)) \in V$*

- *$Inv(v) = \Theta$, $\mathbb{S} = \{(v, \boldsymbol{\eta}) \mid v \in V, \boldsymbol{\eta} \models Inv(v)\}$ is the state space;*
- *$\phi(v, \boldsymbol{\eta}, t) = \boldsymbol{\eta} + t$ for $\boldsymbol{\eta} \models Inv(v)$;*
- *$\Lambda(v, \eta) = \Lambda(v)$ is the exit rate of (v, η);*
- Boundary jump: *for each delay transition $v \xrightarrow{\lambda} v'$ in $\mathcal{C} \otimes \mathcal{G}(\mathcal{A})$, $\mu(\xi, \{\xi'\}) = 1$ whenever $\xi = (v, \boldsymbol{\eta})$, $\xi' = (v', \boldsymbol{\eta})$ and $\boldsymbol{\eta} \models \partial Inv(v)$;*
- Markovian transition jump: *for each Markovian transition $v \xrightarrow{p, X} v''$ in $\mathcal{C} \otimes \mathcal{G}(\mathcal{A})$, $\mu(\xi, \{\xi''\}) = p$ whenever $\xi = (v, \boldsymbol{\eta})$, $\boldsymbol{\eta} \models Inv(v)$ and $\xi'' = (v'', \boldsymbol{\eta}[X := 0])$.*

The flow function here describes that all clocks increase with a uniform rate (i.e., $\dot{x}_1 = 1, \ldots, \dot{x}_n = 1$, or simply $\dot{\mathcal{X}} = 1$) at all locations. The original reachability problem is then reduced to the reachability probability of the set $\{(v, \boldsymbol{\eta}) \mid v \in V_F, \boldsymbol{\eta} \models Inv(v)\}$, given the initial state $(v_0, \mathbf{0})$ and the EPDP $\mathcal{Q}^{\mathcal{C} \otimes \mathcal{A}}$. Let $Pr_v^{\mathcal{Q}^{\mathcal{C} \otimes \mathcal{A}}}(\boldsymbol{\eta})$ stand for the probability to reach the final states $(V_F \times *)$ from $(v, \boldsymbol{\eta})$ in $\mathcal{Q}^{\mathcal{C} \otimes \mathcal{A}}$. Thus, $Pr_v^{\mathcal{Q}^{\mathcal{C} \otimes \mathcal{A}}}(\boldsymbol{\eta})$ can be computed recursively by

$$Pr_v^{\mathcal{Q}^{\mathcal{C} \otimes \mathcal{A}}}(\boldsymbol{\eta}) = \begin{cases} Pr_{v, \lambda}^{\mathcal{Q}^{\mathcal{C} \otimes \mathcal{A}}}(\boldsymbol{\eta}) + \sum_{v \xrightarrow{p, X} v'} Pr_{v, v'}^{\mathcal{Q}^{\mathcal{C} \otimes \mathcal{A}}}(\boldsymbol{\eta}) & \text{if } v \notin V_F \\ 1, & v \in V_F \wedge \boldsymbol{\eta} \models Inv(v) \quad (1) \\ 0, & \text{otherwise.} \end{cases}$$

Let $t_z^*(v, \boldsymbol{\eta})$ denote the minimal time for $\mathcal{Q}^{\mathcal{C} \otimes \mathcal{A}}$ to reach $\partial Inv(v)$ from $(v, \boldsymbol{\eta})$. More precisely,

$$t_z^*(v, \boldsymbol{\eta}) = \inf\{t \mid \phi(v, \boldsymbol{\eta}, t) \models Inv(v)\}.$$

$Pr_{v, \lambda}^{\mathcal{Q}^{\mathcal{C} \otimes \mathcal{A}}}(\boldsymbol{\eta})$ is the probability from (v, η) with a delay and then a forced jump to $(v', \boldsymbol{\eta} + t_z^*(v, \boldsymbol{\eta}))$, onwards evolves to an accepting state, which can be recursively computed by

$$Pr_{v, \lambda}^{\mathcal{Q}^{\mathcal{C} \otimes \mathcal{A}}}(\boldsymbol{\eta}) = exp(-\Lambda(v) t_z^*(v, \boldsymbol{\eta})) \cdot Pr_{v'}^{\mathcal{Q}^{\mathcal{C} \otimes \mathcal{A}}}(\boldsymbol{\eta} + t_z^*(v, \boldsymbol{\eta})).$$

$Pr_{v, v'}^{\mathcal{Q}^{\mathcal{C} \otimes \mathcal{A}}}(\boldsymbol{\eta})$ is the probability that a Markovian transition $v \xrightarrow{p, X} v'$ happens within $t_z^*(v, \boldsymbol{\eta})$ time units, onwards involves to an accepted state, which can be recursively computed by

$$Pr_{v, v'}^{\mathcal{Q}^{\mathcal{C} \otimes \mathcal{A}}}(\boldsymbol{\eta}) = \int_0^{t_z^*(v, \boldsymbol{\eta})} p \cdot \Lambda(v) \exp(-\Lambda(v) s) \cdot Pr_{v'}^{\mathcal{Q}^{\mathcal{C} \otimes \mathcal{A}}}(\boldsymbol{\eta} + s[X := 0]) \, ds.$$

$Pr(\mathcal{C} \models \mathcal{A})$ is reduced to compute $Pr_{v_0}^{\mathcal{Q}^{\mathcal{C} \otimes \mathcal{A}}}(\mathbf{0})$, equivalent to computing the least fixed point of the Eq. (1). That is,

Theorem 1. [10] *For CTMC $\mathcal{C}$ and DTA $\mathcal{A}$, $Pr(\mathcal{C} \models \mathcal{A}) = Pr^{\mathcal{C} \otimes \mathcal{A}} \{Path^{\mathcal{C} \otimes \mathcal{A}}(\lozenge \overline{Q_F})\}$ is the least fixed point of (1).*

Remark 2. Generally, it is difficult to solve a recursive equation like (1). As an alternative, we discuss the augmented EPDP of $\mathcal{Q}^{\mathcal{C} \otimes \mathcal{A}}$ by replacing $\mathcal{A}$ with a bounded DTA resulting from $\mathcal{A}$. As a consequence, using the extended generator of the augmented EPDP, we can induce a partial differential equation (PDE) whose solution is the reachability probability. We will elaborate the idea in the subsequent section.

4 Approximating the Reachability Probability of EPDP

In this section, we present a numerical method to approximate $Pr_{v_0}^{\mathcal{Q}^{\mathcal{C} \otimes \mathcal{A}}}(\mathbf{0})$, as we discussed previously that exactly computing is impossible, at least too expensive, in general. We will first introduce the basic idea of our approach in detail, then discuss its time complexity and convergence property. A key point is that our approach exploits the observation that the flow function of $\mathcal{Q}^{\mathcal{C} \otimes \mathcal{A}}$ is linear, only related to time t, and remains the same at all locations. This enables to reduce computing $Pr_{v_0}^{\mathcal{Q}^{\mathcal{C} \otimes \mathcal{A}}}(\mathbf{0})$ to solving an ODE system.

4.1 Reduction to a PDE System

In this subsection, we first show that $Pr_{v_0}^{\mathcal{Q}^{\mathcal{C} \otimes \mathcal{A}}}(\mathbf{0})$ can be approximated by that of the EPDP of $\mathcal{C}$ and a bounded DTA derived from $\mathcal{A}$, i.e., the length of all its paths is bounded. Then show that the latter can be reduced to solving a PDE system.

Given a DTA $\mathcal{A}$, we construct a bounded DTA $\mathcal{A}[t_f]$ by introducing a new clock y, adding a timing constraint $y < t_f$ to the guard of each transition of $\mathcal{A}$ ingoing to an accepting state in Q_F, and never resetting y, where $t_f \in \mathbb{N}$ is a parameter. So, the length of all accepting paths of $\mathcal{A}[t_f]$ is time-bounded by t_f. Obviously, $Path^{\mathcal{C}}(\mathcal{A}[t_f])$ is a subset of $Path^{\mathcal{C}}(\mathcal{A})$. As $Pr(\mathcal{C} \models \mathcal{A})$ is measurable and $\mathcal{Q}^{\mathcal{C} \otimes \mathcal{A}}$ is Borel right continuous, we have the following proposition.

Proposition 2. *Given a CTMC $\mathcal{C}$, a DTA $\mathcal{A}$, and $t_f \in \mathbb{N}$,*

$$\lim_{t_f \to \infty} Pr(\mathcal{C} \models \mathcal{A}[t_f]) = Pr(\mathcal{C} \models \mathcal{A}). \tag{2}$$

Moreover, if $\mathcal{C}$ is weakly irreducible or satisfies some conditions (please refer to Chap. 4 of [26] for details), then there exist positive constants $K, K_0 \in \mathbb{R}_{\geq 0}$ such that

$$Pr(\mathcal{C} \models \mathcal{A}) - Pr(\mathcal{C} \models \mathcal{A}[t_f]) \leq K \exp\{-K_0 t_f\}. \tag{3}$$

Remark 3. (2) was first observed in [7], thereof the authors pointed out the feasibility of using a bounded system to approximate the original unbounded system in order to simplify a verification obligation. (3) further indicates that such approximation is exponentially convergent w.r.t. $-t_f$ if the CTMC is weakly irreducible.

For a path starting in a state $(v, \boldsymbol{\eta})$ at time y, we use $Path^y_{(v,\boldsymbol{\eta})}[t]$ to denote the set of its locations at time t, and $\hbar_v(y, \boldsymbol{\eta}) = Pr(Path^y_{(v,\boldsymbol{\eta})}[t_f] \in V_F) = \mathbb{E}(1_{Path^y_{(v,\boldsymbol{\eta})}[t_f]\in V_F})$ as the probability of a path reaching V_F within t_f time units, where $1_{Path^y_{(v,\boldsymbol{\eta})}[t_f]\in V_F}$ is the indicator function of $Path^y_{(v,\boldsymbol{\eta})}[t_f] \in V_F$. Then, $\hbar_{v_0}(0, \mathbf{0}) = Pr(\mathcal{C} \models \mathcal{A}[t_f])$ is the probability to reach the set of accepting states from the initial state $(0, \mathbf{0})$, which satisfies the following system of PDEs.

Theorem 2. *Given a CTMC $\mathcal{C}$, a bounded DTA $\mathcal{A}[t_f]$, and the EPDP $\mathcal{Q}^{\mathcal{C}\otimes\mathcal{G}(\mathcal{A}[t_f])} = (\mathcal{X}, V, Inv, \phi, \Lambda, \mu)$, $\hbar_{v_0}(0, \mathbf{0})$ is the unique solution of the following system of PDEs:*

$$\frac{\partial \hbar_v(y, \boldsymbol{\eta})}{\partial y} + \sum_{i=1}^{|\mathcal{X}|} \frac{\partial \hbar_v(y, \boldsymbol{\eta})}{\partial \boldsymbol{\eta}^{(i)}} + \Lambda(v) \cdot \sum_{v \xrightarrow{p,X} v'} p \cdot (\hbar_{v'}(y, \boldsymbol{\eta}[X := 0]) - \hbar_v(y, \boldsymbol{\eta})) = 0, \quad (4)$$

where $v \in V \backslash V_F, \boldsymbol{\eta} \models Inv(v), \boldsymbol{\eta}^{(i)}$ is the i-th clock variable and $y \in [0, t_f)$. The boundary conditions are:

(i) $\hbar_v(y, \boldsymbol{\eta}) = \hbar_{v'}(y, \boldsymbol{\eta})$, *for every* $\boldsymbol{\eta} \models \partial Inv(v)$ *and transition* $v \xrightarrow{\lambda} v'$;
(ii) $\hbar_v(y, \boldsymbol{\eta}) = 1$, *for every vertex* $v \in V_F$, $\boldsymbol{\eta} \models Inv(v)$, *and* $y \in [0, t_f)$;
(iii) $\hbar_v(t_f, \boldsymbol{\eta}) = 0$, *for every vertex* $v \in V \backslash V_F$ *and* $\boldsymbol{\eta} \models Inv(v) \cup \partial Inv(v)$.

Remark 4. Note that the PDE system (4) in Theorem 2 is different from the one presented in [10] for reducing $Pr^{\mathcal{Q}^{\mathcal{C}\otimes\mathcal{A}}}_{v_0}(\mathbf{0})$. In particular, the boundary condition in [10] has been corrected here.

4.2 Reduction to an ODE System

There are several classical methods to solve PDEs. *Finite element method*, which is a numerical technique for solving PDEs as well as integral equations, is a prominent one, of which different versions have been established to solve different PDEs with specific properties. Other numerical methods include finite difference method and finite volume method and so on, the reader is referred to [20, 21] for details. Thanks to the special form of the Eq. (4), we are able to obtain a numerical solution in a more efficient way.

The fact that the flow function (which is the solution to the ODE system $\bigwedge_{x\in\mathcal{X}} \dot{x} = 1 \wedge \dot{y} = 1$) is the same at all locations of the EPDP $\mathcal{Q}^{\mathcal{C}\otimes\mathcal{A}[t_f]}$ suggests that the partial derivatives of $\boldsymbol{\eta}$ and y in the left side of (4) evolve with the same pace. Thus, we can view all clocks as an array, and reformulate (4) as

$$\left[\frac{\partial \hbar_v(y, \boldsymbol{\eta})}{\partial y}, \frac{\partial \hbar_v(y, \boldsymbol{\eta})}{\partial \boldsymbol{\eta}^{(1)}}, \ldots, \frac{\partial \hbar_v(y, \boldsymbol{\eta})}{\partial \boldsymbol{\eta}^{(|\mathcal{X}|)}}\right] \bullet \mathbf{1}$$
$$+ \Lambda(v) \cdot \sum_{v \xrightarrow{p,X} v'} p \cdot (\hbar_{v'}(y, \boldsymbol{\eta}[X := 0]) - \hbar_v(y, \boldsymbol{\eta})) = 0, \quad (5)$$

where $\bullet$ stands for the inner product of two vectors of the same dimension, e.g.,
$(a_1, \ldots, a_n) \bullet (b_1, \ldots, b_n) = \sum_{i=1}^{n} a_i b_i$, and $\mathbf{1}$ for the vector $\overbrace{(1, \ldots, 1)}^{n \text{ times}}$.

By Theorem 2, there exist v_0, y_0 and η_0 such that $v_0 \in V_F$, $y_0 = t_f$, and $\eta_0 \models Inv(v) \vee \partial Inv(v)$. Besides, by the definition of $\mathcal{Q}^{\mathcal{C} \otimes \mathcal{A}[t_f]}$, it follows $\frac{\partial z}{\partial t} = 1$, which implies $dz = dt$, for any $z \in \{y\} \cup \mathcal{X}$. Hence, we can simplify (5) as the following ODE system:

$$\frac{d\hbar_v((y_0, \eta_0) + t)}{dt} + \Lambda(v) \cdot$$

$$\sum_{v \xrightarrow{p, X} v'} p \cdot (\hbar_{v'}((y_0, \eta_0) + t)[X := 0]) - \hbar_v(y_0, \eta_0)) = 0, \quad (6)$$

with the initial condition $v_0 \in V_F$, $y_0 = t_f$, and $\eta_0 \models Inv(v) \vee \partial Inv(v)$, where $v \in V \backslash V_F$. Note that we compute the reachability probability by (6) backwards.

4.3 Numerical Solution

Since $\hbar_v((y_0, \eta_0) + t)$ satisfies an ODE equation, we can apply a discretization method to (6) and obtain an approximation efficiently. To this end, the remaining obstacle is how to deal with the reset part $\hbar_{v'}(y_0 + t, (\eta_0 + t)[X := 0])$. Notice that $X \neq \emptyset \Rightarrow \text{sum}((\eta_0 + t)[X := 0]) + (t_f - y_0 - t)) < \text{sum}(\eta_0 + t) + (t_f - t_0 - t)$, where $\text{sum}(\eta) = \sum_{x \in \mathcal{X}} \eta(x)$. So we just need to solve the ODE system starting from (t_f, η_0) using the descending order over $\text{sum}(\eta)$ in a backward manner. In this way, all of the reset values needed for the current iteration have been computed in the previous iterations. Therefore for each iteration, the derivation is fixed and easy to calculate.

We denote by δ the length of discretization step, the number of total discretization steps is $\lceil \frac{t_f}{\delta} \rceil \in \mathbb{N}$. An approximate solution to (4) can be computed efficiently by the following algorithm.

Line 4 in Algorithm 1 computes a numerical solution to (6) on $[t_f - t, t_f]$ by discretizing $\frac{d\hbar_v((y_0, \eta_0) + t)}{dt}$ with $\frac{1}{\delta}(\hbar_v((y_0, \eta_0) + (t + \delta)) - \hbar_v((y_0, \eta_0) + t))$. A pictorial illustration to Algorithm 1 for the two-dimensional setting is shown in Fig. 5. The blue polyhedron covers all the points we need to calculate. The algorithm starts from $(0, 0, t_f)$, where $\text{sum}(\eta) = x_1 + x_2 = 0$. Then $\text{sum}(\eta)$ is incremented until $2t_f$ in a stepwise manner. For each fixed $\text{sum}(\eta)$, for example $\text{sum}(\eta) = t_f$, the algorithm calculates all discrete points in the gray plane following the direction $(-1, -1, -1)$, and finally reaches the two reset lines. The red line reaching the origin provides the final result.

Algorithm 1. Finding numerical solution to (4)

Input: $\mathcal{C} \otimes \mathcal{G}(\mathcal{A})$, the region graph of the product of CTMC $\mathcal{C}$ and DTA $\mathcal{A}$; t_f, the time bound
Output: A numerical solution for $\hbar_{v_0}(0, \mathbf{0})$, an approximation of $Pr(\mathcal{C} \models \mathcal{A}[t_f])$

1: **for** $n \leftarrow 0$ **to** $|\mathcal{X}| \cdot t_f$ **by** δ **do**
2:      **for each** η in $\{\eta' \mid \text{sum}(\eta') = n \wedge \forall i \in \{1, \ldots, |\mathcal{X}|\}\ 0 \le \eta^{(i)} \le t_f\}$ **do**
3:          **for** t from 0 **down** to $-\min(t_f, \eta)$ **do**
4:              Compute numerical solution to (6) with $(y_0, \eta_0) = (t_f, \eta)$ on $[t_f - t, t_f]$
5:          **end for**
6:      **end for**
7: **end for**
8: **return** numerical solution for $\hbar_{v_0}(0, \mathbf{0})$

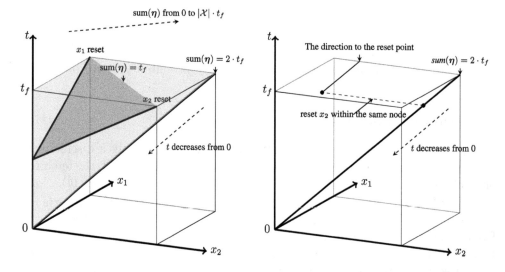

Fig. 5. Illustrating Algorithm 1 (left) and Algorithm 2 (right) for the 2-dimensional setting (Color figure online)

Example 4. Consider the product $\mathcal{C} \otimes \mathcal{G}(\mathcal{A})$ shown in Example 3 (in page 8). For state v_3 in which clock x is 1 and y is arbitrary, the corresponding PDE is

$$\frac{\partial \hbar_{v_3}(y, 1)}{\partial y} + \frac{\partial \hbar_{v_3}(y, 1)}{\partial x} + r_0[0.5 \cdot \hbar_{v_0}(y, 0) + 0.2 \cdot \hbar_{v_4}(y, 0) + 0.4 \cdot \hbar_{v_9}(y, 0) - \hbar_{v_3}(y, 0)] = 0.$$

Since $\text{sum}(y, 0) = y < y + 1 = \text{sum}(y, 1)$, the value for $\hbar_{v_0}(y, 0)$, $\hbar_{v_4}(y, 0)$ and $\hbar_{v_3}(y, 0)$ have been calculated in the previous iterations, thus the value for $\hbar_{v_3}(y, 1)$ can be computed.

To optimize Algorithm 1 for multi-clock objects, we exploit the idea of "lazy computation". In Algorithm 1, in order to determine the reset part for (6), we calculate all discretized points generated by all ODEs. The efficiency is influenced since the amount of ODEs is quite large (the same as the number of states in product automaton). However in Algorithm 2, we only compute the reset part that we need for computing $\hbar_{v_0}(0,\mathbf{0})$. If we meet a reset part $\hbar_v(y, \boldsymbol{\eta}[X := 0])$ which has not been decided yet, we suspend the equation we are computing now and switch to compute the equation leading to the undecided point following the direction of $(-1, \ldots, -1)$. The algorithm terminates since the number of points it computes is no more than that of Algorithm 1. A pseudo-code is described in Algorithm 2.

Algorithm 2. The lazy computation to find numerical solution to (4)

Input: $\mathcal{C} \otimes \mathcal{G}(\mathcal{A})$, the region graph of the product of CTMC $\mathcal{C}$ and DTA $\mathcal{A}$; t_f, the time bound
Output: A numerical solution for $\hbar_{v_0}(0,\mathbf{0})$, an approximation of $Pr(\mathcal{C} \models \mathcal{A}[t_f])$
Procedure dhv$(y, \boldsymbol{\eta})$ //Computing numerical solution for $(y, \boldsymbol{\eta})$
1: **for** t from 0 down to $-\min(t_f, \boldsymbol{\eta})$ by δ **do**
2:     **for** $v \in V$ **do**
3:         Check if $\boldsymbol{\eta}$ satisfies initial and boundary condition from Theorem 2
4:         **for** each Markovian transition $v \xrightarrow{p,X} v'$ **do**
5:             $up = (-t - \delta) \cdot \mathbf{1} + ((t + \delta) \cdot \mathbf{1})[X := 0]$
6:             **if** reset exists and $\boldsymbol{\eta}[X := 0] + up$ is undecided **then**
7:                 call dhv$(t_f, \boldsymbol{\eta}[X := 0] + up)$
8:             **end if**
9:             comput h_v
10:         **end for**
11:     **end for**
12:     execute λ−transition according to Theorem 2
13:     compute $\hbar_v((y_0, \boldsymbol{\eta_0}) + t)$ by equation (6)
14: **end for**
15: mark $\boldsymbol{\eta}$ decided
End Procedure
1: Call dhv$(v_0, t_f, (\mathbf{t_f}))$
2: **return** numerical solution for $\hbar_{v_0}(0,\mathbf{0})$

4.4 Complexity Analysis

Let $|S|$ be the number of the states of the CTMC, and n the number of the clocks of the DTA. The worst-case time complexity of Algorithms 1 and 2 lies in $\mathcal{O}(|V| \cdot \lceil \frac{t_f}{\delta} \rceil^{(n+1)})$, where $|V|$ is the number of the equations in (4), i.e., the number of the locations in the product region graph, that are not accepting. The number of states in the region graph of the DTA is bounded by $n! \cdot 2^{n-1} \cdot \prod_{x \in \mathcal{X}} (c_x + 1)$, denoted by C_b, where c_x is the maximum constant occurring in the guards that constrain x. Note that C_b differs from the bound given in [1], since the boundaries of a region do not matter in our setting and hence can be merged into the region. Thus, the number of states in the product region graph, as well as the number of PDE equations in Theorem 2, is at most $C_b \cdot |S|$. So the total complexity is $\mathcal{O}(C_b \cdot |S| \cdot \lceil \frac{t_f}{\delta} \rceil^{(n+1)})$.

Let $\hbar_{v,n}(y_0, \boldsymbol{\eta_0})$ denote the numerical solution to ODE (6) with $t = -n\delta$, and $\Lambda_{max} = \max\{\Lambda(v_i) \mid 0 \le i \le |S|\}$. Let $N = \lceil \frac{t_f}{\delta} \rceil$. By Proposition 2, $\lim_{t_f \to +\infty} \hbar_v(0,\mathbf{0}) = Pr(\mathcal{C} \models \mathcal{A})$ and $\hbar_v(0,\mathbf{0})$ is monotonically increasing for t_f. In the following proposition, for simplicity of discussion, we assume t_f equal to $N\delta$. Then, the error caused by discretization can be estimated as follows:

Proposition 3. *For $N \in \mathbb{N}^+$ and $\delta = \frac{t_f}{N}$,*

$$|\hbar_{v_0,N}(t_f, t_f \cdot \mathbf{1}) - \hbar_{v_0}(0, \mathbf{0})| = \mathcal{O}(\delta)$$

For function $f(\delta)$, f is of the magnitude $\mathcal{O}(\delta)$ if $\overline{\lim\limits_{\delta \to 0}} \left| \frac{f(\delta)}{\delta} \right| = C$, where C is a constant. From Proposition 3, if we view $\Lambda_{\max}$ and t_f as constants, then the error is $\mathcal{O}(\delta)$ to the step length δ. By Proposition 2, the numerical solution generated by Algorithm 1 converges to the reachability probability of $\mathcal{C} \otimes \mathcal{A}$, and the error can be as small as we expect if we decrease the size of discretization δ, and increase the time bound t_f.

5   Experimental Results

We implemented a prototype including Algorithms 1 and 2 in C and a tool taking a CTMC $\mathcal{C}$ and a DTA $\mathcal{A}$ as input and generating a .c file to store their product in Python, which is used as an input to Algorithms 1 and 2. The first two examples (Examples 5 and 6) come from [10] to show the feasibility of our tool. The last case study is an example of robot navigation from [7]. In order to demonstrate the scalability of our approach, we revise the example with different real-time requirements, which require DTA with different number of clocks. The examples are executed in Linux 16.04 LTS with Intel(R) Core(TM) i7-4710HQ 2.50 GHz CPU and 16 G RAM. The column "time" reports the running time for Algorithm 1, and "time (lazy)" reports the running time for Algorithm 2. All time is counted in seconds.

Example 5. Consider Example 3 with $r_i = 1$, $i = 0, \ldots 3$ and $\delta = 0.01$, experimental result is shown in Table 1. The relevant error when $t_f = 30$ and $t_f = 40$ is 5×10^{-7}.

Table 1. The experimental results for Examples 5 and 6

t_f	Example 5			Example 6		
	$\hbar_{v_0}(0,\mathbf{0})$	time	time (lazy)	$\hbar_{v_0}(0,\mathbf{0})$	time	time (lazy)
20	0.110791	0.8070	0.7232	0.999999	0.1685	0.0002
30	0.110792	1.7246	1.6260	0.999999	0.3453	0.0003
40	0.110792	3.0344	2.8760	0.999999	0.6265	0.0003

Example 6. Consider the reachability probability for the product of a CTMC and a DTA as shown in Fig. 6. A part of its region graph is shown in Fig. 7. Set $r_0 = r_1 = 1$, $\delta = 0.1$, the experimental result is given in Table 1. The relevant error when $t_f = 30$ and $t_f = 40$ is 1×10^{-7}. Note that even for this simple example, none of existing tools can handle it.

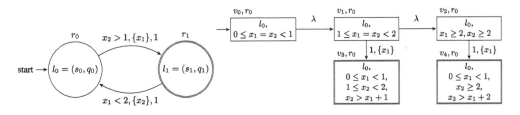

Fig. 6. The product automaton of Example 6

Fig. 7. The reachable product region graph of Fig. 6.

Example 7. Consider a robot moves on a $N \times N$ grid as shown in Fig. 8 (adapted from [7]). It can move up, down, left and right. For each possible direction, the robot moves with the same probability. The cells are grouped with A, B, C and D. We consider the following real-time constraints:

P_1: The robot is allowed to stay in adjacent C-cells for at most T_1 time units, and D-cells for at most T_2 time units;

P_2: The total time of the robot continuously resides in adjacent C-cell and D-cell is no more than T_3 time units, with $T_1 \leq T_3$ and $T_2 \leq T_3$;

P_3: The total time of the robot continuously resides in adjacent A-cell and C-cell is no more than T_4 time units, with $T_1 \leq T_4$.

In this example, we are verifying whether the CTMC satisfies (i) P_1; (ii) $P_1 \wedge P_2$; (iii) $P_1 \wedge P_2 \wedge P_3$. Obviously, P_1 can be expressed by a DTA with one clock, see Fig. 9; to express $P_1 \wedge P_2$, a DTA with two clocks is necessary, see Fig. 10; to express $P_1 \wedge P_2 \wedge P_3$, A DTA with three clocks is necessary, see Fig. 11.

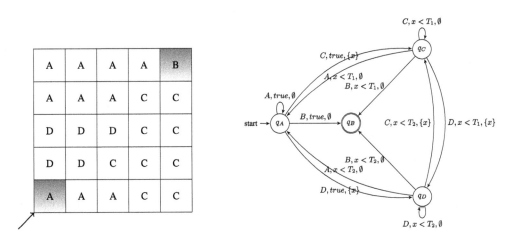

Fig. 8. An example grid

Fig. 9. A DTA with one clock for P_1

The experimental results are summarized in Table 2. The relevant error of $t_f = 20$ and $t_f = 21$ is smaller than 10^{-2}. As can be seen, the running time of our approach heavily depends on the number of clocks. Compared with the

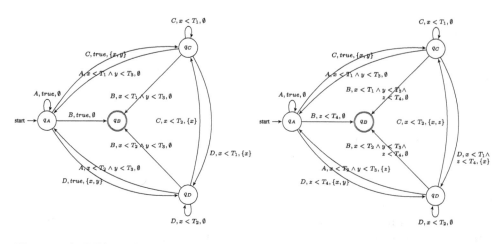

Fig. 10. A DTA with two clocks for $P_1 \wedge P_2$

Fig. 11. A DTA with three clocks for $P_1 \wedge P_2 \wedge P_3$

Table 2. Experimental results for the robot example with $\delta = 0.1$, running time longer than 2700 s is denoted by 'TO' (timeout), the column "#(P)" counts the number of states in the product automaton $\mathcal{C} \otimes \mathcal{G}(\mathcal{A})$, "time([7])" is the running time of prototype in [7] when precision = 0.01, $T_1 = T_2 = 3$, $T_3 = 5$, $T_4 = 7$

		One clock				Two clocks			Three clocks		
N	t_f	#(P)	time	time (lazy)	time([7])	#(P)	time	time (lazy)	#(P)	time	time (lazy)
4	10	39	0.027	0.027	0.011	139	2.583	1.746	733	525.7	141.4
	15		0.049	0.043			7.117	3.445		TO	257.35
	20		0.070	0.071			12.88	5.49		TO	583.76
10	10	232	0.167	0.164	0.087	968	39.41	25.92	5134	TO	1039.7
	15		0.278	0.278			108.48	53.28		TO	TO
	20		0.417	0.421			226.56	89.50		TO	TO
20	10	940	1.142	0.909	1.23	4000	250.1	180.7		TO	TO
	15		1.65	1.54			672.8	375.6		TO	TO
	20		2.54	2.41			1326.8	616.1		TO	TO
30	10	2125	2.38	2.45	6.84	9120	812.9	380.5		TO	TO
	15		4.45	5.42			2058.1	770.8		TO	TO
	20		7.45	7.28			TO	1283.4		TO	TO
40	10	3820	5.62	6.52	20.31	16395	1484.3	759.8		TO	TO
	15		11.97	11.02			TO	1619.9		TO	TO
	20		15.26	16.17			TO	2661.3		TO	TO

results reported in [7] for the case of one clock in this case study (when the precision is set to be 10^{-2}), our result is as fast as theirs, but their tool cannot handle the cases of multiple clocks. In contrast, our approach can handle DTA with multiple clocks as indicated in the verification of P_2 and P_3. Algorithm 2 is much more faster than Algorithm 1 when the number of clocks grows up. To the best of our knowledge, this is the first prototypical tool verifying CTMCs against multi-clock DTA.

6 Concluding Remarks

In this paper, we present a practical approach to verify CTMCs against DTA objectives. First, the desired probability can be reduced to the reachability probability of the product region graph in the form of PDPs. Then we use the augmented PDP to approximate the reachability probability, in which the reachability probability coincides with the solution to a PDE system at the starting point. We further propose a numerical solution to the PDE system by reduction it to a ODE system. The experimental results indicate the efficiency and scalability compared with existing work, as it can handle DTA with multiple clocks.

As a future work, it deserves to investigate whether our approach also works in the verification of CTMCs against more complicated real-time properties, either expressed by timed automata and MTL as considered in [9], or by linear duration invariants as considered in [8].

Acknowledgements. This research is partly funded by the Sino-German Center for Research Promotion as part of the project CAP (GZ 1023), from Yijun Feng, Haokun Li and Bican Xia is partly funded by NSFC under grant No. 61732001 and 61532019, from Joost-Pieter Katoen is partly funded by the DFG Research Training Group 2236 UnRAVeL, from Naijun Zhan is funded partly by NSFC under grant No. 61625206 and 61732001, by "973 Program" under grant No. 2014CB340701 and by the CAS/SAFEA International Partnership Program for Creative Research Teams.

References

1. Alur, R., Dill, D.L.: A theory of timed automata. Theoret. Comput. Sci. **126**(2), 183–235 (1994)
2. Amparore, E.G., Beccuti, M., Donatelli, S.: (Stochastic) model checking in Great-SPN. In: Ciardo, G., Kindler, E. (eds.) PETRI NETS 2014. LNCS, vol. 8489, pp. 354–363. Springer, Cham (2014). https://doi.org/10.1007/978-3-319-07734-5_19
3. Aziz, A., Sanwal, K., Singhal, V., Brayton, R.: Model-checking continous-time Markov chains. ACM Trans. Comput. Log. **1**(1), 162–170 (2000)
4. Baier, C., Cloth, L., Haverkort, B.R., Kuntz, M., Siegle, M.: Model checking Markov chains with actions and state labels. IEEE Trans. Softw. Eng. **33**(4), 209–224 (2007)
5. Baier, C., Haverkort, B., Hermanns, H., Katoen, J.-P.: Model-checking algorithms for continuous-time Markov chains. IEEE Trans. Softw. Eng. **29**(6), 524–541 (2003)
6. Baier, C., Katoen, J.-P.: Principles of Model Checking. MIT Press, Cambridge (2008)
7. Barbot, B., Chen, T., Han, T., Katoen, J.-P., Mereacre, A.: Efficient CTMC model checking of linear real-time objectives. In: Abdulla, P.A., Leino, K.R.M. (eds.) TACAS 2011. LNCS, vol. 6605, pp. 128–142. Springer, Heidelberg (2011). https://doi.org/10.1007/978-3-642-19835-9_12

8. Chen, T., Diciolla, M., Kwiatkowska, M., Mereacre, A.: Verification of linear duration properties over continuous-time Markov chains. ACM Trans. Comput. Log. **14**(4), 33 (2013)

9. Chen, T., Diciolla, M., Kwiatkowska, M., Mereacre, A.: Time-bounded verification of CTMCs against real-time specifications. In: Fahrenberg, U., Tripakis, S. (eds.) FORMATS 2011. LNCS, vol. 6919, pp. 26–42. Springer, Heidelberg (2011). https://doi.org/10.1007/978-3-642-24310-3_4

10. Chen, T., Han, T., Katoen, J.-P., Mereacre, A.: Quantitative model checking of continuous-time Markov chains against timed automata specifications. In: LICS, pp. 309–318 (2009)

11. Chen, T., Han, T., Katoen, J., Mereacre, A.: Model checking of continuous-time Markov chains against timed automata specifications. Log. Methods Comput. Sci. **7**(1) (2011)

12. Chen, T., Han, T., Katoen, J.-P., Mereacre, A.: Observing continuous-time MDPs by 1-clock timed automata. In: Delzanno, G., Potapov, I. (eds.) RP 2011. LNCS, vol. 6945, pp. 2–25. Springer, Heidelberg (2011). https://doi.org/10.1007/978-3-642-24288-5_2

13. Dang, V.H., Zhou, C.: Probabilistic duration calculus for continuous time. Formal Aspects Comput. **11**(1), 21–44 (1999)

14. Davis, M.H.: Markov Models and Optimization, vol. 49. CRC Press, Boca Raton (1993)

15. Dehnert, C., Junges, S., Katoen, J.-P., Volk, M.: A STORM is coming: a modern probabilistic model checker. In: Majumdar, R., Kunčak, V. (eds.) CAV 2017. LNCS, vol. 10427, pp. 592–600. Springer, Cham (2017). https://doi.org/10.1007/978-3-319-63390-9_31

16. Donatelli, S., Haddad, S., Sproston, J.: Model checking timed and stochastic properties with CSL^{TA}. IEEE Trans. Softw. Eng. **35**(2), 224–240 (2009)

17. Feller, W.: An Introduction to Probability Theory and Its Applications, vol. 3. Wiley, New York (1968)

18. Fu, H.: Approximating acceptance probabilities of CTMC-paths on multi-clock deterministic timed automata. In: HSCC, pp. 323–332. ACM (2013)

19. Gao, Y., Xu, M., Zhan, N., Zhang, L.: Model checking conditional CSL for continuous-time Markov chains. Inf. Process. Lett. **113**(1–2), 44–50 (2013)

20. Grossmann, C., Roos, H.-G., Stynes, M.: Numerical Treatment of Partial Differential Equations, vol. 154. Springer, Heidelberg (2007)

21. Johnson, C.: Numerical Solution of Partial Differential Equations by the Finite Element Method. Courier Corporation, Chelmsford (2012)

22. Katoen, J.-P., Zapreev, I.S., Hahn, E.M., Hermanns, H., Jansen, D.N.: The ins and outs of the probabilistic model checker MRMC. Perform. Eval. **68**(2), 90–104 (2011)

23. Kwiatkowska, M., Norman, G., Parker, D.: PRISM 4.0: verification of probabilistic real-time systems. In: Gopalakrishnan, G., Qadeer, S. (eds.) CAV 2011. LNCS, vol. 6806, pp. 585–591. Springer, Heidelberg (2011). https://doi.org/10.1007/978-3-642-22110-1_47

24. Mikeev, L., Neuhäußer, M.R., Spieler, D., Wolf, V.: On-the-fly verification and optimization of DTA-properties for large Markov chains. Formal Methods Syst. Des. **43**(2), 313–337 (2013)

25. Wisniewski, R., Sloth, C., Bujorianu, M.L., Piterman, N.: Safety verification of piecewise-deterministic Markov processes. In: HSCC, pp. 257–266. ACM (2016)

26. Yin, G.G., Zhang, Q.: Continuous-Time Markov Chains and Applications: A Two-Time-Scale Approach, vol. 37. Springer, New York (2012). https://doi.org/10.1007/978-1-4614-4346-9
27. Zhang, L., Jansen, D.N., Nielson, F., Hermanns, H.: Efficient CSL model checking using stratification. Log. Methods Comput. Sci. **8**(2:17), 1–18 (2012)
28. Zhou, C., Hoare, C.A.R., Ravn, A.P.: A calculus of durations. Inf. Process. Lett. **40**(5), 269–276 (1991)

A Counting Semantics for Monitoring LTL Specifications over Finite Traces

Ezio Bartocci[1]([✉]), Roderick Bloem[2], Dejan Nickovic[3], and Franz Roeck[2]

[1] TU Wien, Vienna, Austria
ezio.bartocci@tuwien.ac.at
[2] Graz University of Technology, Graz, Austria
[3] Austrian Institute of Technology GmbH, Vienna, Austria

Abstract. We consider the problem of monitoring a Linear Time Logic (LTL) specification that is defined on infinite paths, over finite traces. For example, we may need to draw a verdict on whether the system satisfies or violates the property "p holds infinitely often." The problem is that there is always a continuation of a finite trace that satisfies the property and a different continuation that violates it.

We propose a two-step approach to address this problem. First, we introduce a counting semantics that computes the number of steps to witness the satisfaction or violation of a formula for each position in the trace. Second, we use this information to make a prediction on inconclusive suffixes. In particular, we consider a *good* suffix to be one that is shorter than the longest witness for a satisfaction, and a *bad* suffix to be shorter than or equal to the longest witness for a violation. Based on this assumption, we provide a verdict assessing whether a continuation of the execution on the same system will presumably satisfy or violate the property.

1 Introduction

Alice is a verification engineer and she is presented with a new exciting and complex design. The requirements document coming with the design already incorporates functional requirements formalized in Linear Temporal Logic (LTL) [13]. The design contains features that are very challenging for exhaustive verification and her favorite model checking tool does not terminate in reasonable time.
Runtime Verification. Alice decides to tackle this problem using runtime verification (RV) [3], a light, yet rigorous verification method. RV drops the exhaustiveness of model checking and analyzes individual traces generated by the system. Thus, it scales much better to the industrial-size designs. RV enables automatic

generation of monitors from formalized requirements and thus provides a systematic way to check if the system traces satisfy (violate) the specification.

Motivating Example. In particular, Alice considers the following specification:

$$\psi \equiv \mathsf{G}(\mathsf{request} \to \mathsf{F}\,\mathsf{grant})$$

This LTL formula specifies that every request coming from the environment must be granted by the design in some finite (but unbounded) future. Alice realizes that she is trying to check a *liveness* property over a set of *finite* traces. She looks closer at the executions and identifies the two interesting examples trace τ_1 and trace τ_2, depicted in Table 1.

The monitoring tool reports that both τ_1 and τ_2 presumably violate the unbounded response property. This verdict is against Alice's intuition. The evaluation of trace τ_1 seems right to her – the request at Cycle 1 is followed by a grant at Cycle 3, however the request at Cycle 4 is never granted during that execution. There are good reasons to suspect a bug in the design. Then she looks at τ_2 and observes that after every **request** the **grant** is given exactly after 2

Table 1. Unbounded response property example.

trace	time	1	2	3	4	5	6	7
τ_1	request	⊤	−	−	⊤	−	−	−
	grant	−	−	⊤	−	−	−	−
τ_2	request	⊤	−	−	⊤	−	−	⊤
	grant	−	−	⊤	−	−	⊤	−

We use "−" instead of "⊥" to improve the trace readability.

cycles. It is true that the last request at Cycle 7 is not followed by a grant, but this seems to happen because the execution ends at that cycle – the past trace observations give reason to think that this request would be followed by a grant in cycle 9 if the execution was continued. Thus, Alice is not satisfied by the second verdict.

Alice looks closer at the way that the LTL property is evaluated over finite traces. She finds out that temporal operators are given *strength – eventually* and *until* are declared as *strong* operators, while *always* and *weak until* are defined to be *weak* [9]. A strong temporal operator requires all outstanding obligations to be met before the end of the trace. In contrast, a weak temporal operator must not witness any outstanding obligation violation before the end of the trace. Under this interpretation, both τ_1 and τ_2 violate the unbounded response property.

Alice explores another popular approach to evaluate future temporal properties over finite traces – the 3-valued semantics for LTL [4]. In this setting, the Boolean set of verdicts is extended with a third unknown (or maybe) value. A finite trace satisfies (violates) the 3-valued LTL formula if and only if all the infinite extensions of the trace satisfy (violate) the same LTL formula under its classical interpretation. In all other cases, we say that the satisfaction of the formula by the trace is unknown. Alice applies the 3-valued interpretation of LTL on the traces τ_1 and τ_2 to evaluate the unbounded response property. In both situations, she ends up with the **unknown** verdict. Once again, this is not what she expects and it does not meet her intuition about the satisfaction of the formula by the observed traces.

Alice desires a semantics that evaluates LTL properties on finite traces by taking previous observations into account.

Contributions. In this paper, we study the problem of LTL evaluation over finite traces encountered by Alice and propose a solution. We introduce a new counting semantics for LTL that takes into account the intuition illustrated by the example from Table 1. This semantics computes for every position of a trace two values – the distances to the nearest satisfaction and violation of the co-safety, respectively safety, part of the specification. We use this quantitative information to make *predictions* about the (infinite) suffixes of the finite observations. We infer from these values the maximum time that we expect for a future obligation to be fulfilled. We compare it to the value that we have for an open obligation at the end of the trace. If the latter is greater (smaller) than the expected maximum value, we have a good indication of a *presumed violation (satisfaction)* that we report to the user. In particular, our approach will indicate that τ_1 is likely to violate the specification and should be further inspected. In contrast, it will evaluate that τ_2 most likely satisfies the unbounded response property.

Organization of the Paper. The rest of the paper is organized as follows. We discuss the related work in Sect. 2 and we provide the preliminaries in Sect. 3. In Sect. 4 we present our new counting semantics for LTL and we show how to make *predictions* about (infinite) suffixes of the finite observations. Section 5 shows the application of our approach to some examples. Finally in Sect. 6 we draw our conclusions.

2   Related Work

The finitary interpretation of LTL was first considered in [11], where the authors propose to enrich the logic with the *weak* next operator that is dual to the (strong) next operator defined on infinite traces. While the strong next requires the existence of a next state, the weak next trivially evaluates to true at the end of the trace. In [9], the authors propose a more semantic approach with *weak* and *strong* views for evaluating future obligations at the end of the trace. In essence the empty word satisfies (violates) every formula according to the weak (strong) view. These two approaches result in the violation of the specification ψ by both traces τ_1 and τ_2.

The authors in [4] propose a 3-valued finitary LTL interpretation of LTL, in which the set {true, false} of verdicts is extended with a third **inconclusive** verdict. According to the 3-valued LTL, a finite trace satisfies (violates) a specification iff all its infinite extensions satisfy (violate) the same property under the classical LTL interpretation. Otherwise, it evaluates to **inconclusive**. The main disadvantage of the 3-valued semantics is the dominance of the **inconclusive** verdict in the evaluation of many interesting LTL formulas. In fact, both τ_1 and τ_2 from Table 1 evaluate to inconclusive against the unbounded response specification ψ.

In [5], the authors combine the weak and strong operators with the 3-valued semantics to refine the inconclusive with {presumably true, presumably false}. The strength of the remaining future obligation dictates the presumable verdict. The authors in [12] propose a finitary semantics for each of the LTL (safety, liveness, persistence and recurrence) hierarchy classes that asymptotically converges to the infinite traces semantics of the logic. In these two works, the specification ψ also evaluates to the same verdict for both the traces τ_1 and τ_2.

To summarize, none of the related work handles the unbounded response example from Table 1 in a satisfactory manner. This is due to the fact that these approaches decide about the verdict based on the specification and its remaining future obligations at the end of the trace. In contrast, we propose an approach in which the past observations within the trace are used to predict the future and derive the appropriate verdict. In particular, the application of our semantics for the evaluation of ψ over τ_1 and τ_2 results in presumably true and presumably false verdicts.

In [17], the authors propose another predictive semantics for LTL. In essence, this work assumes that at every point in time the monitor is able to precisely predict a segment of the trace that it has not observed yet and produce its outcome accordingly. In order to ensure such predictive power, this approach requires a white-box setting in which instrumentation and some form of static analysis of the systems are needed in order to foresee in advance the upcoming observations. This is in contrast to our work, in which the monitor remains a passive participant and predicts its verdict only based on the past observations.

In a different research thread [15], the authors introduce the notion of *monitorable* specifications that can be positively or negatively determined by a finite trace. The monitorability of LTL is further studied in [6,14]. This classification of specifications is orthogonal to our work. We focus on providing a sensible evaluation to all LTL properties, including the non-monitorable ones (e.g., $GF\,p$).

We also mention the recent work on statistical model checking for LTL [8]. In this work, the authors assume a gray-box setting, where the system-under-test (SUT) is a Markov chain with the known minimum transition probability. This is in contrast to our work, in which we passively observe existing finite traces generated by the SUT, i.e., we have a blackbox setting.

In [1], the authors propose extending LTL with a discounting operator and study the properties of the augmented logic. The LTL specification formalism is extended with path-accumulation assertions in [7]. These LTL extensions are motivated by the need for a more quantitative and refined analysis of the systems. In our work, the motivation for the counting semantics is quite different. We use the quantitative information that we collect during the execution of the trace to predict the future behavior of the system and thus improve the quality of the monitoring verdict.

3 Preliminaries

We first introduce *traces* and Linear Temporal Logic (LTL) that we interpret over 3-valued semantics.

Definition 1 (Trace). *Let P a finite set of propositions and let $\Pi = 2^P$. A (finite or infinite) trace π is a sequence $\pi_1, \pi_2, \ldots \in \Pi^* \cup \Pi^\omega$. We denote by $|\pi| \in \mathbb{N} \cup \{\infty\}$ the length of π. We denote by $\pi \cdot \pi'$ the concatenation of $\pi \in \Pi^*$ and $\pi' \in \Pi^* \cup \Pi^\omega$.*

Definition 2 (Linear Temporal Logic). *In this paper, we consider linear temporal logic (LTL) and we define its syntax by the grammar:*

$$\phi := p \mid \neg\phi \mid \phi_1 \vee \phi_2 \mid \mathsf{X}\phi \mid \phi_1 \mathsf{U} \phi_2,$$

where $p \in P$. We denote by Φ the set of all LTL formulas.

From the basic definition we can derive other standard Boolean and temporal operators as follows:

$$\top = p \vee \neg p, \ \bot = \neg\top, \ \phi \wedge \psi = \neg(\neg\phi \vee \neg\psi), \ \mathsf{F}\phi = \top \mathsf{U} \phi, \ \mathsf{G}\phi = \neg\mathsf{F}\neg\phi$$

Let $\pi \in \Pi^\omega$ be an infinite trace and ϕ an LTL formula. The satisfaction relation $(\pi, i) \models \phi$ is defined inductively as follows

$$
\begin{aligned}
(\pi, i) &\models p && \text{iff } p \in \pi_i, \\
(\pi, i) &\models \neg\phi && \text{iff } (\pi, i) \not\models \phi, \\
(\pi, i) &\models \phi_1 \vee \phi_2 && \text{iff } (\pi, i) \models \phi_1 \text{ or } (\pi, i) \models \phi_2, \\
(\pi, i) &\models \mathsf{X}\phi && \text{iff } (\pi, i+1) \models \phi, \\
(\pi, i) &\models \phi_1 \mathsf{U} \phi_2 && \text{iff } \exists j \geq i \text{ s.t. } (\pi, j) \models \phi_2 \text{ and } \forall i \leq k < j, (\pi, k) \models \phi_1.
\end{aligned}
$$

We now recall the 3-valued semantics from [4]. We denote by $[\pi \models_3 \phi]$ the evaluation of ϕ with respect to the trace $\pi \in \Pi^*$ that yields a value in $\{\top, \bot, ?\}$.

$$
[\pi \models_3 \phi] =
\begin{cases}
\top & \forall \pi' \in \Pi^\omega, \pi \cdot \pi' \models \phi, \\
\bot & \forall \pi' \in \Pi^\omega, \pi \cdot \pi' \not\models \phi, \\
? & \text{otherwise.}
\end{cases}
$$

We now restrict LTL to a fragment without explicit $\top$ and $\bot$ symbols and with the explicit F operator that we add to the syntax. We provide an alternative 3-valued semantics for this fragment, denoted by $\mu_\pi(\phi, i)$ where $i \in \mathbb{N}_{>0}$ indicates a position in or outside the trace. We assume the order $\bot <? < \top$, and extend the Boolean operations to the 3-valued domain with the rules $\neg_3\top = \bot$, $\neg_3\bot = \top$ and $\neg_3? =?$ and $\phi_1 \vee_3 \phi_2 = max(\phi_1, \phi_2)$. We define the semantics inductively as follows:

$$\mu_\pi(p,i) \quad = \begin{cases} \top & \text{if } i \leq |\pi| \text{ and } p \in \pi_i, \\ \bot & \text{else if } i \leq |\pi| \text{ and } p \notin \pi_i, \\ ? & \text{otherwise,} \end{cases}$$

$$\mu_\pi(\neg\phi,i) \quad = \neg_3\mu_\pi(\phi,i),$$

$$\mu_\pi(\phi_1 \vee \phi_2,i) = \mu_\pi(\phi_1,i) \vee_3 \mu_\pi(\phi_2,i),$$

$$\mu_\pi(\mathsf{X}\,\phi,i) \quad = \mu_\pi(\phi,i+1),$$

$$\mu_\pi(\mathsf{F}\,\phi,i) \quad = \begin{cases} \mu_\pi(\phi,i) \vee_3 \mu_\pi(\mathsf{XF}\,\phi,i) & \text{if } i \leq |\pi|, \\ \mu_\pi(\phi,i) & \text{if } i > |\pi|, \end{cases}$$

$$\mu_\pi(\phi_1 \,\mathsf{U}\, \phi_2,i) = \begin{cases} \mu_\pi(\phi_2,i) \vee_3 (\mu_\pi(\phi_1,i) \wedge_3 \mu_\pi(\mathsf{X}(\phi_1 \,\mathsf{U}\, \phi_2),i)) & \text{if } i \leq |\pi|, \\ \mu_\pi(\phi_2,i) & \text{if } i > |\pi|. \end{cases}$$

We note that the adapted semantics allows evaluating a finite trace in polynomial time, in contrast to $[\pi \models_3 \phi]$, which requires a PSPACE-complete algorithm. This improvement in complexity comes at a price – the adapted semantics cannot semantically characterize tautologies and contradiction. We have for example that $\mu_\pi(p \vee \neg p, 1)$ for the empty word evaluates to ?, despite the fact that $p \vee \neg p$ is semantically equivalent to $\top$. The novel semantics that we introduce in the following sections make the same tradeoff.

In the following lemma, we relate the two three-valued semantics.

Lemma 3. *Given an LTL formula and a trace $\pi \in \Pi^*$, $|\pi| \neq 0$, we have that*

$$\mu_\pi(\phi,1) = \top \Rightarrow [\pi \models_3 \phi] = \top,$$
$$\mu_\pi(\phi,1) = \bot \Rightarrow [\pi \models_3 \phi] = \bot.$$

Proof. These two statements can be proven by induction on the structure of the LTL formula (see Appendix A.1 in [2]). $[\pi \models_3 \phi] = ? \Rightarrow \mu_\pi(\phi,1) = ?$ is the consequence of the first two.

4   Counting Finitary Semantics for LTL

In this section, we introduce the counting semantics for LTL. We first provide necessary definitions in Sect. 4.1, we present the new semantics in Sect. 4.2 and finally propose a predictive mapping that transforms the counting semantics into a qualitative 5-valued verdict in Sect. 4.3.

4.1   Definitions

Let $\mathbb{N}_+ = \mathbb{N}_0 \cup \{\infty, -\}$ be the set of *natural* numbers (incl. 0) extended with the two special symbols ∞ (infinite) and $-$ (impossible) such that $\forall n \in \mathbb{N}_0$, we define $n < \infty < -$. We define the addition $\oplus$ of two elements $a, b \in \mathbb{N}_+$ as follows.

Definition 4 (Operator $\oplus$). *We define the binary operator $\oplus : \mathbb{N}_+ \times \mathbb{N}_+ \to \mathbb{N}_+$ s. t. for $a \oplus b$ with $a, b \in \mathbb{N}_+$ we have $a + b$ if $a, b \in \mathbb{N}_0$ and $\max\{a, b\}$ otherwise.*

We denote by (s, f) a pair of two extended numbers $s, f \in \mathbb{N}_+$. In Definition 5, we introduce several operations on pairs: (1) the *swap* between the two values ($\sim$), (2) the *increment* by 1 of both values ($\oplus 1$), (3) the *minmax* binary operation ($\sqcup$) that gives the pair consisting of the minimum first value and the maximum second value, and (4) the *maxmin* binary operation ($\sqcap$) that is symmetric to ($\sqcup$).

Definition 7 introduces the counting semantics for LTL that for a finite trace π and LTL formula ϕ gives a pair $(s, f) \in \mathbb{N}_+ \times \mathbb{N}_+$. We call s and f *satisfaction* and *violation witness counts*, respectively. Intuitively, the s (f) value denotes the minimal number of additional steps that is needed to witness the satisfaction (violation) of the formula. The value ∞ is used to denote that the property can be satisfied (violated) only in an infinite number of steps, while $-$ means the property cannot be satisfied (violated) by any continuation of the trace.

Definition 5 (Operations $\sim$, $\oplus 1$, $\sqcup$, $\sqcap$). *Given two pairs $(s, f) \in \mathbb{N}_+ \times \mathbb{N}_+$ and $(s', f') \in \mathbb{N}_+ \times \mathbb{N}_+$, we have:*

$$\sim (s, f) = (f, s),$$
$$(s, f) \oplus 1 = (s \oplus 1, f \oplus 1),$$
$$(s, f) \sqcup (s', f') = (\min(s, s'), \max(f, f')),$$
$$(s, f) \sqcap (s', f') = (\max(s, s'), \min(f, f')).$$

Example 6. Given the pairs $(0, 0)$, $(\infty, 1)$ and $(7, -)$ we have the following:

$$\sim (0, 0) = (0, 0), \qquad \sim (\infty, 1) = (1, \infty),$$
$$(0, 0) \oplus 1 = (1, 1), \qquad (\infty, 1) \oplus 1 = (\infty, 2),$$
$$(0, 0) \sqcup (\infty, 1) = (0, 1), \qquad (\infty, 1) \sqcup (7, -) = (7, -),$$
$$(0, 0) \sqcap (\infty, 1) = (\infty, 0), \qquad (\infty, 1) \sqcap (7, -) = (\infty, 1).$$

Remark. Note that $\mathbb{N}_+ \times \mathbb{N}_+$ forms a lattice where $(s, f) \trianglelefteq (s', f')$ when $s \geq s'$ and $f \leq f'$ with join $\sqcup$ and meet $\sqcap$. Intuitively, larger values are closer to true.

4.2 Semantics

We now present our finitary semantics.

Definition 7 (Counting finitary semantics). *Let $\pi \in \Pi^*$ be a finite trace, $i \in \mathbb{N}_{>0}$ be a position in or outside the trace and $\phi \in \Phi$ be an LTL formula. We define the counting finitary semantics of LTL as the function $d_\pi : \Phi \times \Pi^* \times \mathbb{N}_{>0} \to \mathbb{N}_+ \times \mathbb{N}_+$ such that:*

$$d_\pi(p, i) = \begin{cases} (0, -) & \textit{if } i \le |\pi| \wedge p \in \pi_i, \\ (-, 0) & \textit{if } i \le |\pi| \wedge p \notin \pi_i, \\ (0, 0) & \textit{if } i > |\pi|, \end{cases}$$

$$d_\pi(\neg\phi, i) = \sim d_\pi(\phi, i),$$

$$d_\pi(\phi_1 \vee \phi_2, i) = d_\pi(\phi_1, i) \sqcup d_\pi(\phi_2, i),$$

$$d_\pi(\mathsf{X}\phi, i) = d_\pi(\phi, i+1) \oplus 1,$$

$$d_\pi(\phi \,\mathsf{U}\, \psi, i) = \begin{cases} d_\pi(\psi, i) \sqcup \left(d_\pi(\phi, i) \sqcap d_\pi(\mathsf{X}(\phi \,\mathsf{U}\, \psi), i) \right) & \textit{if } i \le |\pi|, \\ d_\pi(\psi, i) \sqcup \left(d_\pi(\phi, i) \sqcap (-, \infty) \right) & \textit{if } i > |\pi|, \end{cases}$$

$$d_\pi(\mathsf{F}\,\phi, i) = \begin{cases} d_\pi(\phi, i) \sqcup d_\pi(\mathsf{XF}\,\phi, i) & \textit{if } i \le |\pi|, \\ d_\pi(\phi, i) \sqcup (-, \infty) & \textit{if } i > |\pi|. \end{cases}$$

We now provide some motivations behind the above definitions.

Proposition. A proposition is either evaluated before or after the end of the trace. If it is evaluated before the end of the trace and the proposition holds, the satisfaction and violations witness counts are trivially 0 and $-$, respectively. In the case that the proposition does not hold, we have the symmetric witness counts. Finally, we take an optimistic view in case of evaluating a proposition after the end of the trace: The trace can be extended to a trace with i steps s.t. either p holds or p does not hold.

Negation. Negating a formula simply swaps the witness counts. If we witness the satisfaction of ϕ in n steps, we witness the violation of $\neg\phi$ in n steps, and vice versa.

Disjunction. We take the shorter satisfaction witness count, because the satisfaction of one subformula is enough to satisfy the property. And we take the longer violation witness count, because both subformulas need to be violated to violate the property.

Next. The next operator naturally increases the witness counts by one step.

Eventually. We use the rewriting rule $\mathsf{F}\,\phi \equiv \phi \vee \mathsf{XF}\,\phi$ to define the semantics of the eventually operator. When evaluating the formula after the end of the trace, we replace the remaining obligation $(\mathsf{XF}\,\phi)$ by $(-, \infty)$. Thus, $\mathsf{F}\,\phi$ evaluated on the empty word is satisfied by a suffix that satisfies ϕ, and it is violated only by infinite suffixes.

Until. We use the same principle for defining the until semantics that we used for the eventually operator. We use the rewriting rule $\phi \,\mathsf{U}\, \psi \equiv \psi \vee (\phi \wedge \mathsf{X}(\phi \,\mathsf{U}\, \psi))$. On the empty word, $\phi \,\mathsf{U}\, \psi$ is satisfied (in the shortest way) by a suffix that satisfies ψ, and it is violated by a suffix that violates both ϕ and ψ.

Example 8. We refer to our motivating example from Table 1 and evaluate the trace τ_2 with respect to the specification ψ. We present the outcome in Table 2. We see that every proposition evaluates to $(0, -)$ when true. The satisfaction of a proposition that holds at time i is immediately witnessed and it cannot be violated by any suffix. Similarly, a proposition evaluates to $(-, 0)$ when false. The valuations of $\mathsf{F}\,g$ count the number of steps to positions in which g holds. For instance, the first time at which g holds is $i = 3$, hence $\mathsf{F}\,g$ evaluates to

$(2, -)$ at time 1, $(1, -)$ at time 2 and $(0, -)$ at time 3. We also note that $\mathsf{F}\,g$ evaluates to $(0, \infty)$ at the end of the trace – it could be immediately satisfied with the continuation of the trace with g that holds, but could be violated only by an infinite suffix in which g never holds. We finally observe that $\mathsf{G}(r \to \mathsf{F}\,g)$ evaluates to (∞, ∞) at all positions – the property can be both satisfied and violated only with infinite suffixes.

Table 2. Unbounded response property example: $d_\pi(\phi, i)$ with the trace $\pi = \tau_2$.

	1	2	3	4	5	6	7	EOT
r	$\top$	$-$	$-$	$\top$	$-$	$-$	$\top$	
g	$-$	$-$	$\top$	$-$	$-$	$\top$	$-$	
$d_\pi(r, i)$	$(0,-)$	$(-,0)$	$(-,0)$	$(0,-)$	$(-,0)$	$(-,0)$	$(0,-)$	$(0,0)$
$d_\pi(g, i)$	$(-,0)$	$(-,0)$	$(0,-)$	$(-,0)$	$(-,0)$	$(0,-)$	$(-,0)$	$(0,0)$
$d_\pi(\neg r, i)$	$(-,0)$	$(0,-)$	$(0,-)$	$(-,0)$	$(0,-)$	$(0,-)$	$(-,0)$	$(0,0)$
$d_\pi(\mathsf{F}\,g, i)$	$(2,-)$	$(1,-)$	$(0,-)$	$(2,-)$	$(1,-)$	$(0,-)$	$(1,\infty)$	$(0,\infty)$
$d_\pi(r \to \mathsf{F}\,g, i)$	$(2,-)$	$(0,-)$	$(0,-)$	$(2,-)$	$(0,-)$	$(0,-)$	$(1,\infty)$	$(0,\infty)$
$d_\pi(\mathsf{G}(r \to \mathsf{F}\,g), i)$	(∞,∞)	(∞,∞)	(∞,∞)	(∞,∞)	(∞,∞)	(∞,∞)	(∞,∞)	(∞,∞)

We use "$-$" instead of "$\bot$" in the traces r and g to improve the readability.

Not all pairs $(s, f) \in \mathbb{N}_+ \times \mathbb{N}_+$ are possible according to the counting semantics. We present the possible pairs in Lemma 9.

Lemma 9. *Let $\pi \in \Pi^*$ be a finite trace, ϕ an LTL formula and $i \in \mathbb{N}_0$ an index. We have that $d_\pi(\phi, i)$ is of the form $(a, -)$, $(-, a)$, (b_1, b_2), (b_1, ∞), (∞, b_2) or (∞, ∞), where $a \leq |\pi| - i$ and $b_j > |\pi| - i$ for $j \in \{1, 2\}$.*

Proof. The proof can be obtained using structural induction on the LTL formula (see Appendix A.2 in [2]).

Finally, we relate our counting semantics to the three valued semantics in Lemma 10.

Lemma 10. *Given an LTL formula and a trace $\pi \in \Pi^*$ where $i \in \mathbb{N}_{>0}$ is an index and ϕ is an LTL formula, we have that*

$$d_\pi(\phi, i) = (a, -) \;\leftrightarrow\; \mu_\pi(\phi, i) = \top,$$
$$\text{and} \quad \not\exists x < a . \pi' = \pi_i \cdot \pi_{i+1} \cdot \ldots \pi_{i+x}, \mu_{\pi'}(\phi, 1) = \top$$
$$d_\pi(\phi, i) = (-, a) \;\leftrightarrow\; \mu_\pi(\phi, i) = \bot,$$
$$\text{and} \quad \not\exists x < a . \pi' = \pi_i \cdot \pi_{i+1} \cdot \ldots \pi_{i+x}, \mu_{\pi'}(\phi, 1) = \bot$$
$$d_\pi(\phi, i) = (b_1, b_2) \;\leftrightarrow\; \mu_\pi(\phi, i) = ?,$$

where $a \leq |\pi| - i$ and b_j is either ∞ or $b_j > |\pi| - i$ for $j \in \{1, 2\}$.

Intuitively, Lemma 10 holds because we only introduce the symbol "$-$" within the trace when a satisfaction (violation) is observed. And the values of a pair only propagate into the past (and never into the future).

4.3 Evaluation

We now propose a mapping that predicts a qualitative verdict from our counting semantics. We adopt a 5-valued set consisting of true ($\top$), presumably true ($\top_P$), inconclusive (?), presumably false ($\bot_P$) and false ($\bot$) verdicts. We define the following order over these five values: $\bot < \bot_P < ? < \top_P < \top$. We equip this 5-valued domain with the negation ($\neg$) and disjunction ($\vee$) operations, letting $\neg\top = \bot$, $\neg\top_P = \bot_P$, $\neg? = ?$, $\neg\bot_P = \top_P$, $\neg\bot = \top$ and $\phi_1 \vee \phi_2 = \max\{\phi_1, \phi_2\}$. We define other Boolean operators such as conjunction by the usual logical equivalences ($\phi_1 \wedge \phi_2 = \neg(\neg\phi_1 \vee \neg\phi_2)$, etc.).

We evaluate a property on a trace to $\top$ ($\bot$) when the satisfaction (violation) can be fully determined from the trace, following the definition of the three-valued semantics μ. Intuitively, this takes care of the case in which the safety (co-safety) part of a formula has been violated (satisfied), at least for properties that are intentionally safe (intentionally co-safe, resp.) [10].

Whenever the truth value is not determined, we distinguish whether $d_\pi(\phi, i)$ indicates the possibility for a satisfaction, respective violation, in finite time or not. For possible satisfactions, respective violations, in finite time we make a prediction on whether past observations support the believe that the trace is going to satisfy or violate the property. If the predictions are not inconclusive and not contradicting, then we evaluate the trace to the (presumable) truth value $\top_P$ or $\bot_P$. If we cannot make a prediction to a truth value, we compute the truth value recursively based on the operator in the formula and the truth values of the subformulas (with temporal operators unrolled).

We use the predicate pred_π to give the prediction based on the observed witnesses for satisfaction. The predicate $\mathrm{pred}_\pi(\phi, i)$ becomes ? when no witness for satisfaction exists in the past. When there exists a witness that requires at least the same amount of additional steps as the trace under evaluation then the predicate evaluates to $\top$. If all the existing witnesses (and at least one exists) are shorter than the current trace, then the predicate evaluates to $\bot$. For a prediction on the violation we make a prediction on the satisfaction of $d_\pi(\neg\phi, i)$, i.e., we compute $\mathrm{pred}_\pi(\neg\phi, i)$.

Definition 11 (Prediction predicate). *Let s, f denote natural numbers and let $s_\pi(\phi, i), f_\pi(\phi, i) \in \mathbb{N}_+$ such that $d_\pi(\phi, i) = (s_\pi(\phi, i), f_\pi(\phi, i))$. We define the 3-valued predicate pred_π as*

$$\mathrm{pred}_\pi(\phi, i) = \begin{cases} \top & \text{if } \exists j < i \,.\, d_\pi(\phi, j) = (s', -) \text{ and } s_\pi(\phi, i) < s', \\ ? & \text{if } \nexists j < i \,.\, d_\pi(\phi, j) = (s', -), \\ \bot & \text{if } \exists j < i \,.\, d_\pi(\phi, j) = (s', -) \text{ and }, \\ & s_\pi(\phi, i) > \max_{0 \le j < i}\{s' \mid d_\pi(\phi, j) = (s', -)\}, \end{cases}$$

For the evaluation we consider a case split among the possible combinations of values in the pairs.

Definition 12 (Predictive evaluation). *We define the* predictive evaluation *function $e_\pi(\phi, i)$, with $a \leq |\pi| - i$ and $b_j > |\pi| - i$ for $j \in \{1, 2\}$ and $a, b_j \in \mathbb{N}_0$, for the different cases of $d_\pi(\phi, i)$:*

$d_\pi(\phi, i)$		$e_\pi(\phi, i)$
$(a, -)$		$\top$
(b_1, b_2)	*if* $pred_\pi(\phi, i) > pred_\pi(\neg\phi, i)$	$\top_P$
	if $pred_\pi(\phi, i) = pred_\pi(\neg\phi, i)$	$r_\pi(\phi, i)$
	if $pred_\pi(\phi, i) < pred_\pi(\neg\phi, i)$	$\bot_P$
(b_1, ∞)	*if* $pred_\pi(\phi, i) = \top$	$\top_P$
	if $pred_\pi(\phi, i) = ?$	$r_\pi(\phi, i)$
	if $pred_\pi(\phi, i) = \bot$	$\bot_P$
(∞, b_1)		$e_\pi(\neg\phi, i)$
(∞, ∞)		$r_\pi(\phi, i)$
$(-, a)$		$\bot$

where $r_\pi(\phi, i)$ is an auxiliary function defined inductively as follows:

$$r_\pi(p, i) = ?$$
$$r_\pi(\neg\phi, i) = \neg e_\pi(\phi, i)$$
$$r_\pi(\phi_1 \vee \phi_2, i) = e_\pi(\phi_1, i) \vee e_\pi(\phi_2, i)$$
$$r_\pi(\mathsf{X}^n \phi, i) = e_\pi(\phi, i + n)$$
$$r_\pi(\mathsf{F} \phi, i) = \begin{cases} e_\pi(\phi, i) \vee r_\pi(\mathsf{X}\mathsf{F} \phi, i) & \text{if } i \leq |\pi| \\ e_\pi(\phi, i) & \text{if } i > |\pi| \end{cases}$$
$$r_\pi(\phi_1 \mathsf{U} \phi_2, i) = \begin{cases} e_\pi(\phi_2, i) \vee (e_\pi(\phi_2, i) \wedge e_\pi(\mathsf{X}(\phi_1 \mathsf{U} \phi_2), i)) & \text{if } i \leq |\pi| \\ e_\pi(\phi_2, i) & \text{if } i > |\pi| \end{cases}$$

The predictive evaluation function is symmetric. Hence, $e_\pi(\phi, i) = \neg e_\pi(\neg\phi, i)$ holds.

Example 13. The outcome of evaluating τ_2 from Table 1 is shown in Table 3. Subformula $r \to \mathsf{F} g$ is predicted to be $\top_P$ at $i = 7$ because there exists a longer witness for satisfaction in the past (e.g., at $i = 1$). Thus, the trace evaluates to $\top_P$, as expected.

In Fig. 1 we visualize the evaluation of a pair $d_\pi(\phi, i) = (s, f)$ for a fixed ϕ and a fixed position i. On the x-axis is the witness count s for a satisfaction and on the y-axis is the witness count f for a violation. For a value s, respectively f, that is smaller than the length of the suffix starting at position i (with the other value of the pair always being $-$), the evaluation is either $\top$ or $\bot$. Otherwise the evaluation depends on the values s_{max} and f_{max}. These two values

Table 3. Unbounded response property example with $\pi = \tau_2$.

	1	2	3	4	5	6	7	EOT
r	$\top$	$-$	$-$	$\top$	$-$	$-$	$\top$	
g	$-$	$-$	$\top$	$-$	$-$	$\top$	$-$	
$d_\pi(r,i)$	$(0,-)$	$(-,0)$	$(-,0)$	$(0,-)$	$(-,0)$	$(-,0)$	$(0,-)$	$(0,0)$
$e_\pi(r,i)$	$\top$	$\bot$	$\bot$	$\top$	$\bot$	$\bot$	$\top$	?
$d_\pi(g,i)$	$(-,0)$	$(-,0)$	$(0,-)$	$(-,0)$	$(-,0)$	$(0,-)$	$(-,0)$	$(0,0)$
$e_\pi(g,i)$	$\bot$	$\bot$	$\top$	$\bot$	$\bot$	$\top$	$\bot$	?
$d_\pi(\mathsf{F}\,g,i)$	$(2,-)$	$(1,-)$	$(0,-)$	$(2,-)$	$(1,-)$	$(0,-)$	$(1,\infty)$	$(0,\infty)$
$e_\pi(\mathsf{F}\,g,i)$	$\top$	$\top$	$\top$	$\top$	$\top$	$\top$	$\top_P$	$\top_P$
$d_\pi(r \to \mathsf{F}\,g,i)$	$(2,-)$	$(0,-)$	$(0,-)$	$(2,-)$	$(0,-)$	$(0,-)$	$(1,\infty)$	$(0,\infty)$
$e_\pi(r \to \mathsf{F}\,g,i)$	$\top$	$\top$	$\top$	$\top$	$\top$	$\top$	$\top_P$	$\top_P$
$d_\pi(\mathsf{G}(r \to \mathsf{F}\,g),i)$	(∞,∞)	(∞,∞)	(∞,∞)	(∞,∞)	(∞,∞)	(∞,∞)	(∞,∞)	(∞,∞)
$e_\pi(\mathsf{G}(r \to \mathsf{F}\,g),i)$	$\top_P$	$\top_P$	$\top_P$	$\top_P$	$\top_P$	$\top_P$	$\top_P$	$\top_P$

We use "$-$" instead of "$\bot$" in the traces r and g to improve the readability.

represent the largest witness counts for a satisfaction and a violation in the past, i.e., for positions smaller than i in the trace. Based on the prediction function $\mathrm{pred}_\pi(\phi,i)$ the evaluation becomes $\top_P$, ? or $\bot_P$, where ? indicates that the auxiliary function $r_\pi(\phi,i)$ has to be applied. Starting at an arbitrary point in the diagram and moving to the right increases the witness count for a satisfaction while the witness count for a violation remains constant. Thus, moving to the right makes the pair "more false". The same holds when keeping the witness count for a satisfaction constant and moving up in the diagram as this decrease the witness count for a violation. Analogously, moving down and/or left makes the pair "more true" as the witness count for a violation gets larger and/or the witness count for a satisfaction gets smaller.

Our 5-valued predictive evaluation refines the 3-valued LTL semantics.

Theorem 14. *Let ϕ be an LTL formula, $\pi \in \Pi^*$ and $i \in \mathbb{N}_{>0}$. We have*

$$\mu_\pi(\phi,i) = \top \leftrightarrow e_\pi(\phi,i) = \top,$$
$$\mu_\pi(\phi,i) = \bot \leftrightarrow e_\pi(\phi,i) = \bot,$$
$$\mu_\pi(\phi,i) = ? \leftrightarrow e_\pi(\phi,i) \in \{\top_P, \bot_P, ?\}.$$

Theorem 14 holds, because the evaluation to $\top$ and $\bot$ is simply the mapping of a pair that contains the symbol "$-$", which we have shown in Lemma 10.

Remember that $\mathbb{N}_+ \times \mathbb{N}_+$ is partially ordered by $\trianglelefteq$. We now show that having a trace that is "more true" than another is correctly reflected in our finitary semantics. To define "more true", we first need the polarity of a proposition in an LTL formula.

Example 15. Note that g has positive polarity in $\phi = \mathsf{G}(r \to \mathsf{F}\,g)$. If we define τ_2' to be as τ_2, except that $g \in \tau_2'(i)$ for $i \in \{1,\ldots,6\}$, we have $e_{\tau_2'}(\phi,i) = \bot_P$, whereas $e_{\tau_2}(\phi,i) = \top_P$.

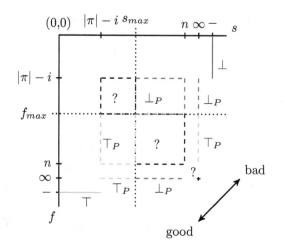

Fig. 1. Lattice for (s, f) with ϕ and $i < |\pi|$ fixed.

Definition 16 (Polarity). *Let* $\#\neg$ *be the number of negation operators on a specific path in the parse tree of* ϕ *starting at the root. We define the polarity as the function* $pol(p)$ *with proposition* p *in an LTL formula* ϕ *as follows:*

$$
pol(p) = \begin{cases} pos, & \text{if } \#\neg \text{ on all paths to a leaf with proposition } p \text{ is even,} \\ neg, & \text{if } \#\neg \text{ on all paths to a leaf with proposition } p \text{ is odd,} \\ mixed, & \text{otherwise.} \end{cases}
$$

With the polarity defined, we now define the constraints for a trace to be "more true" with respect to an LTL formula ϕ.

Definition 17 ($\pi \sqsubseteq_\phi \pi'$). *Given two traces* π *and* π' *of equal length and an LTL formula* ϕ *over proposition* p, *we define that* $\pi \sqsubseteq_\phi \pi'$ *iff*

$$
\forall i \forall p \,.\, pol(p) = mixed \Rightarrow p \in \pi_i \leftrightarrow p \in \pi'_i \text{ and}
$$
$$
pol(p) = pos \Rightarrow p \in \pi_i \rightarrow p \in \pi'_i \text{ and}
$$
$$
pol(p) = neg \Rightarrow p \in \pi_i \leftarrow p \in \pi'_i.
$$

Whenever one trace is "more true" than another, this is correctly reflected in our finitary semantics.

Theorem 18. *For two traces* π *and* π' *of equal length and an LTL formula* ϕ *over proposition* p, *we have that*

$$
\pi \sqsubseteq_\phi \pi' \Rightarrow d_{\pi'}(\phi, 1) \trianglelefteq d_\pi(\phi, 1).
$$

Therefore, we have for $\pi \sqsubseteq_\phi \pi'$ *that*

$$
e_\pi(\phi, 1) = \top \Rightarrow e_{\pi'}(\phi, 1) = \top, \text{ and}
$$
$$
e_\pi(\phi, 1) = \bot \Leftarrow e_{\pi'}(\phi, 1) = \bot.
$$

Theorem 18 holds, because we have that replacing an arbitrary observed value in π by one with positive polarity in π' always results with $d_\pi(\phi,1) = (s,f)$ and $d_{\pi'}(\phi,1) = (s',f')$ in $s' \leq s$ and $f' \geq f$, as with $\pi \sqsubseteq_\phi \pi'$ we have that π' witnesses a satisfaction of ϕ not later than π and π' also witness a violation of ϕ not earlier than π.

Table 4. Making a system "more true".

ϕ	π	$d_\pi(\phi,1)$	$e_\pi(\phi,1)$
p	$-$	$(-,0)$	$\bot$
	$\top$	$(0,-)$	$\top$
$p \wedge \mathsf{X}\,\mathsf{F}\,p$	$- - -$	$(-,0)$	$\bot$
	$\top - -$	$(3,\infty)$	$\bot_P$
$\mathsf{G}\,p$	$-\top\top$	$(-,0)$	$\bot$
	$\top\top\top$	$(\infty,3)$	$\top_P$
$\mathsf{F}\,p$	$- - -$	$(3,\infty)$	$\bot_P$
	$\top - -$	$(0,-)$	$\top$

ϕ	π	$d_\pi(\phi,1)$	$e_\pi(\phi,1)$
$\mathsf{F}\,\mathsf{G}\,p$	$\top - \top - \top$	(∞,∞)	$\bot_P$
	$\top - \top\top\top$	(∞,∞)	$\top_P$
$\mathsf{G}\,\mathsf{F}\,p$	$- - \top - -$	(∞,∞)	$\top_P$
	$\top - \top - -$	(∞,∞)	$\bot_P$
$p \vee \mathsf{X}\,\mathsf{G}\,p$	$-\top\top$	$(\infty,3)$	$\top_P$
	$\top\top\top$	$(0,-)$	$\top$

In Table 4 we give examples to illustrate the transition of one evaluation to another one. Note that it is possible to change from $\top_P$ to $\bot_P$. However, this is only the predicated truth value that becomes "worse", because we have strengthened the prefix on which the prediction is based on, the values of $d_\pi(\phi,i)$ do not change and remain the same is such a case.

5 Examples

We demonstrate the strengths and weaknesses of our approach on the examples of LTL specifications and traces shown in Table 5. We fully develop these examples in Appendix B in [2].

Table 5. Examples of LTL specifications and traces

Specifications	Traces		
$\psi_1 \equiv \mathsf{F}\,\mathsf{X}\,g$	$\pi_1: g: \bot\bot\bot\bot$		$\pi_5: r: \bot\top\top\top\top\bot\top\top$
$\psi_2 \equiv \mathsf{G}\,\mathsf{X}\,g$	$\pi_2: g: \top\top\top\top$		$\quad\ \ g: \bot\top\bot\bot\bot\bot\top\bot$
$\psi_3 \equiv \mathsf{G}(r \to \mathsf{F}\,g)$	$\pi_3: r: \vert\top\vert\vert\top\vert$		$\pi_6: g: \top\top\bot\bot\top\top\bot\bot\top\top\bot\bot\top$
$\psi_4 \equiv \bigwedge_{i \in \{1,2\}} \mathsf{G}(r_i \to \mathsf{F}\,g_i)$	$\quad\ \ g: \bot\bot\top\bot\bot\bot$		$\pi_7: g: \top\top\bot\bot\top\top\bot\bot\top\top\top\top\top$
$\psi_5 \equiv \mathsf{G}((\mathsf{X}\,r)\,\mathsf{U}\,(\mathsf{X}\,\mathsf{X}\,g))$	$\pi_4: r_1: \top\bot\top\bot\top\bot\top$		$\pi_8: r: \top\top\top\top\bot\bot$
$\psi_6 \equiv \mathsf{F}\,\mathsf{G}\,g \vee \mathsf{F}\,\mathsf{G}\,\neg g$	$\quad\ \ g_1: \bot\top\bot\top\bot\top\bot$		$\quad\ \ g: \top\bot\top\bot\top\bot$
$\psi_7 \equiv \mathsf{G}(\mathsf{F}\,r \vee \mathsf{F}\,g)$	$\quad\ \ r_2: \bot\top\bot\top\bot\top\bot$		
$\psi_8 \equiv \mathsf{G}\,\mathsf{F}(r \vee g)$	$\quad\ \ g_2: \top\bot\top\bot\top\bot\top$		
$\psi_9 \equiv \mathsf{G}\,\mathsf{F}\,r \vee \mathsf{G}\,\mathsf{F}\,g$			

Table 6 summarizes the evaluation of our examples. The first and the second column denote the evaluated specification and trace. We use these examples to compare LTL with counting semantics (c-LTL) presented in this paper, to the other two popular finitary LTL interpretations, the 3-valued LTL semantics [4] (3-LTL) and LTL on trucated paths [9] (t-LTL). We recall that in t-LTL there is a distinction between a weak and a strong next operator. We denote by t-LTL-s (t-LTL-w) the specifications from our examples in which X is interpreted as the strong (weak) next operator and assume that we always give a strong interpretation to U and F and a weak interpretation to G.

Table 6. Comparison of different verdicts with different semantics

Spec.	Trace	c-LTL	3-LTL	t-LTL-s	t-LTL-w
ψ_1	π_1	$\perp_P$	?	$\perp$	$\top$
ψ_2	π_2	$\top_P$	?	$\perp$	$\top$
ψ_3	π_3	$\perp_P$	?	$\perp$	$\perp$
ψ_4	π_4	$\top_P$	?	$\perp$	$\perp$
ψ_5	π_5	$\top_P$	?	$\perp$	$\top$

Spec.	Trace	c-LTL	3-LTL	t-LTL-s	t-LTL-w
ψ_6	π_6	$\perp_P$	?	$\top$	$\top$
ψ_6	π_7	$\top_P$	?	$\top$	$\top$
ψ_7	π_8	$\perp_P$	?	$\perp$	$\perp$
ψ_8	π_8	$\perp_P$	?	$\perp$	$\perp$
ψ_9	π_8	$\top_P$	?	$\perp$	$\perp$

There are two immediate observations that we can make regarding the results presented in Table 6. First, the 3-valued LTL gives for all the examples an *inconclusive* verdict, a feedback that after all has little value to a verification engineer. The second observation is that the verdicts from c-LTL and t-LTL can differ quite a lot, which is not very surprising given the different strategies to interpret the unseen future. We now further comment on these examples, explaining in more details the results and highlighting the intuitive outcomes of c-LTL for a large class of interesting LTL specifications.

Effect of Nested Next. We evaluate with ψ_1 and ψ_2 the effect of nesting X in an F and an G formula, respectively. We make a prediction on X g at the end of the trace before evaluating F and G. As a consequence, we find that (ψ_1, π_1) evaluates to **presumably false**, while (ψ_2, π_2) evaluates to **presumably true**. In t-LTL, this class of specification is very sensitive to the weak/strong interpretation of next, as we can see from the verdicts.

Request/Grants. We evaluate the request/grant property ψ_3 from the motivating example on the trace π_3. We observe that r at cycle 2 is followed by g at cycle 3, while r at cycle 5 is not followed by g at cycle 6. Hence, (ψ_3, π_3) evaluates to **presumably false**.

Concurrent Request/Grants. We evaluate the specification ψ_4 against the trace π_4. In this example r_1 is triggered at even time stamps and r_2 is triggered at odd time stamps. Every request is granted in one cycle. It follows that regardless of the time when the trace ends, there is one request that is not granted yet. We note that ψ_4 is a conjunction of two basic request/grant properties and we make independent predictions for each conjunct. Every basic request/grant property is evaluated to **presumably true**, hence (ψ_4, π_4) evaluates to **presumably true**. At this point, we note that in t-LTL, every request that is not granted by the end of the trace results in the property violation, regardless of the past observations.

Until. We use the specification ψ_5 and the trace π_5 to evaluate the effect of U on the predictions. The specification requires that $\mathsf{X}\,r$ continuously holds until $\mathsf{X}\,\mathsf{X}\,g$ becomes true. We can see that in π_5 $\mathsf{X}\,r$ is witnessed at cycles $1-4$, while $\mathsf{X}\,\mathsf{X}\,g$ is witnessed at cycle 5. We can also see that $\mathsf{X}\,r$ is again witnessed from cycle 6 until the end of the trace at cycle 8. As a consequence, (ψ_5, π_5) is evaluated to **presumably true**.

Stabilization. The specification ψ_6 says that the value of g has to eventually stabilize to either true or false. We evaluate the formula on two traces π_6 and π_7. In the trace π_6, g alternates between true and false every two cycles and becomes true in the last cycle. Hence, there is no sufficiently long witness of trace stabilization (ψ_6, π_6) evaluates to **presumably false**. In the trace π_7, g also alternates between true and false every two cycles, but in the last four cycles g remains continuously true. As a consequence, (ψ_6, π_7) evaluates to **presumably true**. This example also illustrates the importance of when the trace truncation occurs. If both π_6 and π_7 were truncated at cycle 5, both (ψ_6, π_6) and (ψ_6, π_7) would evaluate to **presumably false**. We note that ψ_6 is satisfied by all traces in t-LTL.

Sub-formula Domination. The specification ψ_7 exposes a weakness of our approach. It requires that in every cycle, either r or g is witnessed in some unbounded future. With our approach, (ψ_7, π_8) evaluates to **presumably false**. This is against our intuition because we have observed that g becomes regularly true very second time step. However, in this example our prediction for $\mathsf{F}\,r$ dominates over the prediction for $\mathsf{F}\,g$, leading to the unexpected **presumably false** verdict. On the other hand, t-LTL interpretation of the same specification is dependent only on the last value of r and g.

Semantically Equivalent Formulas. We now demonstrate that our approach may give different answers for semantically equivalent formulas. For instance, both ψ_8 and ψ_9 are semantically equivalent to ψ_7. We have that (ψ_8, π_8) evaluates to **presumably false**, while (ψ_9, π_8) evaluates to **presumably true**. We note that t-LTL verdicts are stable for semantically different formulas.

6   Conclusion

We have presented a novel finitary semantics for LTL that uses the history of satisfaction and violation in a finite trace to predict whether the co-safety and safety aspects of a formula will be satisfied in the extension of the trace to an infinite one. We claim that the semantics closely follow human intuition when predicting the truth value of a trace. The presented examples (incl. non-monitorable LTL properties) illustrate our approach and support this claim.

Our definition of the semantics is trace-based, but it is easily extended to take an entire database of traces into account, which may make the approach more precise. Our approach currently uses a very simple form of learning to predict the future. We would like to consider more sophisticated statistical methods to make better predictions. In particular, we plan to apply nonparametric statistical methods (i.e., the Wilcoxon signed-rank test [16]), in combination with our counting semantics, to identify and quantify the traces that are outliers.

References

1. Almagor, S., Boker, U., Kupferman, O.: Discounting in LTL. In: Ábrahám, E., Havelund, K. (eds.) TACAS 2014. LNCS, vol. 8413, pp. 424–439. Springer, Heidelberg (2014). https://doi.org/10.1007/978-3-642-54862-8_37
2. Bartocci, E., Bloem, R., Nickovic, D., Roeck, F.: A counting semantics for monitoring LTL specifications over finite traces. CoRR, abs/1804.03237 (2018)
3. Bartocci, E., Falcone, Y. (eds.): Lectures on Runtime Verification. LNCS, vol. 10457. Springer, Cham (2018). https://doi.org/10.1007/978-3-319-75632-5
4. Bauer, A., Leucker, M., Schallhart, C.: Monitoring of real-time properties. In: Arun-Kumar, S., Garg, N. (eds.) FSTTCS 2006. LNCS, vol. 4337, pp. 260–272. Springer, Heidelberg (2006). https://doi.org/10.1007/11944836_25
5. Bauer, A., Leucker, M., Schallhart, C.: The good, the bad, and the ugly, but how ugly is ugly? In: Sokolsky, O., Taşıran, S. (eds.) RV 2007. LNCS, vol. 4839, pp. 126–138. Springer, Heidelberg (2007). https://doi.org/10.1007/978-3-540-77395-5_11
6. Bauer, A., Leucker, M., Schallhart, C.: Runtime verification for LTL and TLTL. ACM Trans. Softw. Eng. Methodol. **20**(4), 14:1–14:64 (2011)
7. Boker, U., Chatterjee, K., Henzinger, T.A., Kupferman, O.: Temporal specifications with accumulative values. ACM Trans. Comput. Logic **15**(4), 27:1–27:25 (2014)
8. Daca, P., Henzinger, T.A., Křetínský, J., Petrov, T.: Faster statistical model checking for unbounded temporal properties. In: Chechik, M., Raskin, J.-F. (eds.) TACAS 2016. LNCS, vol. 9636, pp. 112–129. Springer, Heidelberg (2016). https://doi.org/10.1007/978-3-662-49674-9_7
9. Eisner, C., Fisman, D., Havlicek, J., Lustig, Y., McIsaac, A., Van Campenhout, D.: Reasoning with temporal logic on truncated paths. In: Hunt, W.A., Somenzi, F. (eds.) CAV 2003. LNCS, vol. 2725, pp. 27–39. Springer, Heidelberg (2003). https://doi.org/10.1007/978-3-540-45069-6_3
10. Kupferman, O., Vardi, M.Y.: Model checking of safety properties. Form. Methods Syst. Des. **19**(3), 291–314 (2001)
11. Manna, Z., Pnueli, A.: The Temporal Logic of Reactive and Concurrent Systems - Specification. Springer, Heidelberg (1992). https://doi.org/10.1007/978-1-4612-0931-7
12. Morgenstern, A., Gesell, M., Schneider, K.: An asymptotically correct finite path semantics for LTL. In: Bjørner, N., Voronkov, A. (eds.) LPAR 2012. LNCS, vol.

7180, pp. 304–319. Springer, Heidelberg (2012). https://doi.org/10.1007/978-3-642-28717-6_24

13. Pnueli, A.: The temporal logic of programs. In: 18th Annual Symposium on Foundations of Computer Science, Providence, Rhode Island, USA, 31 October–1 November 1977, pp. 46–57 (1977)

14. Pnueli, A., Zaks, A.: PSL model checking and run-time verification via testers. In: Misra, J., Nipkow, T., Sekerinski, E. (eds.) FM 2006. LNCS, vol. 4085, pp. 573–586. Springer, Heidelberg (2006). https://doi.org/10.1007/11813040_38

15. Viswanathan, M., Kim, M.: Foundations for the run-time monitoring of reactive systems – fundamentals of the MaC language. In: Liu, Z., Araki, K. (eds.) ICTAC 2004. LNCS, vol. 3407, pp. 543–556. Springer, Heidelberg (2005). https://doi.org/10.1007/978-3-540-31862-0_38

16. Wilcoxon, F.: Individual comparisons by ranking methods. Biom. Bull. $\mathbf{1}$(6), 80–83 (1945)

17. Zhang, X., Leucker, M., Dong, W.: Runtime verification with predictive semantics. In: Goodloe, A.E., Person, S. (eds.) NFM 2012. LNCS, vol. 7226, pp. 418–432. Springer, Heidelberg (2012). https://doi.org/10.1007/978-3-642-28891-3_37

10

Deciding Probabilistic Bisimilarity Distance One for Labelled Markov Chains

Qiyi Tang[(✉)] and Franck van Breugel

DisCoVeri Group, York University, Toronto, Canada
{qiyitang,franck}@eecs.yorku.ca

Abstract. Probabilistic bisimilarity is an equivalence relation that captures which states of a labelled Markov chain behave the same. Since this behavioural equivalence only identifies states that transition to states that behave exactly the same with exactly the same probability, this notion of equivalence is not robust. Probabilistic bisimilarity distances provide a quantitative generalization of probabilistic bisimilarity. The distance of states captures the similarity of their behaviour. The smaller the distance, the more alike the states behave. In particular, states are probabilistic bisimilar if and only if their distance is zero. This quantitative notion is robust in that small changes in the transition probabilities result in small changes in the distances.

During the last decade, several algorithms have been proposed to approximate and compute the probabilistic bisimilarity distances. The main result of this paper is an algorithm that decides distance one in $O(n^2 + m^2)$, where n is the number of states and m is the number of transitions of the labelled Markov chain. The algorithm is the key new ingredient of our algorithm to compute the distances. The state of the art algorithm can compute distances for labelled Markov chains up to 150 states. For one such labelled Markov chain, that algorithm takes more than 49 h. In contrast, our new algorithm only takes 13 ms. Furthermore, our algorithm can compute distances for labelled Markov chains with more than 10,000 states in less than 50 min.

Keywords: Labelled Markov chain · Probabilistic bisimilarity
Probabilistic bisimilarity distance

1 Introduction

A *behavioural equivalence* captures which states of a model give rise to the same behaviour. Bisimilarity, due to Milner [22] and Park [25], is one of the best known behavioural equivalences. Verifying that an implementation satisfies a specification boils down to checking that the model of the implementation gives rise to the same behaviour as the model of the specification, that is, the models are behavioural equivalent (see [1, Chap. 3]).

In this paper, we focus on models of probabilistic systems. These models can capture randomized algorithms, probabilistic protocols, biological systems and many other systems in which probabilities play a central role. In particular, we consider *labelled Markov chains*, that is, Markov chains the states of which are labelled.

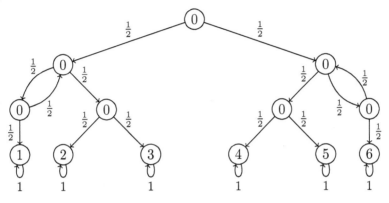

The above example shows how the behaviour of rolling a die can be mimicked by flipping a coin, an example due to Knuth and Yao [19]. Six of the states are labelled with the values of a die and the other states are labelled zero. In this example, we are interested in the labels representing the value of a die. As the reader can easily verify, the states with these labels are each reached with probability $\frac{1}{6}$ from the initial, top most, state. In general, labels are used to identify particular states that have properties of interest. As a consequence, states with different labels are not behaviourally equivalent.

Probabilistic bisimilarity, due to Larsen and Skou [21], is a key behavioural equivalence for labelled Markov chains. As shown by Katoen et al. [16], minimizing a labelled Markov chain by identifying those states that are probabilistic bisimilar speeds up model checking. Probabilistic bisimilarity only identifies those states that behave exactly the same with exactly the same probability. If, for example, we replace the fair coin in the above example with a biased one, then none of the states labelled with zero in the original model with the fair coin are behaviourally equivalent to any of the states labelled with zero in the model with the biased coin. Behavioural equivalences like probabilistic bisimilarity rely on the transition probabilities and, as a result, are sensitive to minor changes of those probabilities. That is, such behavioural equivalences are not robust, as first observed by Giacalone et al. [12].

The *probabilistic bisimilarity distances* that we study in this paper were first defined by Desharnais et al. in [11]. Each pair of states of a labelled Markov chain is assigned a distance, a real number in the unit interval [0, 1]. This distance captures the similarity of the behaviour of the states. The smaller the distance, the more alike the states behave. In particular, states have distance zero if and only if they are probabilistic bisimilar. This provides a quantitative generalization of probabilistic bisimilarity that is robust in that small changes in the transition probabilities give rise to small changes in the distances. For example, we can model a biased die by using a biased coin instead of a fair coin in the above example. Let us assume that the odds of heads of the biased coin, that is, going to the left, is $\frac{51}{100}$. A state labelled zero in the model of the fair die has a *non-trivial* distance, that is, a distance greater than zero and smaller than one, to the corresponding state in the model of the biased die. For example, the initial states have distance about 0.036. We refer the reader to [7] for a more detailed discussion of a similar example.

As we already mentioned earlier, behavioural equivalences can be used to verify that an implementation satisfies a specification. Similarly, the distances can be used to check how similar an implementation is to a specification. We also mentioned that probabilistic bisimilarity can be used to speed up model checking. The distances can be used in a similar way, by identifying those states that behave almost the same, that is, have a small distance (see [3, 23, 26]).

We focus in this paper on computing the probabilistic bisimilarity distances. In particular, we present a *decision procedure* for *distance one*. That is, we compute the set of pairs of states that have distance one. Recall that distance one is the maximal distance and, therefore, captures that states behave very differently. States with different labels have distance one. However, also states with the same label can have distance one, as the next example illustrates.

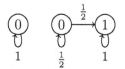

Instead of computing the set of state pairs that have distance one, we compute the complement, that is, the set of state pairs with distance smaller than one. Obviously, the set of state pairs with distance zero is included in this set. First, we decide distance zero. As we mentioned earlier, distance zero coincides with probabilistic bisimilarity. The first decision procedure for probabilistic bisimilarity was provided by Baier [4]. More efficient decision procedures were subsequently proposed by Derisavi et al. [10] and also by Valmari and Franceschinis [30]. The latter two both run in $O(m \log n)$, where n and m are the number of states and transitions of the labelled Markov chain. Subsequently, we use a traversal of a directed graph derived from the labelled Markov chain. This traversal takes $O(n^2 + m^2)$.

The decision procedures for distance zero and one can be used to compute or approximate probabilistic bisimilarity distances as indicated below.

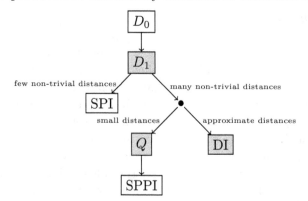

Once we have computed the sets D_0 and D_1 of state pairs that have distance zero or one, we can easily compute the number of state pairs with non-trivial distances. If the number of non-trivial distances is small, then we can use the *simple policy iteration* (SPI) algorithm due to Bacci et al. [2] to compute those distances. Otherwise, we can either compute all distances smaller than a chosen $\varepsilon > 0$ or we can approximate the distances up to some chosen accuracy $\alpha > 0$. In the former case, we first compute a query set Q of state pairs that contains all state pairs the distances of which are at most ε. Subsequently, we apply the *simple partial policy iteration* (SPPI) algorithm due to Bacci et al. [2] to compute the distances for all state pairs in Q. In the latter case, we start with a pair of distance functions, one being a lower-bound and the other being an upper-bound of the probabilistic bisimilarity distances, and iteratively improve the accuracy of those until they are α close. We call this new approximation algorithm *distance iteration* (DI) as it is similar in spirit to Bellman's value iteration [5].

Chen et al. [8] presented an algorithm to compute the distances by means of Khachiyan's ellipsoid method [17]. Though the algorithm is polynomial time, in practice it is not as efficient as the policy iteration algorithms (see the examples in [28, Sect. 8]). The state of the art algorithm to compute the probabilistic bisimilarity distances consists of two components: D_0 and SPI. To compare this algorithm with our new algorithm consisting of the components D_0, D_1 and SPI, we implemented all the components in Java and ran both implementations on several labelled Markov chains. These labelled Markov chains model randomized algorithms and probabilistic protocols that are part of the distribution of probabilistic model checkers such as PRISM [20]. Whereas the original state of the art algorithm can handle labelled Markov chains with up to 150 states, our new algorithm can handle more than 10,000 states. Furthermore, for one such labelled Markov chain with 150 states, the original algorithm takes more than 49 h, whereas our new algorithm takes only 13 ms. Also, the new algorithm consisting of the components D_0, D_1, Q and SPPI to compute only small distances along with the new algorithm consisting of the components D_0, D_1 and DI to approximate the distances give rise to even less execution times for a number of the labelled Markov chains.

The main contributions of this paper are

- a polynomial decision procedure for distance one,
- an algorithm to compute the probabilistic bisimilarity distances,
  an algorithm to compute those probabilistic bisimilarity distances smaller than some given $\varepsilon > 0$, and
- an approximation algorithm to compute the probabilistic bisimilarity distances up to some given accuracy $\alpha > 0$.

Furthermore, by means of experiments we have shown that these three new algorithms are very effective, improving significantly on the state of the art.

2 Labelled Markov Chains and Probabilistic Bisimilarity Distances

We start by reviewing the model of interest, labelled Markov chains, its most well known behavioural equivalence, probabilistic bisimilarity due to Larsen and Skou [21], and the probabilistic bisimilarity pseudometric due to Desharnais et al. [11]. We denote the set of rational probability distributions on a set S by $\text{Distr}(S)$. For $\mu \in \text{Distr}(S)$, its support is defined by $\text{support}(\mu) = \{ s \in S \mid \mu(s) > 0 \}$. Instead of $S \times S$, we often write S^2.

Definition 1. *A labelled Markov chain is a tuple $\langle S, L, \tau, \ell \rangle$ consisting of*

- *a nonempty finite set S of states,*
- *a nonempty finite set L of labels,*
- *a transition function $\tau : S \to \text{Distr}(S)$, and*
- *a labelling function $\ell : S \to L$.*

For the remainder of this section, we fix such a labelled Markov chain $\langle S, L, \tau, \ell \rangle$.

Definition 2. *Let $\mu, \nu \in \text{Distr}(S)$. The set $\Omega(\mu, \nu)$ of couplings of μ and ν is defined by*

$$\Omega(\mu, \nu) = \left\{ \omega \in \text{Distr}(S^2) \;\middle|\; \begin{array}{l} \forall s \in S : \sum_{t \in S} \omega(s, t) = \mu(s) \wedge \\ \forall t \in S : \sum_{s \in S} \omega(s, t) = \nu(t) \end{array} \right\}.$$

Note that $\omega \in \Omega(\mu, \nu)$ is a joint probability distribution with marginals μ and ν. The following proposition will be used to prove Proposition 5.

Proposition 1. *For all $\mu, \nu \in \text{Distr}(S)$ and $X \subseteq S^2$,*

$$\forall \omega \in \Omega(\mu, \nu) : \text{support}(\omega) \subseteq X \text{ if and only if } \text{support}(\mu) \times \text{support}(\nu) \subseteq X.$$

Definition 3. *An equivalence relation $R \subseteq S^2$ is a probabilistic bisimulation if for all $(s, t) \in R$, $\ell(s) = \ell(t)$ and there exists $\omega \in \Omega(\tau(s), \tau(t))$ such that $\text{support}(\omega) \subseteq R$. Probabilistic bisimilarity, denoted $\sim$, is the largest probabilistic bisimulation.*

The probabilistic bisimilarity pseudometric of Desharnais et al. [11] maps each pair of states of a labelled Markov chain to a distance, an element of the unit interval $[0, 1]$. Hence, the pseudometric is a function from S^2 to $[0, 1]$, that is, an element of $[0, 1]^{S^2}$. As we will discuss below, it can be defined as a fixed point of the following function.

Definition 4. *The function $\Delta : [0, 1]^{S^2} \to [0, 1]^{S^2}$ is defined by*

$$\Delta(d)(s, t) = \begin{cases} 1 & \text{if } \ell(s) \neq \ell(t) \\ \displaystyle \min_{\omega \in \Omega(\tau(s), \tau(t))} \sum_{u, v \in S} \omega(u, v)\, d(u, v) & \text{otherwise} \end{cases}$$

Since a concave function on a convex polytope attains its minimum (see [18, p. 260]), the above minimum exists. We will use this fact in Proposition 4, one of the key technical results in this paper. We endow the set $[0,1]^{S^2}$ of functions from S^2 to $[0,1]$ with the following partial order: $d \sqsubseteq e$ if $d(s,t) \leq e(s,t)$ for all $s, t \in S$. The set $[0,1]^{S^2}$ together with the order $\sqsubseteq$ form a complete lattice (see [9, Chap. 2]). The function Δ is monotone (see [6, Sect. 3]). According to the Knaster-Tarski fixed point theorem [29, Theorem 1], a monotone function on a complete lattice has a least fixed point. Hence, Δ has a least fixed point, which we denote by $\mu(\Delta)$. This fixed point assigns to each pair of states their probabilistic bisimilarity distance.

Given that $\mu(\Delta)$ captures the probabilistic bisimilarity distances, we define the following sets.

$$D_0 = \{(s,t) \in S^2 \mid \mu(\Delta)(s,t) = 0\}$$
$$D_1 = \{(s,t) \in S^2 \mid \mu(\Delta)(s,t) = 1\}$$

The probabilistic bisimilarity pseudometric $\mu(\Delta)$ provides a quantitative generalization of probabilistic bisimilarity as captured by the following result by Desharnais et al. [11, Theorem 1].

Theorem 1. $D_0 = \{(s,t) \in S^2 \mid s \sim t\}$.

3 Distance One

We concluded the previous section with the characterization of D_0 as the set of state pairs that are probabilistic bisimilar. In this section we present a characterization of D_1 as a fixed point of the function introduced in Definition 5.

Let us consider the case that the probabilistic bisimilarity distance of states s and t is one, that is, $\mu(\Delta)(s,t) = 1$. Then $\Delta(\mu(\Delta))(s,t) = 1$. From the definition of Δ, we can conclude that either $\ell(s) \neq \ell(t)$, or for all couplings $\omega \in \Omega(\tau(s),\tau(t))$ we have support$(\omega) \subseteq D_1$.

We partition the set S^2 of state pairs into

$$S_0^2 = \{(s,t) \in S^2 \mid s \sim t\}$$
$$S_1^2 = \{(s,t) \in S^2 \mid \ell(s) \neq \ell(t)\}$$
$$S_?^2 = S^2 \setminus (S_0^2 \cup S_1^2)$$

Hence, if $\mu(\Delta)(s,t) = 1$, then either $(s,t) \in S_1^2$, or $(s,t) \in S_?^2$ and for all couplings $\omega \in \Omega(\tau(s),\tau(t))$ we have support$(\omega) \subseteq D_1$. This leads us to the following function.

Definition 5. *The function* $\Gamma : 2^{S^2} \to 2^{S^2}$ *is defined by*

$$\Gamma(X) = S_1^2 \cup \{(s,t) \in S_?^2 \mid \forall \omega \in \Omega(\tau(s),\tau(t)) : \text{support}(\omega) \subseteq X\}.$$

Proposition 2. *The function* Γ *is monotone.*

Since the set 2^{S^2} of subsets of S^2 endowed with the order $\subseteq$ is a complete lattice (see [9, Example 2.6(2)]) and the function Γ is monotone, we can conclude from the Knaster-Tarski fixed point theorem that Γ has a greatest fixed point, which we denote by $\boldsymbol{\nu}(\Gamma)$. Next, we show that D_1 is a fixed point of Γ.

Proposition 3. $D_1 = \Gamma(D_1)$.

Since we have already seen that D_1 is a fixed point of Γ, we have that $D_1 \subseteq \boldsymbol{\nu}(\Gamma)$. To conclude that D_1 is the greatest fixed point of Γ, it remains to show that $\boldsymbol{\nu}(\Gamma) \subseteq D_1$, which is equivalent to the following.

Proposition 4. $\boldsymbol{\nu}(\Gamma) \setminus D_1 = \emptyset$.

Proof. Towards a contradiction, assume that $\boldsymbol{\nu}(\Gamma) \setminus D_1 \neq \emptyset$. Let

$$m = \min\{\boldsymbol{\mu}(\Delta)(s,t) \mid (s,t) \in \boldsymbol{\nu}(\Gamma) \setminus D_1\}$$
$$M = \{(s,t) \in \boldsymbol{\nu}(\Gamma) \setminus D_1 \mid \boldsymbol{\mu}(\Delta)(s,t) = m\}$$

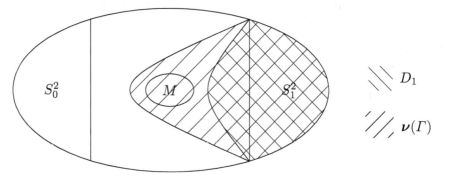

Since $\boldsymbol{\nu}(\Gamma) \setminus D_1 \neq \emptyset$, we have that $M \neq \emptyset$. Furthermore,

$$M \subseteq \boldsymbol{\nu}(\Gamma) \setminus D_1. \tag{1}$$

Since $\boldsymbol{\nu}(\Gamma) \setminus D_1 \subseteq \boldsymbol{\nu}(\Gamma)$, we have

$$M \subseteq \boldsymbol{\nu}(\Gamma) = \Gamma(\boldsymbol{\nu}(\Gamma)) \subseteq S_1^2 \cup S_?^2. \tag{2}$$

For all $(s,t) \in M$,

$$(s,t) \in \boldsymbol{\nu}(\Gamma) \wedge (s,t) \notin D_1 \quad [(1)]$$
$$\Rightarrow (s,t) \in \Gamma(\boldsymbol{\nu}(\Gamma)) \wedge (s,t) \notin S_1^2$$
$$\Rightarrow \forall \omega \in \Omega(\tau(s), \tau(t)) : \mathrm{support}(\omega) \subseteq \boldsymbol{\nu}(\Gamma). \tag{3}$$

For each $(s,t) \in M$, let

$$\omega_{s,t} = \operatorname*{argmin}_{\omega \in \Omega(\tau(s),\tau(t))} \sum_{u,v \in S} \omega(u,v)\,\boldsymbol{\mu}(\Delta)(u,v). \tag{4}$$

We distinguish the following two cases.

– Assume that there exists $(s,t) \in M$ such that $\text{support}(\omega_{s,t}) \cap D_1 \neq \emptyset$. Let

$$p = \sum_{(u,v) \in \nu(\Gamma) \cap D_1} \omega_{s,t}(u,v).$$

By (3), we have that $\text{support}(\omega_{s,t}) \subseteq \nu(\Gamma)$. Since $\text{support}(\omega_{s,t}) \cap D_1 \neq \emptyset$ by assumption, we can conclude that $p > 0$. Again using the fact that $\text{support}(\omega_{s,t}) \subseteq \nu(\Gamma)$, we have that

$$\sum_{(u,v) \in \nu(\Gamma) \setminus D_1} \omega_{s,t}(u,v) = 1 - p. \tag{5}$$

Furthermore,

$$
\begin{aligned}
m &= \boldsymbol{\mu}(\varDelta)(s,t) \\
&= \varDelta(\boldsymbol{\mu}(\varDelta))(s,t) \\
&= \min_{\omega \in \Omega(\tau(s),\tau(t))} \sum_{u,v \in S} \omega(u,v)\,\boldsymbol{\mu}(\varDelta)(u,v) \\
&= \sum_{u,v \in S} \omega_{s,t}(u,v)\,\boldsymbol{\mu}(\varDelta)(u,v) \quad [(4)] \\
&= \sum_{(u,v) \in \nu(\Gamma)} \omega_{s,t}(u,v)\,\boldsymbol{\mu}(\varDelta)(u,v) \quad [(3)] \\
&= \sum_{(u,v) \in \nu(\Gamma) \cap D_1} \omega_{s,t}(u,v)\,\boldsymbol{\mu}(\varDelta)(u,v) + \sum_{(u,v) \in \nu(\Gamma) \setminus D_1} \omega_{s,t}(u,v)\,\boldsymbol{\mu}(\varDelta)(u,v) \\
&= p + \sum_{(u,v) \in \nu(\Gamma) \setminus D_1} \omega_{s,t}(u,v)\,\boldsymbol{\mu}(\varDelta)(u,v) \\
&\geq p + (1-p)m.
\end{aligned}
$$

The last step follows from (5) and the fact that $\boldsymbol{\mu}(\varDelta)(u,v) \geq m$ for all $(u,v) \in \nu(\Gamma) \setminus D_1$. From the facts that $p > 0$ and $m \geq p + (1-p)m$ we can conclude that $m \geq 1$. This contradicts (1).

– Otherwise, $\text{support}(\omega_{s,t}) \cap D_1 = \emptyset$ for all $(s,t) \in M$. Next, we will show that M is a probabilistic bisimulation under this assumption. From the fact that M is a probabilistic bisimulation, we can conclude from Theorem 1 that $\boldsymbol{\mu}(\varDelta)(s,t) = 0$ for all $(s,t) \in M$. Hence, since $M \neq \emptyset$ we have that $M \cap S_0^2 \neq \emptyset$ which contradicts (2).

Next, we prove that M is a probabilistic bisimulation. Let $(s,t) \in M$. Since $M \subseteq \nu(\Gamma) \setminus D_1$ by (1), we have that $(s,t) \notin D_1$ and, hence, $\varDelta(\boldsymbol{\mu}(\varDelta))(s,t) = \boldsymbol{\mu}(\varDelta)(s,t) < 1$. From the definition of $\varDelta$, we can conclude that $\ell(s) = \ell(t)$. Since

$$
\begin{aligned}
m &= \boldsymbol{\mu}(\varDelta)(s,t) \\
&= \sum_{(u,v) \in \nu(\Gamma) \setminus D_1} \omega_{s,t}(u,v)\,\boldsymbol{\mu}(\varDelta)(u,v) \quad \text{[as above]}
\end{aligned}
$$

and $\mu(\Delta)(u, v) \geq m$ for all $(u, v) \in \nu(\Gamma) \setminus D_1$, we can conclude that $\mu(\Delta)(u, v) = m$ for all $(u, v) \in \text{support}(\omega_{s,t})$. Hence, $\text{support}(\omega_{s,t}) \subseteq M$. Therefore, M is a probabilistic bisimulation.   □

Theorem 2. $D_1 = \nu(\Gamma)$.

Proof. Immediate consequence of Proposition 3 and 4.   □

We have shown that D_1 can be characterized as the greatest fixed point of Γ. Next, we will show that D_1 can be decided in polynomial time.

Theorem 3. *Distance one can be decided in* $O(n^2 + m^2)$.

Proof. As we will show in Theorem 5, distance smaller than one can be decided in $O(n^2 + m^2)$. Hence, distance one can be decided in $O(n^2 + m^2)$ as well.   □

4   Distance Smaller Than One

To compute the set of state pairs which have distance one, we can first compute the set of state pairs which have distance less than one. The latter set we denote by $D_{<1}$. We can then obtain D_1 by taking the complement of $D_{<1}$. As we will discuss below, $D_{<1}$ can be characterized as the least fixed point of the following function.

Definition 6. *The function* $\daleth : 2^{S^2} \to 2^{S^2}$ *is defined by*

$$\daleth(X) = S^2 \setminus \Gamma(S^2 \setminus X).$$

The next theorem follows from Theorem 2.

Theorem 4. $D_{<1} = \mu(\daleth)$.

Next, we show that the computation of $D_{<1}$ can be formulated as a reachability problem on a directed graph which is induced by the labelled Markov chain. Thus, we can use standard search algorithms, for example, breadth-first search, on the induced graph.

Next, we present the graph induced by the labelled Markov chain.

Definition 7. *The directed graph* $G = (V, E)$ *is defined by*

$$V = S_0^2 \cup S_?^2$$
$$E = \{ \langle (u, v), (s, t) \rangle \mid \tau(s)(u) > 0 \wedge \tau(t)(v) > 0 \}$$

We are left to show that in the graph G defined above, a vertex (s, t) is reachable from some vertex in S_0^2 if and only if the state pair (s, t) in the labelled Markov chain has distance less than one.

As we have discussed earlier, if a state pair (s, t) has distance one, either s and t have different labels, or for all couplings $\omega \in \Omega(\tau(s), \tau(t))$ we have that $\text{support}(\omega) \subseteq D_1$. To avoid the universal quantification over couplings, we will use Proposition 1 in the proof of following proposition.

Proposition 5. $\mu(\mathbb{1}) = \{\, (s,t) \mid (s,t) \text{ is reachable from some } (u,v) \in S_0^2 \,\}$.

Theorem 5. *Distance smaller than one can be decided in $O(n^2 + m^2)$.*

Proof. Distance smaller than one can be decided as follows.

1. Decide distance zero.
2. Breadth-first search of G, with the queue initially containing the pairs of states that have distance zero.

By Theorem 4 and Proposition 5, we have that s and t have distance smaller than one if and only if (s,t) is reachable in the directed graph G from some (u,v) such that u and v have distance zero. These reachable state pairs can be computed using breadth-first search, with the queue initially containing S_0^2.

Distance zero, that is, probabilistic bisimilarity, can be decided in $O(m \log n)$ as shown by Derisavi et al. in [10]. The directed graph G has n^2 vertices and m^2 edges. Hence, breadth-first search takes $O(n^2 + m^2)$.   □

5   Number of Non-trivial Distances

As we have already discussed earlier, distance zero captures that states behave exactly the same, that is, they are probabilistic bisimilar, and distance one indicates that states behave very differently. The remaining distances, that is, those greater than zero and smaller than one, we call non-trivial. Being able to determine quickly the number of non-trivial distances of a labelled Markov chain allows us to decide whether computing all these non-trivial distances (using some policy iteration algorithm) is feasible.

To determine the number of non-trivial distances of a labelled Markov chain, we use the following algorithm.

1. Decide distance zero.
2. Decide distance one.

As first proved by Baier [4], distance zero, that is, probabilistic bisimilarity, can be decided in polynomial time. As we proved in Theorem 3, distance one can be decided in polynomial time as well. Hence, we can compute the number of non-trivial distances in polynomial time.

To decide distance zero, we implemented the algorithm to decide probabilistic bisimilarity due to Derisavi et al. [10] in Java. We also implemented our algorithm to decide distance one, described in the proof of Theorems 3 and 5.

We applied our implementation to labelled Markov chains that model randomized algorithms and probabilistic protocols. These labelled Markov chains have been obtained from the verification tool PRISM [20]. We compute the number of non-trivial distances for two models: the randomized self-stabilising algorithm due to Herman [14] and the bounded retransmission protocol by Helmink et al. [13].

For the randomized self-stabilising algorithm, the size of the labelled Markov chain grows exponentially in the numbers of processes, N. The results for the randomized self-stabilising algorithm are shown in the table below. As we can see from the table, for systems up to 128 states, the algorithm runs for less than a second. For the system with 512 states, the algorithm terminates within seven minutes. For the case $N = 3$, there are only 12 non-trivial distances. The size is so small that we can easily compute all the non-trivial distances. Section 6 will use the simple policy iteration algorithm as the next step to compute them. The same applies to the case $N = 5$. For $N = 7$ or 9, the number of non-trivial distances is around 11,000 and 200,000, respectively. This makes computing all of them infeasible. Thus, instead of computing all of them, we need to find alternative ways to handle systems with a large number of non-trivial distances. We will discuss two alternative ways in Sects. 7 and 8. Moreover, in this example, as $|D_1| = |S_1^2|$, we know that all the state pairs with distance one are those that have different labels.

N	$|S|$	$D_0 + D_1$	Non-trivial	$|D_0|$	$|D_1|$	$|S_1^2|$
3	8	1.00 ms	12	38	14	14
5	32	6.06 ms	280	304	440	440
7	128	0.77 s	11,032	2,160	3,192	3,192
9	512	378.42 s	230,712	13,648	17,784	17,784

In the bounded retransmission protocol, there are two parameters: N denotes the number of chunks and M the maximum allowed number of retransmissions of each chunk. The results are shown in the table below. The algorithm can handle systems up to 3,526 states within 11 min. In this example, there are no non-trivial distances. As a consequence, deciding distance zero and one suffices to compute all the distances in this case.

N	M	S	$D_0 + D_1$	$|D_0|$	$|D_1|$	$|S_1^2|$
16	2	677	3.0 s	456,977	1,352	1,352
16	3	886	8.6 s	783,226	1,770	1,770
16	4	1,095	17.5 s	1,196,837	2,188	2,188
16	5	1,304	22.8 s	1,697,810	2,606	2,606
32	2	1,349	24.7 s	1,817,105	2,696	2,696
32	3	1,766	69.7 s	3,115,226	3,530	3,530
32	4	2,183	141.0 s	4,761,125	4,364	4,364
32	5	2,600	208.6 s	6,754,802	5,198	5,198
64	2	2,693	235.2 s	7,246,865	5,384	5,384
64	3	3,526	616.4 s	12,425,626	7,050	7,050

6   All Distances

To compute all distances of a labelled Markov chain, we augment the existing state of the art algorithm, which is based on algorithms due to Derisavi et al. [10] (step 1) and Bacci et al. [2] (step 3), by incorporating our decision procedure (step 2) as follows.

1. Decide distance zero.
2. Decide distance one.
3. Simple policy iteration.

Given that we not only decide distance zero, but also distance one, before running simple policy iteration, the correctness of the simple policy iteration algorithm in the augmented setting needs an adjusted proof.

As we already discussed in the previous section, step 1 and 2 are polynomial time. However, step 3 may take at least exponential time in the worst case, as we have shown in [27]. Hence, the overall algorithm is exponential time.

The first example we consider here is the synchronous leader election protocol of Itai and Rodeh [15] which is taken from PRISM. The protocol takes the number of processors, N, and a constant K as parameters. We compare the running time of our new algorithm with the state of the art algorithm, that combines algorithms due to Derisavi et al. and due to Bacci et al. The results are shown in the table below. In this protocol, the number of non-trivial distances is zero. Thus, our new algorithm terminates without running step 3 which is the simple policy iteration algorithm. On the other hand, the original simple policy iteration algorithm computes the distances of all the elements in the set $D_1 \setminus S_1^2$, the size of which is huge as can be seen from the last two columns of the table.

N	K	$|S|$	D_0 + SPI	$D_0 + D_1$ + SPI	Speed-up	$|D_0|$	$|D_1|$	$|S_1^2|$
3	2	26	4 s	1 ms	4,281	122	554	50
3	4	147	49 h	13 ms	13,800,000	7,419	14,190	292
3	6	459	-	214 ms	-	88,671	122,010	916
3	8	1,059	-	3 s	-	508,851	612,630	2,116
4	2	61	812 s	3 ms	305,000	459	3,262	120
4	4	812	-	388 ms	-	145,780	513,564	1,622
4	6	3,962	-	82 s	-	4,350,292	11,347,152	7,922
4	8	12,400	-	2,971 s	-	46,198,188	107,561,812	24,798
5	2	141	-	6 ms	-	2,399	17,482	280
5	4	4,244	-	33 s	-	3,318,662	14,692,874	8,486
6	2	335	-	25 ms	-	14,327	97,898	668

The simple policy iteration algorithm can only handle a limited number of states. For the labelled Markov chain with 26 states ($N = 3$ and $K = 2$) the simple policy iteration algorithm takes four seconds, while our new algorithm takes one millisecond. The speed-up is more than 4,000 times. For the labelled Markov chain with 61 states ($N = 4$ and $K = 2$), the simple policy iteration algorithm runs in 812 s, while our new algorithm takes three milliseconds. The speed-up of the new algorithm is 30,000 times. The biggest system the simple policy iteration algorithm can handle is the one with 147 states ($N = 3$ and $K = 4$) and it takes more than 49 h. In contrast, our new algorithm terminates within 13 ms. That makes the new algorithm seven orders of magnitude faster than the state of the art algorithm. This example also shows that the new algorithm can handle systems with at least 12,400 states.

In the second example, we model two dies, one using a fair coin and the other one using a biased coin. The goal is to compute the probabilistic bisimilarity distance between these two dies. An implementation of the die algorithm is part of PRISM. The resulting labelled Markov chain has 20 states.

As there are only 30 non-trivial distances, we run the simple policy iteration algorithm as step 3. The new algorithm is about 46 times faster than the original algorithm.

$\lvert S\rvert$	D_0+SPI	$D_0 + D_1 + $SPI	Speed-up	Non-trivial	$\lvert D_0\rvert$	$\lvert D_1\rvert$	$\lvert S_1^2\rvert$
20	5.55 s	0.12 s	46.25	30	20	350	198

7 Small Distances

As we have discussed in Sect. 5, for systems of which the number of non-trivial distances is so large that computing all of them is infeasible, we have to find alternative ways. In practice, as we only identify the state pairs with small distances, we can cut down the number of non-trivial distances by only computing those with small distances.

To compute the non-trivial distances smaller than a positive number, ε, we use the following algorithm.

1. Decide distance zero.
2. Decide distance one.
3. Compute the query set

$$Q = \{\, (s, t) \in S^2 \setminus (D_0 \cup D_1) \mid \Delta(d)(s, t) \leq \varepsilon \,\}$$

   where

$$d(s, t) = \begin{cases} 1 \text{ if } (s, t) \in D_1 \\ 0 \text{ otherwise} \end{cases}$$

4. Simple partial policy iteration for Q.

The first two steps remain the same. In step 3, we compute a query set Q that contains all state pairs with distances no greater than ε, as shown in Proposition 6. In step 4, we use this set as the query set to run the simple partial policy iteration algorithm by Bacci et al. [2].

Proposition 6. *Let d be the distance function defined in step 3. For all $(s,t) \in S^2 \setminus (D_0 \cup D_1)$, if $\boldsymbol{\mu}(\Delta)(s,t) \leq \varepsilon$, then $\Delta(d)(s,t) \leq \varepsilon$.*

Given that we not only decide distance zero, but also distance one, before running simple partial policy iteration, the correctness of the simple partial policy iteration algorithm in the augmented setting needs an adjusted proof.

As we have seen before, step 1 and 2 take polynomial time. In step 3, computing $\Delta(d)$ corresponds to solving a minimum cost network flow problem. Such a problem can be solved in polynomial time using, for example, Orlin's network simplex algorithm [24]. As we have shown in [28], step 4 takes at least exponential time in the worst case. Therefore, the overall algorithm is exponential time.

We consider the randomized quicksort algorithm, an implementation of which is part of jpf-probabilistic [31]. The input of the algorithm is the list to be sorted. The list of size 6 gives rise to a labelled Markov chain with 82 states. We compare the running time of the new algorithm for small distances $(D_0 + D_1 + Q + \mathrm{SPPI})$ to the original algorithm $(D_0 + \mathrm{SPI})$ and the new algorithm presented in Sect. 6 $(D_0 + D_1 + \mathrm{SPI})$. The original algorithm $(D_0 + \mathrm{SPI})$ takes about 14 h, the new algorithm which incorporates the decision procedure of distance one takes less than 7 h. For $\varepsilon = 0.1$, the new algorithm for small distances takes 57 min. This makes it about 7 times faster than the algorithm presented in Sect. 6 and about 15 times faster than the original simple policy iteration algorithm. For $\varepsilon = 0.01$, the new algorithm for small distances takes even less time, namely 41 min. As can be seen in the table below, the total number of non-trivial distances is 2,300. The simple partial policy iteration algorithm starts with the query set Q but may have to compute the distances of other state pairs as well. The total number of state pairs considered by the simple partial policy iteration algorithm can be found in the column labelled Total.

ε	$D_0 + D_1 + Q + \mathrm{SPPI}$	$|Q|$	Total	Non-trivial
0.1	57 min	96	1,002	2,300
0.01	41 min	84	842	2,300

8 Approximation Algorithm

We propose another solution to deal with a large number of non-trivial distances by approximating the distances rather than computing the exact values. To approximate the distances such that the approximate values differ from the exact ones by at most α, a positive number, we use the following algorithm.

1. Decide distance zero.
2. Decide distance one.

3. $l(s,t) = \begin{cases} 1 \text{ if } (s,t) \in D_1 \\ 0 \text{ otherwise} \end{cases}$

   $u(s,t) = \begin{cases} 0 \text{ if } (s,t) \in D_0 \\ 1 \text{ otherwise} \end{cases}$

```
   repeat
      for each (s,t) ∈ S² \ (D₀ ∪ D₁)
         if l(s,t) ≠ u(s,t)
            l(s,t) = Δ(l)(s,t)
            u(s,t) = Δ(u)(s,t)
   until ‖l − u‖ ≤ α
```

Again, the first two steps remain the same. Step 3 contains the new approximation algorithm called *distance iteration* (DI). In this step, we define two distance functions, a lower-bound l and an upper-bound u. We repeatedly apply Δ to these two functions until the difference of the non-trivial distances in these two functions is smaller than the threshold α. For each state pair we end up with an interval of at most size α in which their distance lies. To prove the algorithm correct, we modify the function Δ defining the probabilistic bisimilarity distances slightly as follows.

Definition 8. *The function* $\Delta_0 : [0,1]^{S^2} \to [0,1]^{S^2}$ *is defined by*

$$\Delta_0(d)(s,t) = \begin{cases} 0 & \text{if } (s,t) \in D_0 \\ \Delta(d)(s,t) & \text{otherwise} \end{cases}$$

Some properties of Δ_0, which are key to the correctness proof of the above algorithm, are collected in the following theorem.

Theorem 6.

(a) *The function* Δ_0 *is monotone.*
(b) *The function* Δ_0 *is nonexpansive.*
(c) $\mu(\Delta_0) = \mu(\Delta)$.
(d) $\mu(\Delta_0) = \nu(\Delta_0)$.
(e) $\mu(\Delta_0) = \sup_{m \in \mathbb{N}} \Delta_0^m(d_0)$, *where* $d_0(s,t) = 0$ *for all* $s,t \in S$.
(f) $\nu(\Delta_0) = \inf_{n \in \mathbb{N}} \Delta_0^n(d_1)$, *where* $d_1(s,t) = 1$ *for all* $s,t \in S$.

Let us use randomized quicksort introduced in Sect. 7 and the randomized self-stabilising algorithm due to Herman [14] introduced in Sect. 5 as examples. Recall that for the randomized self-stabilising algorithm, when $N = 7$, the number of non-trivial distances is 11,032, which we are not able to handle using the simple policy iteration algorithm. We apply the approximation algorithm to this model and the randomized quicksort example with 82 states and present the results below. The accuracy α is set to be 0.01.

The approximation algorithm for randomized quicksort runs for about 14 min, which is about 3 to 4 times faster than the algorithm for small distances in Sect. 7. For the randomized self-stabilising algorithm with 128 states, the approximation algorithm terminates in about 54 h. Although the number of non-trivial distances for the randomized self-stabilising algorithm is about 5 times of that of the randomized quicksort, the running time is more than 200 times slower. It is unknown whether this approximation algorithm has exponential running time.

Model	$|S|$	Non-trivial	$D_0 + D_1 +$DI
Randomized quicksort	82	2,300	14 min
Randomized self-stabilising algorithm	128	11,032	54 h

9   Conclusion

In this paper, we have presented a decision procedure for probabilistic bisimilarity distance one. This decision procedure provides the basis for three new algorithms to compute and approximate the probabilistic bisimilarity distances of a labelled Markov chain. The first algorithm decides distance zero, then decides distance one, and finally uses simple policy iteration to compute the remaining distances. As shown experimentally, this new algorithm significantly improves the state of the art algorithm that only decides distance zero and then uses simple policy iteration. The second algorithm computes all probabilistic bisimilarity distances that are smaller than some given upper bound, by deciding distance zero, deciding distance one, computing a query set, and running simple partial policy iteration for that query set. This second algorithm can handle labelled Markov chains that have considerably more non-trivial distances than our first algorithm. The third algorithm approximates the probabilistic bisimilarity distances up to a given accuracy, deciding distance zero, deciding distance one and running distance iteration. Also this third algorithm can handle labelled Markov chains that have considerably more non-trivial distances than our first algorithm. Whereas we know that the first two algorithms take at least exponential time in the worst case, the analysis of the running time of the third algorithm has not yet been determined. Moreover, if we are only interested in the probabilistic bisimilarity distances for a few state pairs, with pre-computation of distance zero and one we can exclude the state pairs with trivial distances. We can add the remaining state pairs to a query set and run simple partial policy iteration to get the distances. Alternatively, we can modify the distance iteration algorithm to approximate the distances for the predefined state pairs. The details of these new algorithms will be studied in the future.

Acknowledgements. The authors would like to thank Daniela Petrisan, Eric Ruppert and Dana Scott for discussions related to this research. The authors are also grateful to the referees for their constructive feedback.

References

1. Aceto, L., Ingolfsdottir, A., Larsen, K., Srba, J.: Reactive Systems: Modelling, Specification and Verification. Cambridge University Press, Cambridge (2003)
2. Bacci, G., Bacci, G., Larsen, K.G., Mardare, R.: On-the-fly exact computation of bisimilarity distances. In: Piterman, N., Smolka, S.A. (eds.) TACAS 2013. LNCS, vol. 7795, pp. 1–15. Springer, Heidelberg (2013). https://doi.org/10.1007/978-3-642-36742-7_1
3. Bacci, G., Bacci, G., Larsen, K.G., Mardare, R.: On the metric-based approximate minimization of Markov chains. In: Chatzigiannakis, I., Indyk, P., Kuhn, F., Muscholl, A. (eds.) Proceedings of the 44th International Colloquium on Automata, Languages, and Programming, Warsaw, Poland, July 2017. Leibniz International Proceedings in Informatics, vol. 80, pp. 104:1–104:14. Schloss Dagstuhl - Leibniz-Zentrum für Informatik (2017)
4. Baier, C.: Polynomial time algorithms for testing probabilistic bisimulation and simulation. In: Alur, R., Henzinger, T.A. (eds.) CAV 1996. LNCS, vol. 1102, pp. 50–61. Springer, Heidelberg (1996). https://doi.org/10.1007/3-540-61474-5_57
5. Bellman, R.: A Markovian decision process. J. Math. Mech. **6**(5), 679–684 (1957)
6. van Breugel, F.: On behavioural pseudometrics and closure ordinals. Inf. Process. Lett. **112**(18), 715–718 (2012)
7. van Breugel, F.: Probabilistic bisimilarity distances. ACM SIGLOG News **4**(4), 33–51 (2017)
8. Chen, D., van Breugel, F., Worrell, J.: On the complexity of computing probabilistic bisimilarity. In: Birkedal, L. (ed.) FoSSaCS 2012. LNCS, vol. 7213, pp. 437–451. Springer, Heidelberg (2012). https://doi.org/10.1007/978-3-642-28729-9_29
9. Davey, B., Priestley, H.: Introduction to Lattices and Order. Cambridge University Press, Cambridge (2002)
10. Derisavi, S., Hermanns, H., Sanders, W.: Optimal state-space lumping in Markov chains. In. Process. Lett. **87**(6), 309–315 (2003)
11. Desharnais, J., Gupta, V., Jagadeesan, R., Panangaden, P.: Metrics for labeled Markov systems. In: Baeten, J.C.M., Mauw, S. (eds.) CONCUR 1999. LNCS, vol. 1664, pp. 258–273. Springer, Heidelberg (1999). https://doi.org/10.1007/3-540-48320-9_19
12. Giacalone, A., Jou, C.-C., Smolka, S.: Algebraic reasoning for probabilistic concurrent systems. In: Proceedings of the IFIP WG 2.2/2.3 Working Conference on Programming Concepts and Methods, Sea of Gallilee, Israel, April 1990, pp. 443–458. North-Holland (1990)
13. Helmink, L., Sellink, M.P.A., Vaandrager, F.W.: Proof-checking a data link protocol. In: Barendregt, H., Nipkow, T. (eds.) TYPES 1993. LNCS, vol. 806, pp. 127–165. Springer, Heidelberg (1994). https://doi.org/10.1007/3-540-58085-9_75
14. Herman, T.: Probabilistic self-stabilization. Inf. Process. Lett. **35**(2), 63–67 (1990)
15. Itai, A., Rodeh, M.: Symmetry breaking in distributed networks. Inf. Comput. **88**(1), 60–87 (1990)
16. Katoen, J.-P., Kemna, T., Zapreev, I., Jansen, D.N.: Bisimulation minimisation mostly speeds up probabilistic model checking. In: Grumberg, O., Huth, M. (eds.) TACAS 2007. LNCS, vol. 4424, pp. 87–101. Springer, Heidelberg (2007). https://doi.org/10.1007/978-3-540-71209-1_9
17. Khachiyan, L.: A polynomial algorithm in linear programming. Sov. Math. Dokl. **20**(1), 191–194 (1979)

18. Klee, V., Witzgall, C.: Facets and vertices of transportation polytopes. In: Dantzig, G., Veinott, A. (eds.) Proceedings of 5th Summer Seminar on the Mathematis of the Decision Sciences, Stanford, CA, USA, July/August 1967. Lectures in Applied Mathematics, vol. 11, pp. 257–282. AMS (1967)
19. Knuth, D., Yao, A.: The complexity of nonuniform random number generation. In: Traub, J. (ed.) Proceedings of a Symposium on New Directions and Recent Results in Algorithms and Complexity, Pittsburgh, PA, USA, April 1976, pp. 375–428. Academic Press (1976)
20. Kwiatkowska, M., Norman, G., Parker, D.: PRISM 4.0: verification of probabilistic real-time systems. In: Gopalakrishnan, G., Qadeer, S. (eds.) CAV 2011. LNCS, vol. 6806, pp. 585–591. Springer, Heidelberg (2011). https://doi.org/10.1007/978-3-642-22110-1_47
21. Larsen, K., Skou, A.: Bisimulation through probabilistic testing. In: Proceedings of the 16th Annual ACM Symposium on Principles of Programming Languages, Austin, TX, USA, January 1989, pp. 344–352. ACM (1989)
22. Milner, R. (ed.): A Calculus of Communicating Systems. LNCS, vol. 92. Springer, Heidelberg (1980). https://doi.org/10.1007/3-540-10235-3
23. Murthy, A., et al.: Approximate bisimulations for sodium channel dynamics. In: Gilbert, D., Heiner, M. (eds.) CMSB 2012. LNCS, pp. 267–287. Springer, Heidelberg (2012). https://doi.org/10.1007/978-3-642-33636-2_16
24. Orlin, J.: A polynomial time primal network simplex algorithm for minimum cost flows. Math. Program. **78**(2), 109–129 (1997)
25. Park, D.: Concurrency and automata on infinite sequences. In: Deussen, P. (ed.) GI-TCS 1981. LNCS, vol. 104, pp. 167–183. Springer, Heidelberg (1981). https://doi.org/10.1007/BFb0017309
26. Sen, P., Deshpande, A., Getoor, L.: Bisimulation-based approximate lifted inference. In: Bilmes, J., Ng, A. (eds.) Proceedings of the 25th Conference on Uncertainty in Artificial Intelligence, Montreal, QC, Canada, pp. 496–505. AUAI Press (2009)
27. Tang, Q., van Breugel, F.: Computing probabilistic bisimilarity distances via policy iteration. In: Desharnais, J., Jagadeesan, R. (eds.) Proceedings of the 27th International Conference on Concurrency Theory, Quebec City, QC, Canada, August 2016. Leibniz International Proceedings in Informatics, vol. 59, pp. 22:1–22:15. Schloss Dagstuhl - Leibniz-Zentrum für Informatik (2016)
28. Tang, Q., van Breugel, F.: Algorithms to compute probabilistic bisimilarity distances for labelled Markov chains. In: Meyer, R., Nestmann, U. (eds.) Proceedings of the 28th International Conference on Concurrency Theory, Berlin, Germany, September 2017. Leibniz International Proceedings in Informatics, vol. 85, pp. 27:1–27:16. Schloss Dagstuhl - Leibniz-Zentrum für Informatik (2017)
29. Tarski, A.: A lattice-theoretic fixed point theorem and its applications. Pac. J. Math. **5**(2), 285–309 (1955)
30. Valmari, A., Franceschinis, G.: Simple $O(m \log n)$ time Markov chain lumping. In: Esparza, J., Majumdar, R. (eds.) TACAS 2010. LNCS, vol. 6015, pp. 38–52. Springer, Heidelberg (2010). https://doi.org/10.1007/978-3-642-12002-2_4
31. Zhang, X., van Breugel, F.: Model checking randomized algorithms with Java PathFinder. In: Proceedings of the 7th International Conference on the Quantitative Evaluation of Systems, Williamsburg, VA, USA, September 2010, pp. 157–158. IEEE (2010)

11

Foundations and Tools for the Static Analysis of Ethereum Smart Contracts

Ilya Grishchenko$^{(\boxtimes)}$, Matteo Maffei$^{(\boxtimes)}$, and Clara Schneidewind$^{(\boxtimes)}$

TU Wien, Vienna, Austria
{ilya.grishchenko,matteo.maffei,clara.schneidewind}@tuwien.ac.at

Abstract. The recent growth of the blockchain technology market puts its main cryptocurrencies in the spotlight. Among them, Ethereum stands out due to its virtual machine (EVM) supporting smart contracts, i.e., distributed programs that control the flow of the digital currency Ether. Being written in a Turing complete language, Ethereum smart contracts allow for expressing a broad spectrum of financial applications. The price for this expressiveness, however, is a significant semantic complexity, which increases the risk of programming errors. Recent attacks exploiting bugs in smart contract implementations call for the design of formal verification techniques for smart contracts. This, however, requires rigorous semantic foundations, a formal characterization of the expected security properties, and dedicated abstraction techniques tailored to the specific EVM semantics. This work will overview the state-of-the-art in smart contract verification, covering formal semantics, security definitions, and verification tools. We will then focus on EtherTrust [1], a framework for the static analysis of Ethereum smart contracts which includes the first complete small-step semantics of EVM bytecode, the first formal characterization of a large class of security properties for smart contracts, and the first static analysis for EVM bytecode that comes with a proof of soundness.

1 Introduction

Blockchain technologies promise secure distributed computations even in absence of trusted third parties. The core of this technology is a distributed ledger that keeps track of previous transactions and the state of each account, and whose functionality and security is ensured by a careful combination of incentives and cryptography. Within this framework, software developers can implement sophisticated distributed, transaction-based computations by leveraging the scripting language offered by the underlying cryptocurrency. While many of these cryptocurrencies have an intentionally limited scripting language (e.g., Bitcoin [2]), Ethereum was designed from the ground up with a quasi Turing-complete language[1]. Ethereum programs, called *smart contracts*, have thus found a variety of

---

[1] While the language itself is Turing complete, computations are associated with a bounded computational budget (called gas), which gets consumed by each instruction thereby enforcing termination.

appealing use cases, such as auctions [3], data management systems [4], financial contracts [5], elections [6], trading platforms [7,8], permission management [9] and verifiable cloud computing [10], just to mention a few. Given their financial nature, bugs and vulnerabilities in smart contracts may lead to catastrophic consequences. For instance, the infamous DAO vulnerability [11] recently led to a 60M$ financial loss and similar vulnerabilities occur on a regular basis [12,13]. Furthermore, many smart contracts in the wild are intentionally fraudulent, as highlighted in a recent survey [14].

A rigorous security analysis of smart contracts is thus crucial for the trust of the society in blockchain technologies and their widespread deployment. Unfortunately, this task is quite challenging for various reasons. First, Ethereum smart contracts are developed in an ad-hoc language, called Solidity, which resembles JavaScript but features specific transaction-oriented mechanisms and a number of non-standard semantic behaviours, as further described in this paper. Second, smart contracts are uploaded on the blockchain in the form of Ethereum Virtual Machine (EVM) bytecode, a stack-based low-level code featuring dynamic code creation and invocation and, in general, very little static information, which makes it extremely difficult to analyze.

Our Contributions. This work overviews the existing approaches taken towards formal verification of Ethereum smart contracts and discusses EtherTrust, the first sound static analysis tool for EVM bytecode. Specifically, our contributions are

- A survey on recent theories and tools for formal verification of Ethereum smart contracts including a systematization of existing work with an overview of the open problems and future challenges in the smart contract realm.
- An illustrative presentation of the small-step semantics presented by [15] with special focus on the semantics of the bytecode instructions that allow for the initiation of internal transactions. The subtleties in the semantics of these transactions have shown to form an integral part of the attack surface in the context of Ethereum smart contracts.
- A review of an abstraction based on Horn clauses for soundly over-approximating the small-step executions of Ethereum bytecode [1].
- A demonstration of how relevant security properties can be over-approximated and automatically verified using the static analyzer EtherTrust [1] by the example of the single-entrancy property defined in [15].

Outline. The remainder of this paper is organized as follows. Section 2 briefly overviews the Ethereum architecture, Sect. 3 reviews the state of the art in formal verification of Ethereum smart contracts, Sect. 4 revisits the Ethereum small-step semantics introduced by [15], Sect. 5 presents the single-entrancy property for smart contracts as defined by [15], Sect. 6 discusses the key ideas of the first sound static analysis for Ethereum bytecode as implemented in EtherTrust [1], Sect. 7 shows how reachability properties can automatically be checked using EtherTrust, and Sect. 8 concludes summarizing the key points of the paper.

2   Background on Ethereum

In the following we will shortly overview the mechanics of the cryptocurrency
Ethereum and its built-in scripting language EVM bytecode.

2.1   Ethereum

Ethereum is a cryptographic currency system built on top of a blockchain. Similar to Bitcoin, network participants publish transactions to the network that are
then grouped into blocks by distinct nodes (the so called *miners*) and appended
to the blockchain using a proof of work (PoW) consensus mechanism. The state
of the system – that we will also refer to as *global state* – consists of the state
of the different accounts populating it. An account can either be an external
account (belonging to a user of the system) that carries information on its current balance or it can be a contract account that additionally obtains persistent
storage and the contract's code. The account's balances are given in the subunit
wei of the virtual currency *Ether*.[2]

Transactions can alter the state of the system by either creating new contract
accounts or by calling an existing account. Calls to external accounts can only
transfer Ether to this account, but calls to contract accounts additionally execute
the code associated to the contract. The contract execution might alter the
storage of the account or might again perform transactions – in this case we talk
about *internal transactions*.

The execution model underlying the execution of contract code is described
by a virtual state machine, the *Ethereum Virtual Machine* (EVM). This is *quasi
Turing complete* as the otherwise Turing complete execution is restricted by the
upfront defined resource *gas* that effectively limits the number of execution steps.
The originator of the transaction can specify the maximal gas that should be
spent for the contract execution and also determines the gas price (the amount
of wei to pay for a unit of gas). Upfront, the originator pays for the gas limit
according to the gas price and in case of successful contract execution that did
not spend the whole amount of gas dedicated to it, the originator gets reimbursed
with gas that is left. The remaining wei paid for the used gas are given as a fee
to a beneficiary address specified by the miner.

2.2   EVM Bytecode

Contracts are delivered and executed in *EVM bytecode* format – an Assembler
like bytecode language. As the core of the EVM is a stack-based machine, the
set of instructions in EVM bytecode consists mainly of standard instructions
for stack operations, arithmetics, jumps and local memory access. The classical
set of instructions is enriched with an opcode for the SHA3 hash and several
opcodes for accessing the environment that the contract was called in. In addition, there are opcodes for accessing and modifying the storage of the account

---

[2] One Ether is equivalent to 10^{18} wei.

currently running the code and distinct opcodes for performing internal call and create transactions. Another instruction particular to the blockchain setting is the SELFDESTRUCT code that deletes the currently executed contract - but only after the successful execution of the external transaction.

The execution of each instruction consumes a positive amount of *gas*. The sender of the transaction specifies a gas limit and exceeding it results in an exception that reverts the effects of the current transaction on the global state. In the case of nested transactions, the occurrence of an exception only reverts its own effects, but not those of the calling transaction. Instead, the failure of an internal transaction is only indicated by writing zero to the caller's stack.

3   Overview on Formal Verification Approaches

In the following we give an overview on the approaches taken so far in the direction of securing (Ethereum) smart contracts. We distinguish between verification approaches and design approaches. According to our terminology, the goal of verification approaches is to check smart contracts written in existing languages (such as Solidity) for their compliance with a security policy or specification. In contrast, design approaches aim at facilitating the creation of secure smart contracts by providing frameworks for their development: These approaches encompass new languages which are more amenable to verification, provide a clear and simple semantics that is understandable by smart contract developers or allow for a direct encoding of desired security policies. In addition, we count works that aim at providing design patterns for secure smart contracts to this category.

3.1   Verification

In the field of smart contract verification we categorize the existing approaches along the following dimensions: target language (bytecode vs high level language), point of verification (static vs. dynamic analysis methods), provided guarantees (bug-finding vs. formal soundness guarantees), checked properties (generic contract properties vs. contract specific properties), degree of automation (automated verification vs. assisted analysis vs. manual inspection). From the current spectrum of analysis tools, we can find solutions in the following clusters:

Static Analysis Tools for Automated Bug-Finding. Oyente [16] is a state-of-the-art static analysis tool for EVM bytecode that relies on symbolic execution. Oyente supports a variety of pre-defined security properties, such as transaction order dependency, time-stamp dependency, and reentrancy that can be checked automatically. However, Oyente is not striving for soundness nor completeness. This is on the one hand due to the simplified semantics that serves as foundation of the analysis [15]. On the other hand, the security properties are rather syntactic or pattern based and are lacking a semantic characterization. Recently, Zhou et al. proposed the static analysis tool SASC [17] that extends

Oyente by additional patterns and provides a visualization of detected risks in the topology diagram of the original Solidity code.

Majan [18] extends the approach taken in Oyente to trace properties that consider multiple invocations of one smart contract. As Oyente, it relies on symbolic execution that follows a simplified version of the semantics used in Oyente and uses a pattern-based approach for defining the concrete properties to be checked. The tool covers safety properties (such as prodigality and suicidality) and liveness properties (greediness). As for Oyente, the authors do not make any security claims, but consider their tool a 'bug catching approach'.

Static Analysis Tools for Automated Verification of Generic Properties. In contrast to the aforementioned class of tools, this line of research aims at providing formal guarantees for the analysis results.

A recently published work is the static analysis tool ZEUS [19] that analyzes smart contracts written in Solidity using symbolic model checking. The analysis proceeds by translating Solidity code to an abstract intermediate language that again is translated to LLVM bitcode. Finally, existing symbolic model checking tools for LLVM bitcode are leveraged for checking generic security properties. ZEUS consequently only allows for analyzing contracts whose Solidity source code is made available. In addition, the semantics of the intermediate language cannot easily be reconciled with the actual Solidity semantics that is determined by its translation to EVM bytecode. This is as the semantics of the intermediate language by design does not allow for the revocation of the global system state in the case of a failed call – which however is fundamental feature of Ethereum smart contract execution.

Other tools proposed in the realm of automated static analysis for generic properties are Securify [20], Mythril [21] and Manticore [22] (for analysing bytecode) and SmartCheck [23] and Solgraph [24] (for analyzing Solidity code). These tools however are not accompanied by any academic paper so that the concrete analysis goals stay unspecified.

Frameworks for Semi-automated Proofs for Contract Specific Properties. Hirai [25] formalizes the EVM semantics in the proof assistant Isabelle/HOL and uses it for manually proving safety properties for concrete contracts. This semantics, however, constitutes a sound over-approximation of the original semantics [26]. Building on top of this work, Amani et al. propose a sound program logic for EVM bytecode based on separation logics [27]. This logic allows for semi-automatically reasoning about correctness properties of EVM bytecode using the proof assistant Isabelle/HOL.

Hildebrandt et al. [28] define the EVM semantics in the $\mathbb{K}$ framework [29] – a language independent verification framework based on reachability logics. The authors leverage the power of the $\mathbb{K}$ framework in order to automatically derive analysis tools for the specified semantics, presenting as an example a gas analysis tool, a semantic debugger, and a program verifier based on reachability logics. The derived program verifier still requires the user to manually specify loop invariants on the bytecode level.

Bhargavan et al. [30] introduce a framework to analyze Ethereum contracts by translation into F*, a functional programming language aimed at program verification and equipped with an interactive proof assistant. The translation supports only a fragment of the EVM bytecode and does not come with a justifying semantic argument.

Dynamic Monitoring for Predefined Security Properties. Grossman et al. [31] propose the notion of effectively callback free executions and identify the absence of this property in smart contract executions as the source of common bugs such as reentrancy. They propose an efficient online algorithm for discovering executions violating effectively callback freeness. Implementing a corresponding monitor in the EVM would guarantee the absence of the potentially dangerous smart contract executions, but is not compatible with the current Ethereum version and would require a hard fork.

A dynamic monitoring solution compatible with Ethereum is offered by the tool DappGuard [32]. The tool actively monitors the incoming transactions to a smart contract and leverages the tool Oyente [16], an own analysis engine and a simulation of the transaction on the testnet for judging whether the incoming transaction might cause a (generic) security violation (such as transaction order dependency). If a transaction is considered harmful, a counter transaction (killing the contract or performing some other fixes) is made. The authors claim that this transaction will be mined with high probability before the problematic one. Due to this uncertainty and the bug-finding tools used for evaluation of incoming transactions, this approach does not provide any guarantees.

3.2   Design

The current research on secure smart contract design focuses on the following four areas: high-level programming languages, intermediate languages (for verification), security patterns for existing languages and visual tools for designing smart contracts.

High-Level Languages. One line of research on high-level smart contract languages concentrates on the facilitation of secure smart contract design by limiting the language expressiveness and enforcing strong static typing discipline. Simplicity [33] is a typed functional programming language for smart contracts that disallows loops and recursion. It is a general purpose language for smart contracts and not tailored to the Ethereum setting. Simplicity comes with a denotational semantics specified in Coq that allows for reasoning formally about Simplicity contracts. As there is no (verified) compiler to EVM bytecode so far, such results don't carry over to Ethereum smart contracts. In the same realm, Pettersson and Edström [34], propose a library for the programming language Idris that allows for the development of secure smart contracts using dependent and polymorphic types. They extend the existing Idris compiler with a generator for Serpent code (a Python-like high-level language for Ethereum smart contracts). This compiler is a proof of concept and fails in compiling more advanced contracts (as it cannot handle recursion). In a preliminary work, Coblenz [35] propose Obsidian, an object-oriented programming language that pursues the goal of preventing common bugs in smart contracts such as reentrancy. To this end, Obsidian makes states explicit and uses a linear type system for quantities of money.

Another line of research focuses on designing languages that allow for encoding security policies that are dynamically enforced at runtime. A first step in this direction is sketched in the preliminary work on Flint [36], a type-safe, capabilities-secure, contract-oriented programming language for smart contracts that gets compiled to EVM bytecode. Flint allows for defining caller capabilities restricting the access to security sensitive functions. These capabilities shall be enforced by the EVM bytecode created during compilation. But so far, there is only an extended abstract available.

In addition to these approaches from academia, the Ethereum foundation currently develops the high-level languages Viper [37] and Bamboo [38]. Furthermore, the Solidity compiler used to support a limited export functionality to the intermediate language WhyML [39] allowing for a pre/post condition style reasoning on Solidity code by leveraging the deductive program verification platform Why3 [40].

Intermediate Languages. The intermediate language Scilla [41] comes with a semantics formalized in the proof assistant Coq and therefore allows for a mechanized verification of Scilla contracts. In addition, Scilla makes some interesting design choices that might inspire the development of future high level languages for smart contracts: Scilla provides a strict separation not only between computation and communication, but also between pure and effectful computations.

Security Patterns. Wöhrer [42] describes programming patterns in Solidity that should be adapted by smart contract programmers for avoiding common bugs. These patterns encompass best coding practices such as performing calls at the end of a function, but also off-the-self solutions for common security bugs such as locking a contract for avoiding reentrancy or the integration of a mechanism that allows the contract owner to disable sensitive functionalities in the case of a bug.

Tools. Mavridou and Laszka [43] introduce a framework for designing smart contracts in terms of finite state machines. They provide a tool with a graphical editor for defining contract specifications as automata and give a translation of the constructed finite state machines to Solidity. In addition, they present some security extensions and patterns that can be used as off-the-shelf solutions for preventing reentrancy and implementing common security challenges such as time constraints and authorization. The approach however is lacking formal foundations as neither the correctness of the translation is proven correct, nor are the security patterns shown to meet the desired security goals.

3.3   Open Challenges

Even though the previous section highlights the wide range of steps taken towards the analysis of Ethereum smart contracts, there are still a lot of open challenges left.

Secure Compilation of High-Level Languages. Even though there are several proposals made for new high-level languages that facilitate the design of secure smart contracts and that are more amenable to verification, none of them comes so far with a verified compiler to EVM bytecode. Such a secure compilation however is the requirement for the results shown on high-level language programs to carry over to the actual smart contracts published on the blockchain.

Specification Languages for Smart Contracts. So far, all approaches to verifying contract specific properties focus on either ad-hoc specifications in the used verification framework [25,27,28,30] or the insertion of assertions into existing contract code [39]. For leveraging the power of existing model checking techniques for program verification, the design of a general-purpose contract specification language would be needed.

Study of Security Policies. There has been no fundamental research made so far on the classes of security policies that might be interesting to enforce in the setting of smart contracts. In particular, it would be compelling to characterize the class of security policies that can be enforced by smart contracts within the existing EVM.

Compositional Reasoning About Smart Contracts. Most research on smart contract verification focuses on reasoning about individual contracts or at most a bunch of contracts whose bytecode is fully available. Even though there has been work observing the similarities between smart contracts and concurrent programs [44], there has been no rigorous study on compositional reasoning for smart contracts so far.

4   Semantics

Recently, Grishchenko et al. [15] introduced the first complete small-step semantics for EVM bytecode. As this semantics serves as a basis for the static analyzer EtherTrust, we will in the following shortly review the general layout and the most important features of the semantics.

4.1   Execution Configurations

Before discussing the small-step rules of the semantics, we first introduce the general shape of execution configurations.

Global State. The global state of the Ethereum blockchain is represented as a (partial) mapping from account addresses to accounts. In the case that an account does not exist, we assume it to map to $\perp$. Accounts are composed of a nonce n that is incremented with every other account that the account creates, a balance b, a persistent unbounded storage *stor* and the account's code. External accounts carry an empty code which makes their storage inaccessible and hence irrelevant.

Small-Step Relation. The semantics is formalized by a small-step relation $\Gamma \vDash S \rightarrow S'$ that specifies how a call stack S representing the state of the execution evolves within one step under the transaction environment Γ. We call the pair (Γ, S) a *configuration*.

Transaction Environments. The transaction environment represents the static information of the block that the transaction is executed in and the immutable parameters given to the transaction as the gas prize or the gas limit. These parameters can be accessed by distinct bytecode instructions and consequently influence the transaction execution.

Call Stacks. A call stack S is a stack of execution states which represents the state of the overall execution of the initial external transaction. The individual execution states of the stack represent the states of the uncompleted internal transactions performed during the execution. Formally, a call stack is a stack of regular execution states of the form (μ, ι, σ) that can optionally be topped with a halting state $HALT(\sigma, gas, d)$ or an exception state EXC. Semantically, halting states indicate regular halting of an internal transaction, exception states indicate exceptional halting, and regular execution states describe the state of internal transactions in progress. Halting and exception states can only occur as top elements of the call stack as they represent terminated internal transactions. Halting states carry the information affecting the callee state such as the global state σ that the internal execution halted in, the unspent gas gas from the internal transaction execution and the return data d.

The state of a non-terminated internal transaction is described by a regular execution state of the form (μ, ι, σ). The state is determined by the current global state σ of the system as well as the execution environment ι that specifies the parameters of the current transaction (including inputs and the code to be executed) and the local state μ of the stack machine.

Table 1. Semantic rules for ADD

ADD

$$\frac{\iota.code\,[\mu.\mathsf{pc}] = \mathsf{ADD}}{\mu.\mathsf{s} = a :: b :: s \quad \mu.\mathsf{gas} \geq 3 \quad \mu' = \mu[\mathsf{s} \to (a+b) :: s][\mathsf{pc} \mathrel{+}= 1][\mathsf{gas} \mathrel{-}= 3]}{\Gamma \vDash (\mu, \iota, \sigma) :: S \to (\mu', \iota, \sigma) :: S}$$

ADD-FAIL

$$\frac{\iota.code\,[\mu.\mathsf{pc}] = \mathsf{ADD} \quad (|\mu.\mathsf{s}| < 2 \vee \mu.\mathsf{gas} < 3)}{\Gamma \vDash (\mu, \iota, \sigma) :: S \to EXC :: S}$$

Execution Environment. The execution environment ι of an internal transaction is a tuple of static parameters (*actor, input, sender, value, code*) to the transaction that, i.a., determine the code to be executed and the account in whose context the code will be executed. The execution environment incorporates the following components: the active account *actor* that is the account that is currently executing and whose account will be affected when instructions for storage modification or money transfer are performed; the input data *input* given to the transaction; the address *sender* of the account that initiated the transaction; the amount of wei *value* transferred with the transaction; the code *code* that is executed by the transaction. The execution environment is determined upon initialization of an internal transaction execution, and it can be accessed, but not altered during the execution.

Machine State. The local machine state μ represents the state of the underlying stack machine used for execution. Formally it is represented by a tuple (*gas, pc, m, aw, s*) holding the amount of gas *gas* available for execution, the program counter *pc*, the local memory *m*, the number of active words in memory *aw*, and the machine stack *s*.

The execution of each internal transaction starts in a fresh machine state, with an empty stack, memory initialized to all zeros, and program counter and active words in memory set to zero. Only the gas is instantiated with the gas value available for the execution. We call execution states with machine states of this form *initial*.

4.2 Small-Step Rules

In the following, we will present a selection of interesting small-step rules in order to illustrate the most important features of the semantics.

Local Instructions. For demonstrating the overall design of the semantics, we start with the example of the arithmetic expression ADD performing addition of two values on the machine stack. The small-step rules for ADD are shown in Table 1. We use a dot notation, in order to access components of the different state parameters. We name the components with the variable names introduced for these components in the last section written in sans-serif-style. In addition, we use the usual notation for updating components: $t[c \rightarrow v]$ denotes that the component c of tuple t is updated with value v. For expressing incremental updates in a simpler way, we additionally use the notation $t[c \mathrel{+}= v]$ to denote that the (numerical) component of c is incremented by v and similarly $t[c \mathrel{-}= v]$ for decrementing a component c of t.

The execution of the arithmetic instruction ADD only performs local changes in the machine state affecting the local stack, the program counter, and the gas budget. For deciding upon the correct instruction to execute, the currently executed code (that is part of the execution environment) is accessed at the position of the current program counter. The cost of an ADD instruction consists always of three units of gas that get subtracted from the gas budget in the machine state. As every other instruction, ADD can fail due to lacking gas or due to underflows on the machine stack. In this case, the exception state is entered and the execution of the current internal transaction is terminated. For better readability, we use here the slightly sloppy $\vee$ notation for combining the two error cases in one inference rule.

Transaction Initiating Instructions. A class of instructions with a more involved semantics are those instructions initiating internal transactions. This class incorporates instructions for calling another contract (CALL, CALLCODE and DELEGATECALL) and for creating a new contract (CREATE). We will explain the semantics of those instructions in an intuitive way omitting technical details.

The call instructions initiate a new internal call transaction whose parameters are specified on the machine stack – including the recipient (callee) and the amount of money to be transferred (in the case of CALL and CALLCODE). In addition, the input to the call is specified by providing the corresponding local memory fragment and analogously a memory fragment for the return value.

When executing a call instruction, the specified amount of wei is transferred to the callee and the code of the callee is executed. The different call types diverge in the environment that the callee code is executed in. In the case of a CALL instruction, while executing the callee code (only) the account of the callee can be accessed and modified. So intuitively, the control is completely handed to the callee as its code is executed in its own context. In contrast, in the case of CALLCODE, the executed callee code can (only) access and modify the account of the caller. So the callee's code is executed in the caller's context which might be useful for using library functionalities implemented in a separate library contract that e.g., transfer money on behalf of the caller.

This idea is pushed even further in the DELEGATECALL instruction. This call type does not allow for transferring money and executes the callee's code not only in the caller's context, but even preserves part of the execution environment of the previous call (in particular the call value and the sender information). Intuitively, this instruction resembles adding the callee's code to the caller as

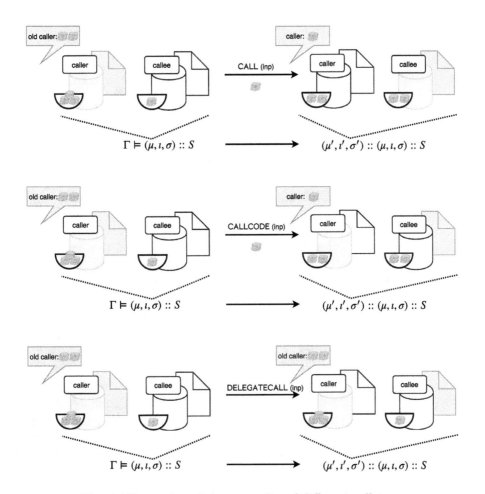

Fig. 1. Illustration of the semantics of different call types

an internal function so that calling it does not cause a new internal transaction (even though it formally does).

Figure 1 summarizes the behavior of the different call instructions in EVM bytecode. The executed code of the respective account is highlighted in orange while the accessible account state is depicted in green. The remaining internal transaction information (as specified in the execution environment) on the sender of the internal transaction and the transferred value are marked in violet. In addition, the picture relates the corresponding changes to the small-step semantics: the execution of a call transaction adds a new execution state to the call stack while preserving the old one. The new global state σ' records the changes in the accounts' balances, while the new execution environment ι' determines the accessible account (by setting the **actor** of the internal transaction correspondingly), the code to be executed (by setting **code**) and further accessible transaction information as the sender, value and input (by setting **sender**, **value** and **input** respectively).

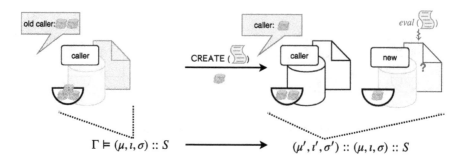

$$\Gamma \vDash (\mu, \iota, \sigma) :: S \longrightarrow (\mu', \iota', \sigma') :: (\mu, \iota, \sigma) :: S$$

Fig. 2. Illustration of the semantics of the CREATE instruction (Color figure online)

The CREATE instruction initiates an internal transaction that creates a new account. The semantics of this instruction is similar to the one of CALL, with the exception that a fresh account is created, which gets the specified value transferred, and that the input provided to this internal transaction, which is again specified in the local memory, is interpreted as the initialization code to be executed in order to produce the newly created account's code as output. Figure 2 depicts the semantics of the CREATE instruction in a similar fashion as it is done for the call instructions before. It is notable that the input to the CREATE instruction is interpreted as code and executed (therefore highlighted in orange) in the context of the newly created contract (highlighted in green). During this execution the newly created contract does not have any contract code itself (therefore depicted in gray), but only after completing the internal transaction the return value of the transaction will be set as code for the freshly created contract.

5   Security Properties

Grishchenko et al. [15] propose generic security definitions for smart contracts that rule out certain classes of potentially harmful contract behavior. These properties constitute trace properties (more precisely, safety properties) as well as hyper properties (in particular, value independence properties). In this work, we revisit one of these safety properties called *single-entrancy* and use this property as a case study for showing how safety properties of smart contracts (that can be over-approximated by pure reachability properties) can be automatically checked by static analysis. For checking value independence properties, in [1] the reviewed analysis technique is extended with a simple dependency analysis that we will not discuss further in this work.

5.1   Preliminary Notations

Formally, contracts are represented as tuples of the form $(a, code)$ where a denotes the address of the contract and *code* denotes the contract's code.

In order to give concise security definitions, we further introduce, and assume all through the paper, an annotation to the small step semantics in order to highlight the contract c that is currently executed. In the case of initialization code being executed, we use $\perp$. We write $S + +S'$ for the concatenation of call stacks S and S'. Finally, for arguing about EVM bytecode executions, we are only interested in those initial configurations that might result from a valid external transaction in a valid block. In the following, we will call these configurations *reachable* and refer to [15] for a detailed definition.

5.2   Single-Entrancy

For motivating the definition of single-entrancy, we introduce a class of bugs in Ethereum smart contracts called *reentrancy bugs* [14,16].

The most famous representative of this class is the so-called DAO bug that led to a loss of 60 million dollars in June 2016 [11]. In an attack exploiting this bug, the affected contract was drained out of money by subsequently reentering it and performing transactions to the attacker on behalf of the contract.

The cause of such bugs mostly roots in the developer's misunderstanding of the semantics of Solidity's call primitives. In general, calling a contract can invoke two kinds of actions: Transferring Ether to the contract's account or Executing (parts of) a contracts code. In particular, Solidity's `call` construct (being translated to a **CALL** instruction in EVM bytecode) invokes the execution of a fraction of the callee's code – specified in the so called *fallback function*. A contract's fallback function is written as a function without names or argument as depicted in the `Mallory` contract in Fig. 3b.

Consequently, when using the `call` construct the developer may expect an atomic value transfer where potentially another contract's code is executed. For illustrating how to exploit this sort of bug, we consider the contracts in Fig. 3.

```
1  contract Bob{
2    bool sent = false;
3    function ping( address c){        1  contract Mallory{
4      if (!sent) { c.call.value(2)();  2    function (){
5            sent = true; }}}           3      Bob(msg.sender).ping(this);}}
```

(a) Smart contract with reentrancy bug   (b) Smart contract exploiting reentrancy bug

Fig. 3. Reentrancy attack

The function `ping` of contract `Bob` sends an amount of 2 *wei* to the address specified in the argument. However, this should only be possible once, which is potentially ensured by the `sent` variable that is set after the successful money transfer. Instead, it turns out that invoking the `call.value` function on a contract's address invokes the contract's fallback function as well.

Given a second contract `Mallory`, it is possible to transfer more money than the intended 2 *wei* to the account of `Mallory`. By invoking `Bob`'s function `ping` with the address of Mallory's account, 2 *wei* are transferred to Mallory's account and additionally the fallback function of Mallory is invoked. As the fallback function again calls the ping function with Mallory's address another 2 *wei* are transferred before the variable sent of contract Bob was set. This looping goes on until all gas of the initial call is consumed or the callstack limit is reached. In this case, only the last transfer of *wei* is reverted and the effects of all former calls stay in place. Consequently the intended restriction on contract Bob's ping function (namely to only transfer 2 *wei* once) is circumvented.

Motivated by these kinds of attacks, the notion of single-entrancy was introduced. Intuitively, a contract is single-entrant if it cannot perform any more calls once it has been reentered. Formally this property can be expressed in terms of the small-steps semantics as follows:

Definition 1 (Single-entrancy [15]). *A contract c is single-entrant if for all reachable configurations* $(\Gamma, s_c :: S)$, *it holds for all* s', s'', S' *that*

$$\Gamma \vDash s_c :: S \rightarrow^* s'_c :: S' + + s_c :: S$$
$$\implies \neg \exists s'' \in \mathcal{S}, c' \in \mathcal{C}_\perp . \Gamma \vDash s'_c :: S' + + s_c :: S \rightarrow^* s''_{c'} :: s'_c :: S' + + s_c :: S$$

This property constitutes a safety property. We will show in Sect. 7 how it can be appropriately abstracted for being expressed in the EtherTrust analysis framework.

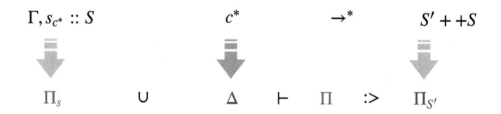

Fig. 4. Simplified soundness statement

6   Verification

Grishchenko et al. [1] developed a static analysis framework for analyzing reachability properties of EVM smart contracts. This framework relies on an abstract semantics for EVM bytecode soundly over-approximating the semantics presented in Sect. 4.

In the following we will review the abstractions performed on the small-step configurations and execution rules using the example of the abstract execution rule for the ADD instruction. Afterwards, we will discuss shortly how call instructions are over-approximated.

6.1 Abstract Semantics

Figure 4 gives an overview on the relation between the small-step and the abstract semantics. For the analysis, we will consider a particular contract c^* under analysis whose code is known. An over-approximation of the behavior of this smart contract will be encoded in *Horn clauses*(Δ). These describe how an abstract configuration (represented by a set of abstract state predicates) evolves within the execution of the contract's instructions. Abstract configurations are obtained by translating small-step configurations to a set Π of facts over state predicates that characterize (an over-approximation of) the original configuration. This transformation is performed with respect to the contract c^* as only all local behavior of this particular contract will be over-approximated and consequently only those elements on the callstack representing executions of c^* are translated. Finally, we will show that no matter how the contract c^* is called (so for every arbitrary reachable configuration $\Gamma, s_{c^*} :: S$), every sequence of execution steps that is performed while executing it can be mimicked by a derivation of the abstract configuration Π_s (obtained from translating the execution state s) using the horn clauses Δ (that model the abstract semantics of the contract c^*). More precisely, this means that from the set of facts $\Pi_s \cup \Delta$ a set Π can be derived that is a coarser abstraction ($<:$) than $\Pi_{S'}$ which is the translation of the execution's intermediate call stack S'. A corresponding formal soundness statement is proven in [1].

6.2 Abstract Configurations

Table 2 shows the analysis facts used for describing the abstract semantics. These consist of (instances of) state predicates that represent partial abstract configurations. Accordingly, abstract configurations are sets of facts not containing any variables as arguments. We will refer to such facts as *closed facts*. Finally, abstract contracts are characterized as sets of Horn clauses over the state predicates (facts) that describe the state changes induced by the instructions at the different program positions. Here only those state predicates are depicted that are needed for describing the abstract semantics of the ADD instruction.

The state predicates are parametrized by a program point pp that is a tuple of the form (id^*, pc) with id^* being a contract identifier for contract c^* and pc being the program counter at which the abstract state holds.[3] The parametrization by the contract identifier helps to make the analysis consider a set of contracts whose code is known (such as e.g., library code that is known to be used by the contract). In this work however we focus on the case where c^* represented by identifier id^* is the only known contract. In addition, the predicates carry the relative call depth cd as argument. The relative call depth is the size of the call stack built up on the execution of c^* (Cf. call stack S' in Fig. 4) and serves as abstraction for the (relative) call stack that contract c^* is currently executed on.

---

[3] Making the program counter a parameter instead of an argument is a design choice made in order to minimize the number of recursive horn clauses simplifying automated verification.

Table 2. Analysis Facts. All arguments in the analysis facts marked with a hat ($\hat{\cdot}$) range over $\hat{D} \cup \textit{Vars}$ where $\hat{D}$ is the abstract domain and *Vars* is the set of variables. All other arguments of analysis facts range over $\mathbb{N}$ with exception of *sa* that ranges over $(\mathbb{N} \to \hat{D}) \cup \textit{Vars}$. Closed facts *cf* are assumed to be facts with arguments not coming from *Vars*.

$$
\begin{array}{lll}
\text{Facts} & f := & \\
\text{Abs. machine state} & \mid & \mathsf{MState}_{pp}\,((size, sa), \hat{aw}, \hat{gas}, cd) \\
\text{Abs. memory} & \mid & \mathsf{Mem}_{pp}\,(\hat{pos}, \hat{va}, cd) \\
\text{Abs. exception state} & \mid & \mathsf{Exc}_{id*}\,(cd) \\
\ldots & \mid & \ldots \\
\text{Abs. configurations} & \Pi := \{cf_1, \ldots, cf_n\} & \\
\text{Horn clauses} & H := \forall x^*.\, \bigwedge_i f_i \implies f & \\
\text{Abs. contracts} & \Delta := \{H_1, \ldots, H_n\} &
\end{array}
$$

The relative call depth helps to distinguish different recursive executions of c^* and thereby improves the precision of the analysis.

As the ADD instruction only operates on the local machine state, we focus on the abstract representation of the machine state μ: The state predicates representing μ are MState_{pp} and Mem_{pp}. The fact $\mathsf{MState}_{pp}\,((size, sa), \hat{aw}, \hat{gas}, cd)$ says that at program point *pp* and relative call depth *cd* the machine stack is of size *size* and its current configuration is described by the mapping *sa* which maps stack positions to abstract values, $\hat{aw}$ represents the number of active words in memory, and $\hat{gas}$ is the remaining gas. Similarly, the fact $\mathsf{Mem}_{pp}\,(\hat{pos}, \hat{v}, cd)$ states that at program point *pp* and relative call depth *cd* at memory address $\hat{pos}$ there is the (abstract) value $\hat{v}$. The values on the stack and in local memory range over an abstract domain. Concretely, we define the abstract domain $\hat{D}$ to be the set $\{\bot, \top, a^*\} \cup \mathbb{N}$ which constitutes a bounded lattice $(\hat{D}, \sqsubseteq, \sqcup, \sqcap, \top, \bot)$ satisfying $\bot \sqsubseteq a^* \sqsubseteq \top$ and $\bot \sqsubseteq n \sqsubseteq \top$ for all $n \in \mathbb{N}$. Intuitively, in our analysis $\top$ will represent unknown (symbolic) values and a^* will represent the unknown (symbolic) address of contract c^*.

Treating the address of the contract under analysis in a symbolic fashion is crucial for obtaining a meaningful analysis, as the address of this account on the blockchain can not easily be assumed to be known upfront. Although discussing this peculiarity is beyond the scope of this paper, a broader presentation of the symbolic address paradigm can be found in the technical report [1].

For performing operations and comparisons on values from the abstract domain, we will assume versions of the unary, binary and comparison operators on the values from $\hat{D}$. We will mark abstract operators with a hat ($\hat{\cdot}$) and e.g., write $\hat{+}$ for abstract addition or $\hat{=}$ for abstract equality. The operators will treat $\top$ and a^* as arbitrary values so that e.g., $\top \hat{+} n$ evaluates to $\top$ and $\top \hat{=} n$ evaluates to *true* and *false* for all $n \in \mathbb{N}$.

Formally, we establish the relation between a concrete machine state μ and its abstraction by an abstraction function that translates machine states to a set of closed analysis facts. Figure 3 shows the abstraction function α_μ that maps a local machine state into an abstract state consisting of a set of analysis facts. The abstraction is defined with respect to the relative call depth cd of the execution and a value abstraction function $\overset{\circ}{\cdot}$ that maps concrete values into values from the abstract domain. The function $\overset{\circ}{\cdot}$ thereby maps all concrete values to the corresponding (concrete) values in the abstract domain, but those values that can potentially represent the address of contract c^*, hence, they are translated to a^* and therefore over-approximated. This treatment might introduce spurious counterexamples with respect to the concrete execution of the real contract on the blockchain (where it is assigned a concrete address). On the one hand, this is due to the fact that by this abstraction the concrete value of the address is assumed to be arbitrary. On the other hand, abstract computations with a always result in $\top$ and therefore possible constraints on these results are lost. However, the first source of imprecision should not be considered an imprecision per se, as the c^*'s address is not assumed to be known statically, thus, the goal of the abstraction is to over-approximate the executions with all possible addresses.

The translation proceeds by creating a set of instances of the machine state predicates. For creating instances of the MState_{pp} predicate, the concrete values aw and gas are over-approximated by $\overset{\circ}{aw}$ and $\overset{\circ}{gas}$ respectively, and the stack is translated to an abstract array representation using the function $\mathsf{stackToArray}$. The instances of the memory predicate are created by translating the memory mapping m to a relational representation with abstract locations and values.[4]

Table 3. Abstraction function for the local machine state μ

$$\alpha_\mu \left((gas, pc, m, aw, s), cd\right) := \{\mathsf{MState}_{(id^*, pc)} \left(\mathsf{stackToArray}\left(s\right), \overset{\circ}{aw}, \overset{\circ}{gas}, cd\right)\}$$

$$\cup \{\mathsf{Mem}_{(id^*, pc)} \left(\overset{\circ}{pos}, \overset{\circ}{v}, cd\right) \mid m\left[pos\right] = v \wedge pos \leq 2^{256}\}$$

$$\mathsf{stackToArray}\left(\epsilon\right) := (0, \lambda x. 0)$$

$$\mathsf{stackToArray}\left(x :: s\right) := let\ (size, sa) = \mathsf{stackToArray}\left(s\right)\ in\ (size + 1, sa^{size}_{\overset{\circ}{x}})$$

6.3   Abstract Execution Rules

As all state predicates are parametrized by their program points, the abstract semantics needs to be formulated with respect to program points as well. More precisely this means that for each program counter of contract c^* a set of Horn clauses is created that describes the semantics of the instruction at this program counter. Formally, a function $(\!|\cdot|\!)^{\{c^*\}}_{pp}$ is defined that creates the required set of rules given that the instruction $inst$ is at position pc of contract c^*'s code.

---

[4] The reason for using a separate predicate for representing local memory instead of encoding it as an argument of array type in the main machine state predicate is purely technical: for modeling memory usage correctly we would need a rich set of array operations that are however not supported by the fixedpoint engines of modern SMT solvers.

Table 4 shows a part of the definition (excerpt of the rules) of $(\!|\cdot|\!)_{pp}^{\{c^*\}}$ for the ADD instruction. The main functionality of the rule is described by the Horn clause 1 that describes how the machine stack and the gas evolve when executing ADD. First the precondition is checked whether the sufficient amount of gas and stack elements are available. Then the two (abstract) top elements $\hat{x}$ and $\hat{y}$ are extracted from the stack and their sum is written to the top of the stack while reducing the overall stack size by 1. In addition, the local gas value is reduced by 3 in an abstract fashion. In the memory rule (Horn clause 2), again the preconditions are checked and then (as memory is not affected by the ADD instruction) the memory is propagated. This propagation is needed due to the memory predicate's parametrization with the program counter: For making the memory accessible in the next execution step, its values need to be written into the corresponding predicate for the next program counter. Finally, Horn clauses 3 and 4 characterize the exception cases: an exception while executing the ADD instruction can occur either because of a stack underflow or as the execution runs out of gas. In both cases the exception state is entered which is indicated by recording the relative call depth of the exception in the predicate $\mathsf{Exc}_{id^*}\,(cd)$.

By allowing gas values to come from the abstract domain, we enable symbolic treatment of gas. In particular this means that when starting the analysis with gas value $\top$, all gas calculations will directly result in $\top$ again (and could therefore be omitted) and in particular all checks on the gas will result in *true* and *false* and consequently always both paths (regular execution via Horn clauses 1 and 2 and exception via Horn clause 4) will be triggered in the analysis.

For over-approximating the semantics of call instructions, more involved abstractions are needed. We will illustrate these abstractions in the following in an intuitive way and refer to [1] for the technical details. Note that in the following we will assume CALL instructions to be the only kind of transaction initiating instructions that are contained in the contracts that we consider for analysis. A generalization of the analysis that allows for incorporating also other call types is presented in [1].

As we are considering c^* the only contract to be known, whenever a call is performed that is not a self-call, we need to assume that an arbitrary contract $c^?$ gets executed. The general idea for over-approximating calls to an unknown contract $c^?$ is that only those execution states that represent executions of contract c^* will be over-approximated. Consequently, when a call is performed, all possible effects on future executions of c^* that might be caused by the execution of $c^?$ (including the initiation of further initial transactions that might cause reentering c^*) need to be captured. For doing this as accurate as possible, we use the following observations:

1. Given that c^* only executes plain CALL instructions the persistent storage of contract c^* can only be altered during executions of c^*.
2. Contracts have a single entry point: their execution always starts in a fresh machine state at program counter zero.

In general, we can soundly capture the possibility of contract c^* being reentered during the execution of $c^?$ by assuming to reenter c^* at every higher call

Table 4. Excerpt of the abstract rules for ADD

$$(\!| \text{ADD} |\!)_{(id*,pc)}^{\{c^*\}} = \{ \text{MState}_{(id^*,pc)} \, ((size, sa), \hat{aw}, \hat{gas}, cd) \wedge size > 1 \wedge \hat{gas} \,\hat{\geq}\, 3$$

$$\wedge\, \hat{x} = sa[size - 1] \wedge \hat{y} = sa[size - 2]$$

$$\Rightarrow \text{MState}_{(id^*, pc+1)} \, ((size - 1, sa_{\hat{x}\,\hat{+}\,\hat{y}}^{size-2}), \hat{aw}, \hat{gas} \,\hat{-}\, 3, cd), \tag{1}$$

$$\text{Mem}_{(id^*,pc)} \, (\hat{pos}, \hat{va}, cd) \wedge \text{MState}_{(id^*,pc)} \, ((size, sa), \hat{gas}, \hat{aw}, cd)$$

$$\wedge\, size > 1 \wedge \hat{gas} \,\hat{\geq}\, 3 \Rightarrow \text{Mem}_{(id^*, pc+1)} \, (\hat{pos}, \hat{va}, cd), \tag{2}$$

$$\text{MState}_{(id^*,pc)} \, ((size, sa), \hat{gas}, \hat{aw}, cd) \wedge size < 2 \Rightarrow \text{Exc}_{id*} \, (cd), \tag{3}$$

$$\text{MState}_{(id^*,pc)} \, ((size, sa), \hat{gas}, \hat{aw}, cd) \wedge \hat{gas} \,\hat{<}\, 3 \Rightarrow \text{Exc}_{id*} \, (cd) \dots \} \tag{4}$$

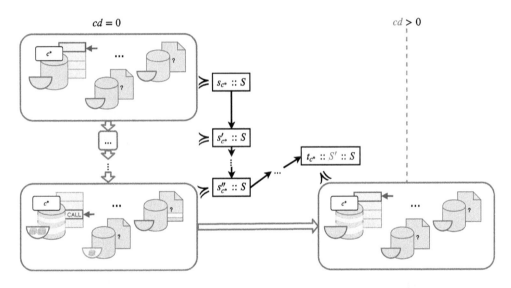

Fig. 5. Illustration of the abstraction of the semantics for the CALL instruction.

level. For keeping the desired precision, we can use the previously made observations for imposing restrictions on the reenterings of c^*: First, we assume the persistent storage of c^* to be the same as at the point of calling (observation 1.). Second, we know that execution starts at program counter 0 in a fresh machine state (observation 2.). This allows us to initialize the machine state predicates presented in Table 2 accordingly at program counter zero. All other parts of the global state and the execution environment need to be considered unknown at the point of reentering as they might have potentially been changed during the execution of $c^?$. This in particular also applies to the balance of contract c^*.

Figure 5 illustrates how the abstract configurations over-approximating the concrete execution states of c^* evolve within the execution of the abstract semantics. We write $\Pi \succcurlyeq S$ for denoting that an abstract configuration Π (here graphically depicted in gray frames) is an over-approximation of call stack S. The depicted execution starts in the initial execution state s_{c^*} of c^*. This is state is over-approximated by assuming the storage and balance of c^* as well as all other information on the global state to be unknown and therefore initialized to ⊤ in the corresponding state predicates of the abstract configuration (denoted in the picture by marking the corresponding state components in red). The execution steps representing the executions of local instructions are mimicked step-wise by corresponding abstract execution steps. During these steps a more refined knowledge about the state of c^* and its environment might be gained (e.g., the value of some storage cells where information is written, or some restrictions on the account's balances, marked in green or blue, respectively). When finally a CALL instruction is executed, every potential reentering of contract c^* (here exemplified by execution state t_{c^*}) is over-approximated by abstract configurations for every call depths $cd > 0$ that consider all global state and environmental information to be arbitrary, but the parts modeling the persistent storage of c^* to be as at the point of calling. In Sect. 7 we will show how this abstraction will help us to automatically check smart contracts for single-entrancy in a sound and precise manner. In addition to these over-approximations that capture the effects on c^* during the execution of an unknown contract, for over-approximating CALL instructions some other abstractions need to be performed that model the semantics of returning:

– For returning it is always assumed that potentially the call failed or returned with arbitrary return values.
– After returning the global state is assumed to be altered arbitrarily by the call and therefore its components are set to ⊤.

For a complete account and formal description of the abstractions, we refer to the full specification of the abstract semantics spelled out in the technical report [1].

7 Verifying Security Properties

In this section, we will show how the previously presented analysis can be used for proving reachability properties of Ethereum smart contracts in an automated fashion.

To this end, we review EtherTrust [1], the first sound static analyzer for EVM bytecode. EtherTrust proceeds by translating contract code provided in the bytecode format into an internal Horn clause representation. This Horn clause representation, together with facts over-approximating all potential initial configurations are handed to the SMT solver Z3 [45] via an API. For showing that the analyzed contract satisfies a reachability property, the unsatisfiability of the corresponding analysis queries needs to be verified using Z3's fixedpoint engine SPACER [46]. If all analysis queries are deemed unsatisfiable then the contract under analysis is guaranteed to satisfy the original reachability query due to the soundness of the underlying analysis.

In the following we will discuss the analysis queries used for verifying single-entrancy and illustrate how these queries allow for capturing contracts that are vulnerable to reentrancy such as the example presented in Sect. 5.

7.1 Over-Approximating Single-Entrancy

For being able to automatically check for single-entrancy, we need to simplify the original property in order to obtain a description that is expressible in terms of the analysis framework described in Sect. 6. To this end, a strictly stronger property named *call unreachability* is presented that is proven to imply single-entrancy:

Definition 2 (Call unreachability [1]). *A contract c is call unreachable if for all initial execution states (μ, ι, σ) such that $(\mu, \iota, \sigma)_c$ is well formed, it holds that for all transaction environments Γ and all call stacks S*

$$\neg \exists s, S'. \, \Gamma \vDash (\mu, \iota, \sigma)_c :: S \rightarrow^* s_c :: S' + +S$$
$$\wedge \; |S'| > 0 \; \wedge \; code\,(c)\,[s.\mu.\mathsf{pc}] \in Inst_{call}$$

With $Inst_{call} = \{ \mathsf{CALL}, \mathsf{CALLCODE}, \mathsf{DELEGATECALL}, \mathsf{CREATE} \}$

Intuitively, this property states that it should not be possible to reach a call instruction of c^* after reentering. As we are excluding all transaction initiating instructions but CALL from the analysis, it is sufficient to query for the reachability of a CALL instruction of c^* on a higher call depth. More precisely, we end up with the following set of queries:

$$\{ \mathsf{MState}_{(id,\,\mathsf{pc})}\,((size, sa), aw, gas, cd) \wedge cd > 0 \mid code\,(c^*)\,[pc] = \mathsf{CALL} \} \qquad (5)$$

As the MState_{pp} predicate tracks the state of the machine state at all program points, it can be used as indicator for reachability of the program point as such. Consequently, by querying the $\mathsf{MState}_{(id^*,\,\mathsf{pc})}$ for all program counters pc where c^* has a CALL instruction and along with that requiring a call depth exceeding zero, we can check whether a call instruction is reachable in some reentering execution.

7.2 Examples

We will use examples for showing how the analysis detects, and proves the absence of reentrancy bugs, respectively. To this end, we revisit the contract Bob presented in Sect. 5, and introduce a contract Alice that fixes the reentrancy bug that is present in Bob. The two contracts are shown in Figure 6.

Detecting Reentrancy Bugs. We illustrate how the analysis detects reentrancy bugs using the example in Figure 6a. To this end we give a graphical description of the over-approximations performed when analyzing contract Bob which is depicted in Figure 7. For the sake of presentation, we give the contract code in Solidity instead of bytecode and argue about it on this level even though the analysis is carried out on bytecode level.

As discussed in Sect. 6.3, the analysis considers the execution of contract Bob to start in an unknown environment, which implies that also the value of the

```
1  contract Bob{                              1  contract Alice{
2    bool sent = false;                       2    bool sent = false;
3    function ping( address c){               3    function ping( address c){
4      if (!sent) { c.call.value(2)();        4      if (!sent) { sent = true;
5                  sent = true; }}}            5                  c.call.value(2)(); }}}
```

(a) Smart contract with reentrancy bug   (b) Smart contract with fixed reentrancy bug

Fig. 6. Examples for contracts showing and being robust against the reentrancy bug.

contract's sent variable is unknown and hence initialized to $\top$. As a consequence, the equality check in line 4 is considered to evaluate to both *true* and *false* in the abstract setting (as $\top$ needs to be considered to potentially equal every concrete value). Accordingly, the analysis needs to consider the then-branch of the conditional and consequently the call in line 4. This call is over-approximated as discussed in Sect. 6.3, and therefore considers reentering contract Bob in an arbitrary call depth. In this situation, the sent variable is still over-approximated to have value $\top$ wherefore the call at line 4 can be reached again which satisfies the reachability query in Eq. 5.

Proving Single-Entrancy. We consider the contract Alice shown in Figure 6b. In contrast to contract Bob, this contract does not have the reentrancy vulnerability, as the guard sent that should prevent the call instruction in line 5 from being executed more than once is set before performing the call. As a consequence, when reentering the contract, the guard is already set and stops any further calls. We show that the analysis presented in Sect. 6 is precise enough for proving this contract to be single-entrant. Intuitively, the abstraction is precise as it considers that the contract's persistent storage can be assumed to be unchanged at the point of reentering. Consequently, the then-branch of the conditional can be excluded from the analysis when reentering and the contract can be proven to be single-entrant. A graphic description of this argument is provided in Figure 8. As for contract Bob, the analysis starts in an abstract configuration that assigns the sent variable value $\top$, which forces the analysis to consider the then as well as the else-branch of the conditional in line 4. When taking the else-branch, the contract execution terminates without reaching a state satisfying the reachability query. Therefore, it is sufficient to only consider the then-branch for proving the impossibility of re-reaching the call instruction. When executing the call in the then-branch, according to the abstract call semantics, the analysis needs to take all abstract configurations representing executions of Alice at higher call depths into account. However, in each of these abstract configurations it can be assumed that the state of the persistent storage (including the sent variable, highlighted in green) is the same as at the point of calling. As at this point sent was already initialized to the concrete value **true**, the then-branch of the conditional can be excluded from the analysis at any call depth $cd > 0$ and consequently the unreachability of the query in Eq. 5 is proven.

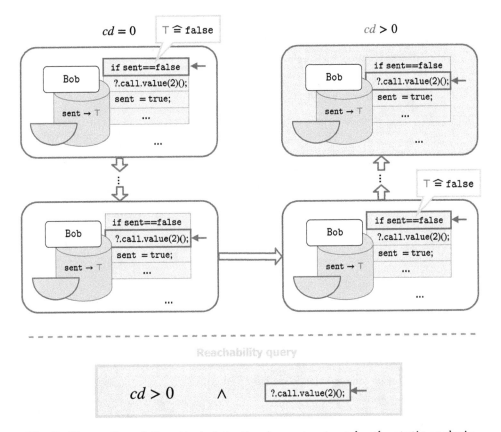

Fig. 7. Illustration of the attack detection in contract Bob by the static analysis.

7.3 Discussion

In this section, we illustrated how the static analysis underlying EtherTrust [1] in principle is capable not only of detecting re-entrancy bugs, but also of proving smart contracts single-entrant. In practice, EtherTrust manages to analyze real-world contracts from the blockchain within several seconds, as detailed in the experimental evaluation presented in [1]. Even though EtherTrust produces false positives due to the performed over-approximations, it still shows better precision on a benchmark than the state-of-the art bug-finding tool Oyente [16]

despite being sound. Similar results are shown when using EtherTrust for checking a simple value independency property.

In general, EtherTrust could be easily extended to support more properties on contract execution – given that those properties or over-approximations of them are expressible as reachability or simple value independency properties. By contrast, checking more involved hyper properties, or properties that span more than one execution of the external transaction execution is currently out of the scope for EtherTrust.

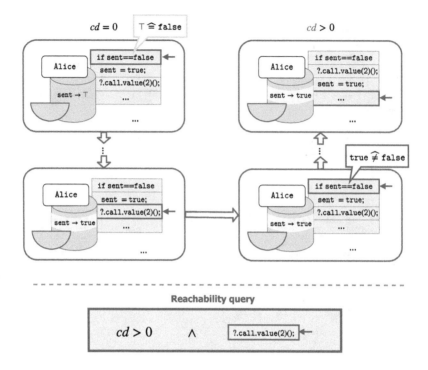

Fig. 8. Illustration of proving single-entrancy of contract `Alice` by the static analysis.

8   Conclusion

We presented a systematization of the state-of-the-art in Ethereum smart contract verification and outlined the open challenges in this field. Also we discussed in detail the foundations of EtherTrust [1], the first sound static analyzer for EVM bytecode. In particular, we reviewed how the small-step semantics presented in [15] is abstracted into a set of Horn clauses. Also we presented how single-entrancy – a relevant smart contract security property – is expressed in terms of queries, which can be then automatically solved leveraging the power of an SMT solver.

Acknowledgments. This work has been partially supported by the European Research Council (ERC) under the European Union's Horizon 2020 research (grant agreement No 771527-BROWSEC), by Netidee through the project EtherTrust (grant agreement 2158), by the Austrian Research Promotion Agency through the Bridge-1 project PR4DLT (grant agreement 13808694) and COMET K1 SBA.

References

1. EtherTrust: Technical report. https://www.netidee.at/ethertrust
2. Nakamoto, S.: Bitcoin: a peer-to-peer electronic cash system (2008). http://bitcoin.org/bitcoin.pdf

3. Hahn, A., Singh, R., Liu, C.C., Chen, S.: Smart contract-based campus demonstration of decentralized transactive energy auctions. In: 2017 IEEE Power & Energy Society Innovative Smart Grid Technologies Conference (ISGT), pp. 1–5. IEEE (2017)

4. Adhikari, C.: Secure framework for healthcare data management using ethereum-based blockchain technology (2017)

5. Biryukov, A., Khovratovich, D., Tikhomirov, S.: Findel: secure derivative contracts for ethereum. In: Brenner, M., Rohloff, K., Bonneau, J., Miller, A., Ryan, P.Y.A., Teague, V., Bracciali, A., Sala, M., Pintore, F., Jakobsson, M. (eds.) FC 2017. LNCS, vol. 10323, pp. 453–467. Springer, Cham (2017). https://doi.org/10.1007/978-3-319-70278-0_28

6. McCorry, P., Shahandashti, S.F., Hao, F.: A smart contract for boardroom voting with maximum voter privacy. In: Kiayias, A. (ed.) FC 2017. LNCS, vol. 10322, pp. 357–375. Springer, Cham (2017). https://doi.org/10.1007/978-3-319-70972-7_20

7. Notheisen, B., Gödde, M., Weinhardt, C.: Trading stocks on blocks - engineering decentralized markets. In: Maedche, A., vom Brocke, J., Hevner, A. (eds.) DESRIST 2017. LNCS, vol. 10243, pp. 474–478. Springer, Cham (2017). https://doi.org/10.1007/978-3-319-59144-5_34

8. Mathieu, F., Mathee, R.: Blocktix: decentralized event hosting and ticket distribution network (2017). https://blocktix.io/public/doc/blocktix-wp-draft.pdf

9. Azaria, A., Ekblaw, A., Vieira, T., Lippman, A.: MedRec: using blockchain for medical data access and permission management. In: International Conference on Open and Big Data (OBD), pp. 25–30. IEEE (2016)

10. Dong, C., Wang, Y., Aldweesh, A., McCorry, P., van Moorsel, A.: Betrayal, distrust, and rationality: Smart counter-collusion contracts for verifiable cloud computing (2017)

11. The DAO smart contract (2016). http://etherscan.io/address/0xbb9bc244d798123fde783fcc1c72d3bb8c189413#code

12. The parity wallet breach (2017). https://www.coindesk.com/30-million-ether-reported-stolen-parity-wallet-breach/

13. The parity wallet vulnerability (2017). https://paritytech.io/blog/security-alert.html

14. Atzei, N., Bartoletti, M., Cimoli, T.: A survey of attacks on Ethereum smart contracts (SoK). In: Maffei, M., Ryan, M. (eds.) POST 2017. LNCS, vol. 10204, pp. 164–186. Springer, Heidelberg (2017). https://doi.org/10.1007/978-3-662-54455-6_8

15. Grishchenko, I., Maffei, M., Schneidewind, C.: A semantic framework for the security analysis of Ethereum smart contracts. In: Bauer, L., Küsters, R. (eds.) POST 2018. LNCS, vol. 10804, pp. 243–269. Springer, Cham (2018). https://doi.org/10.1007/978-3-319-89722-6_10

16. Luu, L., Chu, D.H., Olickel, H., Saxena, P., Hobor, A.: Making smart contracts smarter. In: Proceedings of the 2016 ACM SIGSAC Conference on Computer and Communications Security, pp. 254–269. ACM (2016)

17. Zhou, E., Hua, S., Pi, B., Sun, J., Nomura, Y., Yamashita, K., Kurihara, H.: Security assurance for smart contract. In: 2018 9th IFIP International Conference on New Technologies, Mobility and Security (NTMS), pp. 1–5. IEEE (2018)

18. Nikolic, I., Kolluri, A., Sergey, I., Saxena, P., Hobor, A.: Finding the greedy, prodigal, and suicidal contracts at scale. arXiv preprint arXiv:1802.06038 (2018)

19. Kalra, S., Goel, S., Dhawan, M., Sharma, S.: ZEUS: analyzing safety of smart contracts. In: NDSS (2018)

20. Buenzli, F., Dan, A., Drachsler-Cohen, D., Gervais, A., Tsankov, P., Vechev, M.: Securify (2017). http://securify.ch
21. Mythril. https://github.com/ConsenSys/mythril
22. Manticore. https://github.com/trailofbits/manticore
23. SmartDec: Smartcheck. https://github.com/smartdec/smartcheck
24. Solgraph. https://github.com/raineorshine/solgraph
25. Hirai, Y.: Defining the Ethereum virtual machine for interactive theorem provers. In: Brenner, M., Rohloff, K., Bonneau, J., Miller, A., Ryan, P.Y.A., Teague, V., Bracciali, A., Sala, M., Pintore, F., Jakobsson, M. (eds.) FC 2017. LNCS, vol. 10323, pp. 520–535. Springer, Cham (2017). https://doi.org/10.1007/978-3-319-70278-0_33
26. Wood, G.: Ethereum: a secure decentralised generalised transaction ledger. Ethereum Proj. Yellow Pap. **151**, 1–32 (2014)
27. Amani, S., Bégel, M., Bortin, M., Staples, M.: Towards verifying Ethereum smart contract bytecode in Isabelle/HOL. In: CPP. ACM (2018, to appear)
28. Hildenbrandt, E., Saxena, M., Zhu, X., Rodrigues, N., Daian, P., Guth, D., Rosu, G.: Kevm: A complete semantics of the Ethereum virtual machine. Technical report (2017)
29. Roşu, G., Şerbnut, T.F.: An overview of the K semantic framework. J. Log. Algebraic Program. **79**(6), 397–434 (2010)
30. Bhargavan, K., Delignat-Lavaud, A., Fournet, C., Gollamudi, A., Gonthier, G., Kobeissi, N., Kulatova, N., Rastogi, A., Sibut-Pinote, T., Swamy, N., et al.: Formal verification of smart contracts: short paper. In: Proceedings of the 2016 ACM Workshop on Programming Languages and Analysis for Security, pp. 91–96. ACM (2016)
31. Grossman, S., Abraham, I., Golan-Gueta, G., Michalevsky, Y., Rinetzky, N., Sagiv, M., Zohar, Y.: Online detection of effectively callback free objects with applications to smart contracts. Proc. ACM Program. Lang. **2**(POPL), 48 (2017)
32. Cook, T., Latham, A., Lee, J.H.: Dappguard: active monitoring and defense for solidity smart contracts (2017)
33. O'Connor, R.: Simplicity: a new language for blockchains. arXiv preprint arXiv:1711.03028 (2017)
34. Pettersson, J., Edström, R.: Safer smart contracts through type-driven development. Master's thesis (2016)
35. Coblenz, M.: Obsidian: a safer blockchain programming language. In: 2017 IEEE/ACM 39th International Conference on Software Engineering Companion (ICSE-C), pp. 97–99. IEEE (2017)
36. Schrans, F., Eisenbach, S., Drossopoulou, S.: Writing safe smart contracts in flint (2018)
37. Vyper. https://github.com/ethereum/vyper
38. Bamboo. https://github.com/pirapira/bamboo
39. Formal verification for solidity contracts. https://forum.ethereum.org/discussion/3779/formal-verification-for-solidity-contracts
40. Filliâtre, J.-C., Paskevich, A.: Why3—where programs meet provers. In: Felleisen, M., Gardner, P. (eds.) ESOP 2013. LNCS, vol. 7792, pp. 125–128. Springer, Heidelberg (2013). https://doi.org/10.1007/978-3-642-37036-6_8
41. Sergey, I., Kumar, A., Hobor, A.: Scilla: a smart contract intermediate-level language. arXiv preprint arXiv:1801.00687 (2018)
42. Wöhrer, M., Zdun, U.: Smart contracts: security patterns in the Ethereum ecosystem and solidity (2018)

43. Mavridou, A., Laszka, A.: Designing secure Ethereum smart contracts: a finite state machine based approach. arXiv preprint arXiv:1711.09327 (2017)
44. Sergey, I., Hobor, A.: A concurrent perspective on smart contracts. arXiv preprint arXiv:1702.05511 (2017)
45. de Moura, L., Bjørner, N.: Z3: an efficient SMT solver. In: Ramakrishnan, C.R., Rehof, J. (eds.) TACAS 2008. LNCS, vol. 4963, pp. 337–340. Springer, Heidelberg (2008). https://doi.org/10.1007/978-3-540-78800-3_24
46. Komuravelli, A., Gurfinkel, A., Chaki, S.: Smt-based model checking for recursive programs. Form. Methods Syst. Des. 48(3), 175–205 (2016)

12

Layered Concurrent Programs

Bernhard Kragl[1]([⊠]) [iD] and Shaz Qadeer[2]

[1] IST Austria, Klosterneuburg, Austria
bkragl@ist.ac.at
[2] Microsoft Research, Redmond, USA

Abstract. We present layered concurrent programs, a compact and expressive notation for specifying refinement proofs of concurrent programs. A layered concurrent program specifies a sequence of connected concurrent programs, from most concrete to most abstract, such that common parts of different programs are written exactly once. These programs are expressed in the ordinary syntax of imperative concurrent programs using gated atomic actions, sequencing, choice, and (recursive) procedure calls. Each concurrent program is automatically extracted from the layered program. We reduce refinement to the safety of a sequence of concurrent checker programs, one each to justify the connection between every two consecutive concurrent programs. These checker programs are also automatically extracted from the layered program. Layered concurrent programs have been implemented in the CIVL verifier which has been successfully used for the verification of several complex concurrent programs.

1 Introduction

Refinement is an approach to program correctness in which a program is expressed at multiple levels of abstraction. For example, we could have a sequence of programs $\mathcal{P}_1, \ldots, \mathcal{P}_h, \mathcal{P}_{h+1}$ where $\mathcal{P}_1$ is the most concrete and the $\mathcal{P}_{h+1}$ is the most abstract. Program $\mathcal{P}_1$ can be compiled and executed efficiently, $\mathcal{P}_{h+1}$ is obviously correct, and the correctness of $\mathcal{P}_i$ is guaranteed by the correctness of $\mathcal{P}_{i+1}$ for all $i \in [1, h]$. These three properties together ensure that $\mathcal{P}_1$ is both efficient and correct. To use the refinement approach, the programmer must come up with each version $\mathcal{P}_i$ of the program and a proof that the correctness of $\mathcal{P}_{i+1}$ implies the correctness of $\mathcal{P}_i$. This proof typically establishes a connection from every behavior of $\mathcal{P}_i$ to some behavior of $\mathcal{P}_{i+1}$.

Refinement is an attractive approach to the verified construction of complex programs for a number of reasons. First, instead of constructing a single monolithic proof of $\mathcal{P}_1$, the programmer constructs a collection of localized proofs establishing the connection between $\mathcal{P}_i$ and $\mathcal{P}_{i+1}$ for each $i \in [1, h]$. Each localized proof is considerably simpler than the overall proof because it only needs to reason about the (relatively small) difference between adjacent programs. Second, different localized proofs can be performed using different reasoning methods, e.g., interactive deduction, automated testing, or even informal reasoning.

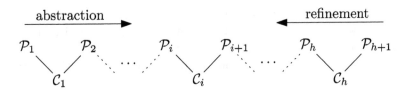

Fig. 1. Concurrent programs $\mathcal{P}_i$ and connecting checker programs $\mathcal{C}_i$ represented by a layered concurrent program $\mathcal{LP}$.

Finally, refinement naturally supports a bidirectional approach to correctness—bottom-up verification of a concrete program via successive abstraction or top-down derivation from an abstract program via successive concretization.

This paper explores the use of refinement to reason about concurrent programs. Most refinement-oriented approaches model a concurrent program as a flat transition system, a representation that is useful for abstract programs but becomes increasingly cumbersome for a concrete implementation. To realize the goal of verified construction of efficient and implementable concurrent programs, we must be able to uniformly and compactly represent both highly-detailed and highly-abstract concurrent programs. This paper introduces layered concurrent programs as such a representation.

A layered concurrent program $\mathcal{LP}$ represents a sequence $\mathcal{P}_1, \ldots, \mathcal{P}_h, \mathcal{P}_{h+1}$ of concurrent programs such that common parts of different programs are written exactly once. These programs are expressed not as flat transition systems but in the ordinary syntax of imperative concurrent programs using gated atomic actions [4], sequencing, choice, and (recursive) procedure calls. Our programming language is accompanied by a type system that allows each $\mathcal{P}_i$ to be automatically extracted from $\mathcal{LP}$. Finally, refinement between $\mathcal{P}_i$ and $\mathcal{P}_{i+1}$ is encoded as the safety of a checker program $\mathcal{C}_i$ which is also automatically extracted from $\mathcal{LP}$. Thus, the verification of $\mathcal{P}_1$ is split into the verification of h concurrent checker programs $\mathcal{C}_1, \ldots, \mathcal{C}_h$ such that $\mathcal{C}_i$ connects $\mathcal{P}_i$ and $\mathcal{P}_{i+1}$ (Fig. 1).

We highlight two crucial aspects of our approach. First, while the programs $\mathcal{P}_i$ have an interleaved (i.e., preemptive) semantics, we verify the checker programs $\mathcal{C}_i$ under a cooperative semantics in which preemptions occur only at procedure calls. Our type system [5] based on the theory of right and left movers [10] ensures that the cooperative behaviors of $\mathcal{C}_i$ cover all preemptive behaviors of $\mathcal{P}_i$. Second, establishing the safety of checker programs is not tied to any particular verification technique. Any applicable technique can be used. In particular, different layers can be verified using different techniques, allowing for great flexibility in verification options.

1.1 Related Work

This paper formalizes, clarifies, and extends the most important aspect of the design of CIVL [6], a deductive verifier for layered concurrent programs. Hawblitzel et al. [7] present a partial explanation of CIVL by formalizing the connection between two concurrent programs as sound program transformations. In this paper, we provide the first formal account for layered concurrent programs to represent all concurrent programs in a multi-layered refinement proof, thereby establishing a new foundation for the verified construction of concurrent programs.

CIVL is the successor to the QED [4] verifier which combined a type system for mover types with logical reasoning based on verification conditions. QED enabled the specification of a layered proof but required each layer to be expressed in a separate file leading to code duplication. Layered programs reduce redundant work in a layered proof by enabling each piece of code to be written exactly once. QED also introduced the idea of abstracting an atomic action to enable attaching a stronger mover type to it. This idea is incorporated naturally in layered programs by allowing a concrete atomic action to be wrapped in a procedure whose specification is a more abstract atomic action with a more precise mover type.

Event-B [1] is a modeling language that supports refinement of systems expressed as interleaved composition of events, each specified as a top-level transition relation. Verification of Event-B specifications is supported by the Rodin [2] toolset which has been used to model and verify several systems of industrial significance. TLA+ [9] also specifies systems as a flat transition system, enables refinement proofs, and is more general because it supports liveness specifications. Our approach to refinement is different from Event-B and TLA+ for several reasons. First, Event-B and TLA+ model different versions of the program as separate flat transition systems whereas our work models them as different layers of a single layered concurrent program, exploiting the standard structuring mechanisms of imperative programs. Second, Event-B and TLA+ connect the concrete program to the abstract program via an explicitly specified refinement mapping. Thus, the guarantee provided by the refinement proof is contingent upon trusting both the abstract program and the refinement mapping. In our approach, once the abstract program is proved to be free of failures, the trusted part of the specification is confined to the gates of atomic actions in the concrete program. Furthermore, the programmer never explicitly specifies a refinement mapping and is only engaged in proving the correctness of checker programs.

The methodology of refinement mappings has been used for compositional verification of hardware designs [11,12]. The focus in this work is to decompose a large refinement proof connecting two versions of a hardware design into a collection of smaller proofs. A variety of techniques including compositional reasoning (converting a large problem to several small problems) and customized abstractions (for converting infinite-state to finite-state problems) are used to create small and finite-state verification problems for a model checker. This work is mostly orthogonal to our contribution of layered programs. Rather, it could be considered an approach to decompose the verification of each (potentially large) checker program encoded by a layered concurrent program.

2   Concurrent Programs

In this section we introduce a concurrent programming language. The syntax of our programming language is summarized in Fig. 2.

$$
\begin{aligned}
Val &\supseteq \mathbb{B} \\
v \in Var &= GVar \cup LVar \\
I, O, L &\subseteq LVar \\
\sigma \in Store &= Var \rightharpoonup Val \\
e \in Expr &= Store \rightharpoonup Val \\
t \in Trans &= 2^{Store \times Store} \\
A &\in Action \\
P, Q &\in Proc \\
\iota, o \in IOMap &= LVar \rightharpoonup LVar
\end{aligned}
$$

$$
\begin{aligned}
gs &\in 2^{GVar} \\
as &\in A \mapsto (I, O, e, t) \\
ps &\in P \mapsto (I, O, L, s) \\
m &\in Proc \cup Action \\
\mathcal{I} &\in 2^{Store}
\end{aligned}
$$

$$
\mathcal{P} \in Prog ::= (gs, as, ps, m, \mathcal{I})
$$

$$
s \in Stmt ::= \texttt{skip} \mid s \; ; \; s \mid \texttt{if } e \texttt{ then } s \texttt{ else } s \mid \texttt{pcall } \overline{(A, \iota, o)} \; \overline{(P, \iota, o)} \; \overline{(A, \iota, o)}
$$

Fig. 2. Concurrent programs

Preliminaries. Let *Val* be a set of *values* containing the Booleans. The set of *variables Var* is partitioned into *global variables GVar* and *local variables LVar*. A *store* σ is a mapping from variables to values, an *expression e* is a mapping from stores to values, and a *transition t* is a binary relation between stores.

Atomic Actions. A fundamental notion in our approach is that of an atomic action. An atomic action captures an indivisible operation on the program state together with its precondition, providing a universal representation for both low-level machine operations (e.g., reading a variable from memory) and high-level abstractions (e.g., atomic procedure summaries). Most importantly for reasoning purposes, our programming language confines all accesses to global variables to atomic actions. Formally, an *atomic action* is a tuple (I, O, e, t). The semantics of an atomic action in an execution is to first evaluate the expression e, called the *gate*, in the current state. If the gate evaluates to *false* the execution *fails*, otherwise the program state is updated according to the transition t. *Input variables* in I can be read by e and t, and *output variables* in O can be written by t.

Remark 1. Atomic actions subsume many standard statements. In particular, (nondeterministic) assignments, assertions, and assumptions. The following table shows some examples for programs over variables x and y.

Command	e	t
$x := x + y$	*true*	$x' = x + y \wedge y' = y$
havoc x	*true*	$y' = y$
assert $x < y$	$x < y$	$x' = x \wedge y' = y$
assume $x < y$	*true*	$x < y \wedge x' = x \wedge y' = y$

Procedures. A *procedure* is a tuple (I, O, L, s) where I, O, L are the *input*, *output*, and *local variables* of the procedure, and s is a *statement* composed from skip, sequencing, if, and parallel call statements. Since only atomic actions can refer to global variables, the variables accessed in if conditions are restricted to the inputs, outputs, and locals of the enclosing procedure. The meaning of skip, sequencing, and if is as expected and we focus on parallel calls.

Pcalls. A *parallel call* (*pcall*, for short) $\texttt{pcall}\ \overline{(A, \iota, o)}\ \overline{(P, \iota, o)}\ \overline{(A, \iota, o)}$ consists of a sequence of invocations of atomic actions and procedures. We refer to the invocations as the *arms* of the pcall. In particular (A, ι, o) is an *atomic-action arm* and (P, ι, o) is a *procedure arm*. An atomic-action arm executes the called atomic action, and a procedure arm creates a child thread that executes the statement of the called procedure. The parent thread is blocked until all arms of the pcall finish. In the standard semantics the order of arms does not matter, but our verification technique will allow us to consider the atomic action arms before and after the procedure arms to execute in the specified order. Parameter passing is expressed using partial mappings ι, o between local variables; ι maps formal inputs of the callee to actual inputs of the caller, and o maps actual outputs of the caller to formal outputs of the callee. Since we do not want to introduce races on local variables, the outputs of all arms must be disjoint and the output of one arm cannot be an input to another arm. Finally, notice that our general notion of a pcall subsumes sequential statements (single atomic-action arm), synchronous procedure calls (single procedure arm), and unbounded thread creation (recursive procedure arm).

Concurrent Programs. A *concurrent program* $\mathcal{P}$ is a tuple $(gs, as, ps, m, \mathcal{I})$, where gs is a finite set of global variables used by the program, as is a finite mapping from *action names* A to atomic actions, ps is a finite mapping from *procedure names* P to procedures, m is either a procedure or action name that denotes the entry point for program executions, and $\mathcal{I}$ is a set of initial stores. For convenience we will liberally use action and procedure names to refer to the corresponding atomic actions and procedures.

Semantics. Let $\mathcal{P} = (gs, as, ps, m, \mathcal{I})$ be a fixed concurrent program. A *state* consists of a global store assigning values to the global variables and a pool of *threads*, each consisting of a local store assigning values to local variables and a statement that remains to be executed. An *execution* is a sequence of states, where from each state to the next some thread is selected to execute one step. Every step that switches the executing thread is called a *preemption* (also called a context switch). We distinguish between two semantics that differ in (1) preemption points, and (2) the order of executing the arms of a pcall.

In *preemptive semantics*, a preemption is allowed anywhere and the arms of a pcall are arbitrarily interleaved. In *cooperative semantics*, a preemption is allowed only at the call and return of a procedure, and the arms of a pcall are executed as follows. First, the leading atomic-action arms are executed from left to right without preemption, then all procedure arms are executed arbitrarily interleaved, and finally the trailing atomic-action arms are executed, again from left to right without preemption. In other words, a preemption is only allowed when a procedure arm of a pcall creates a new thread and when a thread terminates.

For $\mathcal{P}$ we only consider executions that start with a single thread that execute m from a store in $\mathcal{I}$. $\mathcal{P}$ is called *safe* if there is no failing execution, i.e., an execution that executes an atomic action whose gate evaluates to *false*. We write $Safe(\mathcal{P})$ if $\mathcal{P}$ is safe under preemptive semantics, and $CSafe(\mathcal{P})$ if $\mathcal{P}$ is safe under cooperative semantics.

2.1 Running Example

In this section, we introduce a sequence of three concurrent programs (Fig. 3) to illustrate features of our concurrent programming language and the layered approach to program correctness. Consider the program $\mathcal{P}_1^{lock}$ in Fig. 3(a). The program uses a single global Boolean variable b which is accessed by the two atomic actions CAS and RESET. The compare-and-swap action CAS atomically reads the current value of b and either sets b from *false* to *true* and returns *true*, or leaves b *true* and returns *false*. The RESET action sets b to *false* and has a gate (represented as an assertion) that states that the action must only be called when b is *true*. Using these actions, the procedures Enter and Leave implement a spinlock as follows. Enter calls the CAS action and retries (through recursion on itself) until it succeeds to set b from *false* to *true*. Leave just calls the RESET action which sets b back to *false* and thus allows another thread executing Enter to stop spinning. Finally, the procedures Main and Worker serve as a simple client. Main uses a pcall inside a nondeterministic if statement to create an unbounded number of concurrent worker threads, which just acquire the lock by calling Enter and then release the lock again by calling Leave. The call to the empty procedure Alloc is an artifact of our extraction from a layered concurrent program and can be removed as an optimization.

Proving $\mathcal{P}_1^{lock}$ safe amounts to showing that RESET is never called with b set to *false*, which expresses that $\mathcal{P}_1^{lock}$ follows a locking discipline of releasing only previously acquired locks. Doing this proof directly on $\mathcal{P}_1^{lock}$ has two drawbacks. First, the proof must relate the possible values of b with the program counters of all running threads. In general, this approach requires sound introduction of ghost code and results in complicated case distinctions in program invariants. Second, the proof is not reusable across different lock implementations. The correctness of the client does not specifically depend on using a spinlock over a Boolean variable, and thus the proof should not as well. We show how our refinement-based approach addresses both problems.

Program $\mathcal{P}_2^{lock}$ in Fig. 3(b) is an abstraction of $\mathcal{P}_1^{lock}$ that introduces an abstract lock specification. The global variable b is replaced by lock which ranges over integer thread identifiers (0 is a dedicated value indicating that the lock is available). The procedures Alloc, Enter and Leave are replaced by the atomic actions ALLOC, ACQUIRE and RELEASE, respectively. ALLOC allocates unique and non-zero thread identifiers using a set of integers slot to store the identifiers not allocated so far. ACQUIRE blocks executions where the lock is not

```
———————————— (a) P₁ˡᵒᶜᵏ ————————————
var b : bool


proc Main()
  if (*)
    pcall Worker(), Main()

proc Worker()

  pcall Alloc()
  pcall Enter()
  pcall Leave()

proc Alloc() : ()
  skip


proc Enter()
  var success : bool
  pcall success := CAS()
  if (success)
    skip
  else
    pcall Enter()


proc Leave()
  pcall RESET()
  skip

atomic CAS() : (success : bool)
  if (b) success := false
  else    success, b := true, true

atomic RESET()
  assert b
  b := false
```

```
———————————— (b) P₂ˡᵒᶜᵏ ————————————
var lock : int
var linear slots : set<int>


proc Main()
  if (*)
    pcall Worker(), Main()

proc Worker()
  var linear tid : int
  pcall tid := ALLOC()
  pcall ACQUIRE(tid)
  pcall RELEASE(tid)

right ALLOC() : (linear tid : int)
  assume tid != 0 && tid ∈ slots
  slots := slots - tid


right ACQUIRE(linear tid : int)
  assert tid != 0
  assume lock == 0
  lock := tid




left RELEASE(linear tid : int)
  assert tid != 0 && lock == tid
  lock := 0
```

```
———————————— (c) P₃ˡᵒᶜᵏ ————————————



both SKIP()
  skip
```

Fig. 3. Lock example

available (assume lock == 0) and sets lock to the identifier of the acquiring thread. RELEASE asserts that the releasing thread holds the lock and sets lock to 0. Thus, the connection between P_1^{lock} and P_2^{lock} is given by the invariant b <==> lock != 0 which justifies that Enter refines ACQUIRE and Leave refines RELEASE. The potential safety violation in P_1^{lock} by the gate of RESET is preserved in P_2^{lock} by the gate of RELEASE. In fact, the safety of P_2^{lock} expresses the stronger locking discipline that the lock can only be released by the thread that acquired it.

Reasoning in terms of ACQUIRE and RELEASE instead of Enter and Leave is more general, but it is also simpler! Figure 3(b) declares atomic actions with a *mover type* [5], right for *right mover*, and left for *left mover*. A right mover executed by a thread commutes to the right of any action executed by a different thread. Similarly, a left mover executed by thread commutes to the left of any action executed by a different thread. A sequence of right movers followed by at most one non-mover followed by a sequence of left movers in a thread can be considered atomic [10]. The reason is that any interleaved execution can be rearranged (by commuting atomic actions), such that these actions execute consecutively. For $\mathcal{P}_2^{lock}$ this means that Worker is atomic and thus the gate of RELEASE can be discharged by pure sequential reasoning; ALLOC guarantees tid != 0 and after executing ACQUIRE we have lock == tid. As a result, we finally obtain that the atomic action SKIP in $\mathcal{P}_3^{lock}$ (Fig. 3(c)) is a sound abstraction of procedure Main in $\mathcal{P}_2^{lock}$. Hence, we showed that program $\mathcal{P}_1^{lock}$ is safe by soundly abstracting it to $\mathcal{P}_3^{lock}$, a program that is trivially safe.

The correctness of right and left annotations on ACQUIRE and RELEASE, respectively, depends on pair-wise commutativity checks among atomic actions in $\mathcal{P}_2^{lock}$. These commutativity checks will fail unless we exploit the fact that every thread identifier allocated by Worker using the ALLOC action is unique. For instance, to show that ACQUIRE executed by a thread commutes to the right of RELEASE executed by a different thread, it must be known that the parameters tid to these actions are distinct from each other. The *linear* annotation on the local variables named tid and the global variable slots (which is a set of integers) is used to communicate this information.

The overall invariant encoded by the *linear* annotation is that the set of values stored in slots and in local linear variables of active stack frames across all threads are pairwise disjoint. This invariant is guaranteed by a combination of a linear type system [14] and logical reasoning on the code of all atomic actions. The linear type system ensures using a flow analysis that a value stored in a linear variable in an active stack frame is not copied into another linear variable via an assignment. Each atomic action must ensure that its state update preserves the disjointness invariant for linear variables. For actions ACQUIRE and RELEASE, which do not modify any linear variables, this reasoning is trivial. However, action ALLOC modifies slots and updates the linear output parameter tid. Its correctness depends on the (semantic) fact that the value put into tid is removed from slots; this reasoning can be done using automated theorem provers.

3   Layered Concurrent Programs

A layered concurrent program represents a sequence of concurrent programs that are connected to each other. That is, the programs derived from a layered concurrent program share syntactic structure, but differ in the granularity of the atomic actions and the set of variables they are expressed over. In a layered concurrent program, we associate layer numbers and layer ranges with variables (both global and local), atomic actions, and procedures. These layer numbers control the introduction and hiding of program variables and the summarization of compound operations into atomic actions, and thus provide the scaffolding of a refinement relation. Concretely, this section shows how the concurrent programs $\mathcal{P}_1^{lock}$, $\mathcal{P}_2^{lock}$, and $\mathcal{P}_3^{lock}$ (Fig. 3) and their connections can all be expressed in a single layered concurrent program. In Sect. 4, we discuss how to check refinement between the successive concurrent programs encoded in a layered concurrent program.

Syntax. The syntax of layered concurrent programs is summarized in Fig. 4. Let $\mathbb{N}$ be the set of non-negative integers and $\mathbb{I}$ the set of nonempty *intervals* $[a, b]$.

$$[a,b] = \{x \mid a,b,x \in \mathbb{N} \wedge a \leq x \leq b\} \qquad GS \in GVar \rightharpoonup \mathbb{I}$$

$$n, \alpha \in \mathbb{N} \qquad\qquad\qquad\qquad\qquad\qquad AS \in A \mapsto (I, O, e, t, r)$$

$$r \in \mathbb{I} = \{[a,b] \mid a \leq b\} \qquad\qquad IS \in A \mapsto (I, O, e, t, n)$$

$$ns \in LVar \rightharpoonup \mathbb{N} \qquad\qquad\qquad PS \in P \mapsto (I, O, L, s, n, ns, A)$$

$$m \in Proc$$

$$\mathcal{I} \in 2^{Store}$$

$$\mathcal{LP} \in LayeredProg ::= (GS, AS, IS, PS, m, \mathcal{I})$$

$$s \in Stmt ::= \cdots \mid \mathtt{icall}\ (A, \iota, o) \mid \mathtt{pcall}_\alpha\ \overline{(P_i, \iota_i, o_i)}_{i \in [1,k]} \quad (\alpha \in \{\varepsilon\} \cup [1,k])$$

Fig. 4. Layered concurrent programs

We refer to integers as *layer numbers* and intervals as *layer ranges*. A *layered concurrent program* $\mathcal{LP}$ is a tuple $(GS, AS, IS, PS, m, \mathcal{I})$ which, similarly to concurrent programs, consists of global variables, atomic actions, and procedures, with the following differences.

1. GS maps global variables to layer ranges. For $GS(v) = [a,b]$ we say that v is introduced at layer a and available up to layer b.
2. AS assigns a layer range r to atomic actions denoting the layers at which an action exists.
3. IS (with a disjoint domain from AS) distinguishes a special type of atomic actions called *introduction actions*. Introduction actions have a single layer number n and are responsible for assigning meaning to the variables introduced at layer n. Correspondingly, statements in layered concurrent programs are extended with an $\mathtt{icall}$ statement for calling introduction actions.
4. PS assigns a layer number n, a layer number mapping for local variables ns, and an atomic action A to procedures. We call n the *disappearing layer* and A the *refined atomic action*. For every local variable v, $ns(v)$ is the *introduction layer* of v.

   The $\mathtt{pcall}_\alpha$ statement in a layered concurrent program differs from the $\mathtt{pcall}$ statement in concurrent programs in two ways. First, it can only have procedure arms. Second, it has a parameter α which is either ε (*unannotated pcall*) or the index of one of its arms (*annotated pcall*). We usually omit writing ε in unannotated pcalls.
5. m is a procedure name.

The *top layer* h of a layered concurrent program is the disappearing layer of m.

Intuition Behind Layer Numbers. Recall that a layered concurrent program $\mathcal{LP}$ should represent a sequence of $h+1$ concurrent programs $\mathcal{P}_1, \cdots, \mathcal{P}_{h+1}$ that are connected by a sequence of h checker programs $\mathcal{C}_1, \cdots, \mathcal{C}_h$ (cf. Fig. 1). Before we provide formal definitions, let us get some intuition on two core mechanisms: global variable introduction and procedure abstraction/refinement.

Let v be a global variable with layer range $[a,b]$. The meaning of this layer range is that the "first" program that contains v is $\mathcal{C}_a$, the checker program connecting $\mathcal{P}_a$ and $\mathcal{P}_{a+1}$. In particular, v is not yet part of $\mathcal{P}_a$. In $\mathcal{C}_a$ the introduction actions at layer a can modify v and thus assign its meaning in terms of all other available variables. Then v is part of $\mathcal{P}_{a+1}$ and all programs up to and including $\mathcal{P}_b$. The "last" program containing v is $\mathcal{C}_b$. In other words, when going from a program $\mathcal{P}_i$ to $\mathcal{P}_{i+1}$ the variables with upper bound i disappear and the variables with lower bound i are introduced; the checker program $\mathcal{C}_i$ has access to both and establishes their relationship.

Let P be a procedure with disappearing layer n and refined atomic action A. The meaning of the disappearing layer is that P exists in all programs from $\mathcal{P}_1$ up to and including $\mathcal{P}_n$. In $\mathcal{P}_{n+1}$ and above every invocation of P is replaced by an invocation of A. To ensure that this replacement is sound, the checker program $\mathcal{C}_n$ performs a refinement check that ensures that every execution of P behaves like A. Observe that the body of procedure P itself changes from $\mathcal{P}_1$ to $\mathcal{P}_n$ according to the disappearing layer of the procedures it calls.

With the above intuition in mind it is clear that the layer annotations in a layered concurrent program cannot be arbitrary. For example, if procedure P calls a procedure Q, then Q cannot have a higher disappearing layer than P, for Q could introduce further behaviors into the program after P was replaced by A, and those behaviors are not captured by A.

3.1   Type Checker

We describe the constraints that need to be satisfied for a layered concurrent program to be well-formed. A full formalization as a type checker with top-level judgment $\vdash \mathcal{LP}$ is given in Fig. 5. For completeness, the type checker includes standard constraints (e.g., variable scoping, parameter passing, etc.) that we are not going to discuss.

(Atomic Action)/(Introduction Action). Global variables can only be accessed by atomic actions and introduction actions. For a global variable v with layer range $[a, b]$, introduction actions with layer number a are allowed to modify v (for sound variable introduction), and atomic actions with a layer range contained in $[a + 1, b]$ have access to v. Introduction actions must be nonblocking, which means that every state that satisfies the gate must have a possible transition to take. This ensures that introduction actions only assign meaning to introduced variables but do not exclude any program behavior.

(If). Procedure bodies change from layer to layer because calls to procedures become calls to atomic actions. But the control-flow structure within a procedure is preserved across layers. Therefore (local) variables accessed in an if condition must be available on all layers to ensure that the if statement is well-defined on every layer.

(Introduction Call). Let A be an introduction action with layer number n. Since A modifies global variables introduced at layer n, icalls to A are only allowed from procedures with disappearing layer n. Similarly, the formal output parameters of an icall to A must have introduction layer n. The icall is only preserved in $\mathcal{C}_n$.

(Program)
$dom(AS) \cap dom(IS) = \varnothing$
$PS(m) = (\_, \_, \_, \_, h, \_, A_m)$
$AS(A_m) = (\_, \_, \_, \_, r)$
$h + 1 \in r$
$\forall\, A \in dom(AS) : (GS, AS) \vdash A$
$\forall\, A \in dom(IS) : (GS, IS) \vdash A$
$\dfrac{\forall\, P \in dom(PS) : (AS, IS, PS) \vdash P}{\vdash (GS, AS, IS, PS, m, \mathcal{I})}$

(Atomic action)
$AS(A) = (I, O, e, t, r)$
$Disjoint(I, O)$
$\forall\, v \in ReadVars(e, t) : v \in I \vee r \subseteq \widehat{GS}(v)$
$\dfrac{\forall\, v \in WriteVars(t) : v \in O \vee r \subseteq \widehat{GS}(v)}{(GS, AS) \vdash A}$

(Introduction action)
$IS(A) = (I, O, e, t, n)$
$Disjoint(I, O)$
$\forall\, v \in ReadVars(e, t) : v \in I \vee n \in GS(v)$
$\forall\, v \in WriteVars(t) : v \in O \vee GS(v) = [n, \_]$
$\dfrac{Nonblocking(e, t)}{(GS, IS) \vdash A}$

(Procedure)
$PS(P) = (I, O, L, s, n, ns, A)$
$AS(A) = (I, O, \_, \_, \_)$
$Disjoint(I, O, L)$
$\forall\, v \in I \cup O \cup L : ns(v) \le n$
$\dfrac{(AS, IS, PS), P \vdash s}{(AS, IS, PS) \vdash P}$

(Skip)
$\dfrac{}{(AS, IS, PS), P \vdash \mathtt{skip}}$

(Sequence)
$\dfrac{(AS, IS, PS), P \vdash s_1 \quad (AS, IS, PS), P \vdash s_2}{(AS, IS, PS), P \vdash s_1 \,;\, s_2}$

(If)
$PS(P) = (I, \_, L, \_, \_, ns, \_)$
$\forall\, x \in ReadVars(e) : x \in I \cup L \wedge ns(x) = 0$
$\dfrac{(AS, IS, PS), P \vdash s_1 \quad (AS, IS, PS), P \vdash s_2}{(AS, IS, PS), P \vdash \mathtt{if}\ e\ \mathtt{then}\ s_1\ \mathtt{else}\ s_2}$

(Parameter passing)
$dom(\iota) = I' \qquad dom(o) \subseteq O \cup L$
$\dfrac{img(\iota) \subseteq I \cup O \cup L \quad img(o) \subseteq O'}{ValidIO(\iota, o, I, O, L, I', O')}$

(Introduction call)
$PS(P) = (I_P, O_P, L_P, \_, n_P, ns_P, \_)$
$IS(A) = (I_A, O_A, \_, t, n_A)$
$ValidIO(\iota, o, I_P, O_P, L_P, I_A, O_A)$
$n_A = n_P$
$\dfrac{\forall\, v \in dom(o) : ns_P(v) = n_P}{(AS, IS, PS), P \vdash \mathtt{icall}\ (A, \iota, o)}$

(Parallel call)
$\forall\, i \ne j : dom(o_i) \cap dom(o_j) = \varnothing$
$\qquad\qquad dom(o_i) \cap img(\iota_j) = \varnothing$
$\forall\, i : PS(P) = (I_P, O_P, L_P, \_, n_P, ns_P, \_)$
$\qquad PS(Q_i) = (I_i, O_i, \_, \_, n_i, ns_i, A_i)$
$\qquad AS(A_i) = (\_, \_, \_, \_, r_i)$
$\qquad ValidIO(\iota_i, o_i, I_P, O_P, L_P, I_i, O_i)$
$\qquad \forall\, v \in dom(\iota_i) : ns_P(\iota_i(v)) \le ns_i(v)$
$\qquad \forall\, v \in dom(o_i) : ns_i(o_i(v)) \le ns_P(v)$
$\qquad n_i \le n_P \qquad [n_i + 1, n_P] \subseteq r_i$
$\qquad i = \alpha \implies n_i = n_P \wedge O_P \subseteq dom(o_i)$
$\qquad i \ne \alpha \wedge n_i = n_P \implies dom(o_i) \subseteq L_i$
$\dfrac{\exists\, i : n_1 \le \cdots \le n_i \ge \cdots \ge n_k}{(AS, IS, PS), P \vdash \mathtt{pcall}_\alpha\ (Q_i, \iota_i, o_i)_{i \in [1, k]}}$

$\widehat{GS}(v) = [a + 1, b]$ for $GS(v) = [a, b]$

$ReadVars(e) = \{v \mid \exists\, \sigma, a : e(\sigma) \ne e(\sigma[v \mapsto a])\} \,\cup$

$ReadVars(t) = \{v \mid \exists\, \sigma, \sigma', a : (\sigma, \sigma') \in t \wedge (\sigma[v \mapsto a], \sigma') \notin t\}$

$ReadVars(e, t) = ReadVars(e) \cup ReadVars(t)$

$WriteVars(t) = \{v \mid \exists\, \sigma, \sigma' : (\sigma, \sigma') \in t \wedge \sigma(v) \ne \sigma'(v)\}$

$Nonblocking(e, t) = \forall\, \sigma \in e : \exists\, \sigma' : (\sigma, \sigma') \in t$

Fig. 5. Type checking rules for layered concurrent programs

(Parallel Call). All arms in a pcall must be procedure arms invoking a procedure with a disappearing layer less than or equal to the disappearing layer of the caller. Furthermore, above the disappearing layer of the callee its refined atomic action must be available up to the disappearing layer of the caller. Parameter passing can only be well-defined if the actual inputs exist before the formal inputs, and the formal outputs exist before the actual outputs. The sequence of disappearing layers of the procedures in a pcall must be monotonically increasing and then decreasing, such that the resulting pcall in the extracted programs consists of procedure arms surrounded by atomic-action arms on every layer.

Annotated pcalls are only used for invocations to procedures with the same disappearing layer n as the caller. In particular, during refinement checking in C_n only the arm with index α is allowed to modify the global state, which must be according to the refined atomic action of the caller. The remaining arms must leave the global state unchanged.

3.2 Concurrent Program Extraction

Let $\mathcal{LP} = (GS, AS, IS, PS, m, \mathcal{I})$ be a layered concurrent program such that $PS(m) = (\_, \_, \_, \_, h, \_, A_m)$. We show how to extract the programs $\mathcal{P}_1, \cdots, \mathcal{P}_{h+1}$ by defining a function $\Gamma_\ell(\mathcal{LP})$ such that $\mathcal{P}_\ell = \Gamma_\ell(\mathcal{LP})$ for every $\ell \in [1, h+1]$. For a local variable layer mapping ns we define the set of local variables with layer number less then ℓ as $ns|_\ell = \{v \mid ns(v) < \ell\}$. Now the extraction function Γ_ℓ is defined as

$$\Gamma_\ell(\mathcal{LP}) = (gs, as, ps, m', \mathcal{I}),$$

where

$$gs = \{v \mid GS(v) = [a, b] \wedge \ell \in [a+1, b]\},$$
$$as = \{A \mapsto (I, O, e, t) \mid AS(A) = (I, O, e, t, r) \wedge \ell \in r\},$$
$$ps = \{P \mapsto (I \cap ns|_\ell, O \cap ns|_\ell, L \cap ns|_\ell, \Gamma_\ell^P(s)) \mid PS(P) = (I, O, L, s, n, ns, \_) \wedge \ell \leq n\},$$
$$m' = \begin{cases} m & \text{if } \ell \in [1, h] \\ A_m & \text{if } \ell = h+1 \end{cases},$$

and the extraction of a statement in the body of procedure P is given by

$$\begin{aligned}
\Gamma_\ell^P(\text{skip}) &= \text{skip}, \\
\Gamma_\ell^P(s_1 \; ; \; s_2) &= \Gamma_\ell^P(s_1) \; ; \; \Gamma_\ell^P(s_2), \\
\Gamma_\ell^P(\text{if } e \text{ then } s_1 \text{ else } s_2) &= \text{if } e \text{ then } \Gamma_\ell^P(s_1) \text{ else } \Gamma_\ell^P(s_2), \\
\Gamma_\ell^P(\text{icall } (A, \iota, o)) &= \text{skip}, \\
\Gamma_\ell^P(\text{pcall}_\alpha \; \overline{(Q, \iota, o)}) &= \text{pcall } \overline{(X, \iota|_{ns_Q|_\ell}, o|_{ns_P|_\ell})},
\end{aligned}$$

$$\text{for } \begin{aligned} PS(P) &= (\_, \_, \_, \_, \_, ns_P, \_) \\ PS(Q) &= (\_, \_, \_, \_, n, ns_Q, A) \end{aligned} \text{ and } X = \begin{cases} Q & \text{if } \ell \leq n \\ A & \text{if } \ell > n \end{cases}.$$

Thus $\mathcal{P}_\ell$ includes the global and local variables that were introduced before ℓ and the atomic actions with ℓ in their layer range. Furthermore, it does not contain introduction actions and correspondingly all icall statements are removed. Every arm of a pcall statement, depending on the disappearing layer n of the called procedure Q, either remains a procedure arm to Q, or is replaced by an atomic-action arm to A, the atomic action refined by Q. The input and output mappings are restricted to the local variables at layer ℓ. The set of initial stores of $\mathcal{P}_\ell$ is the same as for $\mathcal{LP}$, since stores range over all program variables.

In our programming language, loops are subsumed by the more general mechanism of recursive procedure calls. Observe that $\mathcal{P}_\ell$ can indeed have recursive procedure calls, because our type checking rules (Fig. 5) allow a pcall to invoke a procedure with the same disappearing layer as the caller.

3.3   Running Example

We return to our lock example from Sect. 2.1. Figure 6 shows its implementation as the layered concurrent program $\mathcal{LP}^{lock}$. Layer annotations are indicated using an @ symbol. For example, the global variable b has layer range $[0, 1]$, all occurrences of local variable tid have introduction layer 1, the atomic action ACQUIRE has layer range $[2, 2]$, and the introduction action iSetLock has layer number 1.

First, observe that $\mathcal{LP}^{lock}$ is well-formed, i.e., $\vdash \mathcal{LP}^{lock}$. Then it is an easy exercise to verify that $\Gamma_\ell(\mathcal{LP}^{lock}) = \mathcal{P}_\ell^{lock}$ for $\ell \in [1, 3]$. Let us focus on procedure Worker. In $\mathcal{P}_1^{lock}$ (Fig. 3(a)) tid does not exist, and correspondingly Alloc, Enter, and Leave do not have input respectively output parameters. Furthermore, the icall in the body of Alloc is replaced with skip. In $\mathcal{P}_2^{lock}$ (Fig. 3(b)) we have tid and the calls to Alloc, Enter, and Leave are replaced with their respective refined atomic actions ALLOC, ACQUIRE, and RELEASE. The only annotated pcall in $\mathcal{LP}^{lock}$ is the recursive call to Enter.

In addition to representing the concurrent programs in Fig. 3, the program $\mathcal{LP}^{lock}$ also encodes the connection between them via introduction actions and calls. The introduction action iSetLock updates lock to maintain the relationship between lock and b, expressed by the predicate InvLock. It is called in Enter in case the CAS operation successfully set b to *true*, and in Leave when b is set to *false*. The introduction action iIncr implements linear thread identifiers using the integer variables pos which points to the next value that can be allocated. For every allocation, the current value of pos is returned as the new thread identifier and pos is incremented.

The variable slots is introduced at layer 1 to represent the set of unallocated identifiers. It contains all integers no less than pos, an invariant that is expressed by the predicate InvAlloc and maintained by the code of iIncr. The purpose of slots is to encode linear allocation of thread identifiers in a way that the body of iIncr can be locally shown to preserve the disjointness invariant for linear variables; slots plays a similar role in the specification of the atomic action ALLOC in $\mathcal{P}_2$. The variable pos is both introduced and hidden at layer 1 so that it exists neither in $\mathcal{P}_1^{lock}$ nor $\mathcal{P}_2^{lock}$. However, pos is present in the checker program $\mathcal{C}_1$ that connects $\mathcal{P}_1^{lock}$ and $\mathcal{P}_2^{lock}$.

```
 ───────────────────────────  LP^lock  ───────────────────────────
 var b@[0,1] : bool                    right ACQUIRE@[2,2](linear tid : int)
 var lock@[1,2] : int                    assert tid != 0
 var pos@[1,1] : int                     assume lock == 0
 var linear slots@[1,2] : set<int>       lock := tid

 predicate InvLock                     left RELEASE@[2,2](linear tid : int)
   b <==> lock != 0                      assert tid != 0 && lock == tid
                                         lock := 0
 predicate InvAlloc
   pos > 0 && slots == [pos,∞)         proc Enter@1(linear tid@1 : int)
                                       refines ACQUIRE
 init InvLock && InvAlloc                var success@0 : bool
                                         pcall success := Cas()
 both SKIP@3 ()                          if (success)
   skip                                    icall iSetLock(tid)
                                         else
 proc Main@2()                             pcall_1 Enter(tid)
 refines SKIP
   if (*)                              proc Leave@1(linear tid@1 : int)
     pcall Worker(), Main()            refines RELEASE
                                         pcall Reset()
 proc Worker@2()                         icall iSetLock(0)
 refines SKIP
   var linear tid@1 : int             iaction iSetLock@1(v : int)
   pcall tid := Alloc()                 lock := v
   pcall Enter(tid)
   pcall Leave(tid)                   atomic CAS@[1,1]() : (success : bool)
                                         if (b) success := false
 right ALLOC@[2,2]() : (linear tid : int) else   success, b := true, true
   assume tid != 0 && tid ∈ slots
   slots := slots - tid              atomic RESET@[1,1]()
                                        assert b
 proc Alloc@1() : (linear tid@1 : int)  b := false
 refines ALLOC
   icall tid := iIncr()               proc Cas@0() : (success@0 : bool)
                                       refines CAS
 iaction iIncr@1() : (linear tid : int)
   assert InvAlloc                    proc Reset@0()
   tid := pos                         refines RESET
   pos := pos + 1
   slots := slots - tid
```

Fig. 6. Lock example (layered concurrent program)

The bodies of procedures Cas and Reset are not shown in Fig. 6 because they are not needed. They disappear at layer 0 and are replaced by the atomic actions CAS and RESET, respectively, in $\mathcal{P}_1^{lock}$.

The degree of compactness afforded by layered programs (as in Fig. 6) over separate specification of each concurrent program (as in Fig. 3) increases rapidly with the size of the program and the maximum depth of procedure calls. In our experience, for realistic programs such as a concurrent garbage collector [7] or a data-race detector [15], the saving in code duplication is significant.

4   Refinement Checking

Section 3 described how a layered concurrent program $\mathcal{LP}$ encodes a sequence $\mathcal{P}_1, \ldots, \mathcal{P}_h, \mathcal{P}_{h+1}$ of concurrent programs. In this section, we show how the safety of any concurrent program in the sequence is implied by the safety of its successor, ultimately allowing the safety of $\mathcal{P}_1$ to be established by the safety of $\mathcal{P}_{h+1}$.

There are three ingredients to connecting $\mathcal{P}_\ell$ to $\mathcal{P}_{\ell+1}$ for any $\ell \in [1, h]$— reduction, projection, and abstraction. Reduction allows us to conclude the safety of a concurrent program under preemptive semantics by proving safety only under cooperative semantics.

Theorem 1 (Reduction). *Let $\mathcal{P}$ be a concurrent program. If $MSafe(\mathcal{P})$ and $CSafe(\mathcal{P})$, then $Safe(\mathcal{P})$.*

The judgment $MSafe(\mathcal{P})$ uses logical commutativity reasoning and mover types to ensure that cooperative safety is sufficient for preemptive safety (Sect. 4.1). We use this theorem to justify reasoning about $CSafe(\mathcal{P}_\ell)$ rather than $Safe(\mathcal{P}_\ell)$.

The next step in connecting $\mathcal{P}_\ell$ to $\mathcal{P}_{\ell+1}$ is to introduce computation introduced at layer ℓ into the cooperative semantics of $\mathcal{P}_\ell$. This computation comprises global and local variables together with introduction actions and calls to them. We refer to the resulting program at layer ℓ as $\widetilde{\mathcal{P}}_\ell$.

Theorem 2 (Projection). *Let $\mathcal{LP}$ be a layered concurrent program with top layer h and $\ell \in [1, h]$. If $CSafe(\widetilde{\mathcal{P}}_\ell)$, then $CSafe(\mathcal{P}_\ell)$.*

Since introduction actions are nonblocking and $\widetilde{\mathcal{P}}_\ell$ is safe under cooperative semantics, every cooperative execution of $\mathcal{P}_\ell$ can be obtained by projecting away the computation introduced at layer ℓ. This observation allows us to conclude that every cooperative execution of $\mathcal{P}_\ell$ is also safe.

Finally, we check that the safety of the cooperative semantics of $\widetilde{\mathcal{P}}_\ell$ is ensured by the safety of the preemptive semantics of the next concurrent program $\mathcal{P}_{\ell+1}$. This connection is established by reasoning about the cooperative semantics of a concurrent checker program $\mathcal{C}_\ell$ that is automatically constructed from $\mathcal{LP}$.

Theorem 3 (Abstraction). *Let $\mathcal{LP}$ be a layered concurrent program with top layer h and $\ell \in [1, h]$. If $CSafe(\mathcal{C}_\ell)$ and $Safe(\mathcal{P}_{\ell+1})$, then $CSafe(\widetilde{\mathcal{P}}_\ell)$.*

The checker program $\mathcal{C}_\ell$ is obtained by instrumenting the code of $\widetilde{\mathcal{P}}_\ell$ with extra variables and procedures that enable checking that procedures disappearing at layer ℓ refine their atomic action specifications (Sect. 4.2).

Our refinement check between two consecutive layers is summarized by the following corollary of Theorems 1–3.

Corollary 1. *Let $\mathcal{LP}$ be a layered concurrent program with top layer h and $\ell \in [1, h]$. If $MSafe(\mathcal{P}_\ell)$, $CSafe(\mathcal{C}_\ell)$ and $Safe(\mathcal{P}_{\ell+1})$, then $Safe(\mathcal{P}_\ell)$.*

The soundness of our refinement checking methodology for layered concurrent programs is obtained by repeated application of Corollary 1.

Corollary 2. *Let $\mathcal{LP}$ be a layered concurrent program with top layer h. If $MSafe(\mathcal{P}_\ell)$ and $CSafe(\mathcal{C}_\ell)$ for all $\ell \in [1, h]$ and $Safe(\mathcal{P}_{h+1})$, then $Safe(\mathcal{P}_1)$.*

4.1   From Preemptive to Cooperative Semantics

We present the judgment $MSafe(\mathcal{P})$ that allows us to reason about a concurrent program $\mathcal{P}$ under cooperative semantics instead of preemptive semantics. Intuitively, we want to use the commutativity of individual atomic actions to rearrange the steps of any execution under preemptive semantics in such a way that it corresponds to an execution under cooperative semantics. We consider mappings $M \in Action \rightarrow \{N, R, L, B\}$ that assign mover types to atomic actions; N for non-mover, R for right mover, L for left mover, and B for both mover. The judgment $MSafe(\mathcal{P})$ requires a mapping M that satisfies two conditions.

First, the atomic actions in $\mathcal{P}$ must satisfy the following logical commutativity conditions [7], which can be discharged by a theorem prover.

- *Commutativity:* If A_1 is a right mover or A_2 is a left mover, then the effect of A_1 followed by A_2 can also be achieved by A_2 followed by A_1.
- *Forward preservation:* If A_1 is a right mover or A_2 is a left mover, then the failure of A_2 after A_1 implies that A_2 must also fail before A_1.
- *Backward preservation:* If A_2 is a left mover (and A_1 is an arbitrary), then the failure of A_1 before A_2 implies that A_1 must also fail after A_2.
- *Nonblocking:* If A is a left mover, then A cannot block.

Second, the sequence of atomic actions in preemptive executions of $\mathcal{P}$ must be such that the desired rearrangement into cooperative executions is possible. Given a preemptive execution, consider, for each thread individually, a labeling of execution steps where atomic action steps are labeled with their mover type and procedure calls and returns are labeled with Y (for yield). The nondeterministic *atomicity automaton* $\mathcal{A}$ on the right defines all allowed sequences. Intuitively, when we map the 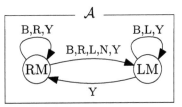 execution steps of a thread to a run in the automaton, the state RM denotes that we are in the right mover phase in which we can stay until the occurrence of a non-right mover (L or N). Then we can stay in the left mover phase (state LM) by executing left movers, until a preemption point (Y) takes us back to RM. Let $\mathcal{E}$ be the mapping from edge labels to the set of edges that contain the label, e.g., $\mathcal{E}(R) = \{RM \rightarrow RM, RM \rightarrow LM\}$. Thus we have a representation of mover types as sets of edges in $\mathcal{A}$, and we define $\mathcal{E}(A) = \mathcal{E}(M(A))$. Notice that the set representation is closed under relation composition $\circ$ and intersection, and behaves as expected, e.g., $\mathcal{E}(R) \circ \mathcal{E}(L) = \mathcal{E}(N)$.

Now we define an intraprocedural control flow analysis that lifts $\mathcal{E}$ to a mapping $\widehat{\mathcal{E}}$ on statements. Intuitively, $x \rightarrow y \in \widehat{\mathcal{E}}(s)$ means that every execution of the statement s has a run in $\mathcal{A}$ from x to y. Our analysis does not have to be interprocedural, since procedure calls and returns are labeled with Y, allowing every possible state transition in $\mathcal{A}$. $MSafe(\mathcal{P})$ requires $\widehat{\mathcal{E}}(s) \neq \varnothing$ for every procedure body s in $\mathcal{P}$, where $\widehat{\mathcal{E}}$ is defined as follows:

$$\widehat{\mathcal{E}}(\texttt{skip}) = \mathcal{E}(B) \quad \widehat{\mathcal{E}}(s_1 \ ; \ s_2) = \widehat{\mathcal{E}}(s_1) \circ \widehat{\mathcal{E}}(s_2) \quad \widehat{\mathcal{E}}(\texttt{if } e \texttt{ then } s_1 \texttt{ else } s_2) = \widehat{\mathcal{E}}(s_1) \cap \widehat{\mathcal{E}}(s_2)$$

$$\widehat{\mathcal{E}}(\texttt{pcall } \overline{A}_1 \overline{P} \ \overline{A}_2) = \begin{cases} \mathcal{E}^*(\overline{A}_1 \overline{A}_2) & \text{if } \overline{P} = \varepsilon \\ \mathcal{E}(L) \circ \mathcal{E}^*(\overline{A}_1) \circ \mathcal{E}(Y) \circ \mathcal{E}^*(\overline{A}_2) \circ \mathcal{E}(R) & \text{if } \overline{P} \neq \varepsilon \end{cases}$$

Skip is a both mover, sequencing composes edges, and if takes the edges possible in both branches. In the arms of a pcall we omit writing the input and output maps because they are irrelevant to the analysis. Let us first focus on the case $\overline{P} = \varepsilon$ with no procedure arms. In the preemptive semantics all arms are arbitrarily interleaved and correspondingly we define the function

$$\mathcal{E}^*(A_1 \cdots A_n) = \bigcap_{\tau \in S_n} \mathcal{E}(A_{\tau(1)}) \circ \cdots \circ \mathcal{E}(A_{\tau(n)})$$

to consider all possible permutations (τ ranges over the symmetric group S_n) and take the edges possible in all permutations. Observe that $\mathcal{E}^*$ evaluates to non-empty in exactly four cases: $\mathcal{E}(N)$ for $\{B\}^*N\{B\}^*$, $\mathcal{E}(B)$ for $\{B\}^*$, $\mathcal{E}(R)$ for $\{R, B\}^* \setminus \{B\}^*$, and $\mathcal{E}(L)$ for $\{L, B\}^* \setminus \{B\}^*$. These are the mover-type sequences for which an arbitrary permutation (coming from a preemptive execution) can be rearranged to the order given by the pcall (corresponding to cooperative execution).

In the case $\overline{P} \neq \varepsilon$ there is a preemption point under cooperative semantics between $\overline{A}_1$ and $\overline{A}_2$, the actions in $\overline{A}_1$ are executed in order before the preemption, and the actions in $\overline{A}_2$ are executed in order after the preemption. To ensure that the cooperative execution can simulate an arbitrarily interleaved preemptive execution of the pcall, we must be able to move actions in $\overline{A}_1$ to the left and actions in $\overline{A}_2$ to the right of the preemption point. We enforce this condition by requiring that $\overline{A}_1$ is all left (or both) movers and $\overline{A}_2$ all right (or both) movers, expressed by the leading $\mathcal{E}(L)$ and trailing $\mathcal{E}(R)$ in the edge composition.

4.2   Refinement Checker Programs

In this section, we describe the construction of checker programs that justify the formal connection between successive concurrent programs in a layered concurrent program. The description is done by example. In particular, we show the checker program $\mathcal{C}_1^{lock}$ that establishes the connection between $\mathcal{P}_1^{lock}$ and $\mathcal{P}_2^{lock}$ (Fig. 3) of our running example.

Overview. Cooperative semantics splits any execution of $\mathcal{P}_1^{lock}$ into a sequence of preemption-free execution fragments separated by preemptions. Verification of $\mathcal{C}_1^{lock}$ must ensure that for all such executions, the set of procedures that disappear at layer 1 behave like their atomic action specifications. That is, the procedures Enter and Leave must behave like their specifications ACQUIRE and RELEASE, respectively. It is important to note that this goal of checking refinement is easier than verifying that $\mathcal{P}_1^{lock}$ is safe. Refinement checking may succeed even though $\mathcal{P}_1^{lock}$ fails; the guarantee of refinement is that such a failure can be simulated by a failure in $\mathcal{P}_2^{lock}$. The construction of $\mathcal{C}_1^{lock}$ can be understood in two steps. First, the program $\widetilde{\mathcal{P}}_1^{lock}$ shown in Fig. 7 extends $\mathcal{P}_1^{lock}$ (Fig. 3(a)) with the variables introduced at layer 1 (globals lock, pos, slots and locals tid) and the corresponding introduction actions (iIncr and iSetLock). Second, $\mathcal{C}_1^{lock}$ is obtained from $\widetilde{\mathcal{P}}_1^{lock}$ by instrumenting the procedures to encode the refinement check, described in the remainder of this section.

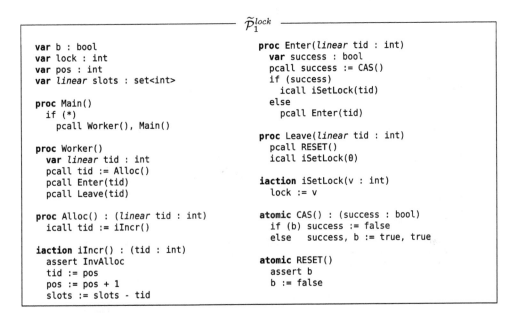

Fig. 7. Lock example (variable introduction at layer 1)

Context for Refinement. There are two kinds of procedures, those that continue to exist at layer 2 (such as Main and Worker) and those that disappear at layer 1 (such as Enter and Leave). $\mathcal{C}_1^{lock}$ does not need to verify anything about the first kind. These procedures only provide the context for refinement checking and thus all invocation of an atomic action (I, O, e, t) in any atomic-action arm of a pcall is converted into the invocation of a fresh atomic action $(I, O, true, e \wedge t)$. In other words, the assertions in procedures that continue to exist at layer 2 are converted into assumptions for the refinement checking at layer 1; these assertions are verified during the refinement checking on a higher layer. In our example, Main and Worker do not have atomic-action arms, although this is possible in general.

Refinement Instrumentation. We illustrate the instrumentation of procedures Enter and Leave in Fig. 8. The core idea is to track updates by preemption-free execution fragments to the shared variables that continue to exist at layer 2. There are two such variables—lock and slots. We capture snapshots of lock and slots in the local variables _lock and _slots and use these snapshots to check that the updates to lock and slots behave according to the refined atomic action. In general, any path from the start to the end of the body of a

$$\mathcal{C}_1^{lock}$$

```
1   macro *CHANGED* is !(lock == _lock && slots == _slots)
2   macro *RELEASE* is lock == 0 && slots == _slots
3   macro *ACQUIRE* is _lock == 0 && lock == tid && slots == _slots
4
5   proc Leave(linear tid)                              # Leave must behave like RELEASE
6     var _lock, _slots, pc, done
7     pc, done := false, false                          # initialize pc and done
8     _lock, _slots := lock, slots                      # take snapshot of global variables
9     assume pc || (tid != 0 && lock == tid)            # assume gate of RELEASE
10
11    pcall RESET()
12    icall iSetLock(0)
13
14    assert *CHANGED* ==> (!pc && *RELEASE*)            # state change must be the first and like RELEASE
15    pc := pc || *CHANGED*                              # track if state changed
16    done := done || *RELEASE*                          # track if RELEASE happened
17
18    assert done                                        # check that RELEASE happened
19
20  proc Enter(linear tid)                               # Enter must behave like ACQUIRE
21    var success, _lock, _slots, pc, done
22    pc, done := false, false                           # initialize pc and done
23    _lock, _slots := lock, slots                       # take snapshot of global variables
24    assume pc || tid != 0                              # assume gate of ACQUIRE
25
26    pcall success := CAS()
27    if (success)
28      icall iSetLock(tid)
29    else
30      assert *CHANGED* ==> (!pc && *ACQUIRE*)          # state change must be the first and like ACQUIRE
31      pc := pc || *CHANGED*                            # track if state changed
32      done := done || *ACQUIRE*                        # track if ACQUIRE happened
33
34      if (*)                                           # then: check refinement of caller
35        pcall pc := Check_Enter_Enter(tid,            #    check annotated procedure arm
36                               tid, pc)  #       in fresh procedure (defined below)
37        done := true                                   #    above call ensures that ACQUIRE happened
38      else                                             # else: check refinement of callee
39        pcall Enter(tid)                               #    explore behavior of callee
40        assume false                                   #    block after return (only then is relevant below)
41
42      _lock, _slots := lock, slots                     # take snapshot of global variables
43      assume pc || tid != 0                            # assume gate of ACQUIRE
44
45    assert *CHANGED* ==> (!pc && *ACQUIRE*)            # state change must be the first and like ACQUIRE
46    pc := pc || *CHANGED*                              # track if state changed
47    done := done || *ACQUIRE*                          # track if ACQUIRE happened
48
49    assert done                                        # check that ACQUIRE happened
50
51  proc Check_Enter_Enter(tid, x, pc) : (pc')          # check annotated pcall from Enter to Enter
52    var _lock, _slots
53    _lock, _slots := lock, slots                       # take snapshot of global variables
54    assume pc || tid != 0                              # assume gate of ACQUIRE
55
56    pcall ACQUIRE(x)                                   # use ACQUIRE to ''simulate'' call to Enter
57
58    assert *ACQUIRE*                                   # check that ACQUIRE happened
59    assert *CHANGED* ==> !pc                           # state change must be the first
60    pc' := pc || *CHANGED*                             # track if state changed
```

Fig. 8. Instrumented procedures Enter and Leave (layer 1 checker program)

procedure may comprise many preemption-free execution fragments. The checker program must ensure that exactly one of these fragments behaves like the specified atomic action; all other fragments must leave `lock` and `slot` unchanged. To track whether the atomic action has already happened, we use two local Boolean variables—`pc` and `done`. Both variables are initialized to *false*, get updated to *true* during the execution, and remain at *true* thereafter. The variable `pc` is set to *true* at the end of the first preemption-free execution fragment that modifies the tracked state, which is expressed by the macro `*CHANGED*` on line 1. The variable `done` is set to *true* at the end of the first preemption-free execution fragment that behaves like the refined atomic action. For that, the macros `*RELEASE*` and `*ACQUIRE*` on lines 2 and 3 express the transition relations of `RELEASE` and `ACQUIRE`, respectively. Observe that we have the invariant `pc ==> done`. The reason we need both `pc` and `done` is to handle the case where the refined atomic action may stutter (i.e., leave the state unchanged).

Instrumenting Leave. We first look at the instrumentation of **Leave**. Line 8 initializes the snapshot variables. Recall that a preemption inside the code of a procedure is introduced only at a pcall containing a procedure arm. Consequently, the body of **Leave** is preemption-free and we need to check refinement across a single execution fragment. This checking is done by lines 14–16. The assertion on line 14 checks that if any tracked variable has changed since the last snapshot, (1) such a change happens for the first time (`!pc`), and (2) the current value is related to the snapshot value according to the specification of `RELEASE`. Line 15 updates `pc` to track whether any change to the tracked variables has happened so far. Line 16 updates `done` to track whether `RELEASE` has happened so far. The assertion at line 18 checks that `RELEASE` has indeed happened before **Leave** returns. The assumption at line 9 blocks those executions which can be simulated by the failure of `RELEASE`. It achieves this effect by assuming the gate of `RELEASE` in states where `pc` is still *false* (i.e., `RELEASE` has not yet happened). The assumption yields the constraint `lock != 0` which together with the invariant `InvLock` (Fig. 6) proves that the gate of `RESET` does not fail.

The verification of **Leave** illustrates an important principle of our approach to refinement. The gates of atomic actions invoked by a procedure P disappearing at layer ℓ are verified using a combination of invariants established on C_ℓ and pending assertions at layer $\ell + 1$ encoded as the gate of the atomic action refined by P. For **Leave** specifically, `assert b` in `RESET` is propagated to `assert tid != nil && lock == tid` in `RELEASE`. The latter assertion is verified in the checker program C_2^{lock} when **Worker**, the caller of `RELEASE`, is shown to refine the action `SKIP` which is guaranteed not to fail since its gate is *true*.

Instrumenting Enter. The most sophisticated feature in a concurrent program is a pcall. The instrumentation of **Leave** explains the instrumentation of the simplest kind of pcall with only atomic-action arms. We now illustrate the instrumentation of a pcall containing a procedure arm using the procedure **Enter** which refines the atomic action `ACQUIRE` and contains a pcall to **Enter** itself. The instrumentation of this pcall is contained in lines 30–43.

A pcall with a procedure arm is challenging for two reasons. First, the callee disappears at the same layer as the caller so the checker program must reason about refinement for both the caller and the callee. This challenge is addressed by the code in lines 34–40. At line 34, we introduce a nondeterministic choice between two code paths—then branch to check refinement of the caller and else branch to check refinement of the callee. An explanation for this nondeterministic choice is given in the next two paragraphs. Second, a pcall with a procedure arm introduces a preemption creating multiple preemption-free execution fragments. This challenge is addressed by two pieces of code. First, we check that lock and slots are updated correctly (lines 30–32) by the preemption-free execution fragment ending before the pcall. Second, we update the snapshot variables (line 42) to enable the verification of the preemption-free execution fragment beginning after the pcall.

Lines 35–37 in the then branch check refinement against the atomic action specification of the caller, exploiting the atomic action specification of the callee. The actual verification is performed in a fresh procedure Check_Enter_Enter invoked on line 35. Notice that this procedure depends on both the caller and the callee (indicated in colors), and that it preserves a necessary preemption point. The procedure has input parameters tid to receive the input of the caller (for refinement checking) and x to receive the input of the callee (to generate the behavior of the callee). Furthermore, pc may be updated in Check_Enter_Enter and thus passed as both an input and output parameter. In the body of the procedure, the invocation of action ACQUIRE on line 56 overapproximates the behavior of the callee. In the layered concurrent program (Fig. 6), the (recursive) pcall to Enter in the body of Enter is annotated with 1. This annotation indicates that for any execution passing through this pcall, ACQUIRE is deemed to occur during the execution of its unique arm. This is reflected in the checker program by updating done to *true* on line 37; the update is justified because of the assertion in Check_Enter_Enter at line 58. If the pcall being translated was instead unannotated, line 37 would be omitted.

Lines 39–40 in the else branch ensure that using the atomic action specification of the callee on line 56 is justified. Allowing the execution to continue to the callee ensures that the called procedure is invoked in all states allowed by $\mathcal{P}_1$. However, the execution is blocked once the call returns to ensure that downstream code sees the side-effect on pc and the snapshot variables.

To summarize, the crux of our instrumentation of procedure arms is to combine refinement checking of caller and callee. We explore the behaviors of the callee to check its refinement. At the same time, we exploit the atomic action specification of the callee to check refinement of the caller.

Instrumenting Unannotated Procedure Arms. Procedure Enter illustrates the instrumentation of an annotated procedure arm. The instrumentation of an unannotated procedure arm (both in an annotated or unannotated pcall) is simpler, because we only need to check that the tracked state is not modified. For such an arm to a procedure refining atomic action Action, we introduce a procedure `Check_Action` (which is independent of the caller) comprising three instructions: take snapshots, `pcall A`, and `assert !*CHANGED*`.

Pcalls with Multiple Arms. Our examples show the instrumentation of pcalls with a single arm. Handling multiple arms is straightforward, since each arm is translated independently. Atomic action arms stay unmodified, annotated procedure arms are replaced with the corresponding `Check_Caller_Callee` procedure, and unannotated procedure arms are replaced with the corresponding `Check_Action` procedure.

Output Parameters. Our examples illustrate refinement checking for atomic actions that have no output parameters. In general, a procedure and its atomic action specification may return values in output parameters. We handle this generalization but lack of space does not allow us to present the technical details.

5 Conclusion

In this paper, we presented layered concurrent programs, a programming notation to succinctly capture a multi-layered refinement proof capable of connecting a deeply-detailed implementation to a highly-abstract specification. We presented an algorithm to extract from the concurrent layered program the individual concurrent programs, from the most concrete to the most abstract. We also presented an algorithm to extract a collection of refinement checker programs that establish the connection among the sequence of concurrent programs encoded by the layered concurrent program. The cooperative safety of the checker programs and the preemptive safety of the most abstract concurrent program suffices to prove the preemptive safety of the most concrete concurrent program.

Layered programs have been implemented in CIVL, a deductive verifier for concurrent programs, implemented as a conservative extension to the Boogie verifier [3]. CIVL has been used to verify a complex concurrent garbage collector [6] and a state-of-the-art data-race detection algorithm [15]. In addition to these two large benchmarks, around fifty smaller programs (including a ticket lock and a lock-free stack) are available at https://github.com/boogie-org/boogie.

There are several directions for future work. We did not discuss how to verify an individual checker program. CIVL uses the Owicki-Gries method [13] and rely-guarantee reasoning [8] to verify checker programs. But researchers are exploring many different techniques for verification of concurrent programs. It would be interesting to investigate whether heterogeneous techniques could be brought to bear on checker programs at different layers.

In this paper, we focused exclusively on verification and did not discuss code generation, an essential aspect of any programming system targeting the construction of verified programs. There is a lot of work to be done in connecting the most concrete program in a concurrent layered program to executable code. Most likely, different execution platforms will impose different obligations on the most concrete program and the general idea of layered concurrent programs would be specialized for different target platforms.

Scalable verification is a challenge as the size of programs being verified increases. Traditionally, scalability has been addressed using modular verification techniques but only for single-layer programs. It would be interesting to explore modularity techniques for concurrent layered programs in the context of a refinement-oriented proof system.

Layered concurrent programs bring new challenges and opportunities to the design of programming languages and development environments. Integrating layers into a programming language requires intuitive syntax to specify layer information and atomic actions. For example, ordered layer names can be more readable and easier to refactor than layer numbers. An integrated development environment could provide different views of the layered concurrent program. For example, it could show the concurrent program, the checker program, and the introduced code at a particular layer. Any updates made in these views should be automatically reflected back into the layered concurrent program.

Acknowledgements. We thank Hana Chockler, Stephen Freund, Thomas A. Henzinger, Viktor Toman, and James R. Wilcox for comments that improved this paper. This research was supported in part by the Austrian Science Fund (FWF) under grants S11402-N23 (RiSE/SHiNE) and Z211-N23 (Wittgenstein Award).

References

1. Abrial, J.-R.: The B-Book - Assigning Programs to Meanings. Cambridge University Press, Cambridge (2005)
2. Abrial, J.-R., Butler, M.J., Hallerstede, S., Hoang, T.S., Mehta, F., Voisin, L.: Rodin: an open toolset for modelling and reasoning in Event-B. STTT **12**(6), 447–466 (2010). https://doi.org/10.1007/s10009-010-0145-y
3. Barnett, M., Chang, B.-Y.E., DeLine, R., Jacobs, B., Leino, K.R.M.: Boogie: a modular reusable verifier for object-oriented programs. In: de Boer, F.S., Bonsangue, M.M., Graf, S., de Roever, W.-P. (eds.) FMCO 2005. LNCS, vol. 4111, pp. 364–387. Springer, Heidelberg (2006). https://doi.org/10.1007/11804192_17
4. Elmas, T., Qadeer, S., Tasiran, S.: A calculus of atomic actions. In: Shao, Z., Pierce, B.C. (eds.) POPL 2009, pp. 2–15. ACM (2009). https://doi.org/10.1145/1480881.1480885
5. Flanagan, C., Qadeer, S.: A type and effect system for atomicity. In: Cytron, R., Gupta, R. (eds.) PLDI 2003, pp. 338–349. ACM (2003). https://doi.org/10.1145/781131.781169
6. Hawblitzel, C., Petrank, E., Qadeer, S., Tasiran, S.: Automated and modular refinement reasoning for concurrent programs. In: Kroening, D., Păsăreanu, C.S. (eds.) CAV 2015. LNCS, vol. 9207, pp. 449–465. Springer, Cham (2015). https://doi.org/10.1007/978-3-319-21668-3_26
7. Hawblitzel, C., Petrank, E., Qadeer, S., Tasiran, S.: Automated and modular refinement reasoning for concurrent programs. Technical report MSR-TR-2015-8, Microsoft Research, February 2015. https://www.microsoft.com/en-us/research/publication/automated-and-modular-refinement-reasoning-for-concurrent-programs/
8. Jones, C.B.: Specification and design of (parallel) programs. In: IFIP Congress (1983)

Permissions

All chapters in this book were first published by Springer; hereby published with permission under the Creative Commons Attribution License or equivalent. Every chapter published in this book has been scrutinized by our experts. Their significance has been extensively debated. The topics covered herein carry significant findings which will fuel the growth of the discipline. They may even be implemented as practical applications or may be referred to as a beginning point for another development.

The contributors of this book come from diverse backgrounds, making this book a truly international effort. This book will bring forth new frontiers with its revolutionizing research information and detailed analysis of the nascent developments around the world.

We would like to thank all the contributing authors for lending their expertise to make the book truly unique. They have played a crucial role in the development of this book. Without their invaluable contributions this book wouldn't have been possible. They have made vital efforts to compile up to date information on the varied aspects of this subject to make this book a valuable addition to the collection of many professionals and students.

This book was conceptualized with the vision of imparting up-to-date information and advanced data in this field. To ensure the same, a matchless editorial board was set up. Every individual on the board went through rigorous rounds of assessment to prove their worth. After which they invested a large part of their time researching and compiling the most relevant data for our readers.

The editorial board has been involved in producing this book since its inception. They have spent rigorous hours researching and exploring the diverse topics which have resulted in the successful publishing of this book. They have passed on their knowledge of decades through this book. To expedite this challenging task, the publisher supported the team at every step. A small team of assistant editors was also appointed to further simplify the editing procedure and attain best results for the readers.

Apart from the editorial board, the designing team has also invested a significant amount of their time in understanding the subject and creating the most relevant covers. They scrutinized every image to scout for the most suitable representation of the subject and create an appropriate cover for the book.

The publishing team has been an ardent support to the editorial, designing and production team. Their endless efforts to recruit the best for this project, has resulted in the accomplishment of this book. They are a veteran in the field of academics and their pool of knowledge is as vast as their experience in printing. Their expertise and guidance has proved useful at every step. Their uncompromising quality standards have made this book an exceptional effort. Their encouragement from time to time has been an inspiration for everyone.

The publisher and the editorial board hope that this book will prove to be a valuable piece of knowledge for researchers, students, practitioners and scholars across the globe.

List of Contributors

Grigory Fedyukovich, Yueling Zhang and Aarti Gupta
Princeton University, Princeton, USA

Bernd Finkbeiner, Christopher Hahn and Hazem Torfah
Reactive Systems Group, Saarland University, Saarbrücken, Germany

Anna Becchi and Enea Zaffanella
Department of Mathematical, Physical and Computer Sciences, University of Parma, Parma, Italy

Daniel J. Fremont and Sanjit A. Seshia
University of California, Berkeley, USA

Chuchu Fan, Umang Mathur, Sayan Mitra and Mahesh Viswanathan
University of Illinois at Urbana Champaign, Champaign, IL, USA

Loris D'Antoni
University of Wisconsin-Madison, Madison, WI, USA

Goran Frehse
Univ. Grenoble Alpes, CNRS, Grenoble INP, VERIMAG, Grenoble, France

Yijun Feng, Haokun Li and Bican Xia
LMAM and School of Mathematical Sciences, Peking University, Beijing, China

George Argyros
Columbia University, New York, NY, USA

Joost-Pieter Katoen
RWTH Aachen University, Aachen, Germany

Naijun Zhan
State Key Laboratory of Computer Science, Institute of Software, Chinese Academy of Sciences, Beijing, China
University of Chinese Academy of Sciences, Beijing, China

Roderick Bloem and Franz Roeck
Graz University of Technology, Graz, Austria

Dejan Nickovi
Austrian Institute of Technology GmbH, Vienna, Austria

Qiyi Tang and Franck van Breugel
DisCoVeri Group, York University, Toronto, Canada

Ilya Grishchenko, Ezio Bartocci, Matteo Maffei and Clara Schneidewind
TU Wien, Vienna, Austria

Bernhard Kragl, Mirco Giacobbe and Thomas A. Henzinger
IST Austria, Klosterneuburg, Austria

Shaz Qadeer
Microsoft Research, Redmond, USA

Index

Printed in the USA
CPSIA information can be obtained
at www.ICGtesting.com
JSHW051351091023
49903JS00006B/111